MANAGING ETHNIC TENSIONS IN MULTI-ETHNIC SOCIETIES

Sri Lanka 1880-1985

K. M. de Silva

UNIVERSITY
PRESS OF
AMERICA

LANHAM • NEW YORK • LONDON

Copyright © 1986 by

University Press of America,® Inc.

4720 Boston Way
Lanham, MD 20706

3 Henrietta Street
London WC2E 8LU England

Printed in the United States of America

Co-published by arrangement with
The Institute of Asian Affairs, Hamburg, and
The International Centre for Ethnic Studies, Kandy/Colombo

Library of Congress Cataloging in Publication Data

De Silva, K. M.
  Managing ethnic tensions in multi-ethnic societies.

    Bibliography: p.
    Includes index.
    1. Sri Lanka—Politics and government.   2. Sri Lanka—
Ethnic relations.   I. Title.
DS489.7.D475   1986   305.8'0095493   86-9116
ISBN 0-8191-5397-4 (alk. paper)
ISBN 0-8191-5398-2 (pbk. : alk. paper)

All University Press of America books are produced on acid-free
paper which exceeds the minimum standards set by the National
Historical Publications and Records Commission.

To my mother,
and to the memory of my father
M.D. deSilva, 1903—1984

CONTENTS

PREFACE

Sri Lanka's current ethnic tensions and conflicts provided a sombre backdrop to the writing of this book. When I began working on it late in 1979 the riots of 1977 still cast a gloomy shadow over the affairs of the island. Dr. Werner Draguhn, Director of the Institute of Asian Affairs, at Hamburg, a frequent visitor to Sri Lanka, invited me to write a short study of Sri Lanka's ethnic problems to be published under the auspices of his institute. For him, as it was for me, the book was a work 'occasioned' — to use Hobbes's words — 'by the disorders of the present time.' The form the book eventually took was influenced greatly by my experience as a member of the Presidential Commission on Development Councils (1979-80), first of all in the exposure it gave me to the constructive and critical use of facts and insights in the analysis of policies and policy options in the management of ethnic tensions at a practical level, and secondly, in the awareness we had of the paucity of studies of the main issues in ethnic conflict and rivalries in Sri Lanka. The first draft of this book was completed in 1981. Its expansion was stimulated by questions raised by readers of that text, questions relating to the background to recent events, issues and controversies, and above all to the historical background. Dr. Draguhn and I both hoped that the book would be ready for publication by the end of 1982, but that was not to be.

The riots of July 1983 compelled me to take a more searching look at many of the chapters I had written. Some were revised and expanded once more, and some fresh material was incorporated in new chapters. The result was a third draft. This in turn was revised substantially in the last quarter of 1985 at Bowdoin

College, Brunswick, Maine in the first few months of my sabbatical year there as Professor of History, and Fulbright Scholar in Residence.

This book is neither intended, nor likely, to provide all the answers to questions relating to the island's ethnic problems: my objective is the more limited and realistic one of helping others to see the complexity of these problems, and of helping them reach their own conclusions on the basis of the data provided in this book. My approach to the problems surveyed in this book is that of a historian, and the treatment of the issues outlined, the analysis of their unfolding over the last one hundred years or so, and the treatment of the sources on which this volume is based, is historical. The Buddhist societies of South and South East Asia, the German Indologist Professor Heinz Bechert pointed out in 1972, are "historically conscious" societies and, I would add, none more so than Sri Lanka. Sri Lankan society carries a huge burden of historical memories and in this book I have tried to show how the pressure of these memories has helped to shape and distort policies and responses to policies over the last 100 years. If the emphasis on the study of policies was influenced by my work on the Presidential Commission on Development Councils, it was strengthened by my association, which began in 1982, with the International Centre for Ethnic Studies (ICES) Kandy/Colombo, Sri Lanka, and its concern with policy-oriented studies.

A decade ago politicians and scholars alike still spoke of *solutions* to ethnic tensions. We are wiser today, admittedly after the event. We are less sanguine, and, hopefully, more realistic. We talk, today, only about the *management* of tensions and rivalries, that is when we do not talk merely of coping with the pressures these set off. It is a chastening experience which leads inevitably to diminished ambitions in facing and resolving the social, political and economic realities of increasing ethnic tensions in Sri Lanka, but hopefully these same diminished ambitions will mark the beginning of the process of evolving realistic policies of managing such tensions on a long-term basis.

I have incurred many debts, intellectual and personal, in the writing of this book. I would like first of all to express my sincerest thanks to Dr. Werner Draguhn who first urged me to write this book, and provided the resources, through his institute, to support the research that went into it. The book has benefitted greatly from my association with the International Centre for Ethnic Studies and the stimulating discussions there on the themes of ethnic conflict and resolution both at seminars and workshops sponsored by the Centre and among my colleagues who work at and for the ICES. My debt to them is very great, even if they may not all agree with the views expressed and conclusions reached in this book. Some of my colleagues at the University of Peradeniya have contributed to the writing of this book in numerous ways. As we sat together seeking answers and solutions to questions and problems directed at us, or placed before us, the discussions we had and the debates we engaged in helped me to clarify my own ideas on the themes surveyed in this book. I would like to make special mention of Professors Gerald Pieris of the Department of Geography, Sirima Kiribamuna of the Department of History, and K.N.O. Dharmadasa of the Department of Sinhalese who very generously gave me access to unpublished research material of theirs. Professor Pieris's assistance in the preparation of the maps for this volume has been invaluable.

There are many others whose assistance was readily available to me when I sought it in the course of gathering data for this book. These included policymakers both at the political and administrative levels. Many of them preferred to remain anonymous, and in acceding to their wishes I have reluctantly decided to make no exceptions to the anonymity of my gratitude to them.

Fortunately there is no need for anonymity in my thanks to three persons who took time off from their busy schedule of administrative and academic work to read and comment on this book in its final form. They are Godfrey Gunatilleke, Director of the Marga Institute, Colombo, Professor Edward Azar, Director of the Center for International Development and Conflict Management of the University of Maryland at College Park, and Professor Myron Wiener of the Massachusetts Institute of Technology.

A generous grant from the research funds of Bowdoin College met the costs incurred in preparing a camera-ready copy of the text of this book. I welcome this opportunity to express my thanks to Professor Paul Nyhus, Chairman of the Department of History at Bowdoin College, who took the initiative in getting me this assistance, and also for the warmth of the reception extended to me as a Visiting Professor in the Department of History at Bowdoin.

The staff of the ICES at Kandy have been a great help to me in the preparation of this book. Ms. Chalani Lokugamage typed several drafts of the text with her customary quiet efficiency; the documents in the appendix were typed by Ms. Ameeta Perera, while Ms. Kanzul Jawahir helped in collecting data for the statistical tables, and Mrs. P. Gamage with the proofs in the conversion of my manuscript to a typescript as well as in checking references in the footnotes and bibliography. I wish to thank all of them.

I would like to convey my appreciation of the unfailing courtesy I received from Ms. Diane deGrasse, Ms. Deborah Gould, Ms. Susan Lamb and Ms. Alice Harding of Type & Design, Brunswick, Maine, who prepared the camera-ready copy of the text of this book. They worked long hours with skill and good humour in producing a final product from a typescript in which handwritten revisions taxed their skills at deciphering a difficult script and, no doubt, their patience as well. My deepest gratitude is due to my wife Chandra whose encouragement sustained me throughout the years that went into the writing of this book.

This book is jointly sponsored by the Institute of Asian Affairs, Hamburg, and the International Centre for Ethnic Studies, Kandy/Colombo, Sri Lanka. The views expressed and the conclusions reached in this book are mine, and do not necessarily reflect those of the two sponsoring institutes. Needless to say, only I should be held responsible for these views and conclusions and for any errors found in this book.

K.M. de Silva
Kandy, Sri Lanka
and
Bowdoin College,
Brunswick, Maine
February 1986

MAPS

DISTRICTS OF SRI LANKA - 1981

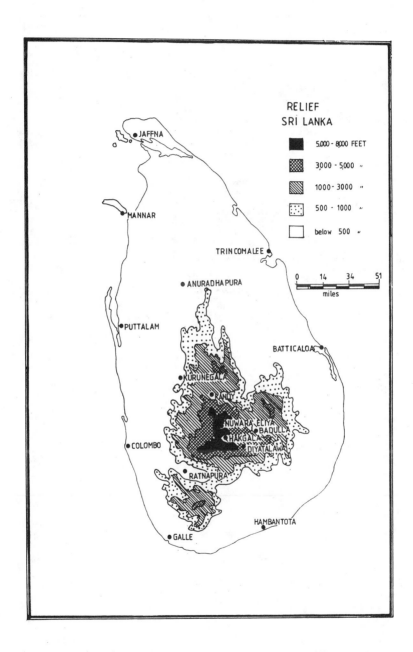

RELIEF
SRI LANKA

| | 5,000 - 8,000 FEET |
| 3,000 - 5,000 " |
| 1000 - 3000 " |
| 500 - 1000 " |
| below 500 " |

JAFFNA

MANNAR

TRINCOMALEE

ANURADHAPURA

PUTTALAM

BATTICALOA

KURUNEGALA

KANDY

NUWARA ELIYA

BADULLA

HAKGALA

DIYATALAWA

COLOMBO

RATNAPURA

HAMBANTOTA

GALLE

0   14   34   51
miles

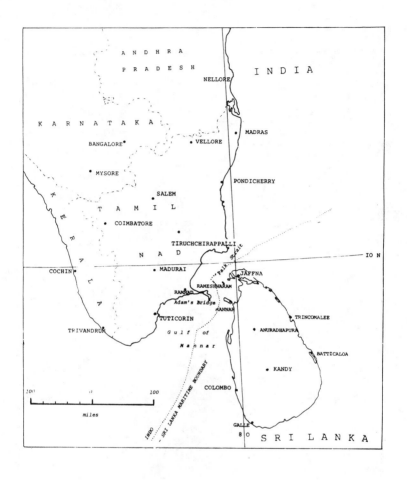

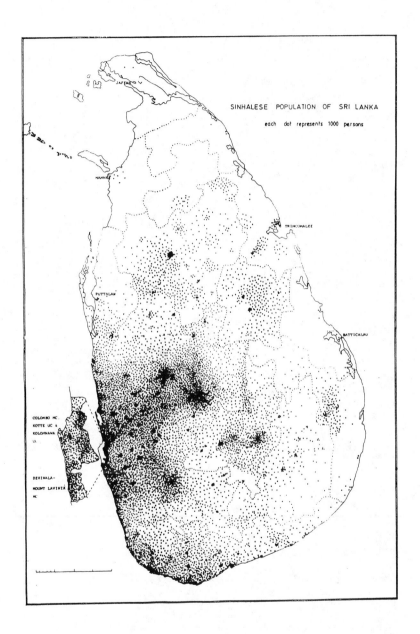

SINHALESE POPULATION OF SRI LANKA

each dot represents 1000 persons

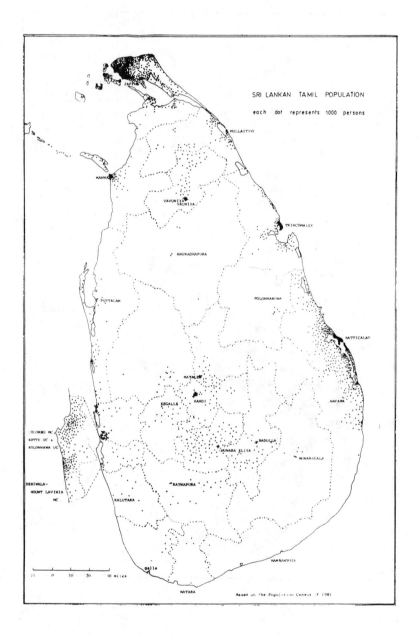

SRI LANKAN TAMIL POPULATION

each dot represents 1000 persons

Based on the Population Census of 1981

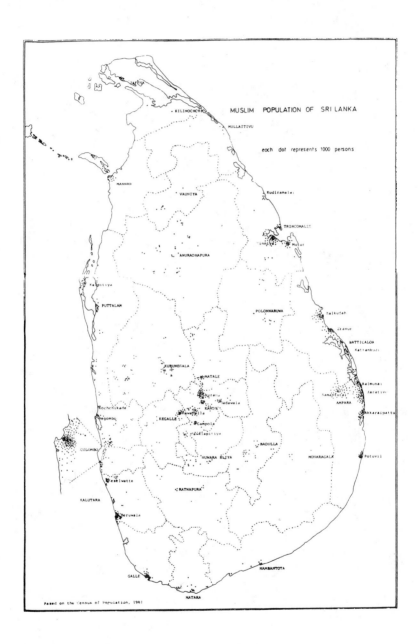

MUSLIM POPULATION OF SRI LANKA

each dot represents 1000 persons

Based on the Census of Population, 1981

PART I

Introduction

Chapter I

Introduction

SRI LANKA — A Case Study in Ethnic Conflict

Few nations in the third world would serve better as a laboratory for the study of ethnic issues than Sri Lanka. The country is small and compact, and has in addition a long history of ethnic tension and rivalries stretching back over several centuries — some would have these go back to the very beginnings of the island's recorded history over two thousand years — and complicated by the processes of change initiated by colonial rule over four centuries and under three western powers in succession from the beginning of the sixteenth century: the Portuguese, the Dutch and the British. No wonder then that the student of the island's affairs is struck by the sheer complexity of its ethnic tensions and rivalries and the enormous difficulties involved in their management if not control and settlement. This same complexity which provides such an excellent introduction to politicized ethnicity for the academic investigator also affords a rigorous testing ground for the skills of the politician and administrator.

Sri Lanka is the smallest of the South Asian states, only 25,332 sq. miles (or 65,610 sq. kilometers) in area, with a maximum distance of 270 miles (435 km) from north to south and 140 miles (225 km) east to west. It lies off the southern coast of India, separated from the Indian sub-continent by a sea which, at its narrowest point, is only 22 miles wide. Due south from the southernmost point in Sri Lanka there is nothing but the ocean and, thousands of miles away, Antarctica.

A small country like Sri Lanka is not normally the focus of international attention. If in recent years it has received such attention this has to do with the ethnic tensions, erupting regularly into clashes, between its two main ethnic groups, the Sinhalese and Tamils.

The current ethnic conflict in Sri Lanka is not a simple, straight-forward confrontation between an oppressed minority and a callous majority. It is a much more complex business, and the Sinhalese Buddhists and the Sri Lanka Tamils are not the only players in this intricate political drama even though, at present, they play the principal roles. The island has one of the most complex plural societies in the world: three important ethnic groups, and as many as four of the world's major religions. The Sinhalese who constitute the majority of the population today, are just short of three quarters of the island's population, while the Sinhalese-Buddhists are just over two-thirds of it. Yet the Sinhalese-Buddhists are all too conscious of their minority status *vis-a-vis* the Tamils of Southern Asia, a consciousness which is accentuated by Sri Lanka's location off the coast of South India, and specifically a close geographical proximity to Tamilnadu. Their sense of ethnic distinctiveness is identified through religion — Theravada Buddhism — and language —Sinhalese.

The complexity of Sri Lanka's pluralism has a dimension which is often neglected if not ignored altogether in discussions of its current ethnic and religious tensions, namely that three of the minorities have loyalties and allegiances which stretch beyond the territorial limits of Sri Lanka to other parts of the world: the Tamil Hindus, the Christians and in particular, the Roman Catholics, and the Muslims. These "extra-territorial" allegiances and loyalties in the case of the first two groups have, in the recent past, caused problems of a political nature to the governments of the island.

Sri Lanka deserves to be known for much more than its ethnic tensions and rivalries, for it is one of the very few functioning democracies of the third world, and although one of the poorer nations of the third world it nevertheless provides its citizens with a quality of life which much wealthier nations have yet to achieve.[1] Both these stem from the fact that Sri Lanka was the first country in Asia to enjoy the benefits of universal suffrage.

Universal suffrage was introduced to the island in 1931, by the British. There was little or no demand for it from Sri Lankan politicians. The first general election under universal suffrage was held in 1931 only two years after Britain herself held her first general election under universal suffrage (in 1929). Up to 1931 the right to vote, in Sri Lanka, had been limited to a mere 4% of the population. This widening of the franchise was a bold decision taken for the avowed purpose of compelling Sri Lanka's political elite to be responsive to the needs of the masses. It was also initiated as an essential prelude to the transfer of power from the British to Sri

Lankans. The latter occurred in 1946-8 and was both smooth and peaceful (in contrast to the cognate process in the British raj), reflecting the moderate tone of the dominant strand in the country's nationalist movement.

In Britain — and in India — the extension of the suffrage to the masses followed upon the growth of political consciousness; in Sri Lanka the process was deliberately reversed. By the time independence came Sri Lanka had had three general elections under universal suffrage; India's first such election came in 1952 over four years after independence. The Sri Lankan electorate has proved to be a highly sophisticated one, politically, and on six occasions beginning in 1956 it has voted a government out of office at a general election. No other country in Asia has such a record. India herself has changed a government through the ballot twice; in 1977 and 1980. The poll at most recent elections has been well over 80% of the electorate.

This highly literate and politicized electorate has used these general elections to ensure that the political elite is indeed responsive to its needs, and through these pressures has succeeded in narrowing the gap between rich and poor far more effectively than in most post-colonial societies; over the last four decades nearly a third of the annual budget has been allocated to social welfare and the establishment of the most extensive social welfare programs in the third world. The state provides free or very inexpensive medical care to the people through a network of clinics and hospitals throughout the island; no tuition fees are charged in state schools — by far the largest number of junior and secondary schools are maintained by the state — and in technical colleges and universities; and until recently there was a system of food subsidies, provided to all citizens irrespective of income. These food subsidies proved to be a heavy financial burden on the national budget and were recently replaced by a system of food stamps to the poorer sections of the population. Almost half the population has access to these food stamps. The literacy rate is 85%, bettered only by Japan and Singapore in Asia; and life expectancy is higher and infant mortality rates much lower than almost all parts of Asia and Africa, and rival those of the southern states of Europe, Spain, Portugal and Yugoslavia.

Again, during most of the period since independence Sri Lanka's economy has been either stagnant or expanding at a moderate pace; levels of unemployment have been high; ethnic (including religious) tensions have been all too prominent a feature of social and political life; and in 1971 a youth revolt assumed the proportions of a miniature civil war. All these are hardly the ingredients regarded by political scientists as essential for the nurturing and survival of a democratic system. Yet despite all this Sri Lanka has sustained a democratic system.

Democratic politics have their less desirable side effects. Not only have the essential processes of democratic politics, the constant need to look for a mandate at a general election, or for popular support on other occasions, made the management of Sri Lanka's ethnic and religious problems an enormously difficult and complicated problem, but also at these general elections ethnic and religious issues — and more particularly the former — have often been the focal points of political contention.

Definitions

The world confronts today the hard reality of the ubiquity, durability and relative permanence of ethnic and cultural loyalties, and of "ethnic identity as one of the most unalterable of man's social characteristics..." Sixty years ago Pareto pointed out that the term ethnicity "is one of the vaguest known to sociology."[2] The efforts of scholars since then to provide greater precision to this term have not succeeded in doing so, and we are reminded that there is still "no standard definition of ethnicity, let alone agreement on its explanation."[3] Like Pareto himself scholars still use the term "merely to designate a state of fact, going in no sense into the question of explaining the fact."[4]

Every step in the process of defining ethnicity has the danger of taking one into a maze of circular reasoning. For instance, while Cynthia Enloe reminds us that the "basic function of ethnicity is to bind the individual to a group ..."[5] she also makes the point that an ethnic group becomes one "because [it] successfully present[s] [itself] as one ..."[6] that, in fact, such a group "must have reality in the minds of members not just in the eye of the beholder."[7] The way out of this maze is difficult, and is only possible through a definition of ethnicity which emphasizes "an awareness of a common identity,"[8] and brings us to three other themes. The first of these is the importance of history, of what could often become, as in the case of Sri Lanka, the burden — indeed a crushing and unbearable burden — of history. Buddhist societies, South Asian (Sri Lankan) and South East Asian are pre-eminently "historically conscious" societies.[9] Closely linked to this is the second, the "politicization of ethnicity," a process which, as Joseph Rothschild shows.

> "...stresses, ideologizes, reifies, modifies and sometimes virtually recreates the putatively distinctive and unique cultural heritages of the ethnic group it mobilizes — precisely at the historical moment when these groups are being thoroughly penetrated by the universal culture of science and technology. Politicization of ethnicity is thus a dialectical process that preserves ethnic groups by emphasizing their singularity and yet also engineers and lubricates their modernization by transforming them into political conflict groups for the modern political arena ..."[10]

And there is thirdly, the elasticity of the term ethnicity, and the wide variety of potential ethnic groups: Barth, for instance, would include "community," "culture," language group, corporation, association or population group.[11] Others speaking from a scholarly interest in or experience of third world nations argue that:

> "Ethnic identity may be perceived according to a variety of terms such as race, culture, religion, language or place of origin of the group's members."[12]

A.J. Stockwell's definition which we quote is based on the Malaysian experience. It fits the Sri Lankan situation admirably, even if it neglects the issue of caste.

References

[1]   J.W. Bjorkman, "Health Policy and Politics in Sri Lanka: Developments in the South Asian Welfare State." *Asian Survey* Vol. XXV(5) May 1985, pp. 537-552.

[2]   V. Pareto, *The Mind and Society: A Treatise on General Sociology* (1923, New York, reprinted 1963), p. 1837.

[3]   Michael Hechter, "The Political Economy of Ethnic Change", *The American Journal of Sociology*, Vol. 79(5), pp. 1151-1178, see p. 1151.

[4]   cited in Hechter, op. cit p. 1151.

[5]   Cynthia Enloe, *Ethnic Conflict and Political Development* (Boston, 1973), p. 187.

[6]   Ibid, p. 16.

[7]   Ibid.

[8]   Paul Brass, *Language, Religion and Politics in North India* (Cambridge University Press, 1974), p. 8.

9   Heinz Bechert, "Buddhism in the Modern States of South East Asia" in B. Grossman (ed) *South East Asia in the Modern World* (Wiesbaden, 1972), p. 130.

10 Joseph Rothschild, *Ethnopolitics: A Conceptual Framework* (New York, 1981), p. 3.

11 F. Barth, (ed) *Ethnic Groups and Boundaries: The Social Organization of Culture Difference*(London, 1969), p. 34.

12 A.J. Stockwell, "The White Man's Burden and Brown Humanity: Colonialism and Ethnicity in British Malaya", in *The Southeast Asian Journal of Social Science*, 10(1), 1982, pp. 44-68, p. 44.

Chapter II

An Anatomy of Sri Lankan Pluralism

A Hydraulic Civilization

From the early centuries of its recorded history, i.e., for over 2000 years, the island of Sri Lanka has had a poly-ethnic society; its main component elements are the Sinhalese and Tamils who have in common an Indian origin, the one primarily North Indian, the other South Indian. The North Indian or, to use a somewhat ambiguous term, 'Aryan' settlement and colonization of Sri Lanka began around 500 B.C. while the Tamil — or, to use another ambiguous term, 'Dravidian' — settlements proper were established a few centuries later.[1] The colonizers confronted an indigenous population about whom the historical records provide only very meager information. Like most dynamic colonizers they soon established an easy and permanent dominance over the indigenes. Nevertheless, these indigenes remained an important if forgotten and subordinate part of the population. The dominant core of the Sri Lankan state system that emerged over the next few centuries was the Sinhalese. There was a distinctive Tamil element too but it was always a much smaller if not subordinate one.

The ancient civilizations of Sri Lanka grew and flourished in the compact plain covering the northern half of the island and stretching southwards along the east coast to a smaller southern plain. This is the dry zone[2] of the island. The earliest settlements were located on the banks of the rivers of this region. Rice was the staple crop and its cultivation was dependent on the vagaries of the North East Monsoon.[3] As the settlements spread there was need to provide protection against not infrequent droughts, and by the first century B.C. a solution had been devised in the form of a highly sophisticated irrigation system remarkably attuned to coping with the geological and geographical peculiarities of the island's dry zone. The construction of canals and channels exhibited an amazing knowledge of trigonometry and the design of the tanks a thorough grasp of hydraulic principles. The broad bases of these dams could withstand the heaviest pressures, while the discharge of water from these reservoirs, or tanks, as these artificial lakes are called today, was regulated with amazing skill and precision. In the third century B.C. or earlier Sri Lankan engineers had discovered the principle of the valve tower or valve pit,[4] a technological *tour de force* which helped establish Sri Lanka as one of the great irrigation civilizations of the ancient world.

The first five centuries of the Christian era constitute the most creative and dynamic phase in the history of irrigation activity in the island. Some of the 'tanks' constructed at this time were man-made lakes of prodigious dimensions. Thus, the Kantalai tank attributed to King Mahasen (274-302) covered an area of 4560 acres. It was served by a canal 25 miles in length, and had a dam 40 to 50 feet high. The Kalavava constructed by King Dhatusena (460-478) was more sophisticated technologically. It covered an area of 7 square miles, had a dam 3½ miles long and 36 to 58 feet high with a spill of hammered granite. A 54 mile canal, 40 feet wide linked it with the capital city of Anuradhapura. The canal was an engineering feat of the highest order for the gradient in its first 27 miles was a mere 6 inches to a mile.[5] By the tenth century there was a vast array of irrigation works spread over a substantial part of the dry zone of the country.

The largest and most spectacular of the 'tanks' of ancient Sri Lanka was located at the second of the great capital cities of this era, Polonnaruva, and was a product of the twelfth century. This was the Parakramasamudra (the sea of Parakrama) which Parakramabahu I (1153-1186) constructed by incorporating within it two smaller tanks. The bund of the Parakramasamudra was nearly 9 miles in length rising to an averge height of 40 feet. Nothing on this scale was attempted thereafter till Sri Lanka regained her independence in 1948.

The monumental scale of the large tanks is positive evidence of a prosperous economy and a well organized state which had so great an agricultural surplus to invest in these projects as well as on religious and public buildings designed on a lavish scale. By itself the irrigation network of ancient Sri Lanka was a tribute to the ingenuity of her engineers and craftsmen, and the organizational skills of her rulers. Nowhere else in South and South East Asia does one find such an abundance of massive irrigation complexes as in the dry zone of Sri Lanka. Indeed, the scale of comparison is not with the Indian subcontinent, but with the major hydraulic civilizations of the ancient world, the fertile Crescent of West Asia, and with China herself. Despite its diminutive size, Sri Lanka belongs to this super-league in regard to irrigation technology and creative achievement in irrigation works, for nowhere else in

> "the pre-modern world was there such a dense concentration of irrigation facilities at such a high technical level."[6]

Buddhism and National Destiny

The introduction of Buddhism to the island around the third century B.C. had an impact on the people as decisive as the development of irrigation technology was in economic activity. Buddhism became in time the state religion and the bedrock of the culture and civilization of the island, so much so that the Sinhalese grew accustomed to regarding themselves as the chosen protectors of Buddhism. Sri Lanka itself was viewed as, "a place of special sancitity for the Buddhism religion", a concept that linked the land, the people, and the Buddhist faith, in brief an intermingling of religion and national identity which has always had the most profound influence on the Sinhalese. Sri Lanka was thus the *Dhammadipa* (the island of the Dhamma) and *Sihadipa* (the island of the Sihala people or the Sinhalese).[7]

From about the fifth century A.D. the *Dhammadipa* and *Sihadipa* concepts were embodied in the ancient Pali chronicles of the island (the *Dipavamsa* and the *Mahavamsa*), and were nourished through embellishment in Sinhalese literature, folk-lore and mythology.[8] Nurtured in an era in which there were no Tamil kingdoms within the island these concepts were in accord with the composition of the island population. While there were probably some Tamil settlements in the Mannar (Mantota) locality, the present centers of the indigenous Tamil population in the Jaffna peninsula and along the eastern coast were inhabited largely by Sinhalese.[9] So complete was the Sinhalese occupation that the term Sihala came to refer to the land as well as its inhabitants.

If Sri Lanka's irrigation network was the basis of a thriving economy with a large agricultural surplus for investment in sustaining a vibrant civilization it was Buddhism that gave dignity and elegance to this civilization and inspired the architectural and sculptural splendors of an'cient Sri Lanka. The two cities of Anuradhapura and Polonnaruva are testimony to the wealth and refinement of Sri Lanka's rulers of old.

The most striking feature of Buddhist Sri Lanka is the *stupa* or *cetiya* which came to the island from Northern India. They generally enshrined relics of the Buddha and the more celebrated *illuminati* of early Buddhism and were (and still are) on that account, objects of veneration. Generally solid hemispherical domes, the *stupas* give a subdued but effective expression to the quintessence of Buddhism — simplicity and serenity. They dominated the skyline of the city of Anuradhapura by their imposing size, awe-inspiring testimony to the state's commitment to Buddhism and to the wealth at its command. The scale of comparison once again is with the largest similar monuments in other parts of the world. The Abhayagiri, for example, was enlarged in the second century A.D. and rose to a height of 280 feet or more, while the Jetavana towered above them all at a height of over 400 feet. Both were taller than the third pyramid at Gizeh in Egypt, and were the wonders of their time. The Jetavana was very likely the largest monument in the whole Buddhist world. It is taller than St. Paul's in London and only slightly lower than St. Peter's in Rome.

Anuradhapura itself was a sprawling city, and at the height of its glory the area it covered (i.e., the city limits in modern parlance) was as extensive as that of most of the great cities of today. Polonnaruva which became the focal point of Sinhalese civilization in the eleventh century, was more compact but contained within its boundaries all the characteristic features of a capital city of ancient Sri Lanka, tanks, *stupas*, palaces and parks and their architectural and sculptural embellishments. It was a gracious cosmopolitan city.

Buddhism became the "established religion" of the Anuradhapura kingdom by the third century B.C. Thereafter, with Budhism and royal authority supporting each other and drawing strength from that, the links were institutionalized. First of all, the ruler, the state and the people were expected to, and did, provide the wherewithal for the maintenance of the *sangha*, the Buddhist order; secondly, state resources were provided for the construction of religious edifices and monuments with their architectural and scriptural embellishments; and third, there was the ruler's duty to protect Buddhism and Buddhist insitutions. All three, and especially the third, form part of the living historical heritage of modern Sri Lanka.

The Tamil Factor

There is no firm evidence on the dates of the first Tamil settlements in the island. Tamil and other literary sources, however, point to substantial urban and trading centers in South India in the third century B.C. It is possible that there were trade relations between these centers and Sri Lanka at this time, and that the island's trade with the West may have been through these South Indian ports. Inevitably traders from South India would have been attracted to the ports and trade centers of the island, and their settlements would, in time, expand in size, wealth and influence. Inevitably too adventurers followed the traders and as early as 237 B.C. two Tamil adventurers usurped the principal Sinhalese throne and ruled here for twenty-two years. Then ten years later came a more significant figure, Elara, who ruled at Anuradhapura for forty-four years, and earned a great reputation for justice and impartial administration.

The long — fifteen year — campaign waged by Dutthagamini, (c 161-137 B.C.), a Sinhalese prince, which culminated in the defeat of Elara is the central theme of the later chapters of the *Mahavamsa* and is developed there into a mythic confrontation between the Sinhalese and Tamils.[10] It is a powerful myth, part cultural, part political which has had a profound influence in shaping popular perceptions of the past, and of the role of the Tamils in Sri Lankan history as the single most powerful and persistent threat confronting the Sinhalese. But the historical evidence we have suggests that there were large reserves of support for Elara among the Sinhalese, and that Dutthagamini, as a prelude to his final decisive encounter with Elara, had to face the resistance of other Sinhalese rivals who appear to have been deeply suspicious of his political ambitions. Moreover, his eventual, and historic, triumph over Elara was much less of a self-conscious victory of Sinhalese proto-nationalism over Dravidian imperialism as much as it was in a very real sense the first significant success of centripetalism over centrifugalism in Sri Lanka's history. His life as it is portrayed in the *Mahavamsa* embodied the collective ideals of the Sinhalese people, and his rule becomes a glorious moment of national history through its fulfillment of national, political and religious aspirations — and his triumph over the Tamils.

It would appear that North Indian settlement and colonization preceded the arrival of 'Dravidian' settlers by several centuries and, as we have seen, Sri Lanka has been from early in its recorded history a multi-ethnic society in which there was a distinct 'Dravidian' element which could not alter the basic 'Aryan' North Indian character of the population. Ethnicity, however, was not an important factor in society of the time of the Dutthagamini-Elara conflict, and it would seem that neither the Sinhalese nor the Tamils could sustain a claim to ethnic purity. More important, there is no reason to suppose that tension was the normal state of affairs between them. It is more appropriate to describe Sri Lanka in the first few centuries after the North Indian settlement as a poly-ethnic society (a conception which emphasizes harmony and a spirit of live and let live) than a plural society (in which tension between ethnic or other distinctive groups is a main feature).

However, by the fifth and sixth centuries A.D. a new factor of instability was introduced into the politics of Sri Lanka with the rise of three Hindu states in South India, of the Pandyas, Pallavas and Colas. The flourishing but very vulnerable irrigation civilization of Sri Lanka's northern plains proved a tempting target for invasion from South India. There was a special quality of hostility in the threat from this quarter from the fact that these Dravidian states of South India were militantly Hindu. South Indian Buddhism, which had maintained a vigorous existence up to this time, literally disappeared under relentless pressure from a resurgent Hinduism bent on its annihilation. The effects of this on the Tamils in Sri Lanka were equally notable: they became more conscious of their ethnicity which they sought to identify in terms of culture, language and religion — 'Dravidian', Tamil and Hindu. Their settlements in the island became sources of support for the South Indian invaders, and as a result Sri Lanka, from being a multi-ethnic polity, became a plural society in which two distinct ethnic groups lived in a state of sporadic tension.

The fluctuating fortunes of these various South Indian states powerfully affected the Sinhalese kingdom and its rulers who were drawn into the turbulent politics of that region — voluntarily or involuntarily — as a necessary condition of its geopolitical position in South Asia. The fact is that the Sinhalese kingdom was rather weaker than the neighboring kingdoms of South India and while for a time it came under the influence if not control of one or other of them it could still maintain its identity by trying and often succeeding in playing one of them off against the other or others. Sri Lanka was by this time a factor in the power politics of South India and often a factor to be reckoned with. By the middle of the ninth century the Sinhalese kingdoms confronted the rapidly expanding Cola empire because of the alliance between the Sri Lanka rulers and the Pandyas. The upshot was a Cola conquest of Sri Lanka in the late 10th century and a Cola domination of the island's affairs for much of the 11th. For 75 years Sri Lanka was ruled as a province of the Cola empire, the only such episode in its history up to that time.

Anuradhapura was destroyed and the Colas established their capital at Polonnaruva largely but not entirely for reasons of security. Though the Sinhalese rulers eventually threw off the Cola yoke they never re-established Anuradhapura as the capital. They remembered how Anuradhapura had been sacked again and again in the past and how dangerously exposed it was to invasion from India. Polonnaruva had the virtue of offering greater security against that peril.

The Polonnaruva kingdom was the last of the great irrigation civilizations of ancient Sri Lanka. Its 11th century history begins with the explusion of the invading Colas after a long war of liberation, and the restoration of a Sinhalese dynasty to the throne under Vijayabahu I. This restoration had hardly been consolidated when there was a relapse into civil war and turmoil, but before anarchy had become all but irreversible a return to order and authority took place under Parakramabahu I. Into his reign (1153-86) and that of Nissanka Malla (1187-96) was crammed a record of activity and constructive achievement in administration, in economic rehabilitation, in religion and culture which could have been stretched comfortably over a much longer period and still deserved to be called splendid and awe-inspiring. But in retrospect the activity appears to have been too frenetic, with an over-extension of the island's economic resources in the restoration of its irrigation network and the architectural splendors of the city of Polonnaruva, and its political power in overseas adventures.

Our main interest in this present work is on the aftermath of the decline and collapse of the Polonnaruva kingdom. With Nissanka Malla's death there was renewed dissension among the Sinhalese and the dynastic disputes contributed to the break-up of the Polonnaruva kingdom. Sinhalese claimants to the throne invited South Indian aid in establishing their claims only to find that the ensuing instability attracted invasions by Cola and Pandya adventurers. The final episode in this was an unmitigated disaster — Magha of Kalinga's campaign of pillage and destruction from which the hydraulic civilizations of Sri Lanka's dry zone never recovered.

After Magha's death in 1255 Polonnaruva and the heartland of the old Sinhalese kingdom were abandoned and the Sinhalese kings and people, faced by repeated invasions from South India, retreated further and further into the hills of the wet zone of the island — in search primarily of security but also of some kind of new economic base for the truncated state they controlled. In the meantime Tamil settlers occupied the Jaffna peninsula and much of the land between Jaffna and Anuradhapura known as the Vanni; they were joined by Tamil soldiers in the invading armies, often mercenaries, who chose to settle in Sri Lanka rather than return to India with the rest of their compatriots. It would appear that by the thirteenth century the Tamils too withdrew from the Vanni, and thereafter their main settlements were confined almost entirely to the Jaffna peninsula and possibly to several scattered settlements near the eastern seaboard. After the thirteenth century with the establishment of a Tamil kingdom in the north of the island, there was in fact a geographical separation of the Sinhalese from the Tamils. The buffer between them were the dry zone forests of the Vanni. The Sinhalese had by now, abandoned the north-central plains and migrated to the south-west quarter of the island where there was more rain, the forests impenetrable, and the terrain rugged when not mountainous.

The distribution of population and its ethnic identity were now in glaring variance with the *Sihadipa* and *Dhammadipa* concepts, which however survived, aided of course, by the readiness with which some Vanni chiefs and Tamil kings put up with the fiction of the Sinhalese kings' overlordship. Even as late as the seventeenth and eighteenth centuries the more or less landlocked kingdom of Kandy, the last of the Sinhalese kingdoms, was known as Sihala and the Sinhalese, wherever they lived, regarded themselves as the 'king's people'. More important still, the pretense of overlordship of the island was maintained despite the obvious impossibility of sustaining it against any serious bid to challenge it.

Until the first quarter of the twentieth century a vast forest belt separated the Sinhalese from the Tamils of the north and the east; but they were not totally isolated from each other, nor was there a break in the social and economic relations between them. Just as real as the historic rivalry if not enmity between the two peoples were the long periods of relatively harmonious social relations, during which the remarkable resilience of the cultural and religious bonds —tenuous at times but strong at others — which they had in common, was repeatedly demonstrated.

The tensions and conflict between the Sinhalese and Tamils

emerging from all this are reflected in the Sinhalese chronicles in which they are often magnified far beyond the reality of historical fact. We begin with the mollifying words of the *sangha* (the Buddhist order) to Duttagamini at the end of the war with Elara. "How shall there be comfort for me, O venerable sirs," Duttagamini asked, "since by me was caused the slaughter of a great host numbering millions?" The *sangha* responded thus:

"From this deed arises no hindrance in the way to heaven. Only one and a half human beings have been slain by thee, O lord of men. The one had come into the (three) refuges, and the other had taken unto himself the five precepts. Unbelievers and men of evil life were the rest, not more to be esteemed than beasts..."[11]

The fact is that the conflict between Duttagamini and Elara was a political one, not an ethnic struggle, but by the time the *Mahavamsa* account of those events was composed ethnicity was already a powerful factor in shaping the Sinhalese sense of national identity.

By the end of the 10th century when the country was confronting the might of the Cola empire, the Sinhalese chronicles incorporate an image of the Tamils as the implacable national enemy. Thus the Colas are likened to "blood sucking yakkas" (devils) "(who) violently destroyed here and there all the monasteries, (and) took all the treasures of Lanka for themselves."[12] Then again there is the Badulla pillar inscription dated to the reign of Udaya III in the middle of the 10th century which urged that; "the office of district headman should not be given to Tamils"; and went on to more personal issues, that "daughters should not be given in marrige to them."[13]

The invasion of Magha of Kalinga lent itself to outbursts of patriotic fervor in the chronicles against the invaders. Magha himself was a Kalinga not a Tamil, but there were Tamils in his army. There is a very long account of atrocities committed by these 'Kerala warriors' or 'Damila warriors', likened to 'warriors of Mara' and 'Kerala devils'. To quote the *Culavamsa*:

"The great scorching fire — King Magha — commanded his countless flames of fire — his warriors — to harass the great forest — the Kingdom of Lanka... the Damila warriors in imitation of the warriors of Mara, destroyed in the evil of their nature, the Laity and the Order."[14]

The other side of the coin is its treatment of Parakramabahu II (1236-1270) and the resistance to Magha's armies where the historical memory is stretched all the way back to Mutasiva's triumph over the 'Damilas Sena and Guttika' in the 3rd century B.C., on then to Duttagamini's triumph over 'Elara of the Cola country', and to

Vattagamini's (103 B.C. and 87-77 B.C.) success against 'five very cruel Damila princes', on to the more recent events of Dhatusena's (455-473) victory over 'six Damila Kings' and Vijayabahu's (1055-1100) days when he expelled the 'Coliyas and Damilas.' One sees here the shaping of a national 'myth', with all these episodes linked together as part of an abiding historical memory of a people fighting to retain their independence against powerful and relentless forces of destruction.

The Colonial Interlude

The establishment and consolidation of Portuguese rule on the littoral in the sixteenth and seventeenth centuries, and the displacement of the Portuguese by the Dutch who ruled much the same region till the end of the eighteenth, had a notable impact on Sri Lanka's pluralism.

Firstly, the fact that neither the Portuguese nor the Dutch were to extend their control of the coastal region to the whole island was an important factor in the emergence of a distinction among the Sinhalese themselves, between those of the south-west littoral, the low-country Sinhalese, and those of the Kandyan areas in the interior. This was based on custom and outlook fostered by colonial rule in the one instance and the absence of it in the other. But the sense of a distinct Kandyan identity was not very sharp throughout these centuries. The political boundaries separating the Kandyan kingdom from the littoral under Western control never sharply defined were in any case remarkably porous. The Sinhalese under Portuguese and Dutch rule tended to regard the Kandyan ruler as king of all the Sinhalese. And there was regular migration of people between the south-west coast and the Kandyan kingdom.

Secondly, the subjugation of the short-lived Jaffna kingdom was one of the more lasting effects of Portuguese rule.[16] The Dutch and the British after them continued the policy of treating the Jaffna region as a mere unit of the larger colonial administrative structure. Nevertheless, for administrative convenience, if not for the sake of good order, the Portuguese and Dutch recognized and maintained the existing distinctions between the Sinhalese and the Tamils. The customary laws of the two peoples were observed. These were strengthened especially by the Dutch who compiled separate codes of law for them.

It was under the Portuguese and Dutch, moreover, that the position of the Muslims who had been in the island from about the eighth and ninth centuries as traders was brought into sharp focus as a distinctive group. Earlier, though they had achieved a dominant commercial position, they were unobtrusive, and there is no record of their having come into conflict with or arousing the jealousies of other groups. The advent of the Portuguese drastically altered the position of the Muslims. The Portuguese followed an uncompromisingly harsh policy towards them. Though the Dutch acted with greater restraint their penchant for legal codes for each ethnic group under their administration served to emphasize rather than blur the identity of the Muslims as a distinct group.

The local presence of the miniscule but influential 'Burgher' community, people of Portuguese and or Dutch extraction stems from this period. The Dutch Burghers were much the more influential of the two. They were an urban group, cut off from the indigenous population by ethnicity and culture, but closely associated with the ruling power. They retained this position under British rule but while many enjoyed elite status most held positions in the lower rungs of the bureaucracy.

The third new element of plurality was in the sphere of religion, through the conversion of Sinhalese and Tamils to Christianity. Christianity was an impinging faith, introduced in all its sectarian variety by the successive western powers who have had control over parts or the whole island. Portuguese Roman Catholicism was a militantly expansionist and aggressively proselytizing faith. The spirit of religious intolerance, and the policy of religious persecution they introduced were very much of a novelty in Sri Lanka where religious tolerance was a well-established tradition. Despite the perennial conflicts between the Sinhalese and the Tamils there had been, in general, mutual tolerance of each other's religions. The vitality of this tradition was demonstrated afresh when the Kandyan kingdom afforded a refuge to the victims of Portuguese and Dutch intolerance, to Muslim refugees from Portuguese persecution, and for Roman Catholic — and especially the harried Roman Catholic clergy — victims of Calvinist persecution. Buddhism suffered greatly under Portuguese rule and so for that matter did Hinduism and Islam. While the Dutch did not actually badger the Buddhists (for fear of offending the Kandyan ruler who regarded himself as the trustee of Buddhist rights in the island) they did not officially countenance Buddhism either, and harassment of Hindus and Muslims continued though not with the same virulence as under the Portuguese.

The material benefits anticipated from association with the established religion were a powerful attraction to elite groups seeking
continuation in office under the Portuguese and Dutch. Converts,
however, were by no means confined to the elite. Forced conversions
there undoubtedly were, especially and by no means only, under
Portuguese rule but it is to the credit of the Portuguese that
conversions to Roman Catholicism have stood the test of persecution
under the Dutch and the disdainful indifference of the British. In
sharp contrast Calvinism did not develop any strong roots among the
people, and its influence did not survive the collapse of Dutch power.
The point to be emphasized, however, is that under Portuguese and
Dutch rule converts to the "official" or "orthodox" version of
Christianity came to be regarded, and treated, as a privileged group.
Though the British were more latitudinarian in outlook the Christian
groups, especially the Anglicans, continued to enjoy favored treatment.

Through much of the nineteenth century and all of the twentieth
the Roman Catholics have constituted nine-tenths of the Christian
community in Sri Lanka. Besides, unlike the Protestants and more
especially the Anglicans who were an elite group the Roman Catholics
came from all strata of society. Together the Roman Catholics and the
Protestants were never more than a tenth of the island's population. A
tenth of the population, however made them the largest Christian
group in all of South Asia, and second only to its Philippines
counterpart if one considers South East Asia as well. They were also a
privileged group with a larger number of persons of elite status than
any other religious group in the island. The privileged position of the
Christian minority became one of the most divisive issues in Sri
Lankan politics in the years before independence and for over two
decades thereafter.

In the nineteenth and twentieth centuries, under British rule — the
whole island was under a single power after many centuries — one new
element of plurality was introduced, and several of those which existed
at the time they established their control over the island assumed new
dimensions of complexity. The new element was immigrant labor from
India to work on the coffee plantations established from the mid-1830s.[17]

The changeover from coffee to other plantation crops in the latter
half of the nineteenth century entailed a fundamental change in the
character of Sri Lanka's immigrant Indian labor. For whereas labor on
the coffee plantations was performed by seasonal migrants, tea and, to

a lesser extent, rubber required a permanent and resident supply of labor. Thus emerged Sri Lanka's Indian problem in its modern form.

Its profoundly disturbing effect was due to several reasons. The vast majority of the immigrants were Tamils; and most of them were concentrated in the plantation districts especially in the Kandyan areas. They were settled in Tamil-Hindu enclaves in Sinhalese areas, their separation from the indigenous society accentuated by the concern of the British administration in the colony with improving working conditions of plantation labor —they were the first, and for long, the only group to receive the benefit of labor legislation. Moreover the scale of migration was such as to make a significant change in the demographic patterns of the regions in which they settled.[18] During some decades in the late nineteenth century immigration from India contributed a higher percentage to the island's population than natural increase.[19]

The conspicuous presence of the migrants in very large numbers has contributed powerfully to the emergence of the Kandyan problem in its contemporary form, especially in the Kandyan aversion to the plantation economy that has been developed in their midst. They have a historic sense of grievance over the land question, the sale of undeveloped land in the Kandyan areas, by the state, for conversion into plantations, and the transfer of these lands into the hands of outsiders. There is also the jealousy and resentment directed at the low-country Sinhalese who have extended and intensified their economic activities in the Kandyan areas with the development of plantation agriculture. The Kandyans themselves have had only a marginal role in plantation activity. But much the most emotion-charged issue is the change in the demographic pattern in many of the Kandyan areas as a result of unrestriced immigration of Indian labor for the plantations.

Caste

Caste, the basis of social stratification in Sri Lankan society, Tamil and Sinhalese, from ancient times is not as important a factor of division today as is ethnicity. But, as we shall presently see, this was not always so. Nevertheless its peculiar feature was that its divisiveness was internal, that is to say within each ethnic group rather than between them. As with practically everything else caste was an Indian transplant which developed its own peculiar characteristics in Sri Lanka (the irony of a Buddhist civilization absorbing a caste system being the most significant of these).

From the beginning there were castes in Sinhalese society which did not resemble Indian castes or sub-castes. The group at the top of the Sinhalese caste hierarchy, the *goyigama*, was no thin upper crust but constituted very nearly half the Sinhalese population. While most castes had a service or occupational role as in Hindu India in general, the distinctive feature of the Sinhalese system, in contrast to its Indian proto-type, was that there was no religious sanction for caste. Thus while there were caste endogamy and taboos of caste avoidance as well, these latter did not cover the whole range of social relations and significantly there was no category of "untouchables" in Sinhalese society except the miniscule *rodi*.[20]

The Sinhalese caste system has been extraordinarily malleable. There was, and is, no rigid stratification on the basis of an immutable order of precedence of castes, and in general a singular pliancy which led Louis Dumont to argue that there was no caste "system among the Sinhalese.[21]

There have been, over the centuries, some remarkable changes recorded in the gradation of Sinhalese castes. In the Sinhalese areas of the littoral, the *salagama*, *karava*, and *durava* rose in importance under western rule. The first distinctive phase in the upward mobility among these castes came in the last quarter of the eighteenth century, largely on account of a belated recognition by the Dutch of the vital importance of the caste occupation of the *salagamas* (cinnamon peeling) to the health of the economy. Upward mobility was more general and much easier under British rule through skilful exploitation of opportunities available to people, to move from traditionally ascribed occupations, the classic example being the *karavas* in the nineteenth century who rose in influence and to unprecedented affluence.[23]

Indeed, the period of British rule was crucial in the transformation of the Sinhalese caste system, but this affected the low-country Sinhalese more than the Kandyans. In the early decades of British rule the government acted on the conviction that the caste system was obnoxious and intolerable, and was opposed to any recognition of caste distinctions. More than once positive declarations were made explicitly and ostentatiously directed against caste discrimination. In the new economy caste affiliations no longer had an inevitable link with occupations, and opportunities became available heedless of caste status. A similar avenue of mobility was opened by the education system. All this meant that the traditional indices of caste distinction, in particular formal caste precedence, were gradually being undermined though not without opposition and recrimination. Caste rivalries in fact became more pronounced in the last quarter of the nineteenth century and seriously affected political activity among the Sinhalese, in the sense that they made it impossible to forge a united front against the British. By the last quarter of the nineteenth century the British became more conservative in their attitudes. They threw their influence behind the *goyigama* establishment against the latter's dynamic, aggressive and affluent *karava* challengers in a well-publicized reversal of the traditional British attitude of not countenancing caste prejudices.[24]

Despite the spread of the plantations the Kandyans were much less affected by the liberalizing effects of the new economy than the low-country Sinhalese. There were no equivalents of the emergent *karava*, *salagama* and *durava* to challenge the primacy of the Kandyan *goyigama*. Thus the relaxation of caste distinctions took longer in the Kandyan areas, and inter-caste regulations had a greater hold there than in the littoral.

The introduction of universal suffrage in 1931 and democratic politics have had a two-fold effect on the Sinhalese caste system. On the one hand because the *goyigama* are the largest group numerically, universal suffrage has enabled them to establish a dominant position in politics by virtue of this fact rather than any recognition and facile acceptance of their caste superiority by others.[25] Secondly, as parliamentary constituencies became smaller in area, minority castes were able to increase their bargaining position *vis-a-vis* the *goyigama*, thus undermining the viability, politically, of a policy of caste discrimination in contemporary Sinhalese society. While overt appeals to caste are rare — unlike in India — the organizational opportunities inherent in political mobilization through recognition of caste identity helped ensure the latter's continued survival as a significant factor in political contests.

Ironically enough caste discrimination prevails practically undisturbed only within the *sangha*, the Buddhist order. Throughout the nineteenth and twentieth centuries caste has been one of the primary factors in Buddhist sectarianism. Entry to the most prestigious *nikaya* (sect) of the *sangha*, the *Siyam nikaya*, is restricted to the *goyigama* caste.[26]

The caste system of the Tamils in Sri Lanka has had much less flexibility than that of the Sinhalese.[27] More important, caste distinctions among the Tamils had as their foundation the religious sanction of the Hindu religion, which made these all the more rigid as a result. In general the Tamil caste system was hardly affected by the rule of the colonial powers which, considering the dynamic influence of English education among the Tamils, is indeed surprising. The Hindu revivalist movement in the second half of the nineteenth century in Sri Lanka strengthened orthodoxy and with it the hierarchical dominance of the *vellalas*, the Tamil counterpart of the *goyigama*. The *vellala* also held a commanding numerical superiority over other Tamil castes with the significant difference that their position, however, was never effectively challenged by the latter. As it turned out, the *vellala* were not only the main beneficiaries of the new opportunites for social and economic advancement that were opened up by the British but they contrived to use the sanctions of Saivite orthodoxy to maintain and consolidate their caste privileges at the expense of those in the lower rungs of the caste hierarchy in Tamil society in Sri Lanka, and in particular in the Jaffna peninsula. Their own insecure status, indeed their marginality in terms of the traditional Hindu caste hierarchy has made them all the more fanatical in defense of their position.[28] Untouchability, virtually non-existent among the Sinhalese, was and still is very much a problem in the Hindu society of Jaffna. The spatial distribution of caste settlements within villages and inter-caste regulations as well as caste endogamy assumed greater meaning in Tamil society. A distinction was drawn not only between "clean" and "unclean" castes — something absent among the Sinhalese — but also within the main classifications.

Demography

We need to complete this introductory chapter by sketching a profile of Sri Lanka's demography. The salient feature of that profile is the overwhelming dominance of the Sinhalese who today form just over 74% of the island's population and at most times during the nineteenth and twentieth centuries, when island-wide census figures were collected, were always at least two-thirds of the population. Most Sinhalese are Buddhists; indeed in religious affiliation 67% of the population are Buddhists. The Tamils — both the indigenous Tamils and the Indian Tamils — constitute the largest minority group, forming a fifth of the population. Right up to independence the Indian Tamils were numerically the larger of the two groups, but their numbers are now steadily declining through repatriation to India and by the late 1980s they will be reduced to about half the number of indigenous Tamils.

Ethnicity divides the Tamils from the Sinhalese and the symbol of a distinctive Tamil identity so far as this division is concerned is language rather than religion, but while language distinguishes the Sinhalese from the Tamils — the two languages have, in fact, two distinctive scripts — it does little to provide any cohesion to the Tamil groups. The vast majority of the Indian Tamils are and always have been plantation workers, and they belong overwhelmingly to the lower strata of the Hindu caste hierarchy.[29] Linguistic ties have proved inadequate so far to override the divisive effects of the *vellala* pride of caste among the Tamil elite groups in Colombo and Jaffna in their relations with the Indian Tamils, and there is in addition the sense of class superiority.

The distribution of the Tamil population has had deeply significant political connotations: the enclaves of plantation workers in the Kandyan areas have been referred to earlier in this chapter; we need to consider the concentration of indigenous Tamils in the Jaffna peninsula and the Northern Province generally where they form an overwhelming majority of the population, and their presence in large numbers along the eastern seaboard and in Colombo where they are a significant minority. If the demographic changes caused by the entry of large numbers of Indian plantation workers to the Kandyan region have been one of the major political issues of modern Sri Lanka, the physical separation of the Tamil population of the north and east from the Sinhalese, till very recently, by a vast forest belt, has had its own no less complicated political problems. It has contributed greatly to the process of ethnic preservation and, in recent times, to the development of Tamil nationalism, and separatist tendencies.

One must remember too that Sri Lanka's population explosion is not a twentieth century phenomenon; it has its beginnings in the middle of the nineteenth century. In 1824 the island's population was a mere 851,941; by 1911 it had reached 4,106,300. Undoubtedly the immigration of Indian plantation workers contributed its share to this increase but the rate of natural growth was, by itself, one of the highest in Asia. This natural increase was greater in the Sinhalese areas of the low country than in almost all other parts of the island.

There was no slackening in the rate of growth of population in the first half of the twentieth century. In the first decade the rate of growth was 15.2% (a population of 4.1 million), 9.6% in the next (4.5 million in 1921) rising to 18% in the decade 1921-1931 (to a population of 5.31 million), and in the period 1931-46 population rose to 6.6 million, an increase of 25%. Density of population rose from 141 per square mile in 1901 to 263 in the mid-1940s, with a marked regional variation that ranged, in 1901, from 500 in the Colombo district to less than 50 in the dry zone areas. There was no change in this pattern of growth in the early twentieth century. The most densely populated part of the island was the south west coast especially the strip extending inwards from the coast and covering the region from Negombo to Matara. Despite this rapid growth in population it remained predominantly rural in all parts of the island including the south west coast and the Colombo district.

One more important facet of population growth attracted more attention than most others — there were expressions of concern from Sri Lankan politicians and British officials alike at overpopulation in parts of the wet zone. By the 1930s population pressure had reached the point where the land resources of the wet zone were clearly incapable of sustaining peasant agriculture against the pervasive pressures of the plantations for land. Up to that time increase in population had been absorbed without resort to any substantial process of internal migration.[30] As a result a deliberate shift of population to the dry zone was encouraged through a process of land colonization especially in the North Central Province. Malaria was, till the 1940s, a formidable obstacle to this process of colonization. But health and transport facilities were improving rapidly and with that the forests that separated the Tamils of the north and east from the Sinhalese were cut down. This moving frontier upset the Tamils who looked upon it with suspicion at first and then increasingly as a palpable threat to the preservation of their majority status in those parts of the north and east where they had such a position.

References

[1] For clarification of terms 'Aryan' and 'Dravidian' see T. Burrow "The Early Aryans" and John R. Marr "The Early Dravidians", Chapters II and IV and pp. 20-29, and 30-37 respectively in (ed) A.L. Basham, *A Cultural History of India* (Oxford, 1975)

[2] The dry zone occupies about two thirds of the land area of the island, consisting largely of the plains of the north-west, north, north-east, east and south-east. The flatness of the plain is broken by scores of rocks and rounded mounds which rise occasionally to heights of over 1000 feet, the erosional remnants of an area levelled over aeons of uninterrupted denudation and weathering. The average annual rainfall is less than 75".

[3] The pattern of the island's rainfall which is convectional is modified to a great extent by two monsoons, the south-west which reaches its peak in July and the north-east in December.

[4] H. Parker, *Ancient Ceylon* (London, 1909), p. 379.

[5] For a review of irrigation in Sri Lanka in these centuries see R.A.L.H. Gunawardane, "Irrigation and Hydraulic Society in Early Medieval Ceylon", *Past and Present*, 53, November 1971, pp. 3-27.

[6] R. Murphey, "The Ruin of Ancient Ceylon", *Journal of Asian Studies* XVI(2), 1967, p. 184.

[7] See K. Malalgoda's perceptive analysis of "Millennialism in Relation to Buddhism", *Comparative Studies in Society and History* VII(4) October 1970, pp. 424-41; L.S. Perera, "The Pali Chronicles of Ceylon" in C.H. Philips (ed.) *Historians of India, Pakistan and Ceylon* (O.U.P., 1961), pp. 29-43; Michael Roberts "Ethnic Conflict in Sri Lanka and Sinhalese Perspectives: Barriers to Accommodation", *Modern Asian Studies* XII(3), 1978, pp. 353-76.

[8] See Heinz Bechert, "The Beginning of Buddhist Historigraphy in Ceylon: The *Mahavamsa* and "Political Thinking"", *Ceylon Studies Seminar*, No. 46, 1974; K. Malalgoda, "Millenialism in Relation to Buddhism", *op. cit.*

[9] K. Indrapala, "Dravidian Settlements in Ceylon and the Beginnings of the Kingdom of Jaffna" (University of London: unpublished Ph.D. dissertation, 1966).

[10] For the historical background see K.M. de Silva, *A History of Sri Lanka*, (London, 1981) pp. 7-16.

[11] *Mahavamsa* (W. Geiger's translation) (Colombo, 1950 reprint) Chapter 25, verses 108-111.

[12] *Culavamsa* (W. Geiger's translation) (Colombo, 1953 reprint) Chapter 55, verses 19-21.

[13] Edited and translated by S. Paranavitana.

[14] *Culavamsa*, Chapter 80, verses 60-71.

[15] *Culavamsa*, Chapter 82, verses 21-26.

[16] On the history of the kingdom of Jaffna, see S. Pathmanathan, *The Kingdom of Jaffna* (Colombo, 1978). See also P.A.T. Gunasinghe, *The Tamils of Sri Lanka: Their History and Role* (Colombo, 1985).

[17] For the immigration of Indian plantation labor to Sri Lanka in the nineteenth century, see, Michael Roberts "Indian Estate Labor in Ceylon during the Coffee

Period, 1830-1880", *The Indian Economic and Social History Review* III(1&2), 1966, pp. 1-52, 101-156. K.M. de Silva, *Social Policy and Missionary Organizations in Ceylon, 1840-55*, pp. 255-281, 299-300. See also H. Tinker, *A New System of Slavery, The Export of Indian Labor Overseas 1830-1920* (London, 1974).

18   See Table IV p. 417 below

9   See Table V p. 418 below.

20   Bryce Ryan's, *Caste in Modern Ceylon:* The Sinhalese System in Transition (New Brunswick, New Jersey, 1953) is still the most comprehensive work on the theme.

21   Louis Dumont, *Homo Hierarchicus* (London, 1972), pp. 262-3.

22   On the emergence of these three new Sinhalese castes see K.M. de Silva, *op. cit.*, pp. 91-92.

23   Michael Roberts, *Caste Conflict and Elite Fomration. The Rise of a Karava Elite in Sri Lanka, 1500-1931.* (Cambridge, 1982).

24   The British attitude to caste rivalry is discussed in K.M. de Silva, *op. cit.*, pp. 216, 243-50, 324-5, 336-344.

25   Janice Jiggins, *Caste and Family in the Politics of the Sinhalese 1947-1976* (Cambridge, 1979).

26   This is discussed in detail in K. Malalgoda, *Buddhism in Sinhalese Society, 1750-1900* (Berkeley, 1976).

27   On the caste system in Jaffna, see Michael Banks, "Caste in Jaffna" in ed. E.R. Leach, *Aspects of Caste in South India, Ceylon and North West Pakistan* (Cambridge, 1960), Cambridge Papers in Social Anthropology No. 2; see also B. Pfaffenberger, *Caste in Tamil Culture: Religious Foundations of Sudra Domination in Tamil Sri Lanka* (New Delhi, 1982).

28   B. Pfaffenberger, *Caste in Tamil Culture, op. cit.*

29   See, R. Jayaraman, "Indian Emigration to Ceylon: Some Aspects of the Historical and Social Background of the Emigrants". *The Indian Economic and Social History Reveiw*, IV(4) December 1967, pp. 319-359. There is also a shorter article by the same author specifically on the theme of caste: "Caste and Kinship in a Ceylon Tea Estate" in *The Economic Weekly*, 22 February 1964, pp. 393-97.
Jayaraman points out that the majority of them belonged to 'non-Brahman and Adi-Dravida' castes of Tamilnadu.

30   It is not that there was no internal migration at all. The plantation regions attracted not merely immigrant labor from South India but local people as well, workers, traders, craftsmen of various sorts, and carters to townships and market centers serving the plantations not to mention others who came into these areas to claim a modest niche in traditional agriculture in the periphery of the plantations.

PART II

Nationalism, Constitutional Reform and The Transfer of Power

PART II

Nationalism, Constitutional Reform and The Transfer of Power

Introduction

The eight chapters (III-X) in part II of this volume cover the last three decades of the nineteenth century. These years mark the first phase in the emergence of nationalism in Sri Lanka, when incipient nationalist sentiment, primarily religious in outlook and content, asserted the need for the primacy of Buddhist values and claimed that Buddhism was in danger of subversion if not submergence. Political overtones in it were visible from its inception, especially in the appeal to the native past as against a contemporary situation of foreign domination. Through the temperance movement, an integral part of the Buddhist revival in the first decade of the twentieth century, it provided an introduction, tentative but astutely restrained, to political activity and became the rallying point of the recovery of national consciousness. But faith in the permanence of British control over the affairs of the island remained largely unshaken, and nobody in public life at the turn of the century could have imagined that Sri Lanka would be independent within 50 years.

Neither the outbreak of the first world war, nor the perverse mishandling of the situation in the island in the wake of the Sinhalese-Muslim riots of 1915, led to a more pronounced radicalization of politics. The keynotes of the emerging reform movement were restraint and moderation. The formation of the Ceylon National Congress in 1919 was evidence of the strength of these attitudes rather than of any notable departure from them.

The 1920s, on the other hand, were characterized by bolder initiatives in politics in the form, firstly, of a significant heightening of working class activity and trade unionism particularly in Colombo and its suburbs. A more intractable problem was the breakdown of the comparative harmony of interests and outlook which had characterized relations between Sinhalese and Tamil politicians in the first two decades of the twentieth century. Foreseeing a transfer of a substantial measure of political power to the indigenous political leadership, minority groups led by the Tamils were increasingly anxious to protect their interests as a prelude to this transfer.

The constitutional reforms introduced in 1931 amounted to the first step towards self-government. Equally significant was the introduction of universal suffrage, which became the main determining factor in the re-emergence of "religious" nationalism, that is nationalism intertwined with Buddhist resurgence and its associated cultural heritage. Again, although the massive rural vote easily swamped the working class vote, universal suffrage strengthened the working class movement and opened the way for it to play an independent role in politics. By the early 1930s Marxists had established themselves in the leadership of the indigenous working class movement. On a different level universal suffrage was largely responsible for the broad impulse towards social welfare, especially in the years 1936-47. Among the most constructive achievements of this era was the purposeful program of restoration of the irrigation schemes of the dry zone, and the settlement of peasant colonists there, under the leadership of D.S. Senanayake, Minister of Agriculture and Lands for 15 years.

The final phase in the transfer of power also began under Senanayake's astute leadership. He was guided by a strong belief in ordered constitutional evolution to dominion status on the analogy of constitutional development in the white dominions. In response to the agitation in Sri Lanka the British goverment appointed the Soulbury Commission in 1944 to examine the constitutional problems there. The constitution that emerged from their deliberations was based substantially on one drafted for Senanayake in 1944 by his advisers. It gave the island internal self-government while retaining some Imperial safeguards in defense and external affairs, but Sri Lanka's leaders pressed, successfully, for the removal of these restrictions, and the island was granted independence, with dominion status, on 4 February 1948. The transfer of power was smooth and peaceful, a reflection of the moderate tone of the dominant strand of the country's nationalist movement. In general the situation in the country seemed to provide an impressive basis for a solid start in nation-building and national regeneration.

Chapter III

Religious Revivalism, Caste Rivalries and Political Quiescence. c. 1870-1900

The Buddhist Revival

One of the common assumptions about the evolution of nationalism in Sri Lanka is that there were two distinct phases in in it, one liberal, moderate and generally concerned about the maintenance of ethnic and religious concord in Sri Lanka's plural society, while the other was populist if not radical and inherently disruptive of communal and religious harmony. The years 1955-6 are treated as the dividing line. Any realistic assessment of the origins and development of modern nationalism in the island must begin however, by demonstrating that any novelty in this second phase was deceptive and that on the contrary the changes inherent in it had their roots in earlier phases of nationalist awakening going back to the last quarter of the nineteenth century.

In Sri Lanka as in many parts of Asia the origins of modern nationalism can be traced back to programs of religious revivalism which were a reaction against missionary enterprise. Religious revival — a Buddhist revival, more specifically — preceded the emergence of political nationalism in the island. It contributed greatly to the latter by providing as it did an ideal basis for the rejection of the pervasive occidental presence and influence in Sri Lankan society. The first phase in the emergence of nationalism would cover the last three decades of the nineteenth century, and its most notable feature was a prolonged but intermittent confrontation between a Buddhist revivalist movement and the strongly entrenched Christian minority, who were a conspicuously privileged group with a larger number of persons of elite status than any other religious group in the island. This confrontation, it must be noted, was primarily a division among the

Sinhalese themselves, and although the Tamils were an influential element among the Christians of all sects the religious controversies that emerged from it never had an ethnic dimension to them.

The Buddhist-Christian Confrontation[1]

The early nineteenth century saw the beginnings of the recovery of Roman Catholicism in the island after the rigorous suppression of it attempted by the Dutch when Calvinist intolerance had replaced an equally harsh or even harsher intolerance by Roman Catholicism directed against the indigenous religions of the Sri Lankan littoral.[2] For much of the first half of the nineteenth century the Roman Catholics had little or no influence on official policies and attitudes which affected the Buddhists. There the pace was set by the Protestants in general and not necessarily the elite Anglican group. But with the passage of time the Roman Catholics asserted themselves and with numbers very much on their side the interaction between Christianity and the indigenous society was often a complex tripartite one, or where the government entered the scene with interests of its own, very often a quadripartite one.

Most of the Protestant missionaries in British Ceylon shared some of the basic assumptions of the secular advocates of Empire — faith in the permanence of British rule being one of them — and identified themselves with the processes of colonial rule to the point which tended to make them appear to the indigenous population as the spiritual arm of the ruling power. To be sure there was no total identity of interests between Christianity and the state, and the missionaries seldom entirely ceased to be critical of the government, but their association, a blend of collaboration and critical appraisal of each other's work, was close enough for the missionary movement to suffer when colonial rule came under attack just as it benefitted enormously from its association with Empire.[3]

With the absorption of the Kandyan kingdom within the crown colony of Ceylon, the British were confronted with one of the most perplexing and intricate problems they were called upon to handle in Sri Lanka, the definition of the state's relations with Buddhism. At the cession of the Kandyan kingdom in 1815 the British had given an undertaking to protect and maintain Buddhism. Nevertheless from the beginning the attitude to Buddhism was one of reluctant neutrality rather than open support. And in the 1840s under Evangelical pressure

the decision was taken to sever the connection between the government and Buddhism. Kandyan opinion viewed this as a gross betrayal
of the solemn undertaking given on the occasion of the signing of the
Kandyan Convention in March 1815. The historical significance of
this could scarcely be exaggerated for it marked the severance of the
traditional bond between Buddhism and the rulers of Sri Lanka which
had lasted almost without interruption from the earliest days of the
ancient Sinhalese kingdom.[4] The withdrawal of the traditional
patronage accorded to Buddhism, and the consequent loss of
precedence and prestige was deeply resented by the Buddhists in
general not merely by the Kandyans. Although a promise was made in
the 1850s that effective administrative machinery for the control of
Buddhist temporalities would be devised, that promise was not
redeemed for several decades thereafter, and even then rather
perfunctorily. As a result the steady decay of Buddhist temporalities
under British rule became one of the persistent complaints of the
Buddhists.

With the Buddhist revival of the last quarter of the nineteenth
century the indigenous element became more assertive if not yet the
dominant one in determining the balance of forces in the complex
interaction between the Christians and the rest of Sri Lankan society.
The government responded with an attempt to turn the Buddhist
movement, which it viewed as an intrinsically conservative force, to its
own advantage. Because the Buddhist movement did not present
demands for constitutional or administrative reform — the two main
points of interest in the incipient formal political activity of the day
—men like Governors Sir William Gregory (1872-77) and Sir Arthur
Gordon (1883-90) were inclined to look upon it with sympathy.
Whatever the motive behind this attitude there was no mistaking the
advantage to the Buddhist movement. A breakthrough came first over
establishing the crucial principle of the state's neutrality in religion. It
came with studied deliberation, and moved from one precedent to
another. The state's neutrality in religious affairs asserted so often in
the mid-1850s and thereafter was demonstrated in a manner at once
open and vigorous by the dis-establishment of the Anglican Church in
1881. With that the separation of church and state was very nearly
complete. But it soon became clear that total separation could not be
made if for no more pressing reason than the revival of Buddhism
which brought with it a persistent demand for state assistance in the
maintenance and supervision of Buddhist temporalities.[5]

Governor Sir Arthur Gordon, for instance, found no difficulty in accepting the principle of the government's neutrality in religious affairs even though he balked at the idea of a formal declaration to that effect which, he felt, carried the implication that the government had indeed been partisan in the past. More important, it would stultify the other related principle in which Gordon believed — that the state had a special obligation towards Buddhism, a judicious patronage of Buddhism which could easily be transformed into a special responsibility towards Buddhism. With this the breakthrough was consolidated.

Of the issues which agitated the Buddhists at this time none was more complex than the vexed one of temple lands — Buddhist temporalities. Gordon, reviving an initiative attempted by Gregory, broke through a barrier of bureaucratic inertia and missionary opposition to give the Buddhists some satisfaction over this long-standing grievance. This he did on the basis of the principle of a special obligation towards Buddhism. The solution he outlined in 1888 was an ordinance of considerable complexity. There was substantial opposition to this bill both within and outside the Legislative Council, but Gordon steered it through to Colonial Office approval in 1889, though not without some concessions to his critics. His predecessor Governor Sir James Longden (1877-83) on the other hand had seen legislation on Buddhist temporalities as a somewhat disagreeable concesion to agitation. Gordon treated it as a matter of conscience and as a fulfillment of an obligation which the British government owed to the Buddhists of the island, who constituted over two-thirds of the population.

The ordinance of 1889 was important because of the principles it embodied rather than for any impact it had on the problems it was devised to remedy. It proved to be too complicated and cumbersome in its working and it did not eliminate or for that matter even significantly reduce corruption and peculation among the trustees of these temporalities. The Buddhist movement regarded this state of affairs as an intolerable scandal, a blot on the reputation of Buddhism in general and continued an agitation for stronger measures to eradicate it. In response to this pressure and in recognition of the validity of the charges levelled by Buddhist activists the Colonial government in the early years of the twentieth century decided on fresh — and more effective — legislation to check if not prevent misappropriation of trust property.

By this time the Buddhist movement was pitching its demands

higher. What it wanted was that the state should assume direct responsibility for the administration of Buddhist temporalities and a more positive, in the sense of a formal, link between the state and Buddhism, in brief a reversion to the position that had existed up to the 1840s when the link had been severed under missionary pressure. But the British government was reluctant to go so far.

By the turn of the century the Buddhist movement had gained greatly in self-confidence. Its leaders turned their attention to what was regarded as one of the great social evils of the day, and one associated with the processes of westernization — intemperence. To the Buddhists the drawing, distilling and sale of arrack and toddy — in short, the use of spiritous liquors — was offensive to the precepts of their religion and the traditional usages of Sinhalese society. Nevertheless the manufacture and distribution of arrack and toddy were controlled by Sinhalese capitalists, many if not most of whom were *karava* Christians.[6] There were also Buddhists of the same and other castes who had large investments in the liquor industry. To the British government, excise duties were a legitimate source of state revenues, and while there was increasing awareness of the harmful effects on village life of excessive alcohol consumption, the reluctance to endanger a valuable source of revenue by the whole-hearted pursuit of temperance objectives overshadowed all that. The Buddhist movement, on the other hand, had no such inhibitions, and by the turn of the century temperance activity was a vitally important facet of the religious revival. Some of the money that went into the support of temperance agitation came from wealth amassed in the liquor trade, conscience-money from Buddhists who thus repudiated a lucrative source of income — there were many prominent Buddhists in this category — or, as was more often the case, from those who had inherited fortunes wholly or partly based on the arrack trade.

By the first decade of the twentieth century, temperance agitation had spread far and wide especially in the Sinhalese areas of the Western and Southern Provinces, and the response it evoked had sufficient passionate zeal in it to sustain the hope that it had potential for development into a political movement. On occasion, temperance agitators indulged in criticism of the government by associating it with the evils of intemperance: and diatribes against foreign vices and Christian values were cleverly scaled down into more restrained and subtle criticism of a 'Christian' government. But while the temperance agitation gave added momentum to the Buddhist movement, it afforded only a tentative and astutely restrained introduction to formal political activity. It is significant that no attempt was made to channel the mass emotion it generated into a sustained and organized political movement. The politicization of the movement, once its appeal to the people became evident, seemed the logical and inevitable next step, but this was never taken. Equally significant was the fact that the mass grassroots support which the temperance agitation generated was achieved without the assistance much less the leadership of such political organizations as existed.

The colonial authorities in the island instinctively got their priorities right. They either ignored these political organizations, or where their aspirations were regarded as an affront or a mild threat to the British position in the island, they were treated with studied contempt. But many British administrators in Sri Lanka were perturbed, from the beginning, by temperance agitation, and they viewed the proliferation of temperance societies with the utmost suspicion, because the Buddhist revival and the temperance movement had by then generated a feeling of hostility to the colonial regime which could, potentially, disturb the hitherto placid political life of the island. Christian missionaries had come to much the same conclusion. 'The political consciousness', they declared in 1910,

> "is almost inevitably anti-British and pro-Hindu [in India], and in Ceylon pro-Buddhist. ...The anti-British feeling becomes anti-Christian feeling: the pro-Hindu or pro-Buddhist feeling develops into a determination to uphold all that passes under the name of Hinduism or Buddhism."

With specific reference to the situation in the island the missionaries noted that,

> "one of the most serious aspects of the Buddhist revival is the attempt to identify Buddhism with patriotism, and to urge upon people that loyalty to the country implies loyalty to the religion... [The Buddhist revival] is hostile to Christianity, representing it as alien, and Buddhism as national and patriotic..."[7]

Though the diagnosis of the malady was swift and accurate, it was as usual more difficult to prescribe a remedy. And no remedy was likely to be effective so long as the root cause of the ailment, the "westernness" of Sri Lankan Christianity was not eliminated. All Christian groups had been oblivious to the value to Christian worship of indigenous art-forms such as music, drumming, dance and even architecture. They had come to Sri Lanka as the apostles of a new faith, as critics of indigenous society and in preaching the gospel —Christianity whether Roman Catholic or Protestant, had generally been an aggressively proselytizing faith — their missionaries had been fortified usually by an unquestioning faith not merely in their own rightness but also in the intrinsic depravity of many traditional customs and beliefs. Indeed there had been a conscious attempt to undermine traditional customs and beliefs and to impose in their place Christian values of the Victorian age. All this had given the Christian community in the island its characteristic feature — cultural alienation. They made no attempt — at least up to the early years of the twentieth century — to blend with the local culture. As a result the Christians, and especially the Protestants, were not only a privileged group but were also alienated from the people at large by an overpowering and seemingly indestructible occidentalism.

The Hindu and Islamic Revival

We turn now to the response of Hinduism and Islam to the challenges posed to them by the dominant religion — Christianity. The recovery of Hinduism in nineteenth century Sri Lanka began a whole generation earlier than that of Buddhism. In a sense Hinduism was in a more advantageous position in resistance to missionary encroachment because it was possible to draw on the tremendous resources of Hinduism in India. Nevertheless in the first half of the nineteenth century — and for that matter even later — the missionary organizations were much stronger in Jaffna and its environs than in most other parts of the island. There were fewer sectarian conflicts among the missionaries working in the north, and their network of schools was far more efficiently run. It would appear that the colonial government was less sensitive to potential risks of occasional or general outbursts of popular hostility to missionary activity in the Tamil areas of the country than with the reaction to mission work among the Buddhists.

The leadership in the Hindu recovery in Sri Lanka was given by Arumuga Navalar, and the structure of Hindu society in contemporary Sri Lanka has been largely influenced by him. The two dominant strands in his work were: a determined effort to stop conversions of Hindus to Christianity; and to preserve the orthodox form of Saivism. To a large extent he was successful in these, especially in the latter. As a counterpoise to the Christian missionary effort he organized Hindu schools for imparting religious and secular education, an example and policy which influenced some eminent Hindu leaders of the nineteenth and early twentieth century.[8] The preservation of the orthodox form of Saivism had two aspects: the renovation and restoration of Hindu temples; and the publication of Saivite religious texts, in both of which Navalar was the pioneer.

Nearly all the Hindu temples in the Jaffna peninsula and the littoral had been destroyed by the Portuguese and the Dutch, and those that had survived were in a state of decay and dilapidation in the nineteenth century. The Hindu temples of Sri Lanka, unlike those in India, are of modest proportions and have rather slender resources for their maintenance. The restoration of the temples was not followed by a restitution of the lands that belonged to them in pre-colonial times. The reconstruction of these temples has continued in contemporary Sri Lanka and is a prominent feature in Hindu life in all parts of the island. Among the Hindus the temple has been and still continues to be the center of cultural activity in the villages, with the annual temple festival the most notable religious and cultural event of the year.

Perhaps Navalar's greatest contribution to the recovery of Hinduism was the publication of a large number of Saivite religious texts. These have helped substantially in sustaining the ideals and preserving the heritage of the Hindus in Sri Lanka primarily, but in South India as well. Some of these publications are still in use as texts for religious instruction in schools. Hindus in Sri Lanka today are, with the exception of a few North Indian traders in Colombo, Saivites belonging to the Siddhanta school of Saivism which is dominant in South India.

The crucial flaw in Navalar's work — and this became evident in the years after independence — was that he was not a social reformer. The Hindu revivalist movement which he led strengthened orthodoxy —as indeed it was intended to — and did little to soften the rigors of the caste system in the Tamil areas of the country. Where the Sinhalese caste system had merely a social sanction the Tamil prototype was deeply embedded in society through the sanctions of Hinduism.

The dark unlovely side of Hinduism and the Hindu caste system lies in the treatment accorded to the so-called "untouchables". From time immemorial these "untouchables" were forbidden entry to Hindu temples, on grounds of "pollution", the most conspicuous act of discrimination in Hindu society directed at them, but by no means the only one. There was also the persistent *vellala* opposition to equal seating in schools which far from abating by the turn of the century reached a peak of emotionalism and violence in the late 1920s and early 1930s. Then again there was the refusal to concede to the *harijans* the right to a seat in buses. Eventually it required government intervention to enforce this right, but attempts to enforce it led to outbreaks of violence in 1930-31, and to a strike by bus drivers and conductors. Previously *harijans* were expected to stand at the back of the bus, or to sit, or squat, on the floor of the bus even though they were required to pay the normal fare. It took decades before *vellalas* accepted this change, and most of them did so with unconcealed reluctance.[9] Discrimination against *harijans* extended to restrictions on entry into cafes and "eating-houses", access to village amenities like wells and cemeteries, and on the clothes they wore — their right to wear shoes was a frequent point of contention. Largely because the *harijan* communities were, and still are, themselves sharply divided by caste rivalries and did not have any common organization to mobilize their resources effectively for bargaining for their rights, there was no improvement in their position until after independence, and the mid-1950s in fact.

In contrast to Hinduism and Christianity, Islam has had a record of harmonious relations with the Buddhist Sinhalese both in the coastal areas and in the Kandyan region. In the latter the Muslims had been afforded a refuge against the vigorous hostility of the Portuguese and the harrassment of the Dutch. There they had been integrated into Kandyan society, though they retained their religious and cultural identity. In the early years of British rule the position of the Muslims of Sri Lanka improved considerably and they became in many ways a privileged group.

In the nineteenth century the Muslims, like the Buddhists and Hindus, faced the challenge of Protestant Christianity, but to a much greater extent than both of them, the Muslims were notable for a refusal to succumb to the blandishments of Christianity. This resistance to conversion to Christianity persisted throughout the nineteenth century, but the survival of Islam in Sri Lanka had been secured, in a sense, at the expense of social if not economic advancement of its adherents. Much of this had to do with the Muslims' response to the school system that developed under British rule and in which Christian missions were a dominant influence. Since the education provided in the schools was primarily an English one, the Muslims of Sri Lanka tended to reject it because of dangers they perceived of a potential erosion of faith in Islam among the younger generation, for education was not only in English but was also largely Christian in content. This manifestation of their zeal for their ancestral faith had rather regrettable consequences for they deliberately sacrificed the social and material benefits that accrued to other communities in the island from the educational process, and by the third quarter of the nineteenth century, the more enlightened Muslim leaders were profoundly disturbed by what they regarded as the backwardness of their community.

The revitalization of the Muslim community has been associated for long with the "charisma" of an Egyptian exiled to the island by the British, Orabi Pasha[10], who is believed to have jolted them out of their conservative seclusion. But much more important were the foresight and tactical skill of a local Muslim leader — M.C. Siddi Lebbe, a lawyer by profession and social worker by inclination — in helping to bring the community to accept the need for a change of outlook. Like Arumuga Navalar, Siddi Lebbe saw the supreme importance of education as a means to the regeneration of his community. The revitalizing process initiated during this phase continued during the first half of the twentieth century.

While the revivalist movements in Hinduism and Islam, in the late-nineteenth century and early-twentieth century, had much in common with the processes of Buddhist resurgence, there were other features in these which set them apart from the Buddhist experience. The Islamic revival benefited greatly from the presence of a charismatic Arab exiled to Sri Lanka; the Hindu recovery was more self-reliant and self-sufficient than the cognate process among the Buddhists and Muslims. As with the Hindus so with the Muslims the processes of recovery were singularly free of any political overtones in the sense of an anti-British or anti-imperialist attitude. In this the contrast with the Buddhist recovery which was never wholly free of such political attitudes could not have been more marked or significant.

Two other points need special mention: there has been much less of an atmosphere of confrontation between Buddhism and Islam — and the Sinhalese and the Muslims — in recent times than between the former and Hinduism. Nevertheless, and this the third point, Buddhist-Hindu rivalry has been much less significant as a point of contention between the Sinhalese and the Tamils than ethnicity and language. There is, in this sense, a striking contrast to pre-independence

India where "communalism" was often defined largely in terms of the deep-rooted hostility to reach other of rival religious groups.

Political Quiescence[11]

Incipient nationalist sentiment was primarily religious in outlook and content — and essentially a re-assertion of Buddhist values. Political overtones in it were visible quite early and became more pronounced in the first two decades of the twentieth century with the vigorous renewal of the temperance movement. These temperance activities were concentrated in the Sinhalese areas of the littoral and there religious revivalism and temperance agitation demonstrated many of the characteristic features of nationalist activity as it emerged after 1955-6.

Nevertheless it is remarkable that a movement as energetic and resourceful as this, and one which drew support from sections of the elite and — more important — from the people at large should have had so little impact and influence on the formal political activity of the elite at the turn of the century and in the first two decades of the twentieth century. There were indeed efforts made to establish an ideological link between religious revival and political nationalism, most notably by men like Anagarika Dharmapala (1864-1931). He saw the political implications and potential of the religious forces that were emerging, and he was among the first to advocate a form of *swaraj* or 'home rule' for Sri Lanka, but the blend of religious enthusiasm, militant nationalism and the advocacy of social reform which Dharmapala stood for evoked little sympathy from the effective political leadership of the day.

Of the distinctive features of the Sri Lanka variant of Asian nationalism the most remarkable is the prominent role played by the "reform" movement within the wider theme of nationalist agitation. 'Constitutionalist', 'moderate' and 'conservative' are some of the terms used to describe the reformers and their political attitudes. Each of these has its uses. What is common to them all is an emphasis on constitutional reform as the major goal of political endeavor.

Though men like Dharmapala responded more positively and perhaps more intelligently to the challenges of the first decade of the twentieth century, the initiative in political issues went almost by default to the "constitutionalists". These latter seldom understood the complexities of the nationalist movement of their day. Steeped in the British Liberal tradition they placed their hopes on the establishment, in the course of time, of a Sri Lanka version of the British system of parliamentary government and the transfer of a substantial measure of political authority to the elected representatives of the people of the country. For many years students of the politics of Sri Lanka, many of whom consciously or unconsciously reflecting these same political attitudes, tended to regard the "constitutionalists" and their political activities as *the* nationalist movement in the island, and they chose to disregard the virile brand of politics associated with the agitation for Buddhist revival and the cultural heritage associated with it and the Sinhalese language.

The Sinhalese elite showed little inclination to take the lead, as they should have done, in political agitation and in the formation of political organizations with a national outlook and membership. By the end of the nineteenth century the Sri Lankan elite had expanded in numbers. Elite status had, by then, become much less dependent on hereditary status and the holding of government office. One of the most far-reaching effects of the development of a capitalist economy based on plantation agriculture and trade was the growth of a new elite which was largely an indigenous capitalist class. The traditional elite whose status was based on hereditary position and the holding of office under the government was soon left far behind in the two most important channels of mobility, the acquisition of an English education, and the amassing of wealth through participation in capitalist enterprise. They were absorbed into this new elite, but even the most enterprising of them — generally the Sinhalese hereditary elite of the low country —were outstripped in wealth if not yet in political influence in the country.

At the end of the nineteenth century the elite had greatly expanded in numbers. It was quite heterogeneous, and neither the common outlook nurtured by an English education nor an anglicized lifestyle gave it anything more than a superficial cohesion. Such homogeneity as it had was derived from its class basis. Whatever their origins once members of this elite had consolidated their fortunes they became members of a single class, an elite representative of but not synonymous with the Sri Lankan capitalist class. This latter was largely low-country Sinhalese in composition; it had a sprinkling of Tamils and other minority groups; Kandyan representation in it was virtually non-existent.

The community of interest engendered by class was shattered by the divisive effect of religious rivalries and caste conflict. One divisive force had not yet emerged, ethnicity, and there were as yet few signs of its becoming as significant as religion and caste. The first two parts of this chapter have dealt with the religious rivalries of this period. We need now to turn, briefly, to the caste problems of the late nineteenth century, and the early years of the twentieth.

Three non-*goyigama* castes, the *karava*, *salagama* and *durava* provided a disproportionate number of men whose success in plantation agriculture, trade and commerce had left them far richer than the generality of the traditional elite. Since the most affluent and assertive segments of the capitalist class were members of these castes, and in particular of the *karava* caste, elite competition became very much a matter of caste rivalry as well. The *karavas* as the most affluent of them all, and the largest non-*goyigama* group numerically in the low country, grew sufficiently self-confident to set out a claim for the top position in the caste hierarchy displacing the *goyigama*, a claim which they supported with elaborate and fanciful theories of caste origin based on myth and distorted historical tradition. They were followed in this by the *salagama* and others as well, with equally extravagant claims to pride of place in the caste hierarchy. When this happened the *goyigamas*, both the traditional elite, as well as the rising men of wealth and education, closed ranks to defend their long accepted status as the most "honorable" of the castes — just as paddy cultivation was the most "honorable" vocation — and their position at the apex of the caste structure.

In the last quarter of the nineteenth century the *goyigama* elite received unexpected support from the colonial administration in Sri Lanka in the person of Governor Gordon. Though the latter was primarily interested in buttressing the traditional elite, he was not averse to extending this assistance on a caste basis to *goyigamas* of all categories whenever they were challenged by competitors from other castes. This policy was continued by his successors over the next two decades at least. One result of this, it must be emphasized, was the re-assertion of caste as an element in elite status, but this only succeeded in preventing the elimination of the traditional elite in the administrative structure, and in particular in the lower rungs of the governing elite. But as regards wealth and education their displacement could not be checked by gubernatorial fiat. It was impossible to exclude a claim to elite status earned by wealth or education (or a combination of these) even when it was not based on caste privilege and hereditary position.

Among the traditional elite it was the Kandyan group whose displacement was well-nigh total. They were left far behind in education, and very few extended their modest land-holdings substantially or converted them into plantations. Instead traditional agriculture was their *forte*, but there were no fortunes to be made in it for the returns on investment in this sphere were meager. To a greater extent than their low country counterparts the Kandyan elite hankered after headmen's posts and the trappings of the past. Gregory did them more harm than good by bringing them in from the cold and into a junior partnership in the colonial administration, for in the long run this proved to be *cul de sac*. Kandyan representation within the capitalist class was miniscule if non-existent.

The colonial administration threw the weight of its influence in support of the traditional elite in what appeared to be the latter's unequal battle with more resourceful newcomers but this did not put an end to elite competition in public life on a caste basis. On the contrary it served to intensify this competition as the *karavas* campaigned to gain a position in public life commensurate with their remarkable, if new-found, affluence. The competition continued in education and philanthropy; for *mudaliyarships*[12] — the title of *mudaliyar* divorced from the traditional system was used as an official 'honor' for other groups as well — and for places in the higher bureaucracy as well as for all posts in government service. But the struggle was keenest in the periodic campaigns to catch the Governor's eye for nomination to the Legislative Council. By the last decade of the nineteenth century on each occasion when the Sinhalese seat was vacant, the *karavas* organized public campaigns to get their man nominated, but to no avail.[13]

This diversion of political energies to caste competition proved to be self-defeating. For one thing it absorbed energies which may have been more profitably engaged in political organization and political activity at a national level. Then again, the passion and zeal these campaigns aroused were all to no purpose and worse still the effect of these campaigns was to divide the Sinhalese elite rather than unite it for a common struggle against the British.

The result was that almost by default some members of the Tamil elite took the leadership in political activity. Contemporary observers were impressed by the energy and enterprise displayed by the Tamils in sharp contrast to the political inertia of their Sinhalese counterparts.

The British colonial administration shared these sentiments originally but soon became suspicious of the Tamil political leadership. On balance they preferred inertia in politics and looked askance at any attempts to disturb it.

How does one account for the initiative and political enterprise of the Tamil leadership? Undoubtedly one factor was the quality of leadership provided by the Tamil representatives in the Legislative Council. The first Tamil representative, A . Coomaraswamy Pulle, was appointed in 1835 but died in 1836. His social background was not that of the traditional elite to which his Sinhalese counterparts clearly belonged. His son Muttu (later Sir Muttu Coomaraswamy) was appointed Tamil representative in 1861 and held that position till 1879. A man of superior talents who made a mark as a legislator in his day and as a friend of men in England like Moncton-Milnes (Lord Houghton), Richard Burton, and Benjamin D'Israeli, he is today best remembered as the father of the great Orientalist Ananda Coomara-swamy. From 1879 to 1898 the seat went to his two nephews Ponnambalam (later Sir Ponnambalam) Ramanathan (1851-1930) and Ramanathan's elder brother P. Coomaraswamy. (Their brother Ponnambalam (later Sir Ponnambalam) Arunachalam (1853-1924) was a distinguished career civil servant who kept up a lively interest in political issues although his official position did not permit him to give public expression to these views or take an initiative in politics. He was to do both in good measure once he retired from public service but that was in the second decade of the twentieth century). The Tamils — and the country in general — were admirably served in the Legislative Council by them.

None of the Sinhalese representatives of their day matched the intellectual dynamism, independence of outlook and political maturity of Ramanathan and his brother. Indeed if nomination to the Sinhalese seat demonstrates the resilience of the traditional elite, that to the Tamil seat shows how a seat in the legislature enabled a family to strengthen and consolidate its elite status. (The Burgher seat was not a monopoly of a single family. It went largely to lawyers of promise and achievement.)

The second factor was the economic one. The economic resources of the Tamil areas were so much more limited than those of the wet zone and while in the whole of the dry zone only the Jaffna peninsula supported an efficient and intensive system of agriculture, the increasing population of the region could not be accommodated in the traditional occupations based on the land.

There were Tamils with investments in plantations and trade but they hardly matched the low-country Sinhalese in these. While the Sinhalese elite showed a preference for commerce and plantation agriculture over politics, and the wealthy and educated Sinhalese, those whose background fitted them for a role of leadership in politics, were engrossed in commercal ventures often to the neglect of their professional activities as well, the educated Tamils turned to the professions, to serve in the bureaucracy especially in the lower clerical grades, and to political agitation, to a much greater extent than their Sinhalese counterparts. The Tamils were well equipped for this. Literacy in English was higher in Jaffna than elsewhere in the island thanks to a superb network of schools run by Christian missionaries. But very soon — certainly before the end of the nineteenth century —educated Tamils found that positions in the bureaucracy were outnumbered by those who aspired to them. Emigration to Colombo for employment had been for long an established feature of life in Jaffna. Now a brain drain began, a steady flow of educated Tamils to what is now Malaysia and Singapore, and a trickle as well to the British colonies in East Africa, as teachers, technicians, and above all as clerks in the lower grades of the public service. This process of emigration continued intermittently till the second decade of the twentienth century when it came to an end. What remained was internal migration to the Sinhalese areas where the competition for clerical posts intensified the rivalry between the Tamils and the Burghers who had established a dominance in this form of employment. Here there was as yet no competition between the Tamils and Sinhalese — unemployment among the educated was not yet a serious problem among the latter.

Tamil students had long been accustomed to going across to India — the Madras presidency particularly — for their university education. There they absorbed the political influences at work in India, and on their return sought to stimulate political activity in the island on the lines of the Indian political movement. The receptivity of the Tamils to the stimulus of Indian nationalism was strengthened by the fact that the Tamil elite, despite its passion for an English education, was much less anglicized than its Sinhalese counterpart. This held true for Tamil Christians as much as for the Hindus. The Tamil lead in politics was sustained over the first two decades of the 20th century.

The third factor lay in the greater cohesion of the Tamil elite. We see very little of the religious tensions that so bitterly divided the Buddhists from the Christians among the Sinhalese, or the caste rivalries which impeded common political activity among them. On the contrary, as we have seen in the previous chapter, the *vellala* had contrived to use the sanctions of Saivite orthodoxy to maintain and consolidate their caste privileges at the expense of those in lower rungs of the caste hierarchy in Tamil society. Like the *goyigamas* among the Sinhalese they had a commanding numerical superiority over all other castes, but unlike the former they faced no serious challenge to their position.

Briefly then, at this stage in the island's political development, ethnicity was not a decisive factor. The decisive forces were religion and caste, and these caused divisions among the Sinhalese themselves rather than dividing the Sinhalese from the other ethnic and religious groups in the island.

References

[1] On the Buddhist-Christian confrontation in the 19th century, see, K.M. de Silva, *Social Policy and Missionary Organizations in Ceylon, 1840-55* (London, 1965); K. Malalgoda, *Buddhism in Sinhalese Society, 1750-1900* (California, 1976). 'The Buddhist-Christian Confrontation in Ceylon, 1800-1880', *Social Compass* XX (2) 1973, pp. 171-200.

[2] S. Arasaratnam, 'Oratorians and Predikants. The Catholic Church in Ceylon under Dutch Rule', review article in *The Ceylon Journal of Historical and Social Studies*, (hereafter) (CJHSS) (1958), pp. 216-22.

C.R. Boxer, 'Christians and Spices. Portuguese Missionary Methods in Ceylon, 1518-1658', *History Today*, VIII (1958), pp. 346-54: 'A Note on Portuguese Missionary Methods in the East: 16th-18th centuries', *Ceylon Historical Journal*, (1960-1), pp. 77-90.

[3] K.M. de Silva, 'Christian Missions in Sri Lanka and their response to nationalism, 1910-1948', in P.L. Prematilake, K. Indrapala, and J.E. Van Lohuizen-de Leeuw (Editors), *Senarat Paranavitana Commemoration Volume. Studies in South Asian Archaeology*, University of Amsterdam, 1978.

[4] K.M. de Silva, *Social Policy and Missionary Organizations in Ceylon, 1840-55, op. cit.*, pp. 29-137.

[5] These issues are reviewed in greater detail by me, in my chapter 'The Government and Religion: Problems and Policies c 1832 to c 1910', in K.M. de Silva (ed) The University of Ceylon. *History of Ceylon*, Vol. III (Colombo, 1973); and in my *A History of Sri Lanka* (London, 1981), Chapter XXV, 'Religion and the Rise of Nationalism, c 1870-1900', pp. 339-355.

6   See, K.M. de Silva, *A History of Sri Lanka,* pp. 350-1; 374-8; The role of this
    small, dynamic caste group in the island's economic and political affairs is
    analyzed in M.W. Roberts, *Caste Conflict and Elite formation. The Rise of a
    Karava Elite in Sri Lanka, 1500-1931* (Cambridge, 1982).

7   Cited in M.T. Price, *Christian Missions and Oriental Civilizations,* (Shanghai,
    1924), pp. 152-3.

8   Apart from a few adulatory essays and pamphlets, there is still no serious study
    of Navalar and the Hindu revival of the nineteenth century. See, A.M.A. Azeez,
    The West Reappraised (Colombo, 1964) pp. 51-62.

9   Jane Russell, *Communal Politics under the Donoughmore Constitution, 1931-1947*
    (Colombo, 1982), *Ceylon Historical Journal,* pp. 9-14. Dr. Russell points out that
    by the 1930s the *vellalas* did face a challenge from the *karaiyar* caste, the Tamil
    counterpart of the *karavas.* Nevertheless, this came 50 years or more after the
    karavas had mounted their own offensive against the *goyigama* leadership.
    Besides the *karaiyars* never matched the *karavas* in wealth and influence.

10 Orabi Pasha, the leader of an abortive uprising against the western powers in
    Egypt in 1882. He spent 19 years of his life (from 1883 to 1901) as an exile in
    Sri Lanka, living mostly in Kandy. See, V. Samaraweera, 'Orabi Pasha n
    Ceylon, 1883-1901', *Islamic Culture,* XLIX October 1976, pp. 219-27.

11 On the politics of this period see K.M. de Silva, *A History of Sri Lanka,* pp.
    315-369.

12 A chief headman, an important position among the 'native' officials in the
    administrative heirarchy.

13 In the period 1833 to 1920 the island's Legislative Council consisted of 16
    members, 10 officials and 6 non-officials, or unofficials as they were called. Of
    the latter, three were European, and there was one for each of the main Sri
    Lankan ethnic groups of this period, the Sinhalese, Tamils and the Burghers.
    All these unofficials were nominated by the Governor of the colony and held
    their posts for life. Reforms introduced on the recommendation of Governor Sir
    Arthur Gordon increased the number of unofficials by two (one for the
    Muslims, and a second Sinhalese member to represent the Kandyans) and also
    introduced the practice of nominating members for a renewable five year term.
    This provided regular opportunities for pressure groups to lobby for their
    candidates.

CHAPTER IV

Political Change, c 1900 - c 1940

The Early Twentieth Century

The pervasive political quiescence of late nineteenth century Sri Lanka continued into the early years of the twentieth. By the first decade of the twentieth century there was greater interest in political and constitutional reform, and greater pressure from the more politically active sections of the elite for a share in the administration of the country. The colonial government in the island disregarded these pressures as it had done in the past. It was in no mood to make concessions to those whom it regarded as political agitators. Faith in the permanence of British rule in the island remained largely unshaken within the colonial administration as well as among influential sections of the elite engaged in political activity.

The most striking feature of nationalist agitation at this time continued to be the dominance within it of the reform movement. The reformers' emphasis on constitutional reform as the major goal of political endeavor, their insistence on the need for a reconciliation of Sri Lankan patriotism with loyalty to Britain, and their belief that these were complementary and not inherently imcompatible still remained unshaken and seemingly unshakeable. Those at the helm of the reform movement showed scant interest in broadening the bases of their political organizations, and were strongly opposed to techniques of agitation that would bring the masses into politics. These attitudes were influential among the mainstream political forces in Sri Lanka throughout the first half of the twentieth century, and beyond that to present times. Although the endeavors of men in the reform movement contributed to the eventual transfer of power from British hands, many of them were not consciously motivated by a desire to shake off the bonds of colonial rule. They did not think this to be possible in their lifetime.

Some of them did play an active and prominent role in the burgeoning temperance movement of the early twentieth century. There they had evoked an enthusiastic response from the people. But as in the past they were not interested in politicizing the movement or in the efforts to forge an ideologial link between a resurgent Buddhism and the incipient nationalist agitation through temperance activity.

The political quiescence which had been impervious to the influences emanating from the Indian sub-continent then in the throes of nationalist agitation, was soon shattered by a combination of international and local events — the outbreak of the first world war, and locally the Sinhalese-Muslim riots of 1915. About this latter we shall have more to say later on in this chapter. Here the point that needs to be made is that the methods used by the colonial authorities in suppressing the riots left bitterness and disillusionment among most sections of the elite. While this ought to have stimulated greater enthusiasm in organized political activity, the immediate effect, curiously enough, was to act as a restraint; the temperance agitation never really recovered its pre-war vitality, or its potential as a surrogate political movement. True, the Ceylon National Congress was established in 1919,[2] but what was significant in this was the long struggle that had to be waged before it could be established, and the lethargy — if not active opposition — of influential members of the elite could be overcome. And if men like Sir Ponnambalam Arunachalam who led the movement for its establishment regarded the Ceylon National Congress as the local counterpart of the Indian National Congress, they were soon in a minority in its governing body. The Ceylon National Congress was from the first an elitist organization dominated by men intent in restricting its political initiatives to the well-worn paths of Sri Lankan reformism with its vision limited by an overpowering pragmatism, and its mobility deliberately restricted by an unconcealed desire not to disturb too much the prevailing placidity of political life in the country.

At the end of the first world war the elite whose emergence we referred to in the previous chapter was not an integral part of the governing elite. At most some sections of it were junior partners in it. Besides, the minorities — Christians and Tamils — were disproportionately represented in it, and the traditional element was still significant even though its power and its numbers were on the wane. At the end of our period, however, it was already the ruling elite; Sinhalese if not yet Sinhalese Buddhists were now dominant although the minorities were still significant, while the traditional elite was very much in the periphery of power and influence, if not of social status.

The principal cause of the change was political. In contrast to the first two decades of the twentieth century the 1920s were characterized by bolder political initiatives, marking in retrospect the first phase in the transfer of power, when the British both in Whitehall and in the colonial administration in the island, for the first time, began to contemplate the possibility — indeed the necessity — of sharing power on a formal basis with the representatives of the indigenous population.

Elite competition in the late nineteenth century and early twentieth, as we have seen, had been a matter of caste rivalry among the Sinhalese rather than a conflict between the Sinhalese and the ethnic minorities, in particular the Tamils. In the years covered in this chapter, these divisions among the Sinhalese persisted and caste was indeed as divisive a force in the early 1920s as it had been earlier. It was a factor in the general elections to the Legislative Council in 1921 and 1924, and a rather embarrassed Ceylon National Congress leadership felt it necessary to adopt a resolution urging its members to desist from raising caste issues at election time.

The electorate at this time was never more than 4% of the total population, forming in effect, the "political nation" — the men of property, education and social standing. However, the increase in the number of voters in the 1920s was large enough to cause a momentous shift in the balance of caste influence among the Sinhalese. The *goyigamas* were able to assert their majority status (it was not the traditional elite who emerged as the dominant factor but rising men of wealth, education and achievement) and the *karava* presence in politics and public life was reduced from a position of salience to one merely of influence.

What this increase in the number of voters did not reflect was the significant politicization of the urban working class of Colombo, the heightening of working class activity and trade unionism which had begun to impinge on the political situation. The urban working class of Colombo was pushing its way into the political arena in the 1920s and with it there appeared the beginnings of a radical challenge to the elite's domination of the country's politics.

The Donoughmore Reforms and Universal Suffrage[3]

The inter-war years, and especially the post-1931 period saw a rapid transformation of the country's constitutional status in contrast to the previous sixty years in which such changes as there were in the constitution had been glacially slow. Once the thaw began the melting process proved to be remarkably rapid. There were three successive increases in the membership of the legislature in just over ten years from 1920: in 1920, 1923-4, and most significantly in 1931. Secondly there was also a distinct qualitative improvement in the status of these members, from nomination by the governor of the colony, to election on the basis of a limited electorate, limited on the basis of property and educational qualifications, to election under universal suffrage which came in 1931.

In 1931 Sri Lanka became the scene of a major departure in British colonial administration, the introduction of universal suffrage to a crown colony. Sri Lanka was the first Asian colony of the British empire and, if one excludes the white settlement colonies which had developed into dominions, the first colony to enjoy this privilege. One has only to set the introduction of universal suffrage against the British experience where it was achieved only after several decades of agitation to realize how revolutionary this step was. That process had stretched from 1832, the year of the great reform bill, to 1929 when the first British general election under universal suffrage was held.

The implementation, in 1931 and after, of many of the recommendations of the Donoughmore Commission published in 1928 mark a crucial watershed in Sri Lanka's political evolution. These changes amounted, in effect, to a crossing of the constitutional barrier towards self-government, a path on which the white dominions had embarked in the mid-nineteenth century. The Donoughmore Commissions had argued that:

> "...[A] good case could be made out for regarding the extension of the franchise as more urgent than any increase of responsible government. When a considerable increase in responsible government is being recommended, therefore, the question of the franchise becomes of first importance".[4]

They proceeded to recommend a form of semi-responsible government in combination with a franchise as near to that of Great Britain under the provisions of the *Representation of the People Act of 1918* as one could get. When the Colonial Office reduced the voting age of women to 21 from 30 in 1931 — the Donoughmore Commission had recommended that while all males should be eligible to vote at 21, women should, in the first instance, get the vote at 30 — the introduction of universal suffrage to Sri Lanka was completed, only three years after the process was completed in Britain itself. There had been, as we shall see, little support for this revolutionary poposal from most of the prominent Sri Lankan politicians of the day, and little to choose between the representatives of the minorities in the country and the Congress leadership on this matter. Most of the former, with Sri Ponnambalam Ramanathan in the lead, were even more strongly opposed to universal suffrage than their counterparts in the Congress.

Universal suffrage was rendered all the more unpalatable to the minorities by the Donoughmore Commission's firm decision to abolish communal electorates which the minorities had come to regard as a political safety net ever since the principle of elective representation had been introduced to the island in the early years of the 20th century. The minorities were unanimous in urging that such electorates be retained. Greatly agitated over the political implications of the introduction of universal suffrage — their fears of a permanent Sinhalese domination of politics to the detriment of minority interests — they were bitterly hostile to the Donoughmore report on account of its attitude to communal electorates. For unlike the Montagu-Chelmsford report on constitutional reform in India which had also been very critical of communal representation, the Donoughmore report took its rejection of communal representation to its logical conclusion by devising an electoral structure which made no concession to "communal" interests. The result, as we shall see in a later chapter (Chapter VI), was that the system of representation remained a controversial political issue over the rest of the decade and into the 1940s.

The leaders of the Ceylon National Congress, who had shown no great enthusiasm for universal suffrage but had acquiesced in it as a *fait accompli* once it was recommended by the Donoughmore Commission had, for their part, cause for concern in the extension of the right to vote to the immigrant plantation workers on almost the same terms as the indigenous population. Sinhalese politicians' fears that this would lead to an increase in the political influence of the European planters, the employers of Indian labor, were easily overshadowed by the alarm they felt over the prospects of a political threat to the inteests of the Sinhalese population of the plantation districts. The Indians were present in some of these latter districts in such large numbers that the Sinhalese, and especially the Kandyan Sinhalese, were thoroughly disturbed at the possibility of an Indian domination of the central highlands of the island if permanent citizenship rights were conferred on the Indian population there without adequate safeguards to protect the interests of the local population.[5]

The Legislative Council adopted the Donoughmore Commission's report by the slimmest of margins, a vote of 19 to 17, and only after prolonged debate. It was adopted at all only because the Colonial Office, at the instance of Governor Sir Herbert Stanley and the colonial administration, and in the face of the determined opposition of the Indian government, imposed restrictions on the franchise of the Indians resident in the island, in modification of the Donoughmore recommendations, by making domicile the standard test for the franchise, and with special provisions for these undomiciled. All British subjects domiciled in Sri Lanka were entitled to vote without reservation. In the case of other residents there were, in addition to the requirement of British nationality, either a literacy or property and income qualification, or a Certificate of Permanent Settlement which could be granted on proof of five years residence. These modifications were incorporated in the *Ceylon State Council (Elections) Order-in-Council 1931* in Articles 7 and 9. Throughout the period 1931 to 1946 the voting rights of Indians resident in the island continued to be a highly sensitive political issue. This — as we shall see in Chapter VI —was partly because the restrictions imposed in 1931 did not prove to be as effective as Sinhalese politicians were assured, and believed, they would be.

In devising a strategy on this question, the Sinhalese, low-country and Kandyan alike, treated the franchise as the most significant issue of all. Controls on immigration seemed at times, especially the period 1939-41, to be just as important, but on closer examination of their campaigns on this it is clear that they regarded the immigration issue as something closely linked with, and indeed inseparable from, the central theme of voting rights.

After the first general election held in 1931 seven members of the legislature attained Ministerial rank, sharing power with the British colonial administration in a dyarchical form of government. Thus the elite whom we saw hovering on the fringes of the governing elite, was now very much an integral part of the latter. Significantly enough, all but one[6] of Sri Lanka's prime ministers of the post-second world war era have been members of the legislature, the State Council, in the Donoughmore era; the one exception being Mrs. Sirimavo Bandaranaike who was herself the wife of a leading political figure of that period. Three of these Prime Ministers, D.S. Senanayake (1947-52), Sir John

Kotalawela (1953-56) and S.W.R.D. Bandaranaike (1956-59) had been Ministers in the Donoughmore period, Senanayake from 1931 to 1947 and the other two from 1936 to 1947. The present President of Sri Lanka, J.R. Jayewardene, had entered the national legislature, for the first time, in 1943. Similarly the three most prominent Marxist leaders of recent times had themselves entered the legislature in the 1930s: Dr. S.A. Wickremesinghe (1931-35), Dr. N.M. Perera (1936-42) and Philip Gunawardene (1936-42).

The grant of universal suffrage was to have the most profound effects on the country's political system. While the full impact of this factor was only felt after independence, pressures were building up for a thorough democraticization of Sri Lanka's politics in the period 1936-47 when the Donoughmore constitution was in operation.

Politicians of the Ceylon National Congress entered the electoral fray in 1931 rather apprehensive about their position because of the massive expansion of the electorate under universal suffrage. They soon found, however, that this made little immediate difference to their political fortunes, even though they fought the first and second general elections to the State Council, in 1931 and 1936, as individuals and not as a group or political party. Their strength lay in the rural constituencies, and the rural vote easily swamped the working class vote which was largely concentrated in and around Colombo and a few other urban and suburban areas.

The principal difference between Britain and Sri Lanka in regard to the franchise was that in Britain the extension of the franchise followed upon the expansion of educational opportunities and the growth of political awareness; in Sri Lanka the process was reversed, with the vote serving as the means of emancipating the people from ignorance, and inculcating an awareness of their political rights and obligations. The contrast was not only with Britain, but with India as well where universal suffrage came after independence while the Indian National Congress had been converted into a political party with a mass base, and a network of party branches throughout the country by the early 1920s. In Sri Lanka a mass electorate preceded the development of modern political parties by nearly two decades, and a party system and general elections fought on party lines came only with independence.

The general election of 1931 followed the pattern of that of 1924 even though universal suffrage had been introduced. In many constituencies Congress candidates contested each other as they had done in 1924. In the absence of genuine party conflict in the contests, candidates in most constituencies resorted to the conventional appeals to caste and religious loyalties, apart from other parochial considerations, which an illiterate and largely unorganized electorate, where the bulk of the electors were casting a vote for the first time, could most readily understand and respond to. A.E. Goonesinha the Labor leader, whose political star seemed on the ascendent in the 1920s won election to the State Council only to find that the new, democratically elected, legislature was an overwhelmingly conservative one. Thus he — the most prominent advocate of universal suffrage among the island's politicians — had much less influence than he expected to have.

When the next elections came in 1936, the Labour Party was superseded on the left of the island's political spectrum by a Marxist party, the Lanka Sama Samaja Party, formed in December 1935 on the eve of the general election. Since this election too was not fought on the basis of parties (save by the small L.S.S.P. contingent) the contests in many electorates were "personalized" in terms of faction (Congress leaders quite often threw their weight against recalcitrant members of their own organization) and more important still, caste and religion, which were openly advanced as the main criteria of the merits of candidates. Nor were such appeals confined to the rural and, presumably, more backward areas.

While the growth of parties and party organizations were alike surprisingly tardy despite the impetus given by the enormous increase in the electorate in 1931 and 1936, universal suffrage had a powerful influence on the political process in many other ways. We shall refer, in this chapter, to just one of these. Though the rural vote established its dominance from the outset universal suffrage strengthened the working class movement and opened the way for it to play an independent role in politics.[7] By the early 1930s the Marxists had established themselves in the leadership of the indigenous working-class movement. That influence may well have been stronger and more powerful in its political impact if the indigenous working class, despite its increasing politicization and militancy, had not been numerically smaller than the immigrant plantation workers. Immigrant Indian labour also formed a small but influential section of the urban working class.

The trade-union movement on the plantations and elsewhere among the immigrant Indians had its own leadership whose hold on these workers was not and has never been successfully challenged by the indigenous working class leaders. Politically the influence of the immigrant working class was vitiated by the fact that they were seen to be a large foreign element whose presence in the country posed a powerful threat to the interests of the Sinhalese. As a result the working class movement in Sri Lanka was divided into two separate and mutually suspicious if not hostile sections, to the great advantage of the Congress leadership of this period, and their successors after independence.

The Kandyan Response[8]

In the final phase of their rule over the island, the two decades beginning in 1920, the colonial administration in the island had to adjust itself to the reality of political pressure for constitutional reforms, that is to say, for a transfer of a share of political power to local politicians. They began by reacting to this with scarcely concealed displeasure, and resorted to that classic device of all rulers of plural societies — a policy of *divide et impera*, winning over, first of all, a section of the Sinhalese, the Kandyans. There was now manifested a fresh point of division among the Sinhalese with competition between the Kandyans and the low country Sinhalese a noteworthy factor in the country's politics. The Kandyans emerged as a countervailing conservative force in politics, in opposition to the leaders of the nationalist movement. They served as collaborators of the British in that they counselled retarding the pace of political advance, out of a sense of grievance against the low-country Sinhalese.

In the first half of the nineteenth century Kandyan resistance had been the major political problem that confronted the British in Sri Lanka. But Kandyan resistance to the British petered out in the two or three decades after the suppression of the 'rebellion' of 1848, and disappeared for ever thereafter. By a deliberate change of policy the British converted the Kandyans from a suspect group into a bloc of loyalists.

The Kandyan problem in the sense of a 'traditional' nationalism guided by an aristocratic leadership ceased to be a serious threat to the continued stability of British rule. Between the 1880s and the attainment of independence, the Kandyans mostly took satisfaction in a new role, that of associates of the British, and a counterweight to the reform and nationalist movements dominated by the elite of the low country. The leaders of Kandyan opinion seldom showed much sympathy for the political aspirations of these movements. They stood aloof and suspicious when not positively hostile. The tradition of Kandyan "resistance" was invoked not against the British but against the "constitutionalist" leadership. Nevertheless, the memory of Kandyan resistance and of the Kandyan kingdom as the last independent Sinhalese kingdom persisted, to provide some inspiration for the more forward looking "reformers" and those among the latter who came to form the nucleus of a genuine "nationalist" movement basing itself on Sinhalese tradition.

The Emergence of Sinhalese-Tamil Rivalries

More importantly, the British won over the Tamils. As a result, from the 1920s, politics began to reflect more clearly the pluralism of the Sri Lanka polity.[9]

However, once the constitutional barrier to self-government was passed with the adoption of the Donoughmore constitution in 1931, there was very little evidence of this policy of *divide et impera*. Behind the policy decision to introduce universal suffrage lay the assumption that the broadening of the bases of political activity anticipated from this would lead to a greater measure of national integration, which latter was regarded as essential to a smooth transfer of power.

Nevertheless dissension and mutual suspicion between the Sinhalese and the Tamils was one of the unfortunate but inevitable consequences of the concentration of energies on constitutional reform, and the increasing prospect of the transfer of political power from the British to the indigenous political leadership. Minority groups led by the Tamils were opposed to any positive measures of constitutional progress towards responsible government unless they included a scheme of checks and balances to protect their interests. Two issues gave rise to more anguish and more controversy than most others: the representative system — discussed in Chapter VI — and posts in the bureaucracy, a theme discussed below in Chapter VIII.

In the last decade of the nineteenth century and in the early years of the twentieth there was, as we have seen, a remarkable contrast between Tamils and the Sinhalese in their political attitudes: the former were far ahead in political consciousness and receptivity to nationalist ideas then emerging in the Indian sub-continent. This lead they maintained till the early 1920s. During this period they did not regard themselves as a minority, but aspired to equality with the Sinhalese as one of two majority groups in the island as indeed their enfranchised segment was under the restricted franchise then prevailing. This state of affairs was too good to last. In democratic politics, which the political leadership of the island was pledged to uphold, numbers were inevitably a decisive factor. Soon numbers began to count, and when that happened, or was seen to be happening, the artificiality of the "two majority communities" concept was easily exposed.

In the early 1920s the crucial issues involved in the fundamental problem of Tamil politics — their relationship with the Sinhalese within the larger Sri Lanka polity — were dramatized in the careers of two distinguished Tamil politicians who dominated the politics of the island at this time, the brothers Ponnambalam Arunachalam and Ponnambalam Ramanathan. Their careers afford a study in contrasts as regards their aspirations for the people of this country: Arunachalam stood for harmonious association between the Sinhalese and Tamils in nationalist politics and nation-building, for mutual trust and responsive co-ordination of sectional interests in the struggle for a common goal or *swaraj*. He viewed the Sinhalese and Tamils as associates in the building up (and eventually in the government) of a poly-ethnic polity.

Ramanathan, in contrast, emphasized the virtues of a separate identity for the Tamils, of a Tamil nationalism to be fostered in collaboration with the British and if necessary in opposition to Sinhalese nationalism. Ramanathan was much less visionary and idealistic than his brother: he was a last-ditch opponent of universal suffrage and a fervent advocate of *vellala* privileges.[10] An acute awareness of the disadvantages inherent in the numerical inferiority of the Tamils was the major premise of his arguments, and the basis too of his insistence on the need to protect the special interests of the Tamils through emphasizing their distinctive communal identity. In this last phase of British rule the logical conclusion of Ramanathan's policies was unabashed collaboration with the imperial power in return for the protection of minority interests and rights, and an insistence on a special if not privileged status as the price of acceptance of the eventual transfer of power by the British. There were two basic considerations: the emphasis on Tamil nationalism as something essentially divergent from, if not positively hostile to, Sinhalese nationalism; and secondly, the rejection, tacit or explicit, of Arunachalam's concept of a poly-ethnic polity and a Sri Lanka nationalism. There was a hard-headed pragmation in all this, for the events of the mid-nineteen fifties were to demonstrate that, for the Sinhalese themselves, the concept of a Sri Lankan nationalism could hardly hold its own against the compelling attractions of Sinhalese nationalism. Besides, Arunachalam's eventual disenchantment with the Congress served to underline the fact that, for many Sinhalese, 'responsive co-operation' between the Sinhalese and Tamils pre-supposed the acceptance by the Tamils of an essentially subordinate position by virtue of their numerical inferiority, and that their status in a Sri Lankan polity could seldom be anything more than that of a junior partner.

There was thus a breakdown in the general harmony of interests and outlook which had characterized relations between Sinhalese and Tamil politicians in the first two decades of the twentieth century. National unity and ethnic harmony which the Ceylon National Congress was expected to epitomize proved illusory within three years of its establishment. At this stage in the island's political evolution under British rule, the Sinhalese and Tamils were viewed as its *two* majority communities; with the smaller ethnic groups being regarded as the minorities. The situation changed fundamentally after 1922; instead of two majority communities and the minorities, there was now just one majority community, the Sinhalese, with the Tamils beginning to think of themselves — and being thought of as — a minority community. This has remained so ever since.

The Muslim Response

Among the Muslims the revitalizing process initiated during the last quarter of the nineteenth century continued during the first half of the twentieth century. There was little or no political content in this process in the sense of a hostility to British rule, much less any anxiety to replace it with a national regime. It was one of self-awareness and self-realization, and intrinsically inward looking. The Muslims in general, were well behind the Tamils and the Sinhalese in the formulation of political demands and in the pressure for constitutional reform. In this they followed the pattern set by their co-religionists in British India of the late 19th and early 20th century.

And then came the Sinhalese-Muslim riots of 1915. These were by far the most virulent outbreak of communal violence in Sri Lanka since the establishment of British rule. The outcome of the riots was to strengthen the trend towards collaboration with the British which was, in any case, quite strong among Muslim leaders already.

The riots of 1915[11] were in essence a communal disturbance directed against the Muslims but more especially a section of the Muslim community called the Coast Moors, who were in the main recent immigrants from South India. The ubiquitous activities of the Coast Moors in retail trade brought them in contact with the people at indigent levels — they were reputed to be readier than their competitors to extend credit but sell at higher prices — and this earned them the hostility alike of the people at large, and their competitors among Sinhalese traders (mainly low country Sinhalese) who had no compunctions about exploiting religious and 'racial' sentiments to the detriment of their well established rivals. Since the low country Sinhalese traders were a powerful driving force within the Buddhist movement, religious sentiment gave a sharp ideological focus and a cloak of respectability to sordid commercial rivalry. The rivalry became more pronounced because the Coast Moors were not only tenacious in the protection of their trading interests, but were also more vociferous than the indigenous Muslim community in the dogged and truculent assertion of their civic rights, which stemmed no doubt from their familiarity with such matters in India. This streak of obduracy and their insensitivity to traditional rites and customs of other religious groups, at a time when there was a resurgence of Buddhism, led them inexorably into confrontation and conflict with the Sinhalese Buddhist masses.

After initially treating the riots as a communal disturbance pure and simple, the British authorities in the island came to regard them as part of an organized conspiracy against the British by the Sinhalese. Although there was no evidence to suggest that the riots were anything other than communal in nature, British officials in the island chose to believe their own fanciful theory of a sinister political motive in the riots, and this belief lay behind a series of panic measures of inexplicable harshness taken against the alleged leaders of such an anti-British movement, namely the Sinhalese Buddhists, and especially those associated with the temperance movement. They were the first to be arrested and jailed notwithstanding that many of them had used their influence in the restoration of order, and in protecting the lives and property of potential victims of mob violence. The list of detainees reads like a roll-call of the nationalist leaders of the future: the Senanayake brothers, F.R., D.S., and D.C., D.B. Jayatilaka, W.A. de Silva, C. Batuwantudawe, and Edmund and Dr. C.A. Hewavitharana (brothers of the well-known religious leader Anagarika Dharmapala). The recently established Young Lanka League also came under suspicion and its active members, of whom the youthful A.E. Goonesinha was most prominent, were arrested and detained. The colonial administration seemed determined to detain any Sinhalese who had shown the slightest inclination to challenge authority in the past.

The methods employed for dealing with the disturbances shattered Sri Lankan — and especially Sinhalese — illusions about the colonial administration's commitment to justice and fair play and their sense of grievance was aggravated by the persistent refusal of the colonial authorities to investigate charges of excesses committed by the military and others during the suppression of the riots. In the Legislative Council, Ponnambalam Ramanathan[12] rose to the defense of the Sinhalese leaders in a series of impassioned speeches notable alike for fearless condemnation of the manner in which the disturbances were suppressed and the cogently argued refutation of the conspiracy theory. For two years or more Ramanathan combined his public condemnation of the excesses committed under martial law, with persistent though fruitless appeals for redress of grievances.

The Sinhalese political leaders and their allies among the Tamils kept up the agitation for this for a decade or more. And as a result the Muslims closed ranks and stood firmly in support of the British. One saw little here of the post-war political activism of the Muslim *elite* that led in India to a brief but lively alliance between the Indian National Congress under Gandhi and the Muslim leadership in that country. True the Khilafat movement in India had its repercussions among the Muslims in Sri Lanka as well, but largely as a result of the 1915 riots, the local version of it neither attracted any enthusiastic support from the mainstream Muslim leadership nor developed the positively anti-British tone that it had in India. The Sri Lankan Muslims did not turn away from their traditional policy of association with the imperial power.

Indeed, as we shall see in a later chapter of this book, throughout the next two decades the Muslims formed part of a phalanx of minorities under Tamil leadership which accepted the need for collaboration with the British in return for the protection and consolidation of the rights of minorities as the price for accepting any significant measures of constitutional reform leading to representative government. It was not until the early and mid-1940s, on the eve of the transfer of power, that the Muslims as a whole broke away from the Tamils to support the Sinhalese leaders in their political campaigns for independence.

The Christian Minority Under Pressure

The Christian missions found to their surprise and relief that the pressure from the Buddhist movement relaxed somewhat in the inter-war years. In the early years of the century the Buddhist movement in the hands of men like the Anagarika Dharmapala had been almost the mirror image of Protestant Christianity in techniques of propaganda. The new Buddhist revivalist was old missionary writ large.[13] Dharmapala grasped as few of his contemporaries did, the political implications of the Buddhist resurgence and he never lost sight of the need to set this latter within the wider framework of the rise of nationalism in Asia. But he was at the same time a vocal and uncompromising advocate of a Sinhalese-Buddhist domination of the island. His propaganda bore a remarkable similarity to that of the great champion of the Hindu resurgence in Western India, Tilak. While his political skills — and achievements — did not match Tilak's — his blending of religious fervor and national pride, of a sophistsicated internationalism with a coarse insularity served as a model for the Buddhist activists of post-independence Sri Lanka.

After the first world war this brand of militant Buddhism receded to the background for over a generation. This was not due to any decline of interest in Buddhism or Buddhist activity but because of a mood of restraint and excessive caution in politics which spilled over into religious activity when the new leaders of the reform movement F.R. Senanayake (1884-1925) and D.B. Jayatilaka took control of the Buddhist movement as well and kept a tight rein on religious enthusiasm. Their approach to the religious problems of the day was in every way a contrast to Dharmapala's and they set the tone in Buddhist activity right up to the time of Jayatilaka's retirement from active politics in 1943. Jayatilaka was the most prominent Buddhist leader of the day. His dual role of elder statesman in political and religious affairs enhanced his prestige in both and this he used with considerable finesse to curb what he regarded as extremism.[14]

In the nineteen thirties, with the introduction of universal suffrage, politicians of the first (1931-1935) and the second (1936-1947) State Councils, unlike their predecessors in the reformed Legislative Council of the 1920s, became subject to the pressures of a popular electorate. Buddhist pressure groups could now work, through the democratic process, to influence legislators much more effectively, if also more unobtrusively. Significantly the Buddhist temporalities question was settled very early and Ordinance 19 of 1931 conceded the demand which Buddhist opinion had made for several decades for the administration of Buddhist temporalities under state supervision. An Ordinance which was passed in 1942 for the preservation of the sacred city of Anuradhapura was based on sober necessity but lent itself to some recrudescence of Dharmapala's ideas.

When Buddhist activists turned their attention to the composition of the Legislative Council they found irrefutable evidence of the reduction of the Buddhists to an uninfluential minority. Indeed no Buddhist had been returned to the Legislative Council in 1921 when all elected Sinhalese members had been Christians, Protestant or Roman Catholic. In the elections of 1924 therefore there was strong pressure from Buddhist activists, Congress disapproval notwithstanding, to make religion an issue at the elections, and the cry of Buddhism in danger was raised in a number of constituencies in which Buddhist candidates faced Christian opponents. It had the desired effect of ensuring the election of a large number of Buddhists. The situation improved dramatically with the introduction of universal suffrage. At the general election of 1931 there were 38 Sinhalese returned as elected members of the new Legislature. Of these 28 were Buddhists or claimed to be one since it was now politically advantageous to be a Buddhist. Thus the Buddhists had a clear majority in the Legislature for the first time.

Two Brands of Nationalism

Sinhalese Buddhists were awakening to a new political awareness, and by the very nature of democratic "parliamentary" politics there were political groups who sought to build a political program emphasizing the traditional cultural and religious patterns associated with Buddhism. The most notable of these groups was S.W.R.D. Bandaranaike's Sinhala Maha Sabha. There are few doubts now about the viability of religio-cultural nationalism as a major political force, or —

more important — of the validity of its appeal to a democratic electorate, but its potentially divisive effect on a plural society such as Sri Lanka's deterred the moderate leadership in the Board of Ministers from giving their support to such a program with any enthusiasm. The Sinhala Maha Sabha had no such restraints. They urged that the Sri Lankan polity must be essentially Buddhist and Sinhalese in orientation. In the late 1930s it took issue with the Ceylon National Congress on the latter's concept of a "Ceylonese" or Sri Lankan national entity in which the ethnic and religious minorities retained their distinctive identities while conceding to the Sinhalese Buddhists a primacy in the Sri Lankan polity in recognition of their majority status in a democratic society. The Sinhala Maha Sabha would not accept this position, and insisted on an assertion of Sinhalese-Buddhist preeminence in the most unmistakable terms.

Neutrality in religious affairs was a cardinal feature of state policy under the Donoughmore Constitution as it had been in the past but there was greater readiness to underline a sense of a special obligation to foster Buddhism. This pragmatic concession to political realities was devised by the duumvirate of D.B. Jayatilaka and D.S. Senanayake (F.R. Senanayake's younger brother and political heir). Adhering to the western concept of a secular state, they would not go beyond this in their response to pressure from vociferous Buddhist groups such as the Sinhala Maha Sabha and the All-Ceylon Buddhist Congress for a more thorough-going reconstruction of the island's polity to reflect the supremacy of the Sinhalese-Buddhists rather than merely their primacy. The duumvirate drew a distinction between a government in which Buddhists were the predominant influence, and a Buddhist government. The former they preferred and were indeed comitted to, both because it was compatible — quite unlike the latter — with the requirements of their negotiations on the transfer of power and, not less important, their personal inclinations: the latter they strongly opposed because of its political implications. The influence of D.B. Jayatilaka was crucial in this. Along with D.S. Senanayake he succesfully postponed an open confrontation between a militant Buddhist movement urging the establishment of a Sri Lanka polity on traditional Sinhalese-Buddhist lines, and those who were committed to the maintenance of the liberal ideal of a secular state in which the lines between state power and religion were carefully demarcated, and scrupulously respected. (The Marxists too, at this stage, remained dogmatically unresponsive to this brand of Sinhalese-Buddhist nationalism, often dismissing it as mere chauvinism.) It required D.B. Jayatilaka's retirement from active politics in 1943 (and his death in 1944) to open the way for a new generation of militant Buddhist activists, many of whom were members of the Sinhala Maha Sabha, to take control of the Buddhist movement. They were men nursing a sense of outrage and indignation at what they regarded as the historic injustices suffered by their religion under Western rule. As we shall see in the next chapter they led the attack on the Christian minority and in particular the Roman Catholics on the schools issue, but found a major obstacle to the success of their enterprise in D.S. Senanayake, the most powerful and convincing if not the most articulate advocate of a broad-based Sri Lankan nationalism which sought to bring all ethnic and religious groups in the island under its umbrella. The nation in this context not only subsumed all these groups but was defined in all-inclusive terms, co-extensive with the island.

References

1   See, K.M. de Silva, *A History of Sri Lanka*, pp. 373-388.

2   On the formation of the Ceylon National Congress see K.M. de Silva, 'The formation and character of the Ceylon National Congress, 1917-1919', (CJHSS) X, 1967, pp. 70-102.

3   The impact of universal suffrage on Sri Lanka is reviewed in K.M. de Silva (ed) *Universal Franchise, 1931-1981; the Sri Lankan Experience*, (Colombo, the Government Press, 1981).

4   *Report of the Special Commission on the Constitution*, 1928 (hereafter the *Donoughmore Report*), p. 42.

5   For further discussion of this see below, Chapter VI.

6   There is also the present Prime Minister of Sri Lanka, R. Premadasa. He is excluded from consideration here as he is not a head of government.

7   See, Michael Roberts, 'Labour and the Politics of Labour in the late Nineteenth and Early Twentieth Century', *Modern Ceylon Studies* (hereafter *MCS*) 5(2) 1974, pp. 179-208.

8   See, K.M. de Silva, 'The Ceylon National Congress in Disarray, I, 1920-1: Sir Ponnambalam Arunachalam leaves the Congress'. *CJHSS* n.s. 11(2) 1972, pp. 97-117; and 'The Ceylon National Congress in Disarray, II: the triumph of Sir William Manning, 1921-1924, *CJHSS* n.s. III(1) 1973, pp. 16-35.
See also, K.M. de Silva, *A History of Sri Lanka*, pp. 389-401.

9   The same references as for footnote 7 above.

[10] In January 1930, for instance, Ramanathan led a delegation of Tamil politicians to see the Governor Sir Herbert Stanley to protest against equal seating in the dining hall at the Teachers Training College at Kopay on the north of the island. See Jane Russell, *Communal Politics under the Donoughmore Constitution, 1931-1947*, p. 11.

[11] For discussion of the riots and their historical significance, see, 'The 1915 Riots in Ceylon: a Symposium', *Journal of Asian Studies*, XXIX(2) 1970, pp. 219-66; and Ceylon Studies Seminar, 1969/70 series 'A Symposium on the 1915 Communal Riots'. See also, A.P. Kannangara, 'The Riots of 1915 in Sri Lanka: A Study in the Roots of Communal Violence', *Past and Present*, 102 (1984) pp. 130-165.

[12] He was at this time the elected member for the 'Educated Ceylonese' electorate.

[13] See, G. Obeysekera, 'Religious symbolism and political change in Ceylon', *MCS* 1(1) 1970, pp. 43-63.

[14] This theme is discussed in K.M. de Silva, 'Christian Missions in Sri Lanka and their response to nationalism, 1910-1948', in P. L. Prematilake *et al* (eds) *Senerat Paranavitana Commemoration Volume*.

Chapter V
Education Reform, Language Policy and Ethnic Rivalries, c 1920 - 1945

The Contraction of Missionary Enterprise

The inter-war period was a decisive phase in the reconciliation of the Christian minority to a diminished role in the affairs of the country — if not yet a ready acceptance of Buddhist dominance in the Sri Lanka polity. In the early 1920s the Christian groups in the island began, at last, to face up to the implications of the changes brought about by the rise of nationalism. They responded to this with efforts to make the missions and churches indigenous institutions less conspicuously under European leadership and direction, a change at variance with missionary thinking and practice in Sri Lanka in the nineteenth century.

This process of coming to terms with nationalism was a "re-indigenization" movement,[1] the revival of indigenous names, forms of dress and the cultivation of the native arts and crafts among the Christians. In most Christian churches a Sinhalese or Tamil prayer book — a faithful translation from the English — had been the only concession to the native culture, and no attempt had been made to adapt modes of worship to a national, that is to say Sinhalese and Tamil, form. The Anglicans, surprisingly enough, were in the forefront of the "re-indigenization" movement, in the use of forms of worship native to Sri Lanka, and in the adoption of the traditional architecture in church building.

A second aspect of this trend was the attempt to seek an autonomous status for the Christian missions and churches, self-supporting, self propagating and indigenous. This was a long-drawn out process largely because of the practical and mundane problem of financial independence from the parent societies in Europe and the United States. The extent of independence achieved varied from mission to mission but it would be true to say that at the time the island achieved its independence few if any at all were substantially self-supporting. Besides the most articulate spokesmen of the "re-indigenization" movement were more often than not British missionaries rather than native Christians. And almost up to the time of independence "indigenization" of the top rungs of the hierarchy of the Christian churches in the island proceeded much more slowly than in the cognate process in politics and the bureaucracy.

Thirdly, the Buddhist resurgence and the growth of nationalism led to a sober realism about the limits of evangelical activity. Expansion gave way to consolidation and contraction. Besides the missions could no longer afford to dissipate their energies in sectarian disputes. At the turn of the century there had been little co-operation among the Christian groups working in the island. But with the World Missionary Conference held in Edinburgh in 1910 the first permanent instrument of Christian co-operation outside the Roman Catholic Church was established — this was the greatest achievement of that conference: its impact began to be felt in Sri Lanka in the 1920s and after, and its influence fitted neatly into the practical necessity of closing ranks in the face of a resurgent Buddhism. Nevertheless this co-ordination of activity did not encompass the Roman Catholics who stood aloof from the other Christian groups.

That is not to say there were no differences in attitude among the various Christian missions or obstacles to this policy of accommodation. Most of these centered on education and the schools, and the conflicts regarding them determined the pattern of relations between the Buddhist majority and Christian minority both in the later years of British rule and in the years after independence. Indeed the "re-indigenization" movement as a whole was essentially a Protestant one, and the Roman Catholics lagged well behind.

Education Reform

Beginning in the mid-1930s a purposeful effort was made to give the island's education system a new orientation, more secular and less elitist in outlook and also to enlarge considerably the role of the state at the expense of the missions which up to this time had dominated education. The mission schools, organized on denominational lines, came increasingly under attack. These had been, for long, distrusted as instruments of religious conversion. The rivalry and competition between the missions for enlarging their spheres of influence in education was regarded, not unfairly, as being wasteful of resources, and unhealthy in its encouragement of sectarianism especially through exploitation of the widespread desire for education in their schools. There was all too often an insistence on a study of the Christian scriptures by all students in these schools irrespective of whether or not they were Christians. All denominations of Christians zealously avoided recruitment of non-Christians to the teaching staff of their schools especially in the larger secondary schools in the towns; and even in the village schools where employment of Buddhists and Hindus could not be avoided a distinct preference was shown for Christians.

There were often more damaging accusations. The system of education in the mission schools encouraged their pupils to detach themselves from the larger Sri Lankan community if not to identify themselves with the metropolitan country and to develop a contempt for their own national cultures. When the missions sought to rebut these charges by pointing out that the students educated in their schools were often the pioneers of the movement for political reform, their critics contended that the liberating effects of a purely secular nature which flowed from the education provided in the mission schools were not always those which were anticipated or even encouraged by the missionaries. At any rate the general purpose of education imparted in the mission schools was not to prepare Sri Lankans for self-rule so much as to make British rule more humane and palatable to the people of the country.

Concentration of attention on education as a means of religious conversion tended to divert attention from the more constructive achievements of the missionaries in education. If the mission schools were seldom designed for purposes unrelated to evangelization, their students nevertheless did find opened out to them new vistas of secular knowledge, and their intellectual horizons were widened.

For, as E.F.C. Ludowyk points out, the missionaries scored their greatest success,

> "by providing an English rather than a Christian education ... coloured by certain values derived from the teacher's own education in his homeland. For all its inadequacies and misdemeanours this kind of education had most effect through the contact of the pupil with persons whose qualities of mind and character had much to give them. One can only regret that contact such as these were available only to so few ..."[2]

In the 1930s pressures for radical reform of the denominational system were intensified and as a result the use of the educational process as a means of conversion to Christianity, at last, received an effective check. Nevertheless there was considerable resistance to the education reforms envisaged and not merely from the Christian groups. This well organized and prolonged resistance succeeded in delaying their implementation and in eliminating some of the more far-reaching aspects which were regarded as being specially dangerous to the denominational system. The strength of this resistance to education reform stemmed from a combination of factors, personal and institutional: the instinctive distrust of the changes envisaged which many of the more influential political leaders of the day (most notably D.S. Senanayake) demonstrated; many members of the State Council, although themselves Buddhists, were alumni of mission schools and were susceptible to influence by the missions; but there was more than a sentimental attachment to the old school involved in this, for these legislators had a deep-seated regard for the positive achievements of mission schools and were unwilling to have these jeopardized by the precipitate adoption of radical reform; and finally, the defense of the denominational principle was by no means confined to the Christian missions. The managers and heads of denominational schools controlled by Buddhists and Hindus many of whom were State Councillors (some of them were members of the Board of Ministers and others members of the Executive Committee of Education itself) recognized that protection of their own vested interests in education could only be achieved by the maintenance of the *status quo*. In 1944 the State Council resolved that it was desirable that members of the Executive Committee of Education should cease to be managers or teachers in assisted schools, but the members at whom this resolution was directed ignored it and continued with their dual role, oblivious to the conflict of interests it clearly involved.

It took seven years to prepare legislation to transfer power from the Board of Education[3] to the Executive Committee of Education. The delays inherent in the cumbersome machinery of the Donoughmore constitutional system were aggravated by the calculated obstruction of those who regretted the transfer of power from a body which was dominated by denominational interests, to one in which the opponents and critics of this principle were likely to have control.[4] When the Education Ordinance of 1939 eventually emerged for debate in the State Council spokesmen for denominational interests opposed it tooth and nail. They succeeded in securing the adoption (by the State Council by a vote fo 27 to 26) of an amending clause which read: "This Ordinance is not designed to give effect to any policy aimed against denominational schools". This was adopted in the face of the opposition of the Minister of Education, C.W.W. Kannangara.

The Education Ordinance of 1939 heralded the beginning of nearly a decade of radical and acutely controversial education reforms in which the Minister's determination to push a policy of far-reaching change through the legislature was resisted not merely by denominational interests but also by influential colleagues in the Board of Ministers itself. The most far-reaching and controversial of these changes was the proposal for a system of "free"[5] education at all levels — primary, secondary and tertiary. "Free" education had been confined in the past to the state schools. Now this was to be extended to denominational schools as well, principally through a revision of the mode of financial assistance provided by the state to these schools — the grants-in-aid system as it was called. While the reforms proposals envisaged the continuation of these maintenance grants by the state, they went well beyond the conventional grants-in-aid system by making provision for the payment of salaries of teachers in the denominational schools, provided however that tuition fees were abolished. The Christian missions viewed these propsoals with deep suspicion. The dilemma they faced was that while the payment of teachers salaries would relieve them of a heavy burden, entry into the new scheme of "free" education posed the danger of increased state interference in, if not bureaucratic control of, their schools. Yet to opt out of the scheme was to lose the maintenance grants on which the vast majority of these schools depended for survival. Only the few elite denominational schools could survive without grants-in-aid from the state.

These education proposals were debated in the State Council in the latter half of 1944.[6] The debate in the State Council developed into a bitter confrontation between the protagonists of the scheme and the advocates of denominationalism and reflected all too accurately the passions this issue aroused in the country at large where one significant feature was the entry into national politics of members of the *sangha*, the Buddhist order. The *sangha's* involvement was spearheaded by a group of young, highly politicized and radicalized *bhikkhus* from religious institutions in and around Colombo, most notably the prestigious Vidyalankara *pirivena*.

They enthusiastically supported the reforms initiated by the Minister of Education C.W.W. Kannangara. Like most articulate members of the *sangha* they too regarded the existing school system as a bastion of Christian privilege, and this despite the immeasurably improved position of the Buddhists in education, especially if one looked back to what it had been in the first quarter of the 20th century, to go back no further. Indeed this distinct and continuing improvement made them more resentful of the prestige and influence which the Christian clergy and their schools still enjoyed. For the radicalized *bhikkhus*, the so-called political *bhikkhus*, this struggle over education reform also had the additional advantage of being a means of discrediting powerful opponents of these reforms in the Board of Ministers and in the State Council, the most prominent of whom was D.S. Senanayake. While the lay leaders of the Buddhist movement and the established — and more conservative if not conventional — *bhikkhu* leaders, were not inclined to reject their support in the battles over education reform, they were quite often distinctly uneasy at these attempts to widen the range of conflict, to bring the Sri Lankan political elite, the emerging establishment led by D.S. Senanayake, within the scope of the struggle for elite displacement.

Most of the leaders of the Vidyalankara pressure group had spent some time in India as students, often in Bengal, and while resident there had been drawn into the political struggles of the subcontinent. All of them had imbibed there the current orthodoxies of Indian nationalism, as well as Marxism, and on their return turned to political activity with the newly established Marxist party, the Lanka Sama Samaja Party, and other radical political groups.

When the State Council endorsed these education proposals in June 1945 the Vidyalankara *bhikkhus* were seen to have achieved a notable success in this their first major political struggle — the campaign to have the education proposals of 1943 accepted by the national legislature. (But their political campaign also provoked considerable opposition from the more 'orthodox' Buddhists, lay and clerical).

There was one more phase in this battle on education reform: the translation of the education reforms proposals endorsed by the State Council in 1945 into legislation. This phase, in which the political *bhikkhus* played a prominent role in winning public support for the legislation prepared by Kannangara, is reviewed in a later chapter of this present work.

The fact that the opposition to the "free" education scheme came mainly from the Roman Catholics[7] explains to some extent the irony of a situation where the bitterness of the Buddhists against the injuries and neglect suffered at the hands of Christians during the period of Western rule should be directed against the Roman Catholics rather than the Protestants who, for the last two centuries or more, enjoyed special favors from the ruling imperial powers. That bitterness was a factor in Sri Lankan politics till at least the mid-1960s, and did not entirely disappear till the early 1970s.

Language Policy

The two decades beginning in 1930 which were such a decisive phase in the evolution of Sri Lanka's modern education system, also saw the emergence of language policy as a major national political issue, and a divisive one. A change in the medium of instruction in schools was a central issue in the education reforms of this period, but language policy was much wider in scope and potential impact than that. Some of the principal political figures involved in the language controversies of this period were to play a similar role of prominence in the more strident and passionate controversies on language in the mid-1950s when language became the primary political issue of the day and when, indeed, language became the very core of the ethnic conflicts that erupted and nationalism itself took on a linguistic form. For them this was, historically — and although they would not know it at that time — a dress rehearsal for the political dramas of the mid-1950s and early 1960s in which, moreover, the roles they played were often quite different from the ones in which we see them in this chapter.

Pressure for the replacement of English as the official language by Sinhalese and Tamil began in the 1920s. As in most other things at this time Sri Lanka was following the lead set by India in this, and as usual, several decades after the emergence and development of similar movements in India. There was, naturally enough, greater momentum for this change with the Donoughmore reforms and the introduction of universal suffrage.

The *swabasha* movement as this came to be called was, in its origins, a protest against the privileges of the English educated — and English speaking — elite and its monopoly of all important positions in public life and in the bureaucracy. Between the English educated and the vernacular educated was a formidable class barrier with its contrast in status and wealth exacerbated by the conflict of cultures. The island's education system was notable for its bifurcation between a privileged

English education sector to which access was quite limited, on the one hand, and the vernacular schools, the largest segment in the school system, on the other. From the outset agitation for education reform — and in particular the use of the mother tongue in the education process — was an integral part of the *swabasha* movement.

Jaffna took the lead in the *swabasha* agitation from as early as 1925 with the Jaffna Youth Congress in the forefront of it. They retained their lead in this till well into the 1930s. Thus in 1934 we see the Northern Province Teachers Association adopting a resolution demanding "free and compulsory education with teaching in the vernaculars as far as possible in all subjects except English".

With the establishment of the State Council in 1931 the national legislature served as a forum for the *swabasha* agitation. This was especially true of the second State Council (1936-47). Earlier, in 1932 G.K.W. Perera, a backbencher had moved a resolution to amend the standing orders of the State Council to allow Sinhalese and Tamil to be used in conducting its business. Although the resolution had wide support it fell short of the two-thirds majority required to amend these standing orders.[8] Two years later he moved another resolution with a wider perspective: that the vernaculars be used in the administrative system and the courts. That resolution was adopted but little if anything at all was done to translate it into official policy.

Early in 1935 the Ceylon National Congress published a memorandum on reform in education in which it called for the introduction of the vernaculars as media of education. By this time agitation for *swabasha* was in full swing, and it was closely linked with education reform. The agitation was led by a small group of highly articulate and politicized school teachers in some of the prestigious English secondary schools. In the Sinhalese areas it included some who became outstanding politicians — C.W.W. Kannangara (Minister of Education, 1936-47), W. Dahanayaka, a future Cabinet Minister (1956-59, 1965-70) and Minister of Education (1956-1959) who became for a short time, Prime Minister (1959-60) and P. de S. Kularatne — not to mention T.B. Jayah, a Malay educationist and politician who achieved Cabinet rank in the first post-independence government. In Jaffna their counterparts had scored a spectacular if temporary success in leading a boycott of elections to the first State Council.[9] This small band of nationalists among teachers in English schools set out to canvass the support of the vernacular speaking masses for the goal of national independence; they believed and worked on the basis that a compre-

hensive system of national education was a *sine quo non* for the mobilization of the masses and that a change in the medium of instruction in the
English schools was essential to bridge the gap between the two nations
— the English educated and English speaking elite — and the people at
large. To be sure not all teachers in the English medium schools
supported them. On the contrary, the anglicized intelligentsia, including the majority of the English teaching profession, was generally
either hostile to the changes they advocated, or were lukewarm at best
to their demands.

Through the mid-1930s and late-1930s the *swabasha* movement grew
in strength. Within the national legislature there was, first of all, the
pressure from the LSSP, the newly established Marxist party. In 1936
Philip Gunawardene one of its leaders, moved that the proceedings in
the law courts and entries in police records be allowed in Sinhalese and
Tamil.[10] Many of the *swabasha* agitators linked with the Southern
Province Teachers Association were now in the State Council, with
Kannangara in the key position of Minister of Education. Two years
later, in 1939, the Ceylon National Congress adopted a resolution to the
effect that Sinhalese and Tamil be made the official languages.
Nevertheless, although there was by now a greater sense of urgency in
all this, progress made did not match the enthusiasm for the cause and
the public support it was generating in the country, especially for the
use of the mother tongue in education.

Critics of this latter had already picked on a potentially deleterious
flaw. While English education had become the badge of social and
cultural superiority, and elevated the English educated to the position
of a privileged minority, the national establishment, the English
language served a politically useful role as an important unifying factor
in the country. The first Principal of the Ceylon University College —
and as usual at this time a British expatriate — Robert Marrs, pointed to
the possibility that the triumph of *swabasha* would bring to an end the
two nations system as it existed only to create an equally dangerous one
detrimental to national cohesion, on the basis of the two languages
Sinhalese and Tamil.

What today would be seen as an unusually prescient observation was
dismissed by *swabasha* enthusiasts then as arrant nonsense or worse
from a prejudiced and hostile source. They believed that bilingualism
—Sinhalese and Tamil — would be an ideal unifying force, and in the
beginning there were encouraging signs of this actually happening. In
1938-40 the Hindu Board of Education, which controlled all the Hindu

schools in the north of the island, adopted a policy of introducing Sinhalese as a compulsory subject in all their schools. The Jaffna Youth Congress, in 1938, moved that "the teaching of Sinhalese and Tamil be made compulsory in all schools in Ceylon". The fact of the matter, however, was that the viability of Sinhalese-Tamil bilingualism was largely impaired by the general lack of enthusiasm for Tamil among the Sinhalese including educationists and the elite, the natural complacency of a majority community. The result was that the agitation for *swabasha* continued, and succeeded — in the 1950s and 1960s — in its objective of replacing English as the medium of instruction with Sinhalese and Tamil, quite oblivious to the need to establish a unifying link in place of that language. Two nations on the basis of class and language, were indeed eventually replaced by a similar division on the basis of Sinhalese and Tamil. But this, so far as the 1940s and 1950s were concerned, was yet to be.

With the introduction of the Education Ordinance of 1939 for debate in the State Council, there began nearly six years of concentration on education reform in general, and in particular on the medium of instruction. As we have seen, the Executive Committee of Education had formed itself into a Special Committee by co-opting educationists, and after long deliberation this special committee produced a report in 1943. Among the main recommendations was one on language: the replacement of English by the mother tongue of the student as the medium of instruction in schools.

It is against this background that one needs to consider the resolution introduced on 22 June 1943 by Sri Lanka's present President, J.R. Jayewardene, then a newcomer to the national legislature beginning a career in politics which was to span a period of over 40 years. The chief feature of this motion was its comprehensiveness; and by setting out these issues in detail he also demonstrated the complex nature of the *swabasha* problem. Jayewardene had been largely responsible for infusing a new spirit of commitment to nationalism within the Ceylon National Congress and he and his close associates had succeeded in pushing the Congress to supporting the *swabasha* movement. Indeed he had been instrumental in getting that body to adopt a resolution in 1939 urging that Sinhalese and Tamil be made the official languages.

When he formally moved this resolution on 30 November 1943 it became immediately controversial because of its exclusion of Tamil as a national language. By the time the debate commenced in May 1944 Jayewardene himself sought to include Tamil along with Sinhalese as the two national languages. Instead with his consent an amendment was moved by a Tamil member, V. Nalliah, whereby the words "and Tamil" were included in the original of the motion wherever the word "Sinhalese" occurred.[11]

Jayewardene's resolution read as follows originally: "That with the object of making Sinhalese the official language within a reasonable number of years, this Council is of the opinion

(a) That Sinhalese should be made the medium of instruction in all schools.

(b) That Sinhalese should be made a compulsory subject in all public examinations.

(c) That legislation be introduced to permit the business of the House to be conducted in Sinhalese.

(d) That a Commission be appointed to choose for translation and to translate important books of other languages into Sinhalese.

(e) That a Commission should be appointed to report on all steps that need to be taken to effect the transition from English into Sinhalese."[12]

There were several noteworthy features of the debate that ensued. (Ironically enough the debate was conducted in English; the standing orders of the State Council would not permit the use of the indigenous languages in debates.) The first was the unconcealed reluctance of D.S. Senanayake to give his support to the change in language policy envisaged in the motion both in its original and amended forms.

Secondly, there was the attitude of S.W.R.D. Bandaranaike, the future champion — in the mid-1950s — of Sinhalese as the sole official language of Sri Lanka. Speaking on the motion he argued that

"...there is no question that one of the most important ingredients of nationality is language, because it is through the vehicle of language that the aspirations, the yearnings and triumphs of a people through the centuries are enshrined and preserved. Therefore all that it means to a nation from the psychological, from the sentimental, from the cultural points of view, the value of nationality from all those points of view are expressed through the medium of language. That is why language is such an important ingredient of nationality."[13]

More specifically he made his position unmistakably clear on the role of Tamil as an official language.

"...What is the object of having Sinhalese alone as the official language?" he asked, and went on to answer the question thus:

"...If the objection is that it is rather awkward to have more than one official language, I would like to point out that other countries are putting up with more than two official languages and are carrying on reasonably satisfactorily...I do not see that there would be any harm at all in recognizing the Tamil language also as an official language. It is necessary to bring about that amity, that confidence among the various communities which we are all striving to achieve within reasonable limits. Therefore, on the second point, I have no personal objection to both these languages being considered official languages, nor do I see any particular harm or danger or real difficulty arising from it..."

But his position was far from being unambiguous. Thus he was the only member to abstain from voting on a resolution moved by T.B. Jayah, a Malay nominated member, that sections (a), (b), (c) and (d) of the amended motion be deleted and that item (e) should read as follows:

"That a Commission should be appointed to report on all steps that need to be taken to effect the transition from English into Sinhalese and Tamil."

Of the twelve State Councillors who voted for Jayah's resolution only D.S. Senanayake was a Sinhalese; all the Moors and T.B. Jayah voted for it as did all the Tamils present on that occasion except V. Nalliah. Of the 25 members who voted against, 23 were Sinhalese, the others being V. Nalliah and H.R. Freeman, an Englishman who had retired from the elite Ceylon Civil Service and was the elected representative of the Anuradhapura constituency.[15] Again, once the State Council adopted Jayewardene's resolution, and when the question of implementing the resolutions arose Bandaranaike insisted that "...none of these recommendations should be given effect to immediately."

The third noteworthy feature about the debate — and this is especially important in regard to the future — was that whatever support there was in official circles and from established politicians to have Tamil recognized along with Sinhalese as an official language, Sinhalese Buddhist opinion expressed a strong and vocal dissent.[16] They wanted only one official language, Sinhalese. At this time — 1944-45 —their opposition to the two-language principle carried much less weight than it was to do within a decade of the State Council's adoption of this resolution.

Fourthly, it is necessary to emphasize the lack of enthusiasm for change in language policy among the elite and in the higher bureaucracy. Certainly the minorities other than the Tamils had their reservations on it, and the Tamils themselves as we shall see, were beginning to have second thoughts.

The implementation of these recommendations owed much to the energy and initiative of J.R. Jayewardene. In mid-1945 he succeeded in getting a Select Committee of the State Council appointed to chart the steps and stages in the implementation of official language policy. Taking advantage of D.S. Senanayake's absence from the island for two months from mid-July 1945 in London where he had gone for negotiations with the Colonial Office for reform of the island's constitution, the Board of Ministers was persuaded to appoint a Select Committee of the State Council, with J.R. Jayewardene as Chairman.[17]

In 1946 the Committee issued its report.[18] In support of its strong appeal for *swabasha,* it cited, in particular, the disabilities which affected vernacular education and especially education in Sinhalese and the compelling need to overcome these. The Committee recommended a ten year transition period at the end of which English would cease to be the language of government.

It is necessary to conclude this survey on education and language policy with a reference to a new, and from the point of view of the future, an ominous development — a change of attitude on the part of the Tamils in regard to language and education in the 1940s. During the 1930s struggle over education reform Hindu and Muslim educationalists were willing co-billigerents in weakening the hold of the Christians, particularly the Roman Catholics, on education. The State Councillors from the Northern Province all voted for the education bill of 1939 but they all voted against Kannangara's education bill of 1945 as they did in 1944 for Jayah's amending resolution on J.R. Jayewardene's language motion.

They were, in a sense, reacting against the more flagrant manifestations of Sinhalese-Buddhist chauvinism on the part of bodies such as the Sinhala Maha Sabha, and of some members of the *sangha* who had entered the political arena on issues relating to education and language.[19] Nor were such utterances confined to *bhikkhus* and the rank and file of the Sinhala Maha Sabha. For instance a speech by Bandaranaike in his dual role of member of the Ceylon National Congress and leader of the Sinhala Maha Sabha, in 1939 argued or appeared to argue, the case for assimilation of the Tamil minority by the Sinhalese.

> "What is this country?" he asked. "Is it the land of the people? If it is
> the people I do not know of any country which has progressed to the goal
> of freedom by embracing all communities and all cultures in their acti-
> vities".[20]

By the late 1930s even the moderates among Sri Lanka Tamil politicians expressed fears of assimilationist policies eroding the cultural identity of the Tamils. But it was G.G. Ponnambalam, the supremely eloquent successor to Arunachalam and Ramanathan as the principal leader of the Tamils, who put this view across with his customary zest.

> "A Sinhalese Christian can become a Sinhalese Buddhist, but a Tamil cannot become a Sinhalese. That is a metamorphosis through which we cannot go."[21]

The fears of the Tamils, in regard to this, were clearly exaggerated, often wilfully so by some Tamil politicians who wanted an easy road to political success. But if assimilation was at worst a remote threat, there was, on any realistic assessment of the situation little likelihood of Tamil and Hinduism being accepted on a basis of equality with Sinhalese and Buddhism. Besides, neither Sinhalese educationalists nor politicians made a serious attempt to foster Sinhalese-Tamil bilingualism in the English schools outside the Northern Province and this lack of reciprocity was treated as evidence of insensitivity on the part of the majority community on the larger issue of national integration. It was partly on account of this that Jayewardene's resolution on official languages attracted so much criticism from Tamil politicians within the State Council, and was gleefully seized upon by communal extremists among the Tamils outside it to justify their alarmist views.

Ponnambalam himself, in the course of the debate, asserted that

> "if the object of this resolution was to usher in the cultural and literary renaissance of the Sinhalese, I should be the first to support it, even unamended. But I cannot be blind to the fact that the motion as it stands, invites this House to accept the language of a section of the people as the only official language and the medium of instruction and medium of normal official intercourse. It is merely one of the first steps that one would take to advance the theory of one race, one religion, one language."[22]

He went on to ask:

> "Where is all this talk of the psychological deficiency of imparting instruction in a foreign language if in point of fact two million of the people of this country are to be consigned to receive their future instruction through a foreign language — Sinhalese".[23]

He argued that it was better to retain English as the official language rather than make any change to promote the vernaculars

> "...As long as there are two races, two linguistic communities, if we are to avoid creating a local Pakistan, with two sections of the people speaking two different languages confined to two different areas, we must have a common language, and that language must be English".[24]

Implicit in all his arguments on this and other occasions was the belief that the English language provided a neutral medium for fair competition between the two communities.

Not all Tamil politicians — and certainly not many Tamil educationists — endorsed Ponnambalam's support of the *status quo* on language with the same enthusiasm or conviction. And of course, there was the small minority who took a diametrically opposite view. Among them the most notable was V. Nalliah. It would be appropriate to conclude this chapter by quoting an extract from his speech during the debate on J.R. Jayewardene's resolution on language:

> "...It is ridiculous that we should call ourselves a people fighting for
> independence and Dominion Status and still be conducting the business
> of the country in a language not understood by the large majority. If those
> who do not know Sinhalese or Tamil have decided to remain in Ceylon it
> is high time they learnt one of the languages. I do not see any reason why
> we, as Tamils, should stand in the way of Sinhalese being the official
> language in the Tamil areas, and it is quite possible that both languages
> will be used for purposes of administration".[25]

References

1   For a study of the 're-indigenization" movement, see, K.M. de Silva, 'Christian Missions in Sri Lanka and their response to nationalism, 1910-1948', in P.L. Prematileke, *et al* (eds), *Senarat Paranavitana Commemoration Volume* pp. 221-233.

2   E.F.C. Ludowyk, *The Modern History of Ceylon,* (London, 1966), p. 116.

3   The Board of Education was established under Ordinance 1 of 1920. There was a substantial weightage in favor of denominational interests in its membership, and this became more pronounced with the passage of time.

4   In the State Council, the Executive Committee of Education formed itself into a Special Committee by co-opting educationists, and after long deliberation this Special Committee produced a report in 1943 which recommended radical changes in educational policy — *Sessional Paper*, hereafter *(S.P.)* XXIV of 1943.

5   "Free" education as it applied to Sri Lanka has been till very recently nothing more than the abolition of tuition fees.

6   Among those who spoke up in criticism of the system of denominational education were S.W.R.D. Bandaranaike (*Hansard* [State Council] 24 January 1945, column 492). The chief proponents of demoninationalism were G.A.H. Wille (a nominated Burgher representative) and G.C.S. Corea, Minister of Labour, Industry and Commerce.

7   The difference between the Roman Catholics and Protestants as regards the education of the children in their flock needs to be explained. The former brought pressure to bear on Roman Catholic parents to send their children to Roman Catholic schools and the larger (and better) of such schools had a majority of Roman Catholic pupils; there were no such pressures by Protestant churches and in very few (if any) Protestant schools was there a majority of pupils who were Protestants (even using the term widely to cover all Protestant denominations).

8   *Hansard* [State Council] 1932 column 3118, ff, G.K.W. Perera's motion of 9 March.

9   On the Jaffna boycott see, Jane Russell, 'The Dance of the Turkey-Cock — The Jaffna Boycott of 1931' in *CJHSS*, n.s. VIII(1), pp. 47-64. See also S. Kadiragamar 'The Jaffna Youth Congress' in the *Handy Perimpanayagam — A Memorial Volume*, (Jaffna 1980), pp. 1-112, particularly pp. 71-82.

10 *Hansard* [State Council] 1936 Vol. I Column 881, Philip Gunawardene's motion of 3 July 1936. The resolution was adopted by a majority of 34 to 4 with 1 member declining to vote.

11 The voting on this amendment was 29 for and 8 against. Among those voted for were D.S. Senanayake, S.W.R.D. Bandaranaike, and G.G. Ponnambalam, *Hansard* [State Council] 1944 Vol. I columns 816-7.

12 *Hansard* [State Council] Vol. I 1944, column 745.

13 Ibid., columns 816-7.

14 Ibid.

15 The motion, in its final form, was carried by a majority of 27 votes to 2.

16 K.N.O. Dharmadasa, 'The Rise of Sinhalese Language Nationalism: A Study in the Sociology of Language' (unpublished Ph.D. thesis, Monash 1979), pp. 472-84.

17 The Select Committee was appointed on 20 September 1946.

18 *S.P.* XXII of 1946.

19 For discussion of this see, K.N.O. Dharmadasa op. cit., pp. 384 ff.

20 *Ceylon Daily News*, 25 January 1939.

21 *Hansard* [State Council] 1939 column 960.

22 Ibid., column 764.

23 Ibid., column 765.

24 Ibid.

25 Ibid., column 759.

Chapter VI

The Higher Bureaucracy and Elite Conflict c 1920 - 1948

"A just distribution of places of honour and emolument in the community is the mark of a wise ruler, as by satisfying the legitimate ambitions it largely contributes to the contentment of the people."[1]

In this comment he made in 1917 in the course of a speech that was to become famous, Sir Ponnambalam Arunachalam, retired a short while earlier from the Ceylon Civil Service and beginning a new career in politics, was giving expression to one of the main grievances of the Sri Lankan elite, namely the vigor with which the British administration in the island had protected the portals of the higher bureaucracy against any significant entry of Sri Lankans to it.

Arunachalam argued that progressive indigenization — Ceyloni-zation as the process was then called — was the only means of retaining in the island the wealth of administrative experience which left with every departing and retiring European* in the higher bureaucracy. As in India so in Sri Lanka the mounting pressure from the elite for concessions on this confronted a stubborn resistance from the British administrators no less than from Whitehall. But it was impossible to ignore it altogether, or to be entirely unresponsive to it.[2] And in Sri Lanka as in India the ensuing competition for posts in the bureaucracy figured so prominently in the 'communal' controversies of the last two decades of British rule that many contemporary

---

* The term 'European' was used by the Colonial Office as well as by Sri Lankan politicians and journalists to refer to British members of the higher bureaucracy and technical services during British rule in the island. Among the British officials of this period were a few colonials from the British West Indies and from India, who had successfully competed for nomination to the island's higher bureaucracy at the annual examination held for this purpose.

observers saw the communal or ethnic tension of the day as nothing more than a sordid struggle for jobs in the administration between sections of what they called "the middle class".[3] While competition was eager for all categories of posts in the bureaucracy, it was fiercest in regard to positions in the higher bureaucracy, and the prestigious technical services including the judiciary. Our concern in this chapter is with the competition that arose over positions in the higher bureaucracy and the technical services. While ethnic conflict in Sri Lanka was, and is, much more than a mere struggle for posts in the bureaucracy, yet its importance as a factor in that conflict, and as one that still generates more bitterness than most others, is as unmistakable as it is unlikely to diminish in significance.

The appointment in 1918 of a committee of the Legislative Council to report on the question of Sri Lankan entry to the higher bureaucracy represented the first significant response on the part of the colonial administration in the island to this pressure. The Sri Lankan elite was gratified to note that this committee's principal recommendation was that up to a third of the places in the elite Ceylon Civil Service should be reserved for Sri Lankans, and that this proportion should be increased gradually till it reached 50% in due course. Along with this it recommended the abolition of the much maligned and obviously inferior local division of the Ceylon Civil Service, and the introduction of a local examination for the recruitment of Sri Lankans to the higher bureaucracy. Both these were major concessions to Sri Lankan pressures, and amounted in the first case to the elimination of a grievance, and in the second to the conferment of an advantage in eliminating the need to travel to London to sit the examination. There was at the same time an insistence on the continued recruitment of Europeans to, and employment of Europeans in, the Ceylon Civil Service.

As so often happens a seemingly radical recommendation of an official Commission of Inquiry was merely a recognition of a change that was already taking place. Because of war time conditions more Sri Lankans had entered the higher bureaucracy; and educated Sri Lankan youths who had served in the British armed forces in the European battlefields were accommodated in the Ceylon Civil Service even though their educational qualifications fell far short of those normally insisted upon.

When a second Committee was apppointed in 1921 to report on what further steps needed to be taken to implement the recommendations of the 1918 Committee its investigations revealed that the Sri Lankan element in the higher bureaucracy had increased substantially. Their numbers kept increasing. The virtual monopoly which Europeans held in the higher bureaucracy was over by the late 1920s. In 1907 only 13% of the positions in the Ceylon Civil Service (i.e., twelve out of 90 posts) were held by Sri Lankans; but by 1925 this had risen to 32% or forty-three out of 135 posts.

Yet one needs to remember that while in 1925 32% of the posts in the Ceylon Civil Service were occupied by Sri Lankans, that change was remarkable largely in comparison to previous decades. Even in 1925 almost all Sri Lankans in the higher bureaucracy were in the judicial branch of the service, then as in the past distinctly inferior to the key administrative branch of the service. Only two Sri Lankans stand out as exceptions, C.L. Wickremesinghe, a Sinhalese, and P. Saravanamuttu, a Tamil. The former was in the judicial branch till 1917, and became in time Assistant Government Agent, and eventually the first Sri Lankan Government Agent (he was Government Agent of the North Central Province), while the latter after a similar spell of service in the judiciary became Additional Assistant Government Agent Colombo in 1923 and rose to be Tea and Rubber Commissioner in the 1940s. Even as late as 1935 seven of the nine positions of Government Agent, the administrative heads of the nine provinces in the island, were held by Europeans, and their dominance here continued till 1946 when they still held five of the posts as against two each for the Sinhalese and the Sri Lanka Tamils.[4]

Apart from the key Civil Service, European dominance of the technical departments, with the single exception of the Department of Health, continued into the 1930s. In the Health Department, Sri Lankans held 67% of the posts of Colonial Surgeons and Assistant Colonial Surgeons as early as 1907. By 1919 the medical profession was almost entirely Sri Lankan and although at the beginning there was a preponderance of Burghers, the Sinhalese were a majority by 1925. The position was quite different in other technical departments, such as the Public Works Department, Irrigation, Posts and Telegraphs and the Railway. There the European dominance was so marked that a select committee of the Legislative Council was appointed in 1928 to investigate ways and means of increasing the number of Sri Lankans in these technical departments; it made a rather conventional and predictable recommendation that steps be taken to train Sri Lankans to fill some of these positions.

The Donoughmore Reforms and the Higher Bureaucracy

In regard to "Ceylonization" of the higher bureaucracy, as in so many other aspects of the country's political and administrative system, the report of the Donoughmore Commission was a path-breaking document. The major premise of its argument here was that the higher bureaucracy must be largely manned by Sri Lankans, and while it accepted the need for the retention of a small core of Europeans in it, the Donoughmore Commission came out strongly in favor of a progressive reduction of the European element in the bureaucracy.

In the first State Council there was near unanimity of opinion among Sri Lankan members that the time had come to place restrictions on the recruitment of Europeans to the higher bureaucracy and the judiciary. In 1932 the State Council urged that the recruitment of Europeans to these services be stopped. A resolution to this effect was adopted in 1933, and another was tabled in 1934. These had the enthusiastic support of the Board of Ministers who in 1934 persuaded the then Governor Sir Edward Stubbs to back them in this demand to Whitehall. But to no avail for Sir Philip Cunliffe-Lister, then Secretary of State for the Colonies, refused this request with the comment that

"... the maintenance of an European element in the Civil Service [is]
a matter of profound importance..."[5]

He was merely reflecting the conventional wisdom of the Colonial Office where a senior official, H.R. Cowell, remarked that:

"... the maintenance of European officers is essential to the proper exercise by the Governor of the power reserved to him in the constitution, and would still be essential ... so long as the Governor is ultimately responsible for the administrtion to the S[ecretary] of S[tate]."[6]

Yet within two years of this reiteration of the Whitehall's conventional stand on this issue the recruitment of Europeans to the Ceylon Civil Service came to an end. The last European cadet to the Ceylon Civil Service was appointed in 1937; by 1938 all vacancies in the service were filled by Sri Lankan recruits. By 1946 the composition of the Ceylon Civil Service showed a remarkable change: although many of the senior positions were still held by Englishmen, the more numerous lower posts were now a monopoly of young Sri Lankans.

This same process is seen in the manning of the technical departments. After an initial insistence on a core of Europeans to be maintained by regular recruitment their numbers actually dropped drastically and then recruitment ceased altogether in all the technical departments during the second world war. Two processes were at work here: the reluctance of young Europeans to enter a service in which their prospects of future advancement seemed so obviously limited by impending political changes; and a notable increase in the number of technically qualified Sri Lankans ready to fill all the vacancies available. There was, as with the Ceylon Civil Service, a third process as well: Sri Lankan legislators and politicians insistent on the complete "Ceylonization" of the technical departments.

The Donoughmore recommendations hastened other processes of change within the higher bureaucracy, one of which was the creation of a Judicial Service distinct from the Ceylon Civil Service. There had been, indeed, no clear demarcation of administrative and judicial functions within the higher bureaucracy, and nearly all positions in the judiciary save the Supreme Court could be and were held by members of the Ceylon Civil Service. As we have seen the judicial posts were regarded as distinctly inferior in function and status to the coveted revenue positions which carried with them both greater power in the execution of policy, and greater influence in the making of it. With the growth and expansion of the legal profession there was increasing pressure from Sri Lankan lawyers for appointments to the judicial service; in time members of the Civil Service themselves welcomed the entry of lawyers. Official recognition of the need for a separation of judicial from administrative functions came in 1924 with the recommendations of the Retrenchment Committee, and the appointment of a Select Committee of the Legislative Council in 1926 to consider the establishment of a separate judicial service. It was after 1931 with the introduction of the Donoughmore Constitution that the most fundamental changes came. In 1936 a separate judicial service was created and that became a monopoly of professional lawyers almost all of whom were Sri Lankans.

Secondly, there was the traditional element in the bureaucracy the native headmen as they were called. They had their own hierarchy with the *Maha Mudaliyar*, the Governor's principal aide, at the top. Even as late as the first decade of the twentieth century the British colonial administration in the island was bent on protecting the interests of this group and sustaining them as a counterweight to the more assertive political element in the elite. But as this latter grew in numbers and influence in the 1920s their agitation against the traditional elite grew correspondingly stronger. The traditional elite was viewed as a relic of the past, a 'feudal' element whose powers and influence were incompatible with the creation of a modern bureaucracy and whose privileges were indefensible in a society which was becoming more democratic in aspiration and attitudes. The Donoughmore Commission was not inclined to be more sympathetic to the traditional elite than the latter's critics among the Sri Lankan elite. The Commissioners described the traditional element in the bureaucracy as

"a mechanism more suited to the more primitive stage of Colonial Government and it is more than possible that Ceylon is outgrowing that stage."[7]

The legislators of the Donoughmore era (1931-47) were, if anything, even more persistent than most of their predecessors of the Legislative Councils of the 1920s in pressing for the abolition of the traditional element in the bureaucracy. With the political system based on universal suffrage introduced in 1931, and the social and economic changes of the 1930s of which rapid improvements in literacy were a significant feature, this traditional element in the bureaucracy was more than ever an anachronism. The appointment of a Commission on the Headman System in 1934 was to mark a vital stage in the process of its elimination. That Commission recommended a new administrative mechanism to replace it; one feature of it was the replacement of the Chief Headmen and *Rate Mahatmayas* by Divisional Revenue Officers appointed on the results of a competitive examination, and by the transfer of much of the powers of the village level headmen to local government institutions.[8] But the village level headmen survived with their powers reduced, and recruitment to their ranks now established on a different basis from the past, i.e., it had less to do with the traditional criteria than political patronage, which now became the rule.

Replacement of Chief Headmen (the *Rate Mahatmayas*) by D.R.O.'s began in 1938; some of the former survived till the mid-1940s. In 1946 the abolition of these posts was complete.

We need to turn now to one important feature of the transformation of the bureaucracy which we have surveyed here — the change in the ethnic composition of the Sri Lankan element in it.[9] In 1870 all seven Sri Lankans in the Ceylon Civil Service had been Sinhalese; by 1907 that monopoly had been broken and the figures were six Burghers, four Sinhalese and two Tamils respectively. In 1925 there were forty-three Sri Lankans in the higher bureaucracy, of whom fourteen (35%)

were Burghers, seventeen (40%) Sinhalese and twelve (22%) Tamils. By 1946 Sri Lankan dominance was established, and of the Sri Lankans in the Ceylon Civil Service, the figures were sixty-nine, thirty-one, and sixteen for the Sinhalese, Tamils and Burghers respectively. Although the Sinhalese had 60% of the posts held by Sri Lankans, Tamils and Burghers were still significantly larger in number here than their relative proportions of the total population.

In the technical services — Medical, Engineering and Surveying — there was a similar gradual assertion of Sinhalese majority status, and once more it was a change from an original Burgher dominance. Indeed the preponderance of Burghers in the Department of Health and the Public Works Department (PWD) had been even greater than in the Ceylon Civil Service. Thus, in 1925 when there were only four Sri Lankan Provincial Engineers, and all of them were Burghers, while of twenty-four Sri Lankan District Engineers in the PWD as many as thirteen were Burghers as against six Sinhalese and five Tamils.

In the PWD as in the Ceylon Civil Service the Sri Lanka Tamils had a larger number of posts than the Tamils relative proportion of the total population. By 1946 Sinhalese held thirty-five out of sixty-seven of the principal executive positions, — civil list posts as they were called —in the PWD in the hands of Sri Lankans; there were seventeen Tamils and fifteen Burghers. Thus while the Sinhalese held a majority of such posts it is nevertheless significant that they are almost equalled by the two minorities put together.

The Civil Medical Department had been for decades a preserve of the Burghers. In 1870 of 23 Sri Lankan Colonial Surgeons and Assistant Colonial Surgeons as many as 21 were Burghers; in 1907 all six Sri Lankan Colonial Surgeons were Burghers and 31 out of 61 Medical Officers. At this time Sinhalese doctors constituted only 23% of the total number of Sri Lankans in the medical service of the government. By 1925 the Sinhalese were represented in larger numbers in the service, and their majority position was consolidated by the large number of new recruits to the service from among them.

The pattern is different if one considers the medical profession as a whole and not merely those in government service. Thus in 1921 31% of the physicians and medical practitioners were low-country Sinhalese, 3% were Kandyan Sinhalese, thus making a total of 34% of Sinhalese; the Burghers were 12%, but the Sri Lanka Tamils constituted 44% of the total. Indeed in the medical profession as a whole the Sri Lanka Tamils were dominant, followed by the Sinhalese, while the Burghers had lost their earlier supremacy although they still had a remarkably large number in that profession considering their position as a miniscule minority of the population. Here, by the end of British rule the Sinhalese were in a clear majority: there were in 1946, 205 Sinhalese doctors as against 25 Burghers and 115 Tamils.

In the legal profession however the Sinhalese had established their dominance by 1921, with 50% of the lawyers (46% low-country Sinhalese and 4% Kandyans) while the Sri Lanka Tamils were 28% and the Burghers 16%. Again in absolute numbers the Sinhalese were dominant, while the Burghers and Tamils, especially the former had representation which was clearly disproportionate to their numbers in the total population. This position the Sinhalese retained over the next two decades till the end of British rule and it was reflected in the judicial service as well. In 1946, five out of nine Sri Lankan judges of the Supreme Court were Sinhalese, while three were Burghers and only one was a Tamil. But in the lower rungs of the judiciry there was still a dominance of minority members in the Sri Lankan representation: as against twenty-one Sinhalese, there were eleven Burghers and thirteen Tamils.

Expansion

The transformation of the bureaucracy we have surveyed in this chapter has other significant features. One such was its increase in size. There had been a notable expansion in the departmental organization of the administration in the late 19th century when a considerable widening of government activities had occurred. In the first decade of the 20th century a number of new government departments were created, largely as a result of a continuing enlargement of the scope of governmental activities. But these were overshadowed by the expansion which came in the 1930s, one which also saw a diversification of and a greater emphasis on specialization in administrative functions. Here the stimulus came from the social and economic policies followed under the Donoughmore system which necessitated a steady increase in the number of government departments. This rate of growth was sustained and accelerated under wartime conditions and needs. All this meant that the number of places in the bureaucracy, at all levels, increased as never before and not least in the executive and technical grades: it meant greater opportunites for the educated Sri Lankans to enter the elite through the administrative system.

Secondly, from the late 1920s, the Civil Service which formed the major instrument of colonial administration in the island was confronted with the difficult task of coping with the pressures of elected representatives, pressures which became ever stronger with the introduction of the Donoughmore Constitution. Ministers and legislators sought to convert the administrative machine which had evolved under colonial rule into an effective instrument for the implementation of policies of economic and social change, the significance of which, and the need for which, not every member of the higher bureaucracy understood or sympathized with.

There already was, by the end of British rule in 1946-8, a displacement of the bureaucracy from its traditional colonial role of being an integral part of the governing elite; instead the political elite was now dominant; it had become the ruling elite, and did not pretend to accept any significant role for the bureaucracy as part of the governing elite although quite often the politicians and the Sri Lankan element in the higher bureaucracy had a common outlook on many issues. The process was naturally reinforced by the adoption of a parliamentary system of government after 1947 and the dominant position the political executive occupied in such a system.

Thirdly, the transformation in the ethnic composition of the higher bureaucracy, and the technical departments which we have surveyed earlier in this chapter did reflect increased competition among the elite for places and positions. That competition may indeed have been more bitter had it been from the outset a struggle between the Sinhalese and Tamils. On the contrary it was for most of this period a struggle between the Burghers, and the Tamils, with the Sinhalese entering the picture only later.

The miniscule Burgher community, as we have seen, had a dominant position in the higher bureaucracy and in the professions. This was due to two factors: literacy in English, their mother-tongue; and a greater readiness on the part of the British to use them, rather than the emerging educated elements among other sectors of the population, as intermediaries, not indeed between themselves and the people at large for which they used the traditional elite, but in the higher reaches of the bureaucracy. By the end of this period the Burghers had lost their early advantages in literacy in English, and more ominous still the position of English as the language of administation was being challenged. It was far from being displaced either as the language of administration or of instruction in schools, but the days of its dominance were clearly at an end.

The Burghers were too small in numbers to put up a fight; with independence in the offing they began a process of emigration in large numbers, to Australia mainly, but to Britain as well. Thus one factor in the competition was eliminated, leaving the struggle to the Tamils and the Sinhalese. For the Tamils or the Tamil elite, emigration was not yet a remedy. On the contrary one phase of their emigration was quite clearly over — that to Malaya and Singapore which came to an end in the 1920s. Thus many more turned to employment in the south of the island — at all levels. This occurred at a time when the Sinhalese themselves were more inclined than in the past to seek government employment.

Ironically enough the Sri Lankan elite came into its own at a time when its economic strength was being sapped by the inter-war depression in international trade. The inter-war years were on the whole a long period of depression, reflecting a decline in the growth of world trade, first because of the world war of 1914-9, and and secondly as a result of the economic dislocation in Europe in the 1920s and the great economic depression of the 1930s. The export sector of Sri Lanka's economy reflected this trend. There was an improvement in the late 1930s and with the outbreak of the second world war when after the Japanese had overrun most of South East Asia, Sri Lanka became the sole supplier of rubber to the allied powers. The improvement may have been greater if the price of rubber had not been artificially restrained and had been permitted to reflect the true market forces. Nevertheless, despite this regeneration of the productive capacity of the plantation sector of the economy at this time, it could hardly be said that it's capacity to generate profits and employment had recovered to what it had been in the halcyon days before the first world war.

These trends affected the Sinhalese sector of the elite more than others because their stake in the plantations had been greater than that of other sections of the Sri Lankan elite. This inevitably strengthened a trend toward a search for employment in the professions and in government service and this in turn exacerbated existing rivalries within the elite.

Looking back at the 1930s and 1940s one sees the beginnings of a great social revolution, the full effects of which were felt only in the

1950s. This concerned, in the first place, the expansion of education at every level, primary, secondary and tertiary. Literacy both in English and in the local languages was on the increase. And at last the University College established in 1921 as a halfway house to a national university provided the not-so-very affluent with higher education at a reasonable financial cost. The children of the affluent still went across to Britain and Europe for their education, sometimes after a brief spell at the University College. In 1942 the University College severed its formal links with the University of London and became the University of Ceylon.[10] There was almost simultaneously a rapid and consistent increase in the intake of students to the University, and the impact of this on social mobility and the expansion of the elite was immediately noticeable. Just as the establishment of a Medical College and the Law College in the last quarter of the nineteenth century had given a great filip to the growth of these two professions, so now there was a similar growth in other professions, teaching at the University and secondary schools, for instance, quite apart from providing the administrative service — including the higher bureaucracy — with its rapidly expanding needs of trained manpower. Education was by now a much more important route to elite status than it had been in the past.

It also aggravated competition between Sinhalese and Tamil elites. Because of the overwhelming numerical dominance of the Sinhalese in Sri Lanka even a small but steady increase in literacy among them meant a large increase in the number of literates in general, and in those in search of positions in the administrative system.

The fact is that the Sinhalese were reasserting their majority status, and there were among them many who were distinctly unhappy that the gains were not coming quicker than they did. Whereas in an earlier age progress was measured over decades, now they wanted it all speeded up. What they aspired to was a domination of public life by Sinhalese Buddhists commensurate with that achieved by them in the Legislature and in politics.

Up to 1946 the contest was muted for two reasons: firstly, expansion of the public service and the higher bureaucracy in particular kept pace with the number of recruits available through the University of Ceylon, and the expanding network of secondary schools. In fact the mid-1940s saw unemployment reduced to the barest minimum. Secondly, the transfer of power had still to be negotiated and thus the complete assertion of the power of the Sinhalese was postponed — in particular the domination of the Sinhalese Buddhists. The minorities, ethnic and religious, still had a significant, if no longer a commanding, role in public life, and this the Sinhalese Buddhists resented. It was because of this sense of grievance of theirs that elite conflict took on a fiercer outlook by the mid-1950s.

There was besides the additional complication of an emphasis on the national languages in education and the administration. At the outset of the campaign for this the Tamil elite, like an influential section of the Sinhalese elite, had been in favor of it. By the late 1930s they began to lose much of their earlier enthusiasm for it. Looking ahead into the near future the Tamil elite regarded the impending changes in language policy as a threat to their advantageous position in Sri Lanka's public life.[11] By the end of the period, one observes a distinct sense of insecurity among the Tamils. The familiar protective umbrella of British rule was about to be removed, and the Tamils did not relish the prospect of facing life ahead without it, or at least without a viable alternative for it. Their sense of loss was all the more poignant for being, in fact, one of relative deprivation, the loss of an advantageous if not a privileged position.

References

[1]   Sir Ponnambalam Arunachalam, 'Our Political Needs' in (ed) S.W.R.D. Banda-ranaike, *The Handbook of the Ceylon National Congress, 1919-1928.* (Colombo, 1928), pp. 90-91.

[2]   See, P.T.M. Fernando, 'The Ceylon Civil Service. A Study of Recruitment Policies, 1880-1920', *M.C.S.*, (1) (1) 1970, pp. 64-83.

[3]   See, G.C. Mendis, 'The Rise of the Middle Class and the Beginnings of Communalism', in his *Ceylon Today and Yesterday* (Colombo, 2nd ed, 1963) pp. 126-136. This chapter originally appeared in the *University of Ceylon Review* 1(1) 1943 under the title 'The Causes of Communal Conflict in Ceylon', pp. 41-49.

[4]   See, S.J. Tambiah, 'Ethnic Representation in Ceylon's Higher Administrative Services, 1870-1946' in the *University of Ceylon Review*, XIII (2&3) 1955 pp. 113-134.

[5]   C O 54/960. File 34227/2, Cunliffe-Lister's Secret Despatch to Stubbs, 14 December 1934.

[6]   C O 54/960, File 34227/2, H.R. Cowell's minute of 9 February 1935.

[7]   *The Donoughmore Report*, p. 122.

8   *S.P. XXVII of 1935, Report of the Commission on the Headman System.*

9   The analysis here is based on S. J. Tambiah, 'Ethnic Representation in Ceylon's Higher Administrative Services, 1870-1946' pp. 127-134.

10 On the early years of the University of Ceylon, see, D.L. Jayasuriya "Development in University Education' The Growth of the University of Ceylon, 1942-65", in The *University of Ceylon Review* XXIII (1&2) 1965.

11 Jane Russell, 'Language, Education and Nationalism — The Language Debate of 1944', *CJHSS*, n.s. VIII(2), 1982, pp. 38-64.

Chapter VII

The Representative System
And Ethnic Rivalries
c 1929 - 1943

Territorial Versus Communal Representation

Few political problems had generated more controversy and done more in fomenting ethnic hostility since the early 1920s than the questions relating to the mode of representation in the national legislature. It remained at the centre of political controversy throughout the next two decades.

At the root of the controversy were the diametrically opposed views on this held by the Sinhalese on the one hand, and minority representatives on the other: from the early years of the 20th century the Sinhalese political leadership had generally insisted on territorial electorates, and an elected majority in a national legislature based on such electorates; the minorities were apprehensive of so far-reaching a change. They were accustomed, or grew accustomed, to nominated representation on a communal basis, or to election through communal or special electorates. Besides, they could argue with much justice, that given the pattern of the spatial distribution of ethnic groups in the island, territorial representation was, in effect, a form of 'communal' representation with a built-in and overwhelming advantage to the Sinhalese.[1]

The suspicions of the minorities were exploited by men like Governor Sir Henry Manning who in 1920 devised an electoral arrangement which, while apparently conceding territorial representation to a large extent, diluted it with communal electorates to accommodate the demands of the minorities.[2] This patently obvious attempt to aggravate existing differences between these groups was deeply resented by the Sinhalese leadership who saw this new electoral system as a capitulation to the demands of the minorities. One result was the collapse of the harmonious relations that had existed for a decade or so between the Sinhalese and Tamil political leaderships. Ramanathan broke away more abruptly, and with greater conviction in his new role of minority leader than did his brother Arunachalam. More significantly Ramanathan led the minorities in solid formation and, in collusion with Manning, sought to thwart the political ambitions of the Sinhalese. The Muslims, for instance, readily worked with Ramanathan to protect their interests against those of the Sinhalese majority.[2] Their acceptance of Ramanathan's leadership which lasted till his death in 1930, and of a role of junior partner in a minorities' bloc in the national legislature under Tamil leadership which lasted much longer than that, are reviewed in Chapter VIII of this present work. Here, we need to note that they were among the principal beneficiaries of the system of communal representation, and were also among the most dogged defenders of that system.

The arrival of the Donoughmore Commissioners in the island in 1928 had the immediate effect of exacerbating communal and political rivalries in the island with groups and individuals making exaggerated claims and demands in the hope of influencing the Commission's work and the political-constitutional structure they would recommend. For one thing the question of universal suffrage became an important, and divisive, issue in the island's politics. The minorities found universal suffrage just as unpalatable and indeed even more so than those Sinhalese who took a stand against it. For universal suffrage would not only democratise the electorate, but would guarantee the permanent Sinhalese domination of politics. Ramanathan came out strongly against it on behalf of the Tamils: indeed his opposition to universal suffrage was more vehement than that of the Congress leadership. The Muslim leadership was equally uneasy if not nervous about the impact of universal suffrage on the political prospects of their community.

Thus despite all its attractive features the Donoughmore report satisfied none of the important political groups in Sri Lanka. The minorities were bitterly hostile largely on account of its forthright condemnation of communal electorates and for devising an electoral structure that made no concessions to "communal" interests. Minority representatives protested bitterly that a decisively significant measure of political power had been transferred to Sri Lankans with, what they regarded as, totally inadequate safeguards for protecting their — the minorities' — interests. Nor — as we have seen — did the principle of universal suffrage make the Donoughmore proposals more palatable to the minorities.

All the minority representatives, including the Muslims, voted against the adoption of the Donoughmore proposals when these came up for debate in the Legislative Council. The proposals secured a very slim margin of acceptance, 19 votes to 17. Thereafter Ramanathan made a well publicized but totally fruitless visit to Whitehall to persuade the Colonial Office to reject the Donoughmore proposals. On behalf of the Muslims, T.B. Jayah sent a memorandum entitled "Muslims and Proposed Constitutional Changes in Ceylon" to the Colonial Office, complaining that the Muslims were "aggrieved that they were forced to submit to a scheme wholly unacceptable to them."[3] Jayah too followed Ramanathan's lead in a visit to London for much the same purpose. He fared no better than his more eloquent and more politically astute senior colleague.

The Delimitation Commission of 1930

The Donoughmore Commission had recommended 65 elected members in the new Legislature, the State Council; the Colonial Office, quite inexplicably, reduced this to 50 and in so doing aggravated the problem of minority representation in the State Council. The Tamils of the Northern and Eastern Provinces, for instance, had been accustomed to a ratio of 2:1 in terms of Sinhalese to Tamil seats in the Legislature in the 1920s; now they faced one of 5:1 which although a more accurate reflection of the demographic pattern in the country was nevertheless an alarming proposition for it was as though all their fears of an overwhelming Sinhalese domination of the Sri Lanka polity were on the verge of fulfilment.

They found the Ceylon National Congress, now that the principle of communal representation against which they had fought for so long had at last been abandoned, in a generous and accommodating mood. They readily accepted weightage in representation for the Northern and Eastern Provinces, and the former in particular. Thus two Congress representatives George E. de Silva and S.W.R.D. Bandaranaike appearing before the Delimitation Commission appointed in 1930 to demarcate boundaries of the 50 elected seats in the State Council, declared themselves "very anxious to conserve the present representation in the North and Eastern Provinces", and urged the creation of two additional seats for these areas, additional presumably to the number they would be entitled to on a population basis.[4] They were joined in this by the Labor leader A.E. Goonesinha who acknowledged the

> "heartburning of the Tamils owing to their losing a great deal of representation and also their 2:1 proportion." "In the interests of the country as a whole" he urged "they should give more representation to the Northern Province than was necessary in order that there might be a contented people."[5]

Not all Sinhalese politicians were inclined to be so accommodating on this issue of weightage in representation for the Tamils of the Northern and Eastern Provinces. Indeed a great many Sinhalese who appeared before the Delimitation Commission were as hostile to weightage in representation as they were to communal representation; more often than not they confused the one for the other and gave the impression of believing that conceding the principle of weightage in representation carried with it the inherent danger of its eventual transformation into communal representation.[6]

Representatives of Tamil opinion had uniformly asked for an allotment of 7 seats for the Northern Province, three more than their numbers warranted. And some of them, H.A.P. Sandarasegera for instance, focussed attention on the decline in their representational fortunes and contrasted this with "the over-representation" of the Kandyans which was certain to obtain in the new situation where the Colonial Office had imposed restrictions on the voting rights of Indians in modification of the Donoughmore proposals. This resulting over-representation of the Kandyans, was advanced by Sandarasegera — and other Tamils — as a justification for the creation of additional seats in the Northern and Eastern Provinces.[7]

Proposals for weightage and special constituencies were not confined to the Tamils and other minorities. There were similar requests from some Sinhalese on a caste basis. But all such claims, requests and demands were rejected by the Delimitation Commission of 1930 who proceeded, in accordance with their terms of reference, to carve out constituencies on a fairly uniform basis of one per 100,000 persons much to the chagrin of the minorities.[8] The "artificial uniformity" of this delimitation became one of the grievances complained of by the Tamil community in the late 1930s.[9] There was some justification for the rigidity with which the Delimitation Commissioners adhered to their terms of reference in the exercise of their duty, in view of the difficulties of resolving the conflicting claims made on behalf of ethnic, caste, religious and regional groups at a time when the ascertainment of population figures was sufficiently formidable by itself.

They settled on 50 elected members on the basis of single-member constituencies. There were 7 nominated State Councillors to represent minorities. The smaller minorities benefitted from this: the Muslims, the European and the Burghers. There were only two seats in which a Muslim candidate had any real chance of winning: Colombo Central and Batticaloa South. Only in 1931 when a Muslim won this latter seat did a Muslim candidate secure election at a general election under the Donoughmore system. The defeated Muslim candidate at Colombo Central was nominated to the State Council in 1931 and 1936.

The seven Executive Committees into which members of the national legislature, the State Councillors, were divided under the Donoughmore Constitution chose their own chairmen and in so doing also elected them as Ministers who, seven in all, constituted the Board of Ministers along with the three Officers of State appointed by the Governor. It was a system which found little favor among Sri Lankan politicians. One unexpected result of the election to the Board of Ministers after the first general election of 1931 was that two minority members, one a Muslim and the other an Indian, were elected, defeating better known and seemingly more influential candidates. Indeed if the Jaffna boycott had not taken place there could well have been a third minority member elected to the Board, a Sri Lankan Tamil. There was a second unexpected result which flowed from this election: the Executive Committee system now had a new set of champions — the minorities. They came to regard it as an essential safeguard of minority rights in a situation where communal electorates to which they were accustomed had been abolished. The mainstream politicians with the Sinhalese in the lead found that there could be no consensus on constitutional reform, much less unanimity of opinion on it, in a Board of Ministers constructed in this form. Thus there were two fundamentally opposed attitudes on the Executive Committees: the mainstream politicians of the Ceylon National Congress wished to see the Executive Committees eliminated and a quasi-Cabinet system established in their place; the minorities were overly protective of this system seeing in it a guarantee of minority representation in the Board of Ministers.

When the elections of 1936 took place the Sinhalese leadership devised a strategy to capture all seven elected places in the Board of Ministers and succeeded in doing so on the basis of a formula for the planned dispersal of their supporters into the seven communities. The scheme itself was devised by a Tamil, C Suntheralingam, Professor of Mathematics at the University College, Colombo, one of the several able advisers whom D.S. Senanayake gathered round himself. The scheme had two objectives: first, to demonstrate that the Executive Committee system did not after all give the minorities the protection they sought, that in fact there was no real need to retain it; the second was that a "Pan-Sinhalese" ministry would ensure a unanimity of opinion on constitutional reform, a condition which the Colonial Office appeared to insist upon.

Looking back on this election one feels that the Sinhalese leadership had made a serious error of judgement. The practical demonstration that the minorities had "no better chance of getting elected [to the Board of Ministers] under the existing method than under some modification"[10] of it was criticized — and deserved to be criticized —as "showing a singular lack of statesmanship."[11] If this argument in support of their action advanced by the ministers could be described as "ill-advised", their second argument was "disingenuous."[12] The unanimity of views on constitutional reform within the Board of Ministers this achieved did not change the situation, so far as the Colonial Office critics of this policy was concerned, "except for the worse."[13]

In 1944 the Soulbury Commission pointed out that:

> "In requiring unanimity, the Secretary of State had clearly intended to convey that he was not prepared to consider proposals for constitutional reform unless they were supported by the minority members of the Board as well as by the Sinhalese. To eliminate the minority not merely failed to satisfy the condition; it gave strong grounds for the belief that they had been excluded precisely because they could not be induced to accept the majority proposals. Moreover as a result of the creation of the Pan-Sinhalese Ministry, the minorities had grown still more alarmed, and it became more difficult than ever to reach a measure of agreement on constitutional reform in the State Council and in the country as a whole."[14]

By the time this criticism appeared in print a Tamil member had been elected in place of D.B. Jayatilaka who retired at the end of 1943. This was Arunachalam Mahadeva, son of Sir Ponnambalam Arunachalam. His election heralded the end of the Pan-Sinhalese Ministry.

The "Fifty-Fifty" Campaign

The question of minority representation which had receded to the background for about five years after 1931 was revived again during the early months of the administration of Governor Sir Andrew Caldecott in 1937 when a reform of the constitution was being considered. For two years beginning with the middle of 1937 pressures and counterpressures, claims and counter claims, reached such a pitch of intensity that Caldecott was constrained to comment in 1939 that "... all our political fissures radiate from the vexed question of minority representation."[15]

And so indeed they did for this was the climax of the so-called "fifty-fifty" campaign directed by the Tamil leader G.G. Ponnambalam on behalf of the coalition of minorities he had organized. Dr. Jane Russell whose recently published doctoral dissertation is the most comprehensive and perceptive study of Tamil politics in this period has pointed out that

> "the proposals of the minorities were as variable as the permutation of interests in the coalition itself. The multifarious proposals formulated by each section of the coalition came to be included in the umbrella term "Fifty-Fifty" — a term which became a shibboleth to the minorities."[16]

The term "fifty-fifty" she adds, was in fact no more than a slogan, a simplification of a rather complex set of proposals which were first devised by G.G. Ponnambalam in 1937. His scheme involved a complicated system of multiple weightages in a combination of territorial and communal representation which was supposed to ensure the re-instatement of the constitutional concept of "balanced representation" by which no single ethnic group could out-vote a combination of the others.[17] It was, in brief, a return to the electoral system of the 1920s — the so-called Manning constitutions — but modified to accommodate the principle of universal suffrage.

"Fifty-fifty", then, did not always mean an equal division of seats between the Sinhalese on the one hand and the minorities on the other. What Ponnambalam originally asked for was a ratio of 13:7 Sinhalese seats to Tamil, to be awarded on a territorial and geographical basis. It amounted to a very considerable weightage in favor of the Sri Lanka Tamils, and as justification for it Ponnambalam advanced the historical precedent of the 2:1 ratio of Sinhalese and Sri Lanka Tamils of the early 1920s. However, an agreement on the ratio of minority members to Sinhalese in the State Council eluded this coalition of minorities despite several modifications of the formula, or ratio, devised to secure as wide a range of support within it as was possible.

In June 1937 at a secret conference of the minorities at which representatives of all minority communities were present a ratio of 1:1 or "fifty-fifty" was first formulated, and was put up for the consideration of Caldecott by a deputation from the minorities. The outcry which followed this demand, an outcry not only from the Sinhalese but from a large and influential section of the Sri Lanka Tamils themselves and Muslims, compelled the coalition to adopt a more moderate stand. The ratio of 1:1, "fifty-fifty", was changed to "sixty-forty". Although H.W. Amarasuriya, the President of the Ceylon National Congress at that time — 1938 — provisionally agreed to this proposal, he had no support from the Congress in general or from the duumvirate that ran the Board of Ministers: D.B. Jayatilaka and D.S. Senanayake.

Nor did the minorities find the Governor Sir Andrew Caldecott more favorably disposed towards these claims than Jayatilaka and Senanayake. He was in fact inflexibly opposed to their scheme in all its permutations. In June 1938 he informed the Secretary of State for the Colonies that:[18]

> "I have made known my opposition to what is called here the 'fifty-fifty' demand. That is that seats in the State Council should be apportioned half to 'the majority community' i.e. the Sinhalese, and half to the 'minority communities'. I am similarly opposed to the 'sixty-forty demand' and to any other form of fractional representation on a race basis. The elected seats must in my opinion continue to be filled on a territorial franchise though (as will emerge later in this despatch) I would gladly see the electoral areas so constituted as to afford a chance of more seats for members of minority communities ... My reason for opposition to the 'fifty-fifty demand' or to any modification of it is that any concession to the principle of communal representation would perpetuate sectionalism (which I believe to be anathema to thinking people in Ceylon of all races) and preclude the emergence of true political issues. To ease the present position by affording a chance of more seats for minority candidates is one thing; to introduce the principle of representation of minorities on any mathematical formula is quite another."
>
> "... I am in favour of re-shaping, and adding to the number of, electoral areas in order to afford more chances for minority candidates. Redelimitation is also necessary in the Kandyan area in order that the

Kandyan interest, which is that of an agricultural peasantry, may not be swamped by the Indian interest which is that of plantation labour..."[19]

Caldecott stated that he had had a number of specific proposals for these purposes, but that he was not prepared to sponsor any of them until they were examined by a delimitation committee. He recommended the following terms of reference for that committee:

"To consider the present electoral areas of the island and to advise what changes or additions could be reasonably made with a view to affording more chances for the return of candidates belonging to the minority communities and to securing adequate representation of the Kandyan rural interest."[20]

Caldecott's forthright rejection of what was popularly called the "fifty-fifty" demand was an unexpected and insuperable setback to Ponnambalam and other advocates of it. Nor were other British observers of the Sri Lankan political scene more sympathetic or more impressed. Thus, in 1944, the Soulbury Commissioners reviewing the "fifty-fifty" campaign commented:

"... that any attempt by artificial means to convert a majority into a minority is not only inequitable but doomed to failure".[21]

Indeed the rhetorical excesses of this campaign, and the political posturing associated with it alienated large sections of Sinhalese opinion. Apart from conferring a greater political acceptability to political organizations such as the Sinhala Maha Sabha (which was in many ways a mirror image of the Tamil Congress in its commitment to ethnic identity as the central motivating force in political organization and activity), it also lost the support of minority groups such as the Muslims who came to view the renewed "50-50" program as a truculent, dogged and intrinsically self-destructive pursuit of excessive political demands. More important, memories of it lingered on long after the campaign itself had been abandoned, and the suspicions it aroused were kindled afresh when demands for a federal political structure emerged in the late 1940s from Tamil politicians whose entry into national politics had been through the "50-50" campaign.

Voting Rights of Immigrant Indians

Throughout the period 1931 to 1943 the voting rights of Indians resident in the island continued to be a highly sensitive political issue. This was — as we shall see — partly because the restrictions imposed in 1931 did not prove to be as effective as Sinhalese politicians were assured, and believed, they would be. There was also, in 1937, a controversy over the franchise of Indian plantation workers in local government elections at the village level.

Europeans, Burghers and Indian plantation workers had been excluded from the franchise in elections to Village Committees under the provisions of Ordinance 13 of 1889. The rationale for this denial of voting rights was that none of these groups paid taxes to such committees, never formed an integral part of the village community served by such committees and could not possibly benefit from the social objects these councils were designed to serve. When this ordinance was amended in 1924 this exclusion was retained. Representatives of Indian opinion in the island acquiesced in it on that occasion, and indeed raised no objections on it till 1937.

In 1937 a more comprehensive amendment of Ordinance 13 of 1889 was attempted and implemented on the initiative of S.W.R.D. Bandaranaike, the Minister of Local Government. Plantations were included within the area of operations of such committees and, in addition to the existing commutation tax, provision was made for a land tax on an acreage basis as an alternative method of village taxation. But the more controversial amendment had to do with the continued exclusion of Indian plantation workers from the franchise while Europeans and Burghers were now given the right to vote at Village Committee elections. Representatives of Indian opinion reversed their previous and long-established acceptance of the exclusion of Indian plantation workers from the franchise at Village Committee level, and protested against their exclusion under the terms of Bandaranaike's amending ordinance, charging that it was a clear case of ethnic discrimination.[22]

More important still, G.G. Ponnambalam made a significant entry into this debate as a champion of the rights of the Indians.[23] In the early 1930s when the *Ceylon (State Council Elections) Order-in-Council* of 1931 had imposed restrictions on the voting rights of the Indians resident in the island, in modification of the recommendations of the Donoughmore scheme, Tamil politicians in Jaffna and elsewhere had paid little or no heed to the protests emanating from among the Indian Tamil leadership in the island.[24] When Ponnambalam in a notable reversal of this attitude emerged as a defender of the rights of the Indian Tamils, he was hoping thereby to enlarge the composition of the minorities coalition he led.

In so doing he risked jeopardizing the support the Sinhalese leadership had extended to the principle of weightage in representation as a concession to the Sri Lankan Tamils. But that risk he was willing to take. From then on advocacy of unrestricted voting rights for Indians in Sri Lanka became a staple element in Ponnambalam's political campaigns in the late 1930s and early 1940s.

If anything Ponnambalam's intervention strengthened the resolve of Sinhalese politicians to stand firm against the inclusion of plantation workers in yet another area of political activity when their numbers on the electoral roll in the country had increased far beyond the limits envisaged by them — the Sinhalese politicians — in accepting the restrictions on the voting rights of Indians devised and introduced through the *Ceylon (State Council Elections) Order-in-Council* in 1931. As a result of the controversy that ensued the bill as passed by the State Council was not approved, in that form, by the Colonial Office. Instead, at the suggestion of the then Secretary of State for the Colonies, the amending bill was itself amended by the exclusion from the Village Committee franchise of all plantation workers irrespective of ethnic identity. The vast majority of plantation workers were Indians but by making the restriction general rather than specific the amendment was made more acceptable to the colonial administration in the island if not to representatives of Indian opinion.

This restriction, devised in 1938, survived till the end of 1977 when, at last, it was removed from the statute book by the present UNP government.

Much of the opposition to the extension of the franchise in Village Committee elections to the Indian plantation workers stemmed from dissatisfaction among Sinhalese politicians with the working of Articles 7 and 9 of the *Ceylon (State Council Elections) Order-in-Council.* This latter article had been devised to provide enfranchisement of Indians who had difficulty in proving domicile of choice under Article 7 where the requirement was five years of residence. Applicants for Certificates of Permanent Settlement under Article 9, were required not merely to make a declaration that they were permanently settled in the island but also to renounce claims to rights, and privileges, which under the existing laws of the land were not common to all British subjects. Also registration under Article 7 was found to be much easier than anticipated, partly at least, because British officials in charge of enforcing the law were inclined to be less exacting and demanding than the spirit if not letter of the law warranted, to say nothing of the assurances given on these matters to local politicians in 1931. Indeed

the route to registration through Article 7 proved to be so uncompli-
cated that not many Indians resorted to Article 9, which soon became
an abandoned and ill-maintained path as a result. The number of
Indians registered as voters stood at around 100,000 in 1931; it rose to
143,000 in 1936, and to 235,000 in 1939.[25] This steep increase led to
strong protests from Sinhalese politicians against what they described
as laxity in registration procedure. The Governor, Sir Andrew
Caldecott, responded by tightening rules and regulations on registration in 1940, and by 1943 the number of Indians on the electoral
registers had dropped to 168,000. Even so only 2% of Indian
registrations were obtained by means of Certificates of Permanent
Settlement under Article 9. Thus Sinhalese grievances against
registration procedure remained almost undiminished from what they
were before 1940 while Indian opinion was resentful at the insistence
on a stricter adherence to the requirements of the law in regard to
registration of Indians as voters.

Competition between immigrant and indigenous workers in the city
and suburbs of Colombo was especially marked in the aftermath of the
great depression of the early 1930s. As a result we now see for the first
time the working-class movement in Sri Lanka become sharply divided
into two separate if not mutually suspicious groups. There was also the
increasing unpopularity of another element in the Indian community,
infinitely smaller in numbers than either the Indian plantation
workers or the Indian urban working class, but scattered throughout
the island, the Indian traders and money-lenders. Between them they
controlled much of the island's import-export trade in consumer
goods, the wholesale and retail distribution of rice and other food
items, and were prominent, ubiquitous and inevitably unpopular as
the most accessible source of ready money at a time when banks were
few in number and content with financing the plantations and big
commercial houses.

The Kandyans had always felt threatened by the plantation workers
in their midst. The Indians were present in their regions in such large
numbers that the Kandyans were greatly perturbed at the prospect of
Indian domination of the plantation districts if permanent citizenship
rights were conferred without, what the Kandyans regarded as,
adequate safeguards on the Indian population in their midst. They took,
and have always taken, the lead in the insistence on rigid rules and
regulations for the grant of citizenship to the Indians. Ever since
universal suffrage was recommended by the Donoughmore Commis-

sioners, the Kandyans found that the established Sinhalese politicians — like D.S. Senanayake, D.B. Jayatilaka and S.W.R.D. Bandaranaike — were willing converts to their cause.

With the depression of the late 1920s and early 1930s working class Indians in the urban areas, especially in and around Colombo, were resented as competitors in a tight labor market. The plantation workers were seen — to a greater extent than in the past — as a privileged group, and trade union leaders like A.E. Goonesinha, who had earlier worked with the Indian trade union leaders and championed the cause of the underprivileged workers, indigenous and Indian alike, turned against the latter.

Above all else the depression focused attention on the Indian money-lenders foreclosing on mortgages on land, and on Indian traders who had established themselves as the most efficient of them all, and had consolidated their position against their indigenous rivals. The commanding position attained in their respective spheres by the money lenders and traders brought the Indian community as a whole under attack from the Sri Lankan political elite or at least its dominant low-country Sinhalese segment.

The strains and tensions that resulted from these controversies over the franchise for Indians in the island, and the question of immigration are neatly summarized in the following extract from an official report submitted by a delegation from the Ceylon National Congress to the Ramgarh sessions of the Indian prototype in 1940.[26] The chief spokesman of the Sri Lankan delegation was its leader J.R. Jayewardene at a notably Indophile phase in his political career in a political *milieu* in which Indophilia was greatly in vogue among politicians.

"We had an interview with Mahatma Gandhi on Wednesday 20th March [1940] and his first words to us [were] 'It is an unfortunate thing that is happening to Indians in Ceylon.' We explained to him that the problem was an economic one and that the Indians in Ceylon apart from the labourers and a few others, were mainly exploiters. Petty traders and Chettiars have captured the entire import and export trade. The people of Lanka only see this side of India. Gandhiji replied, 'Yes, that is too true. The fault is on both sides.'"

The Congress delegation assured him that

"there was no racial animosity against Indians as made clear by the receptions accorded to Pandit Nehru. Till poet Tagore, Gandhiji, Pandit Nehru and a few other eminent Indians came to Lanka our people met only the exploiting Chettiars and the immigrant Indian labourers. Gandhiji replied, 'Unfortunately we have not many Nehrus or many men of the same calibre. Wrong people if sent might spoil everything.'

> We asked him what Ceylon could expect from a free India. Many in
> Lanka prefer to remain as a dominion in the British empire than to be
> free and run the risk of being exploited by India which could easily
> swamp Lanka. Gandhiji laughed and said, 'Ceylon has nothing to fear
> from a free India.' "

In November 1940, D.S. Senanayake led an official Ministerial level
delegation (the other members were S.W.R.D. Bandaranaike and
G.C.S. Corea, and the Financial Secretary of the day, a British civil
servant H.J. Huxham), to New Delhi to discuss questions relating to
the franchise of Indians resident in the island, and also the problems of
immigration from India to Sri Lanka, with the Indian government. No
headway was made towards a settlement of outstanding issues on this
occasion as well as in 1941, when a senior Indian civil servant, Sir Girja
Bajpai, led an Indian delegation to Colombo. As we shall see in Chapter
IX of this book, a settlement of this problem figured prominently in
the negotiations with Whitehall on the transfer of power in Sri Lanka.

Weightage In Representation

The third distinctive phase in the complex question of the
minorities, universal suffrage and representation, came in the years
1943-44. Needless to say it coincided with a vitally important phase in
the transfer of power in Sri Lanka, with the drafting of a new
constitutional system for the island under the terms set out by
Whitehall in May-July 1943.

"The representation clauses," as Sir Ivor Jennings remarked all too
accurately, "were undoubtedly the most contentious ... [and the] task
of the Ministers was exceedingly difficult."[27] The Ministers were
required to produce a scheme which had to satisfy three quarters of all
the members of the State Council, and to cope with demands for
balanced representation. They were acutely aware that any such
scheme had little chance of acceptance by the State Council if balanced
representation presupposed the creation of some form of communal
electorates. There were also the echoes of the "fifty-fifty" campaign of
the mid-1930s. The revived campaign was not quite as vociferous as
the original one. It had become merely part of the political ritual of the
day, lacking in both conviction and political viability. One by one all
the other minorities had abandoned their support for it, leaving
Ponnambalam's Tamil Congress established in 1944 as its sole
advocate.

Caldecott had made his own position clear in 1937: he would have nothing to do with "fifty-fifty" or "sixty-forty" in determining the ratio of representation between the Sinhalese and the minorities. He had advised that a Committee should be set up in order to create additional seats in the State Council and to ensure the return of more members belonging to the minorities. On this Re-delimitation Committee, as he called it, he placed most of his hopes for a settlement of the question of minority rights, and he persisted in advocating it for over four years even after the Colonial Office, which had endorsed it in 1940, lost interest in it thereafter.

However, one important advantage flowed from all the controversies surrounding the "fifty-fifty" campaign of 1937-8; weightage in representation to the benefit of the minorities was politically acceptable to the Sinhalese leaders no less than to Caldecott. Indeed, many of them had declared their support for it as early as 1930 during the sessions of the Delimitation Commission of that year.

The advantages of weightage in representation were many; its beneficiaries were also many. Sinhalese politicians welcomed it because of its avoidance of communal representation; by reducing the size of constituencies both in area and population in those parts of the country where the minorities were the, or a, dominant element, comparatively homogeneous constituencies which were not specifically communal could be demarcated by a future Delimitation Commission; the sparsely populated areas which were also, coincidentally, the areas with larger concentrations of minorities, would increase their representation, and this appealed to the minority groups such as the Muslims who were growing increasingly disenchanted with Ponnambalam's campaign for balanced representation. The Kandyans were among the principal beneficiaries of weightage in representation, a point on which both Caldecott and the Sinhalese political leadership of the day were agreed; and there was an element also of equity in that the sparsely populated backward areas (some of wich were Kandyan) would have greater representation, and thus greater influence politically, than they may have had if population figures were the sole criterion in demarcating constituencies.

Thus one of the unexpected results of the campaign for balanced representation was to give weightage in representation a salience and a wide political acceptability which it may not have otherwise had. Weightage in representation helped both those whom it was primarily designed to benefit — the minorities — as well as the more backward groups and areas among the Sinhalese who became in time its principal beneficiaries and most vociferous supporters.

References

1   See, K.M. de Silva, "The Ceylon National Congress in Disarray' Parts I and II, in *CJHSS, n.s. II(2) 1972, pp. 97-117, and n.s. III(1) 1973, pp. 16-35 respectively.*

2   *Ibid.*

3   C.O. 54/900 File 73290/10, T.B. Jayah's Memorandum of 27 July 1930.

4   *The Ceylon Daily News*, 11 March 1930 cited in Jane Russell, *Communal Politics under the Donoughmore Constitution, 1931-1947*, p. 31.

5   *The Ceylon Daily News*, 26 February 1930; cited in Jane Russell, *op. cit.*, p. 31.

6   Jane Russell, *op. cit.*, pp. 31-2.

7   *Ibid.*, pp. 32-33.

8   *S.P..*, XI of 1930.

9   J. Russell, *op. cit.*, pp. 33-5.

10 *The Soulbury Report, Report of the Commission on Constitutional Reform*, Cmd 6677 (London, 1945), p. 19.

11 *Ibid*

12 *Ibid*

13 *Ibid*

14 *Ibid*

15 This extract is from Caldecott's confidential dispatch of 28 October 1939 to the Secretary of State for the Colonies, Malcolm McDonald. It is cited by him in his "personal and most secret" letter of 23 December 1941 to Gent (a Senior Colonial Office Servant) in C.O. 54/950 File 55541, Part I.

16 J. Russell, *op. cit.*, p. 230.

17 *Ibid*, p. 231.

18 *Cmd* 5910. *Correspondence Relating to the Constitution of Ceylon*. Caldecott's dispatch to Malcolm McDonald, 13 June 1938, p. 3, para 5.

19 *Ibid.*, pp. 3-4, para 6.

20 *Ibid.*, p. 4, para 6.

21 *The Soulbury Report*, p. 70.

22 S.U. Kodikara, *Indo-Ceylon Relations since Independence* (Colombo, 1965), pp. 79-81.

23 J. Russell, *op. cit.*, p. 410.

24 *Ibid.*, p. 52.

25 S.U. Kodikara, *op. cit.*, pp. 79 ff. and *Soulbury Report*, p. 55.

26 Printed in M.W. Roberts (ed) *Documents of the Ceylon National Congress and*

Nationalist Politics in Ceylon, 1929-1950 (4 vols, Colombo, 1978), IV, pp. 2764-5. (Hereafter, Roberts, *Documents*).

27   Sir W. Ivor Jennings, *The Constitution of Ceylon* (O.U.P. 1949) p. 33. Jennings was Vice Chancellor of the University of Ceylon, and also adviser on constitutional reform to D.S. Senanayake.

Chapter VIII

The Muslim Minority
At The Crossroads
c 1920 - 1943

Introduction

Sri Lanka's Muslim minority began the game of competitive politics with a number of formidable disadvantages, the first of which was its small size, never more than 6% to 7% of the island's population. Secondly, they are also geographically dispersed unlike Sri Lanka's Tamils who form a clear majority in the Jaffna peninsula and most of the other parts of the Northern Province, as well as in the Batticaloa district of the Eastern Province. In no district do the Muslims constitute a majority; in all except the present Amparai district of the Eastern Province (then part of the Batticaloa district) they are a small minority. There is a concentration of Muslims in the city of Colombo. This geographical dispersal of the Muslim community has been a perennial problem to them because of its political implications in regard to representation in the legislature, a recurring theme in this present chapter.

Then again their ethnicity is identified in terms of religion and culture, not language. Today most Muslims speak the language of the district in which they live; a great many are bilingual, speaking both Sinhalese and Tamil. During the period surveyed in this chapter most Muslims spoke Tamil. Indeed Tamil had been for long the *lingua-franca* of maritime trade in the Indian Ocean region, and the Muslims as a trading and sea-faring community had been exposed for centuries to the influence of that language. More importantly, the *Quaran* was translated into Tamil, and thus even Sinhalese-speaking Muslims had perforce to be proficient in Tamil up to now for that reason. (It is only recently that the *Quaran* has translated into Sinhalese). Unlike the Tamils —and unlike the Muslims of Tamilnadu — however, the Muslims have no great emotional commitment to the Tamil language and have demonstrated little reluctance to adopting Sinhalese as a medium of instruction in schools, and as the principal if not the sole national language. But they have also found it exceedingly difficult to abandon Tamil altogether.

Fourthly, the Sri Lanka Muslims consist of several distinct groups between whom the common link was their religion. A controversy which broke out during this period over the use of the terms Moor and Muslim focused attention on the divisions among them.[1] Which of the two was more appropriate for the community? Those who preferred and indeed took pride in calling themselves 'Moors' emphasized their Arabic heritage and the historical origins of their community, and its strong indigenous roots in Sri Lanka. They were clearly the majority group. The others felt that this term was too exclusive and even elitist, and that the term Muslim would help bring in a number of other Islamic groups in the island who had come there in Dutch and British times. Most of these were small in number, but many of them — like the Borahs, Memons, Sindhis and others — were extremely powerful economically through their control of a great deal of the island's import-export trade. It would also include Muslims of Indian origin living in the island as well as, of course, the small Malay community. The distinction between Moor and Muslim led to the formation of two separate political associations during this period, the All Ceylon Muslim League, and the All Ceylon Moors Association.

Ethnic stereotypes popular in the island had the Muslims as largely a trading and business community. But this is to ignore the fact that most of the Muslims were cultivators (as in the Eastern Province) or part of the urban poor (as in the city of Colombo). Nevertheless it would be true to say that to a larger extent than all the other ethnic groups in the island, the Muslims had a penchant for trade at all levels, so much so that the Muslims played no part at all in the rivalry for places in the bureaucracy in this period, and Muslim representation in the professions was miniscule.

Ramanathan's Allies

The keynote of Muslim politics of this period was one of self-preservation. While their national leadership was pragmatic and hard-headed, they were also generally timid and over-cautious in national politics. Their objectives were limited. What they attempted to do —

and did successfully — was to safeguard, sustain and advance their distinctive cultural identity. They sought and obtained state support for this in two distinct fields: first, in the consolidation and recognition of the personal laws of the Muslims. *The Muslim Marriage and Divorce Registration Ordinance 27 of 1929* (which became operative from 1937) set up a system of domestic relations courts presided over by Muslim judges (*quazis*) and explicitly recognized the orthodox Muslim law of marriage and divorce; and the same process may be observed in respect of inheritance, in the *Muslim Intestate Succession and Wakfs Ordinance of 1931*. Secondly, there was the field of education. Here again, and more especially with regard to the former, it was a trend which began from the earliest years of British rule. On the divisiveness of education — dividing Muslim from Tamil — we shall have more to say later in this chapter.

Turning to competitive politics the mood of the Muslim community for a decade or more after the riots of 1915 was a mixture of fear and suspicion of Sinhalese nationalism, and in that mood they were eagerly receptive to the blandishments of the British administration — especially of men like Governors Sir William Manning and Sir Hugh Clifford — intent on using the minorities as a brake on nationalist agitation: and also to the clever political manipulations of some of the Tamil leaders, most notably Sir Ponnambalam Ramanathan, who had turned against his erstwhile Sinhalese allies and supporters in the early 1920s.

Thus there was little or no support from among the Muslims for the major constructive political achievement of the Sinhalese and Tamil leadership in the years 1917-9, the establishment of the Ceylon National Congress. The Muslims stood aloof, somewhat apprehensive of this new political organization. At that time the political prestige of the Tamil leaders was at its peak. Twice Ramanathan had been elected over a Sinhalese rival to the "Educated-Ceylonese Electorate". His first victory in 1911 had been over a formidable opponent, Dr. (later Sir) Marcus Fernando, in a hard fought election campaign, the first national election campaign in Sri Lanka. Then in 1917 he crushed his second Sinhalese opponent to a humiliating defeat. Then again, even more significant, the political program that culminated in the establishment of the Ceylon National Congress in 1919 was led by Ramanathan's equally distinguished brother, Sir Ponnambalam Aruna-chalam, whose leadership was readily acknowledged and accepted by the Sinhalese political leaders of the day. Indeed at this time the political establishment of the emerging nationalist movement had a dual leadership in terms of ethnic origin: the Tamils achieved a status within it of equality with the numerically much larger Sinhalese majority.

This alliance between the Muslims and Tamils was based only partly on Muslim fears of Sinhalese domination colored by memories of the 1915 riots. It was due also to a lack of self-confidence on the part of the Muslim leadership. None of their leaders could match the political skills and personal prestige of Ramanathan, and so they preferred to follow him on a campaign in which admittedly, they saw their interests coincide with those of the Tamils.

While their acceptance of Tamil leadership at this stage was a natural development given the depth of their disillusionment with the Sinhalese, the fact that this leadership lay with Ramanathan is evidence of the brevity of public and communal memories. For Ramanathan had been at the center of a controversy in the mid- and late-1880s over his publicly expressed views on the ethnicity of the Muslims of Sri Lanka, the Moors as he preferred to call them. Speaking on the debate on the *Mohammedan Marriage Ordinance* in 1885, Ramanathan argued that the Moors of Ceylon were Tamils in 'nationality' and 'Mohammedans' in religion. These unorthodox views gave great offense to the Muslims, and they were attacked with considerable vigor in the *Muslim Friend*, a journal edited by Siddi Lebbe. Far from re-tracing his steps, Ramanathan made a more comprehensive statement of his views in 1888 in a lecture on "The Ethnology of the 'Moors' of Ceylon" delivered at the Royal Asiatic Society's Ceylon branch, then at the height of its prestige as the island's premier — indeed, the only — learned society.[2]

Part of the bitterness that Ramanathan's views on the ethnicity of the Muslims caused was due to suspicions — admittedly not without foundation in fact — that he had ulterior political motives. This was a time when an expansion of the Legislative Council was in the offing, and there was to be a seat for the Muslims. Ramanathan as representative of the Tamil community was often inclined to talk expansively on behalf of the Tamil-speaking peoples of Sri Lanka, a categorization which enabled him to place the Muslims within the scope of his tutelage as a legislator. In this claim as in so many other ways Ramanathan was the precursor of views and attitudes of the mainstream of Tamil politics of the future. Then, as now, however, the Muslims rejected this claim and refused this tuteglage.

The Muslim rejection of Ramanathan's views did not stop in the 1880s. Twenty years later — in 1907 — the attack was renewed on a more systematic basis by I.L.M. Abdul Azeez,[3] in a pamphlet, which significantly enough was re-published in 1957 at the height of the language conflict in Sri Lanka, and at a time when a similar attempt was made by the Tamil leadership to speak on behalf of the Muslims as well in a coalition entitled the Tamil speaking peoples of Sri Lanka. This, however, is to anticipate events. In the 1920s the Muslims' acceptance of Ramanathan's leadership, just a few years after his passionate defense of the Sinhalese leadership in the aftermath of the riots of 1915, was a triumph of hope over experience. On this occasion the hope was fulfilled in ample measure. They remained Ramanathan's allies till his death in 1930. Indeed their acceptance of Tamil leadership on political issues lasted for some time after his death.

None of the Muslim representatives in the Legislative Council were major political figures. All were conservatives in political attitude and were either somewhat diffident in expressing their views or gave silent but unswerving support to the British administration and later on to Ramanathan. The impression one has of them is of men who were distinctly uncomfortable in the parry and thrust of debate in the national legislature. They were solid, upright men whose integrity, personal and political, was seldom in doubt, but they were not men who could capture the imagination of the masses, and move them to stirring deeds.

W.M.A. Rahiman had served in the Legislative Council from 1900 to 1917, when N.H.M. Abdul Cader replaced him and remained a member till 1923. They were both nominated members. Abdul Cader was one of three Muslims elected to the Legislature in 1924 through a communal island-wide electorate. The others were Mohammed Macan Markar, and T.B. Jayah, a Malay. Of them Jayah was the only one without a business or trading background: he was an educationist. Eventually Jayah emerged as the spokesman for Muslim interests in regard to political and constitutional reform, but that leadership came to him by default and largely because Macan Markar, for all his great wealth and personal standing in his community, was not a good speaker and not given to setting out his thoughts and views in writing. Not that Jayah himself was an accomplished speaker, but at least he had the intellectual skills to make a coherently argued case for his community when that was called for. And even Jayah, in his days in the Legislative Council, was very much in the shadow of Ramanathan.

He deferred to the latter on most constitutional and political issues, for example in their opposition to the Donoughmore proposals, as we have seen in the previous chapter.

A Realignment Of Forces

We turn now to a review of the Muslim community in Sri Lanka and its attitude to the nationalist movement in the decade after the introduction of the Donoughmore constitution. The political attitudes we have described in the previous section persisted in this phase as well, till the early 1940s.

The Muslims like the other minorities had deep misgivings about their position under the new system. Their apprehension turned to dismay when it became known that instead of the 65 constituencies recommended by the Donoughmore report there were to be only 50, and these were to be single member constituencies. For the Muslims this was a bitter blow; when the report of the Delimitation Commision of 1930 was published it was evident that there was not one single constituency in which they had a majority position. There were only 3 (Colombo Central and 2 Eastern Province seats) in which they had a fair chance of success. As it was, their worst fears were fulfilled when only one Muslim won election to the State Council, Mohammed Macan Markar, who was returned by the Batticaloa South electorate. Jayah lost Colombo Central. With one nominated member (M.K. Saldin) the Muslims now had only two members in a house of 60 (50 elected, 7 nominated and 3 Officers of State) where previously under the Manning constitution and its system of communal electorates they had 3 elected members.

However, there was some consolation for them in Macan Markar's election as Minister of Transport and Works. They had one member in the Board of Ministers. Because of the Jaffna boycott[4] four seats in the Northern Province were vacant, and the Tamils lost the opportunity of getting one of their number elected to a Ministerial post. Instead there was one Indian Tamil, Perianan Sunderam[5], who held a Ministerial post during the first State Council (1931-1935). It was to take 42 years thereafter before another member of that community won a place in the Cabinet.

There was a vacuum in the minorities leadership in the State Council. Ramanathan had died in 1930 and there was no one, neither

Peri Sunderam nor any of the other elected Tamil members, to step comfortably into his shoes. Here was an opportunity for a Muslim to take the leadership but Macan Markar was clearly not the man for it. Despite his considerable business acumen and long political experience he lacked the breadth of vision and parliamentary skills for such a role. Above all he was too rigidly conservative in political outlook, and he lacked the common touch. Within the Board of Ministers, however, he together with Perianan Sunderam ensured that there would be no unanimity of opinion on matters of constitutional reform, so long as adequate measures were not taken to compensate the minorities for the advantages they were asked to forgo. The Sinhalese politicians were insistent on the introduction of the Cabinet form of government, and were hostile to the Executive Committee system which, as both Macan Markar and Peri Sunderam knew only too well, gave the minorities some chance of securing election to a Ministerial post. At least it had given them that chance in 1931. By 1934 however, G.G. Ponnambalam was in the State Council, and he quickly took over the leadership of the minorities in their political campaigns.[6]

The general election of 1936 was an unmitigated disaster for the Muslims. Not one single Muslim was elected. Without Mohammed Macan Markar his seat was lost; Jayah lost again at Colombo Central. The need for a more equitable form of representation, one that would guarantee the election of a reasonable number of Muslims, became now a battle cry of the community. To compensate the Muslims for their losses, two members were nominated, Jayah himself, despite his defeat, and a newcomer who was to make a notable contribution in paving the way for a change of policy among the Muslims in relation to the nationalist movement and the transfer of power. This was A.R.A. Razik who later became Sir Razik Fareed after independence on receiving a knighthood, the son of W.M.A. Rahiman the Muslim representative in the Legislative Council from 1900 to 1917.

From this time onwards the Muslims' response to nationalism can be viewed in terms of the differences in attitude to political and social reform of T.B. Jayah and A.R.A. Razik. These differences, subtle and muted at first, became more pronounced in time as Razik gained greater confidence and influence both within the Muslim community and the national legislature. Some of these differences were demonstrated in the controversy that broke out over the terms Moor and Muslim, with Razik as the advocate of the first and Jayah of the second.

By 1942 we see the beginnings of change in the Muslim attitude to the nationalist movement. In that year their ranks in the State Council were strengthened when Dr. M.C.M. Kaleel won a by-election to the Colombo Central seat caused by the unseating of A.E. Goonesinha.[7] The poll was small (only 25% of the total) and there were a number of Sinhalese candidates none of whom was a national figure. In this low poll Kaleel won a narrow victory. Then again Razik, who had up to this time been a member of the Executive Committee of Local Administration, switched over to the Education Committee on 10 March 1942 and that Committee now had two Muslim members (the other being Jayah).

From this time onwards concentration of attention on education in a bid to give a boost to Muslim education brought Razik into conflict with the Tamils. This was especially so with regard to the Eastern Province where such Muslim schools as there were had mostly Tamil school teachers, or where Muslims attended Tamil schools. Razik deplored this state of affairs, and used his influence through the Executive Committee on education to build the resources of Muslim schools and to secure the appointment of more Muslim teachers. The insensitivity of the Tamils to this brought home to men like Razik the need to emphasize the Muslim identity in the national education system. Combined with this the tactless remarks of some Tamil politicians who argued that Tamils could well represent Muslim interests in the Eastern Province, drove men like Razik into an alliance with the Sinhalese.

The change of attitude was illustrated by the voting patterns in the State Council on J.R. Jayewardene's motion, debated in May 1944, on making Sinhalese the national language of Sri Lanka.[8] The difference in attitude between Razik and Jayah was clearly seen on this issue. When J.R. Jayewardene first introduced his motion in 1943 there was much opposition to it on the grounds that it made no provision for Tamil. By the time the motion came up for debate in 1944 Jayewardene had agreed to amend it to include Tamil along with Sinhalese as the national languages. With the mover's consent a Tamil member, V. Nalliah, moved an amendment "that the words 'and Tamil' be added after the word 'Sinhalese' wherever the latter occurs." The amendment was debated and put to a vote on 25 May 1944. It was carried by 29 votes to 8. Jayah voted for the amendment; Razik joined 7 others in voting against it. Among those who voted against were 2 European appointed members and a Burgher who were opposed to the whole idea of Sinhalese and Tamil replacing English as the official language. But there were four Sinhalese who voted against, because they wanted Sinhalese as the sole national language: Razik joined them in this.

Razik's speech on this occasion[9] — a brief speech — is worth quoting. He said:

> "I feel that in the best interest of Lanka, my mother country, I must stand up for the motion of the honourable member for Kelaniya [J.R. Jayewardene]; that is that Sinhalese should be the official language of the country. However, there is not the slightest doubt that this cannot be done in a hurry in a year or two, or even in 10 years. I certainly feel that in the best interests of Lanka and her people one language will bring unity among our people. We are really divided at the present moment. Each community has its own language. But if we all take to one language, then we will not think in terms of Tamils, Moors, Sinhalese, Burghers, Malays and so on."

If Razik staked out his own distinct territory in this speech, he joined together with Kaleel in supporting Jayah's amendment to the main motion which would have the effect of leaving the implementation of the policy on language dependent on the recommendations of a Commission to be appointed by the house. This amendment attracted only 12 supporters. There were 25 who voted against it.

When we look back on it today this debate on language policy was clearly one of the landmark events of the last years of British rule. Yet curiously enough the Sinhalese leadership — as we have seen in Chapter V of this book — was divided on it, while the Tamils were not. But it was equally clear that no longer could the Tamils take Muslim support for granted in their political campaigns. When G.G. Ponnambalam's vociferous campaign for balanced representation had begun in 1937 he counted on the support of the Muslims — who naturally enough were in a disgruntled mood in the aftermath of the debacle of the general election of 1936 and was encouraged by the response he evoked. This campaign — "the 50-50" campaign as[10] it was called — enjoyed the sympathy and support of the Muslims in its earliest phase. But that support became less enthusiastic in time, and was withdrawn by the early 1940's as the political alliance between the Tamils and Muslims came apart over conflicting attitudes on the transfer of power.

References

[1]   Very little research has been done on this interesting theme. Some of the issues are outlined in the pamphlets issued on behalf of the main participants in the contro-

versy. See for instance, a pamphlet entitled *Who are the Ceylon Moors* (author, S.L. Mohamed) the first of a series issued by The Moors' Direct Action Committee, Colombo, 1950.

[2]   P. Ramanathan, 'The Ethnology of the 'Moors' of Ceylon'. *The Journal of the Royal Asiatic Society, Ceylon Branch*, Vol. X(36) 1888, pp. 234-262.

[3]   I.L.M. Abdul Azeez, *A Criticism of Mr. Ramanathan's Ethnology of the 'Moors' of Ceylon* (published by the Moors' Union) (Colombo, 1907), Reprinted by the Moors' Islamic Cultural Home, (Colombo, 1957).

[4]   On the Jaffna boycott see, Jane Russell, 'The Dance of the Turkey-cock — the Jaffna boycott of 1931', *CJHSS* n.s. VIII(1) pp. 47-67.

[5]   Elected uncontested to the Hatton seat (in a plantation district in Central Sri Lanka) he was chosen Chairman of the Executive Committee of Labour, Industry and Commerce, and therefore a member of the Board of Ministers.

[6]   See, K.M. de Silva, *A History of Sri Lanka* pp. 431-5 for the background.

[7]   Goonesinha was unseated for election offenses committed during the campaign for the Colombo North seat at a by-election held on 25 February 1942.

[8]   See above Chapter V.

[9]   *Hansard* (State Council) 1944, Vol. I p. 812, A.R.A. Razik's speech of 25 May 1944.

[10]   See above Chapter VII.

Chapter IX

Pluralism And The Transfer Of Power

Senanayake's Hour of Triumph

When the ageing D.B. Jayatilaka retired from active politics in late 1943 the old duumvirate gave way to a single leader — D.S. Senanayake. The ten years following upon the former's retirement mark the dominance of Senanayake in Sri Lanka's politics, his successful negotiation of the transfer of power and the establishment and consolidation of his authority as the first Prime Minister of the island.

The transition from a dual to a single leadership marked a change of style in leadership rather than any significant change of policy. Senanayake saw nothing dishonorable in a pragmatic acceptance of constitutional reform in installments. In this there was a continuity with policies pursued under the old dual leadership. But Senanayake quickly demonstrated that he was more skilled than Jayatilaka in the exercise of political power and the exploitation of political influence and patronage.

He was much less inclined than Jayatilaka to share power with the Ceylon National Congress of which both were founding members. Significantly, Senanayake had never served as President of that organization; Jayatilaka had done so on several occasions. At the end of 1942 Senanayake had indicated his displeasure with the new policies and outlook of the new model Congress led by J.R. Jayewardene, and Senanayake's son, Dudley, by refusing to serve any longer on its Executive Committee. From that to severing his links with the Congress altogether was but a short stop, and one he took in 1943 even before Jayatilaka's retirement. In his attitude to the Congress there were two main considerations: firstly, his views on the transfer of power, and secondly, distancing himself from an organization which had lost the support of the minorities and which showed few signs of being able to win it back.

Under his leadership Sri Lanka was seeking membership of an exclusive club — the countries that ranked as dominions —in which the conventions, practices and precedents for securing admission were determined by the older members. The goal, then, was Dominion Status, and the process of attaining this was to be essentially imitative of the white dominions of Canada, Australia and New Zealand, whose constitutional evolution to that status had been in measured stages, and in association not in opposition to Great Britain. The underlying assumption was that self-government would come through the legislature becoming progressively more representative and exercising wider control over the executive until it approximated to a dominion parliament. Majority opinion in the Ceylon National Congress as reflected by J.R. Jayewardene, for instance, was opposed both to the objective he set for the country, and the policies and tactics for its attainment adumbrated by Senanayake: they would have independence rather than Dominion Status.

Senanayake was much more sensitive than the majority of his colleagues and associates in the national leadership to the political implications that flowed from the plural nature of Sri Lankan society, and showed a greater concern for political and constitutional concessions to the minorities to win their support for a joint program of action on the transfer of power. Thus he readily accepted the proposition that the Sri Lanka polity would hold no special privileges for any single ethnic group, and much less any section of an ethnic group. He neither lent support nor gave any encouragement to those —like S.W.R.D. Bandaranaike and his adherents in the Sinhala Maha Sabha — who urged that the principle of the religious neutrality of the state be abandoned and with that, by implication, the concept of Sri Lanka as a secular state. More important, however, was that in regard to these Senanayake placed himself, consciously and deliberately, in opposition to the current of opinion — influential and becoming even more so — representated by Bandaranaike and the Sinhala Maha Sabha, which saw the Sri Lanka polity as one that was essentially Sinhalese and Buddhist in character and which insisted on the need to evolve policies on the transfer of power and the post-independence phase of national development based on this perception. At isssue, then, was a battle between two intrinsically conflicting concepts of nationalism.[1]

But first we need to turn to a brief review of the main issues on the transfer of power as they emerged in 1943. Caldecott had patiently put together a consensus on constitutional reform[2] in 1938-9. This dissolved in the face of world events and their impact on local politics. At the beginning of 1942 the moderate wing — by far the most influential — of the nationalist movement was no longer bound by the consensus of 1938-9, and had set out Dominion Status as their objective. Within a year the youthful new leadership within the Ceylon National Congress had carried through a change of policy in which independence rather than Dominion Status became the main political objective of that body. It needed all D.S. Senanayake's personal prestige and tenacity of purpose to stand up against this powerful current of opinion, and to insist instead that the goal of Sri Lanka's constitutional evolution should continue to be Dominion Status.[3]

The 'official mind' of Whitehall was insensitive to the political perils that faced Senanayake in his commitment to a political goal about which most Asian politicians of the British empire still harbored deep suspicions. Nehru for instance had not, at this stage, committed himself to accepting Dominion Status as equivalent to independence. No Asian or Caribbean colony had yet achieved the status of a dominion and thus — to most officials at Whitehall — Senanayake seemed to be unduly optimistic, if not naive, in arguing that his country was mature enough for this new status, and ignorant of the complex constitutional problems that had to be overcome before Sri Lanka achieved Dominion Status.[4] Caldecott himself in his letters and dispatches to the Colonial Office showed clearly that he shared Whitehall's views on this matter.[5]

Whitehall's decision, announced officially through Caldecott in December 1941, was to defer consideration of constitutional reform in Sri Lanka till after the war was over when the position would be examined afresh by a Committee or Conference. This decision clearly disappointed the Board of Ministers, but they reacted to this as was customary with them with a polite note of disagreement and continued to press for a more positive gesture from Britain.

Soon Japan's entry into the war and the uninterrupted and — for the Allied powers — demoralizing successes she achieved initially, overrunning British, French and Dutch colonial territories in South East Asia, and the Philippines as well, left Sri Lanka as one of the few strategically important territories controlled by the Allied powers, and above all one in which the political leadership was strongly committed to support the Allied cause. Caldecott in his dispatches to Whitehall urged that this new situation called for a more convincing and forthright statement on constitutional reform than that issued in December 1941, if the goodwill and co-operation of the Board of Ministers were to be retained and the wholehearted participation of the people of Sri Lanka in the war effort secured. The pressure from Caldecott and the cogency of his arguments had some effect on the thinking of the War Cabinet which considered it politic to issue a fresh declaration on constitutional reform in the island. A declaration was issued in December 1942 but it satisfied neither Caldecott, nor the Commander-in-chief of the island, Sir Geoffrey Layton,[6] who took

> "...a very serious view of what may happen if it is not possible, by some new declaration to meet the desires and aspirations of the more moderate elements in Ceylon. They expect[ed] immediate and progressive loss of co-operation and decrease of war-effort, coupled with the deflection of now moderate opinion toward intransigent nationalism and the demand for the right of secession".[7]

More important, Caldecott and Layton responded to this with their own proposals in the form of a draft declaration of policy on constitutional reform in Sri Lanka for Whitehall approval as a substitute for that sent in December 1942.[8] The principles enunciated in that were eventually endorsed by Whitehall and published in the island on 26 May 1943, using much the same phraseology contained in the document sent home by Caldecott and Layton. It offered "full responsibility for government under the Crown in all matters of Civil administration". The only matters to be reserved would be external relations and defense "while of course, the proposals [did] not include the right of secession."

In urging the War Cabinet to give its support to the proposals set out by Caldecott and Layton, Oliver Stanley as Secretary of State for the Colonies gave four reasons.[9] Of these the first was that it would be difficult to prevent a very serious deterioration in Ceylon's war effort "unless we go as far as this", especially because of

> "the vital importance of Ceylon, both as a strategical base and as the source of essential war materials, rubber in particular".

Secondly, he pointed out that the Ministers had worked an admittedly difficult constitution with great goodwill and achieved an unexpected degree of success. In the circumstances it would be natural for them to compare the definite promises made to India, where,

> "with all respect to India's war effort, the political element at least has been largely non-co-operative, with the indefinite hopes held out to Ceylon, where the elected members have thrown themselves heart and soul into war production. This comparison may lead to the argument that more can be obtained from His Majesty's Government by making trouble than by methods of co-operation".

Thirdly, there was the hope that the declaration would encourage Sinhalese politicians to turn their minds to a settlement with the minorities and "to a realistic appreciation of their future relations with India" by which Stanley obviously meant the difficulties that had arisen over the political status and voting rights of Indians in Sri Lanka, on which the Colonial Office and the India Office held quite substantially different views.

And finally he pointed out that even under the declaration of December 1942,

> "When we come after the war to a discussion of this question, we shall have to offer a great deal, if not all, of what is now contained in the Governor's proposed declaration. We shall, however, have lost the goodwill which we should gain by making the declaration now, and proposals which today, it is believed, will stabilise the situation, may by that time fall far short of the majority view".

He conceded however, that "very real difficulties [could] arise if [these] proposals are accepted". Among these the first in importance was the crucial issue of minority rights.

> "The only definite safeguard, for the various minorities lies in the requirement of approval [of any new constitutional framework] by three-fourths of the State Council. [Stanley] had feared that the discussion of constitutional reform would exacerbate the communal position and that we might risk losing the co-operation of the minorities in the war effort, but [he had] received the expressed assurance of the Commander-in-Chief and the Governor that they do not share this fear..." Secondly, a popular government "will assume for the first time complete financial responsibility just at a time when the post-war financial and economic problems of Ceylon may be most acute."

There were, finally, the questions relating to British commercial interests in the island. With regard to this the declaration adopted a sensible and pragmatic attitude in conceding that there were, indeed, "no specific safeguard[s] for British commercial interests in Ceylon," but pointing out that such safeguards could not be inserted in it because..."

> "the promises made to India contain no such provision. Nor is there

any definite safeguard for Indian commercial interests; but India would
not be without bargaining power for this purpose.'

Although the proposals outlined on 16 May 1943 fell short of
Dominion Status (which D.S. .Senanayake had set forth as the
objective he aimed at), and far short of the goal of independence
(which the Ceylon National Congress advocated) the Board of
Ministers under D.S. Senanayake's leadership preferred to accept this
offer as one further stage in the constitutional advancement of the
country and as the basis of further negotiations.

The Ministers' Draft Constitution

The first task that confronted D.S. Senanayake was to draft a
constitution on the basis of the conditions laid down in the declaration
of 26 May 1943 and the clarification of this given on 11 July 1943.[10]
The requirement that such a draft constitution needed to win the
approval of three-quarters of all the members of the State Council
practically ensured that it would have to be nothing less than a national
consensus on constitutional reform.

The working committee of the Congress, in the meantime, set about
the business of influencing the process of constitution-making which
D.S. Senanayake had undertaken in response to the Whitehall
declaration of May/July 1943. The framework of a constitution for a
free Lanka was drafted and this was sent along to the Board of
Ministers. The guiding spirit behind this initiative was J.R. Jayewardene, while the draft itself was prepared by J.A.L. Cooray, his associate
in the secretariat of the Congress.

For our purposes the most significant feature of Cooray's draft was
the incorporation in it of a comprehensive and justiciable Bill of
Rights.[11] Senanayake himself was not unsympathetic to the view that a
Bill of Rights was a useful means of allaying the fears of minorities with
regard to their position in an independent Sri Lanka, but he was
dissuaded from supporting it by the arguments of his principal adviser
on constitutional affairs, Sir Ivor Jennings, for whom the applicability
of the Westminster constitutional model to the Sri Lankan situation
was an unalterable article of faith. Jennings would not give any serious
consideration to the incorporation of a Bill of Rights in the
Constitution. On his advice therefore the Board of Ministers decided
against a Bill of Rights but included instead a provision based on
Section 5 of the *Government of Ireland Act* of 1920, prohibiting

legislation infringing on religious freedom or discriminating against persons of any community or religion. The draft Constitution prepared by the Board of Ministers in 1944 contained a clause (Clause 8) prohibiting Parliament from enacting laws which discriminated against ethnic or religious groups, restricted or prohibited the free exercise of any religion, or conferred on "persons of any community or religion any privileges or advantages which are not conferred on persons of other communities or religions." This was transferred, with only minor additions, to the constitution on which the transfer of power was effected in 1947-8, the Soulbury Constitution — section 29(2).

In retrospect it would seem that this was no substitute for a Bill of Rights, and the protection afforded to minorities in the Soulbury Constitution proved to be far from adequate. But at the time of the transfer of power the constitutional guarantees against discriminatory legislation in the new constitution seemed sufficient for the purpose they were intended to serve.

J.R. Jayewardene on his part persisted with his advocacy of a Bill of Rights even after it had been omitted from the Ministers' Draft Constitution[12] but to no avail. Over 30 years later however — in 1977-8 as Prime Minister and soon to become the first Executive President of the island — he had the satisfaction of seeing the second republican Constitution of Sri Lanka incorporate a justiciable Bill of Rights. J.A.L. Cooray was one of his constitutional advisers on this latter occasion as he was in 1943.

The Ministers' Draft Constitution addressed itself to the thorny question of representation, and devised a structure which found wide acceptability. Indeed it lasted with only minor modifications till 1978. One of its most noteworthy features was the incorporation of the principle of weightage in representation to allay the fears of the minorities and to provide greater electoral influence to the backward areas of the country. The province was the unit adopted for demarcation of constituencies. There was to be a constituency for each 75,000 persons ascertained to the nearest 75,000 in a province. While this naturally favored the more densely populated parts of the country, weightage diluted the population formula through the provision of an additional constituency for every 1000 square miles of area. This area weightage varied from a minimum of 1 in the Western Province, to 4 each in the Northern and Eastern Provinces (dominated by the Tamils and Muslims) and the North Central Province. The weightage in the

North Central Province was designed to benefit the Kandyans. The other comparatively backward Kandyan Provinces, Uva and the North Western Province, were to gain 3 seats each on the area rule. The effect of this weightage was as follows: the Northern and Eastern Provinces would get 9 and 7 MPs instead of 5 and 3 which was all they were entitled to on a purely population basis; the weightage was even more favorable in the North Central Province, with 5 MPs instead of 1. In Uva and the North Western Province the figures were 7 and 10 instead of 4 and 7 respectively.

The Draft Constitution recognized that "No system of representation would necessaily ensure that all sections of the community would be adequately represented."[13] Provision was therefore made for the nomination of up to six members by the head of state "where he considers that any important interest was not adequately represented."[14] This too was designed with the minorities, or rather the smaller minorities, in mind.

The preparation of a draft constitution that would meet the requirements of the Whitehall declaration of 1943 was a challenge to the statesmanship and political acumen of Senanayake and the Board of Ministers. They — and his advisers — worked with remarkable speed, and by the beginning of 1944 a draft — the Minister's Draft Constitution[15] as it came to be called — was ready for submission to Whitehall. On the whole it bore the stamp of Senanayake's influence, especially in the concessions made to the minorities. The speed with which they had completed their work was due mainly to the fact that nobody outside the Board of Ministers, not even members of the State Council, had been invited to participate in the preparation of the draft constitution. While this was not contrary to the terms of the declaration of 1943, it was nevertheless one of the criticisms of the draft constitution raised by the more vocal representatives of Tamil opinion and British business interests in the island.

In regard to external affairs a major concession had been made by 1943. This was with regard to the question of Indians resident in the island, their right to the franchise, and the problem of immigration to the island from British India. Under the Donoughmore constitution external affairs came under the purview of the Chief Secretary of the island, one of the three British Officers of State in the Board of Ministers. The dispatch of an official mission to India in November 1940 under D.S. Senanayake's leadership meant that, with regard to the Indian problem in Ceylon, the Board of Ministers was given the right to negotiate on behalf of the country. This was taken a stage further when a Ceylon Government representative to New Delhi was appointed — D.B. Jayatilaka — who took up the post in 1943. Thus at the time D.S. .Senanayake assumed the leadership in the negotiations on the transfer of power, the Board of Ministers had been conceded the right to speak on behalf of the country on one of the most crucially important aspects of its external relations.

The Soulbury Commission

Under the terms of the declaration of May 1943 it was envisaged that this draft constitution would be examined by a "suitable commission or conference" after victory over the Axis powers had been achieved. Once the draft was ready — by February 1944 — Senanayake and the Board of Ministers pressed for an immediate consideration of their scheme. Senanayake argued that urgent local circumstances made an early decision on the constitution a matter of vital necessity. He was supported in this by Caldecott and Layton, but the most convincing case for the appointment of a constitutional commission before the ending of hostilities was made by Lord Louis Mountbatten who, as Supreme Allied Commander, South-East Asia Command, was consulted, and whose views helped greatly in overcoming the original reluctance of the Colonial Office and the War Cabinet to concede Senanayake's request.[16] The decision could well have gone against Senanayake had Mountbatten not intervened.

The official announcement on the appointment of a Commission to visit the island was made on 5 July 1944, but far from being received with cordiality and a sense of satisfaction at the extraction of an important concession, it was greeted in Ministerial circles in Colombo with undisguised dismay. And not merely Ministerial circles. The Ceylon National Congress, naturally enough, was even more forthright in criticism. The point at issue was the widening of the Commission's terms of reference well beyond that set out in the declaration of May 1943, from merely an examination of the draft Constitution prepared by the Board of Ministers, under the terms of that declaration, to include consultation with "various inteests, including the minority communities, concerned with the subject of constitutional reform in Ceylon". Senanayake and his colleagues in the Board of Ministers argued that this amounted to an abrogation of one of the terms of the declaration of 1943, and urged that the work of the Commission should be restricted to the scope set out in that declaration which meant in effect that it should be limited to an examination of the Ministers' Draft Constitution. They added that the requirement of approval of such a constitution by at least three-quarters of the members of the State Council gave sufficient protection to the interests of the minorities.

The Ministers' protests had no effect on Whitehall's thinking and the terms of reference of the Commission were left unchanged when the announcement was made of the appointment of a Chairman (Lord Soulbury) and members of the Commission on 20 September 1944. Given the anxieties of the minorities with regard to the protection of their legitimate rights in any new constitutional arrangements, Whitehall could hardly have come to any other decision. Contrary to the impression created in Sri Lanka that the widening of the Commission's terms of reference stemmed from pressure from Caldecott and his British advisers in the island on behalf of the minorities, the initiative had come from Whitehall, apparently in response to criticisms made by the minorities' representatives (mostly the Tamils) that they had not been consulted in the formulation of constitutional proposals submitted to Whitehall in 1944. Senanayake believed that Caldecott had let him down over this and as a result relations between them were rather strained in the last few months of Caldecott's tour of duty as Governor.

Senanayake and the Board of Ministers resolved on an official boycott of the Commission, as an expression of their disapproval at the widening of its terms of reference. The Ceylon National Congress, at a special session, rejected the July 1944 declaration, came out in support of an all-party conference on constitutional reform and resolved to boycott the Soulbury Commission.

So far as the Minsters were concerned the boycott of the Commission meant, in practice, merely that they did not appear before it at its public sittings. Intermediaries conveyed their views to the Commissioners and Senanayake and the Ministers met them informally especially at receptions for the Commission. Above all, although the Ministers did not present their draft constitution before the Commission, the latter regarded the examination of that document as its main task during its stay in the island. The Congress leadership however, took the decision to boycott the Commission much more seriously.

Up to the appointment of the Soulbury Commission things had gone Senanayake's way. Not only had he succeeded in keeping the process of drafting a constitution under his control, he had also guided it so astutely that he was able to win the backing of the Board of Ministers for the final document. Now, however, doubts were cast about his ability to get things done. His critics within the State Council, and all those within that body and in the Congress who had resented being left out of the process of drafting the Constitution, and negotiating the next step in the transfer of power, sensed the possibility of exploiting the weakening of his position, to make their own views on the constitution known, and their influence felt in the process of drafting a constitution. Not that Senanayake entirely minded it, for it had the advantage — such as it was — of giving Whitehall and the Soulbury Commissioners a sobering comparative perspective in which Senanayake's moderation came through with greater clarity than it may have done through his own efforts.

His critics moved a resolution in the State Council calling upon the Board of Ministers to draft a constitution for a free Lanka, a constitution of the "recognized Dominion type".[17] This initiative was immediately successful, and indeed an amendment to this resolution, pledging support to the Whitehall declaration of 1943 was beaten soundly by 26 votes to 4. Under the provisions of the Donoughmore constitution the Board of Ministers was bound by this resolution, and a bill making provision for such a constitution was introduced at the next sessions of the State Council by S.W.R.D. Bandaranaike.

A word, at this stage, is necessary on 'The Free Lanka' bill. If our readers wonder how it was that a draft consitution was produced with such speed, i.e., between November 1944 and the beginning of February 1945, the answer is that it was in fact based on the Ministers' Draft Constitution. Apart from certain minor dissimilarities incidental to the variance in intentions of the two bills, the Free Lanka bill diverged from the Ministers' Draft Constitution only in regard to the provisions dealing with the powers of the Governor General. These powers were, of necessity, much more limited in the former because it deliberately placed control over defense and external affairs with the Cabinet and not with the Governor General as envisaged in the Whitehall declaration of May 1943.

The Soulbury Commission was in the island and engaged in its task of examining witnesses and documents when the State Council debated the Free Lanka bill. British officials in the island and in

Whitehall, recognized this debate for what it was, a piece of political theatre, set in an atmosphere of unreality, and therefore not to be taken too seriously.

In the meantime, D.S. Senanayake had decided on his own course of action. Once the Commission left the island he was anxious to be in London in time for the publication of their report. If the report was favorable he would ask for more, for Dominion Status, in fact, but if it was unsatisfactory he would repudiate it, and refuse to be any longer bound by the Declaration of 1943 which the British Government itself had discarded. In a conciliatory gesture Whitehall readily consented to extend an invitation to D.S. Senanayake to visit London. The latter left for London in early July 1945, but arrived there in mid-July 1945 only to find that events were moving with remarkable rapidity. There was, first of all, the landslide electoral defeat suffered by the Conservative party led by Winston Churchill, the wartime Prime Minister. This meant inevitably that no immediate response was likely from the new Labour government to the Soulbury proposals. Senanayake met G.H. Hall, the new Secretary of State for the Colonies, on 9 August and was then given a copy of the Soulbury report. To his great surprise and satisfaction he found that the Soulbury Commissioners had, in fact, endorsed the main principles of the Ministers' Draft Constitution. There were adjustments and modifications no doubt but none of any real substance. But more important, the minorities' political campaign during the period of the Soulbury Commission's visit to the island had had little impact on the Commission's thinking.[18]

On the international scene — and this is the second point — the war in the East was over with dramatic suddenness, and this too contributed to the delay in the review of the Soulbury proposals, for the Labour government's energies were now concentrated on the urgent task of formulating policy on the diplomatic and political consequences of Japan's defeat. The change in the international situation also affected Senanayake's attitude to the Soulbury proposals. Had circumstances been different — that is to say, had the war with Japan not come to so sudden an end — Senanayake would have been elated to find that the Soulbury Commissioners had endorsed the main principles of the Ministers' Draft Constitution of 1944. But the war was over, and there was therefore no reason for accepting anything short of Dominion Status.

In his discussions with Whitehall, he seized on the remaining obstacle to the attainment of Dominion Status by Sri Lanka: the limits on her external sovereignty in regard to defense and external affairs laid down in the 1943 declaration, and adhered to by both the Soulbury report and the Ministers themselves in their Draft Constitution of 1944. In both these, bills relating to defense and external affairs fell into the category which the Governor-General was empowered to "reserve" for approval by Whitehall, to ensure that "only legislation conforming with the policy of the Imperial Defence Authorities may be enacted by the Parliament of Ceylon". The Governor-General's powers in regard to defense were not limited to the control of legislation. Where "legislation was required for the implementation of long-range Imperial Defence policy or for other reasons" it was envisaged that the Governor-General would explain what was required to the Prime Minister who would then get his Cabinet to introduce such legislation. But if "for political or other reasons" the government was unwilling to introduce such legislation the Governor-General was empowered to meet this situation by means of a Governor-General's ordinance.[19]

The Soulbury Commissioners endorsed this procedure, but went beyond it in situations "which may not be capable of being dealt with by normal constitutional methods or by a Governor General's ordinance". They referred to "the emergency of war or a grave national emergency in which normal constitutional machinery has either broken down or become ineffective".[20] The Soulbury Report argued that in "order to deal with either of these emergencies it may be necessary for His Majesty in Council to legislate by Order in Council" and proceeded to "recommend, therefore, that this power be reserved to His Majesty in Council and that an express provision to this effect be inserted in the Constitution."[21] It was Senanayake's contention that this elaborate procedure was unworkable in practice because of its complexity. This now became one of the main arguments in Senanayake's case for the immediate grant of Dominion status without the intermediate stage envisaged in the Soulbury Report.

What in the meantime, of the Labour government's response to the Soulbury proposals? On 11 September the Cabinet decided that it would accept the Soulbury Report as the basis on which the island's new Constitution would be framed. But it was firmly opposed to the immediate grant of Dominion Status. Hall conveyed the gist of these decisions to Senanayake on 17 September. The latter returned home, disappointed that the main objective had not been attained, but convinced that it would not take long for the island to achieve self-government. The Labour government's priorities in the dissolution of Empire were India (including Burma) first and then Palestine, and the Cabinet would not be diverted from this to the solution of less important problems.

For Senanayake there were two other important advantages. Firstly, the fact that the obstacle to the immediate grant of Dominion Status was not the minority problems of Sri Lanka but the complex issues of the transfer of power in the Indian empire gave an entirely new and much more satisfactory perspective to the problems that confronted him. Dominion Status, he believed, was now in the offing. Secondly, before his return home he had obtained one vital concession — questions relating to citizenship, the Colonial Office agreed, were to be treated as falling within the ambit of powers of the Sri Lanka government under the new Constitution, a theme to which we shall turn in Chapter X.

The Transfer of Power

The publication of the Soulbury Report was followed by a White Paper[22] embodying the decisions of the British government on the new constitution for Sri Lanka, and clarifying the point that though there was to be no immediate grant of Dominion Status, it was merely postponed pending the successful working of the new Constitution. The reference to the evolutionary character of constitutional development was made at the suggestion of Clement Attlee, the British Prime Minister. The people of Sri Lanka were assured that the British Government was in sympathy with their desire "to advance towards Dominion Status and they were anxious to co-operate with them to that end". Senanayake and his colleagues in the Board of Ministers were unaware that the British Cabinet thought in terms of a further revision of the Constitution after six years: the reference to the six year period was omitted from the final draft of the White Paper only because Whitehall felt that it would be impolitic to lay down a specified period of time, not because it was regarded as too long a period.[24]

The publication of the Soulbury Report, and the White Paper had one major political consequence: it guaranteed Senanayake's triumph over his critics in the Board of Ministers and the State Council. As we shall see in the next chapter the State Council endorsed his motion for the acceptance of the White Paper on constitutional reform by an overwhelming majority of 51 votes to 3, far above the majority of three-quarters of the membership of the State Council which the British government had laid down as a requirment in 1943 and was now reluctant to insist upon for fear that it could not be achieved. Senanayake's motion for the acceptance of the Soulbury proposals was seconded by none other than Bandaranaike. When George E. de Silva gave the blessings of the Ceylon National Congress to these proposals in a long speech (prepared by J.R. Jayewardene himself) Senanayake's triumph was complete.

In less than two years after the publication of the White Paper Senanayake's objective — Dominion Status — was achieved. In early 1947 with the general elections to the new Parliament scheduled for August-September 1947, Senanayake pressed Whitehall for a more precise statement of policy on the attainment of Dominion Status. India's independence was announced by the British Cabinet on 20 February 1947, and with the partition of the Indian sub-continent into the states of India and Pakistan and the grant of independence to Burma, the way was clear for Dominion Status for Sri Lanka. Arthur Creech-Jones, Hall's successor at the Colonial Office, was much more receptive to the request for Dominion Status from Senanayake. The negotiations at Whitehall were handled by O.E. (later Sir Oliver) Goonetileke on Senanayake's behalf. Senanayake and his associates were facing increasing pressure from left-wing forces, apart from other critics, and the immediate grant of Dominion Status was now seen in Whitehall as an urgent if not compelling necessity to guarantee their success in the forthcoming general elections and a smooth transfer of power. In recognition of this the British Government made the official announcement on 18 June 1947 that the island would receive "fully responsible status within the British Commonwealth of Nations".[24]

References

[1]   On this see, K.M. de Silva 'Nationalism and its impact' in *CJHSS* n.s. IV (1&2) pp. 62-72.

[2]   The consensus included: a further and significant measure of constitutional reform stopping short of responsible government; a reversion to the conventional quasi cabinet form of government associated with this new status; a Chief Minister appointed by the Governor and commanding the support of the legislature; and weightage in representation for the minorities as compensation for the abandonment of the executive committee system.

[3]   K.M. de Silva, "The Transfer of Power in Sri Lanka — A Review of British

Perspectives", *CJHSS* n.s. IV (1&2) pp. 8-19.

[4] See, K.M. de Silva 'The Model Colony — Reflections on the Transfer of Power in Sri Lanka', in A.J. Wilson and D. Dalton, (eds) *The States of South Asia* (London, 1982) pp. 77-88.

[5] For Caldecott's views on this see, K.M. de Silva 'The Transfer of Power in Sri Lanka — A Review of British Perspectives' *CJHSS* n.s. IV (1&2) p. 12.

[6] On 5 March 1942 Sir Geoffrey Layton was appointed Commander-in-Chief of the British forces in the island. His powers extended well beyond the armed services to the civil government as well. Layton's powers were so wide-ranging that clashes with the civil government — the Governor and the Board of Ministers — seemed inevitable. In practice this did not happen. He established a surprisingly effective and even cordial working relationship with Senanayake, and the Board of Ministers. The latter gave their unstinted support to the war effort.

[7] C.O. 54/980 file 55541/5. Secret Cabinet Paper W.P. (43) 129 of 27 March 1943; see also Caldecott's "personal and secret" dispatches to Stanley, 27 January and 17 February 1943.

[8] C.O. 54/980 File 55541/5 Caldecott's "personal and secret" dispatches to Stanley, 27 January 1943 and 17 February 1943.

[9] C.O. 54/980 File 55541/5 Stanley's Secret Cabinet Paper, W.O. (43) 129 of 27 March 1943 entitled *Ceylon Constitution*.

[10] For this declaration and clarification see *S.P.* XVII of 1943.

[11] J.A.L. Cooray, *Constitutional and Administrative Law of Sri Lanka*, (Colombo, 1973) pp. 508-10.

[12] Among the resolutions that came up for discussion at the 26th annual sessions of the Ceylon National Congress held on 27 and 28 January 1945 was a Declaration of Fundamental rights. See Roberts, *Documents*, II pp. 1569-70.

[13] *S.P.* XIV of 1944, para 9, on page 5.

[14] *Ibid.*

[15] *S.P.* XIV of 1944.

[16] See, Mountbatten's telegram of 22 May 1944 (marked 'top secret') to the Chief of Staff, C.O. 54/986 file 55541/5, War Cabinet 77(44) conclusions of meeting of 13 June 1944.

[17] The resolution was moved by Susantha de Fonseka, the Deputy Speaker who was not a member of the Congress at this time.

[18] See, K.M. de Silva, *A History of Sri Lanka*, pp. 449-461, and K.M. de Silva "The Model Colony: Reflections on the Transfer of Power in Sri Lanka" in A.J. Wilson and D. Dalton (eds) *The States of South Asia*, pp. 77-88.

[19] See, Sections 39(1-4) of *S.P.* XIV of 1944, and the *Soulbury Report* (1945) pp. 93-5, paragraphs 349-358.

[20] *The Soulbury Report*, p. 93.

[21] *Ibid.*

[22] *Cmd* 6690, "Ceylon, statement of policy on Constitutional Reform."

[23] See, K.M. de Silva "The Model Colony: Reflections on the Transfer of Power in Sri Lanka", *op. cit.*, pp. 77-83.

[24] *Ibid.*

Chapter X

Senanayake's Political Settlement And Its Critics, 1947 - 1952

We need to begin this chapter with a brief but close look at the voting in the State Council debate of 8 and 9 November 1945 on Whitehall's reforms proposals. One feature of it has been referred to in the previous chapter namely the unexpected overwhelming majority of 51 to 3 which Senanayake won. Our interest in this present chapter is on other features of the vote beginning with the discomfiture of the Tamil Congress and the vivid manifestation of the failure of its political campaign, a failure compounded by the support given by the Muslim representatives to Senanayake and their unmistakable opposition to the Tamil demands. There was also the case of three dissenters, two representatives of Indian interests, and the third, W. Dahanayake, the irrepressible sole representative of radical and socialist opinion in the legislature on that occasion.

Outside the legislature there was the vocal opposition of a small group of Buddhist activists, most notably the 'political *bhikkhus*' of the Vidyalankara *pirivena*, but this was more significant for presaging the potential strength of these forces in the country in the years to come than for any immediate serious threat to Senanayake and the emerging political establishment.

Ponnambalam's Discomfiture

The publication of the Soulbury report, and its endorsement of all the principal features of the Ministers' Draft Constitution were a severe setback to Ponnambalam and his recently formed ethnic party, the Tamil Congress. Their well-documented charges of ethnic discrimination had been carefully scrutinized by the Commission. The latter's rejection of these was all the more telling for being so balanced and fair in their assessment of the charges.[1] Similarly the "50-50" campaign which had run out of steam by the early 1940s, had been revived with the arrival of the Soulbury Commission in the island. It lacked the vitality and much of the fervor of the original campaign. It failed to impress the Commission just as it had failed to impress Caldecott from the outset. Indeed the former's rejection of it was just as forthright as Caldecott's, and even more cogently argued than his criticisms.[2]

Like Senanayake, G.G. Ponnambalam himself left for London, once the Soulbury Commissioners completed their assignment in the island. There he sought to use such influence as he had — including the support of a powerful lobby of British businessmen with investments in Sri Lanka — to gain support for his views in Whitehall. In this he was following in the footsteps of Ramanathan who, in 1930, had made a well-publicized but eventually futile mission to London to oppose the Donoughmore reforms. Ponnambalam was no more successful in 1945 than Ramanathan had been in 1930. Unlike Ramanathan he did not carry the battle to the national legislature when the reforms proposals were debated there. Ponnambalam was a notable absentee at the debate of 8 and 9 November. He left the Tamil representatives leaderless on that occasion, and one by one they made their peace with Senanayake, and gave these proposals their support, although in most cases not with any great enthusiasm.

The debate of 8 and 9 November 1945 marked the culmination of a decade of blighted hopes for the Tamil community, which began in 1930 with the death of Ramanathan, and the boycott of the general election of 1931, which the Jaffna Youth League successfully imposed on their reluctant senior politicians. Ramanathan had opposed the Donoughmore proposals because they disturbed the *status quo* too much; the Jaffna Youth League's opposition was for quite different reasons — namely, that the reforms did not disturb the *status quo* sufficiently. As advocates of *swaraj*, they opposed the Donoughmore scheme because the constitutional system it proposed fell short of self-government. In their eyes Jaffna seemed once more to be setting the pace in politics. Initially the boycott did create a favorable impression among the political *avant garde* in Colombo, but that neither lasted very long nor spread to the more prominent Sinhalese politicians.[3] What the latter remembered were Ramanathan's die-hard opposition to these reforms, and his last minute visit to London to lobby the Colonial Office against them, and they remembered also the effusions of other Tamil leaders against the reforms. Thus when the Jaffna Youth League acted in emulation of Indian nationalism, most Sinhalese saw the boycott as a parody of Ulster sectionalism. Nor were British officialdom in Colombo or London more sympathetic to the boycott than the average Sinhalese politician.

The boycott failed to make the impact it was intended to have, and in 1934 elections were held to fill the vacancies in the legislature caused by the boycott. Ponnambalam entered the legislature on this occasion and quickly established his leadership of Tamil politics in the legislature and the country. Now only 10 years later he appeared to have taken Tamil politics once more to a *cul de sac*; his absence at the debate was as notable for being a confession of failure as it was evidence of a change of attitude and policy, a change which ultimately led him to a seat in Senanayake's cabinet in 1948.

Eventually all five Tamils who participated in the debate voted in favor, beginning with Arunachalam Mahadeva, (Arunachalam's son) who was Minister of Home Affairs. Of the others only one member, J.G. Rajakulendran, spoke on behalf of the Tamil Congress. (The problem was that the position of the Tamil Congress within the legislature did not reflect its wide support among the Tamils). And there was, of course, V. Nalliah who did not follow Ponnambalam's lead. At the general election of 1947 he won his seat, while all the Tamils who spoke and voted on this occasion lost theirs. Ponnambalam inflicted a severe defeat on Mahadeva in a prestige battle for the key Jaffna seat. But this is to anticipate events.

Ponnambalam's discomfiture had many other features, but none so important as the forthright repudiation of Tamil leadership of minority politics in the island by the Muslims on this occasion. Despite the latter's anxiety to be assured of a fair share of seats in the future national legislature, they preferred to agitate on their own, and most significantly, to back the Sinhalese leadership in the latter's political campaigns.

The Muslims' Response

When the State Council debated the Free Lanka bill all three Muslim members supported it. Jayah and Kaleel spoke in favor and Razik and Kaleel voted for it (Jayah was not present at voting time). And then on 9 November 1945 on the historic vote on the acceptance of the Soulbury reforms, all the Muslim members voted in favor. Two of them spoke on that occasion, Jayah and Razik, and their speeches were a study in contrasts.[4]

Jayah's speech was, as usual with him, unexciting. This was not the moment, he said, "for jubilation or exultation or even for mutual recrimination ... [or] to speak of the discomfiture of the minority communities or of the victory of the majority community." But unexciting or not, the points he made were all the more effective because they came from him: first, that the Muslim members of the Council had the fullest backing of the Muslim community in the island in the stand they took on these reforms; and secondly, that

> "When the Muslim Members of this Council decided to take a definite stand at the time the 'Sri Lanka' bill was introduced, they did so for one and for one reason only. That reason was that where the political freedom of this country was involved, they were prepared to go to any length, even to the point of sacrificing advantages and benefits as a result of such action."

The recrimination that Jayah eschewed there was in full measure in Razik's speech, and it was recrimination directed against the Tamils. He spoke with a zest and enthusiasm which was lacking in the phlegmatic contributions of Jayah. He spoke on behalf of the All-Ceylon Moors Association which had entrusted to him "the pleasant task of announcing to the House that they pledge their support to the resolution" moved by D.S. Senanayake.

> "... As my community and I have always stood by him I must say that in this hour of his triumph we join hands with him in the forward march to the goal of Dominion Status to which he aspires ..."

Razik emphasized the historic links between the Muslims — or Moors as he called them — and the Sinhalese who "have lived together for centuries ... in amity and accord ... ." This, in fact, was the central theme of his speech. "Mistakes have been made in the past," he stated but his "fervent plea" was that these would not be repeated, and "in a spirit of fellowship and understanding" he offered "the hand of fellowship to my Sinhalese brethren... ."

What set him apart from Jayah were the frequent criticisms he made of the Tamils in his speech, not sparing even their leader G.G. Ponnambalam. He began his speech thus:

> "After the five pathetic speeches made by my good friends the hon. Member for Kankesanthurai (Mr. Natesan), the hon. Member for Mannar (Mr. Tyagaraja) and others, I feel that I should say how we the Moors, have been placed in the past in spite of the treatment we

received, not at the hands of the Sinhalese, but at the hands of the other communities. I say this as a solace to the Tamil community. We have been heard even without representation! I remember the time when we, the Ceylon Moors, were told that as we speak a sort of Tamil, we can be put down as a Tamil-speaking community and represented by Tamil Members! We had to bow even to that, and very unfortunately."

"I can appreciate the feelings and the thoughts that passed through the minds of my very good friends. But I am afraid I cannot help them. If they had stood by the Sinhalese community as the Moors and I, as their representative, have done, I am sure that today would be a very happy day for them as it is for me and my community. Whatever I say with regard to the Tamil community, I am not saying in the spirit of 'vengeance is sweet.' I say it as a solace to them."

He returned to this theme time and again in his speech, and especially in the extract we quote below. But it was always subsidiary to the central theme: the Muslims were now allies of the Sinhalese.

"Now Sir, I admire my good friend the hon. Member for Point Pedro (Mr. Ponnambalam). He is in England now. I admire him for the courage of his convictions, for the splendid flight he has put up for his cause, whether it was right or wrong. He, with his wonderful organizing ability, baited the Moors to join in the demand for his famous '50-50' representation. Did the Moors lose faith in the Sinhalese community by doing so? No, Sir! I want this to be remembered by the Sinhalese community in their hour of triumph..."

"And at the same time, I would ask the Tamil community to understand our attitude, and not to misunderstand us — that in so solidly standing with the Sinhalese community, we only did the correct thing. It was not animosity or even malice that prevented us from joining hands with our friend the hon. Member for Point Pedro. It was our political sagacity, if I may say so, and a sense of justice that made us stand up and fight side by side with the Sinhalese in the cause of attaining Dominion Status. Let us now, Sinhalese, Tamils and Moors, march together towards the early securing of Dominion Status..."

Razik's speech on this occasion reflected more faithfully than Jayah's the fundamental shift that had occurred in the political thinking of the Muslims. He exploited this mood more effectively, and hoped no doubt that his community would benefit politically from the change in attitude he had expressed with such optimism and sense of purpose. Soon, the two main Muslim political associations, the All Ceylon Muslim League, and the All Ceylon Moors Association would join Senanayake in his political initiative of a new national political party — the United National Party. That too would set the Muslims apart from the Tamils. The latter always had their ethnic political parties with a regional base; the Muslims had preferred to join the major national political party. This difference in political behavior has continued over the three decades and more since independence.

The Indian Problem

The unresolved issues relating to the position of the Indians in the Sri Lanka polity, and the conflicting grievances involved in these had been ventilated afresh when the Soulbury Commission arrived in the island in late 1944. Spokesmen for the Indian community argued that Indians resident in the island had been clearly discriminated against in regard to the franchise, and urged that this subject as well as immigration in general should be among those reserved for the British government under the terms of the declaration of July 1943. The Soulbury Commission devoted a chapter of its report[5] to these issues but came down very much on the side of the Board of Ministers in declaring that the policies pursued by the latter on the franchise

"did not seem to His Majesty's Government to involve any racial discrimination against Indians, whereas some of the Indians' protests amounted in effect to a claim to a position of privilege rather than of equality."

Besides, in paragraph 242 it recommended that:

"(i) Any Bill relating solely to the prohibition or restriction of immigra- into Ceylon shall not be regarded as coming within the category of Bills which the Governor General is instructed to reserve for the signification of His Majesty's pleasure; ...

(ii) Any Bill relating solely to the franchise shall not be regarded as coming within the category of Bills which the Governor-General is instructed to reserve for the signification of His Majesty's pleasure".

The Indian leadership in the island was bitterly disappointed at this setback, and began a campaign of opposition to the reforms embodied in the Soulbury report. When that happened J.R. Jayewardene was constrained to complain to Nehru that no Indian

"who seeks freedom for India, can object to the recommendations, in para 242(i) and (ii). The Ceylon Indian Congress, however, while pleading for Ceylon's independence, in the same breath insists, that the British government should include in the Constitution articles relating to immigration, and the Indian franchise, in accordance with the demands of the [Ceylon Indian] Congress. Mr. Aney [Indian Government representative in Colombo] is now in Simla to press this point of view on the British Raj. I do hope for the sake of friendly feelings, which

you, as well as many others, in India, and in Ceylon wish to promote
between our two countries, he will not be successful."[6]

Aney did not succeed in his mission to Simla but returned to
Colombo to continue the battle here.

With the publication of the British Government's White Paper of
October 1945 the focus of attention shifted to the State Council. There
as we have seen, the major point of interest was how large a majority
Senanayake would secure in support of his motion recommending
acceptance of the White Paper. Although there were fears that a
majority of three-quarters of the membership of the State Council was
beyond Senanayake's reach he would not abandon his quest for a
massive majority, and in the event he got one as near to unanimity as
was possible. Thanks to a concerted campaign of persuasion all
waverers in the ranks of the minorities were won over, and when the
debate began on 8 November the tide turned so strongly in his favor
that only one vote eluded him, that of W. Dahanayake, a Sinhalese
radical who wanted nothing short of independence.

When the vote was taken on 9 November two others joined
Dahanayake in opposition to Senanayake's motion, which was
approved by 51 members. Two Indian representatives voted against
the resolution. They themselves had been inclined to vote in favor
even though the *quid pro quo* they asked for was not forthcoming, but
M.S. Aney, seated in the house, sent down a note asking them to vote
against the motion. It was, as Governor Sir Henry Monck-Mason-
Moore observed in a confidential letter to a senior official at the
Colonial Office, "a stupid and improper piece of interference"[7] on the
part of the representative of the Indian government.

Senanayake was elated at the majority he had won.[8] But Aney's
indiscretion did not pass unnoticed. If nothing else it would have
confirmed fears of potential undue Indian influence on the affairs of
Sri Lanka once both India and Sri Lanka had won their independence.
No doubt it would have strengthened his resolution to stand firm
against any major concessions to the Indians on the franchise and
immigration.

Indeed relations between Senanayake and his associates on the one
hand and the leadership of the Indian community in the island on the
other remained strained throughout the year 1946-7. In a letter dated
22 May 1946 to Nehru George E. de Silva, as President of the Ceylon
National Congress[9], explained the Sri Lankan leadership's position thus:

"... The new Constitution," he declared, "... gives Ceylon for the first time the right to determine the future composition of her population and the right to prohibit or restrict immigration into Ceylon without any overriding powers being vested in the British Government.

"Surely you will agree that the powers granted to Ceylon under the new Constitution, ... are consistent with her progress towards freedom, and that the request of the Ceylon Indian Congress to the British Government to include in the Constitution articles relating to franchise and immigration in accordance with its demands is a negation of that freedom? The Ceylon Indian Congress also talks of a general strike as a protest. As a protest against what? Against Ceylon's march to freedom; against vesting in the people of Ceylon the right to determine the composition of the country's population and the rights which its citizens should be entitled to? Surely you will not accept for India any restriction on the freedom that Britain will soon give her? Then why should Ceylon not enjoy freedom as full and as unqualified as yours?

"As Mr. Senanayake has informed you," the letter continued, "the relations between India and Ceylon, and any questions relating to Indians in Ceylon which are not already settled, will be the subject of negotiations between a free India and a free Ceylon; until then your influence should be used to prevent misguided actions by those Indians in Ceylon who are adopting tactics so correctly criticized by you in your latest book."[10]

The negotiations de Silva referred to in his letter to Nehru began at the end of December 1947 in New Delhi. The discussions were the third of the decade. The first had been in November 1940 when Sri Lanka had put forward proposals to: accept Indians of the third generation born in the island as Sri Lankan citizens; to grant voting rights — with specified restrictions — to Indians with a domicile of choice; and to allow all Indians with less than five years residence the right to work but no possibility of acquiring political rights for themselves or their children. The aim was to reduce the number of Indians in the island, and where necessary to repatriate them. The Indian side in the negotiation stuck to one single theme: political rights for all Indians after 5 years residence,[11] which had been their position ever since the Donoughmore report had been published. The talks failed; the two sides were too far apart in their respective demands. The negotiations held in Colombo in September 1941 saw both sides in a more conciliatory tone, the Sri Lankans more so than the Indians. The Sri Lankans offered the status of permanent settlers — with the right to vote — to all Indians with a minimum of 7 years residence in the island,[12] with all those admitted to the country thereafter being treated as temporary residents. A major concession had been made but the Indian side still had reservations and so these talks failed too. However, the six point formula which the Sri Lankan delegation offered in 1941 became the basis of the talks in New Delhi in 1947.[13]

Two things had happened since then to strengthen Senanayake's hand: first, the Soulbury Commissioners had themselves considered this problem in all its ramifications, and, as we have seen, came down heavily on the side of Sri Lankans. They had been convinced that the Sri Lankan political leadership had made a genuine effort to reach an agreement on this issue. Secondly, independence was in the offing, and Sri Lanka was now in a stronger position — as a would be Dominion talking to another Dominion — to get a favorable settlement.

The substance of the offer on this occasion was the grant of citizenship to all Indians who had lived in the island for a "prescribed number of years." Senanayake defined the prescribed period as seven years continuous residence for married persons and ten for single persons with 31 December 1945 as the operative date. This in fact was a much more generous offer than the one made in 1941, but Nehru held out for a qualification of 8 years for all persons, married or single, with 1 January 1948 as the qualifying date.[14] Professor Hugh Tinker, a severe critic of Sri Lankan politicians in their attitude to the Indian minority in the island, blames Nehru for the failure of these talks: as a result of his rigidity, and refusal to bargain or compromise, on what he thought were matters of principle,[15] a unilateral settlement was imposed by Senanayake's independent government in 1948-9.

The Left-Wing Opposition

W. Dahanayake's negative vote in the debate was significant for being the only one cast in protest at the inadequacy of the offer made to Sri Lanka. He would have independence or nothing. At this time he was not yet a member of the Trotskyist LSSP but acted the role of a radical gadfly in the legislature.

In Sri Lanka in the meantime the challenge that Senanayake and his associates faced from the Marxists and radicals gathered momentum with the release of the LSSP leaders from jail in early 1947. They had been incarcerated by the British authorities in 1941 as security risks. Their two members in the national legislature, Philip Gunawardene and Dr. N.M. Perera, were among those jailed, and also among those who broke jail shortly after their imprisonment. They escaped to India, and were re-arrested sometime in 1947. After their release they seized the opportunity to project themselves as the most stalwart opponents of the imperial connection, and the most genuinely nationalist of all the political groups in Sri Lanka. They denounced the Soulbury report, the White Paper of 1945 and the new Constitution, and the promise of independence as part of a cynical deal between the imperial power and its pliant agents in Sri Lanka led by Senanayake.

In staging its return to a prominent role in national politics the LSSP sought also to undermine the Communist Party's influence in left-wing politics. Their contention was that the latter had been associated with the country's political establishment through their policy of seeking an accommodation with the party of the national consensus, that is to say, with the Ceylon National Congress, till the end of November 1945.

The LSSP turned almost at once to industrial action to regain the primacy there that they had lost to the Communists. They organized a series of major strikes between 1945 and 1947 culminating in the general strike of 1947, the most noteworthy demonstration of solidarity by the working class and white collar workers up to that time. These strikes were as much political demonstrations as they were trade disputes — one of the demands of the strikers was a rejection of the new constitution — and the Board of Ministers was inclined to treat these, particularly the general strike, as a serious bid for political power by the Marxists. The "moderates" had come into their inheritance, and the radicals, in the sense of the Marxist left, were demonstrating their determination to deprive them of it.

The Political Bhikkhus

The so-called political *bhikkhus* continued their campaign against what they regarded were the conservative forces of Sri Lankan society. In that sense they were allies of the radical and Marxist left. They found a determined opponent in D.S. Senanayake. With regard to language policy and educational reform which Buddhist activists treated as matters of special concern, he was distinctly, if not positively, opposed to their demands. His opposition to the language reforms adopted by the State Council in 1944 on the basis of J.R. Jayewardene's resolution has been referred to earlier in this book. To Kannangara's education reforms he was, if anything, even more vehemently opposed. In both instances the peculiar constitutional structure of the Donoughmore system gave individual Ministers and backbenchers greater independence and permitted a fuller play of individual initiative, than a conventional cabinet form of government would allow. Thus Senanayake could signal his lack of sympathy for these reforms but was powerless to prevent either the adoption of these reforms proposals or their implementation.

A bill to give effect to the State Council's decisions of June 1945 on education reform took several months to prepare, and when at last it appeared before the State Council as the Education Ordinance of 1947, denominational interests led by the Roman Catholics strained every nerve to have the debate postponed, in the hope, no doubt, that with the dissolution of the State Council and elections to the new Parliament due, the delay would give denominational pressure groups the opportunity of influencing the preparation of a more congenial piece of legislation drafted by someone other than C.W.W. Kannangara.

There was soon a polarization of conflicting educational forces with the Roman Catholics in the vanguard of the resistance, and a "Central Free Education Defense Committee" representing Buddhist interests taking the issue before the electorate in an island-wide campaign. The political *bhikkhus* were in the forefront of the agitation in support of the bill. If the Roman Catholics were intent on securing a postponement of the bill, Buddhist activists were determined to use pressure on State Councillors, soon to face election in the new Parliament, to have the ordinance adopted. They had the enthusiastic support of the Marxists on this issue, as well as of Bandaranaike and the Sinhala Maha Sabha. J.R. Jayewardene too supported these reforms against the opposition of D.S. Senanayake: they shared a common hostility to the political *bhikkhus*, but the former's antipathy to them did not extend to the education reforms they so enthusiastically supported.

Petitions were presented to the State Council on behalf of the two contending parties. The hierarchy of the Roman Catholic church presented a memorandum to Kannangara against his new education ordinance. A Roman Catholic State Councillor presented a petition against the bill in the legislature. But petitions and the collection of signatures for them were matters in which the Roman Catholics were no match for the *bhikkhus*. All the petitions submitted in support of the bill were either presented or organized by *bhikkhus*: one such petition was a mammoth scroll containing 192,292 signatures.

The campaign in support of the ordinance had the effect of silencing its opponents in the Council; as prospective candidates at the forthcoming general election they would not risk losing popular support by opposing a bill which had so clearly captured the people's imagination. Thus when the vote was taken at the second reading of the bill on 15 May 1947 it was passed unanimously. A large number of *bhikkhus* were seated in the Council's gallery savoring their triumph and it was generally accepted that they had played a decisive role in Kannangara's success.

Senanayake had to concede victory, but despite the success achieved by the supporters of the bill, a concession was extracted under which "assisted" denominational schools which did not enter the "free" education scheme were to receive grants in aid on the old basis till 30 September 1948, after which all aid would cease. The deadline was subsequently extended after independence.

The "Free Education" campaign was the highwater mark of the influence the 'political *bhikkhus*' of Vidyalankara had on policy making and public opinion in the 1940s. They sought to rouse public opinion against the official policy adopted by the Board of Ministers and their political allies, on the transfer of power; and they intervened in the campaigning for seats in the new Parliament. In the first of these, their views reflected the influence of the Marxist parties, in particular the LSSP, on their thinking; in the second, their intervention was on behalf of the Marxist parties in general, and in particular against key individuals in the newly formed United National Party (UNP).

Early in 1947 they had expressed their dissatisfaction with Senanayake's policies on the transfer of power, and the concept of Dominion Status. On 6 January 1947 at a meeting held in the Kelaniya temple, a statement of policy which came to be called "The Kelaniya Declaration of Independence" was adopted. It affirmed that,

> "We, the *sangha* of Sri Lanka ... do hereby declare and publish on behalf of the people that Sri Lanka claims its right to be a Free and Independent Sovereign State, that it has resolved to absolve itself from all allegiance to any other power, State or Crown, and that all political connection between it and any other state is hereby dissolved ... ."[16]

During the election campaign of 1947 the political *bhikkhu* leadership were prominent speakers at the meetings organized by the Marxist parties against Senanayake and the newly formed United National Party — the sucessor to the Ceylon National Congress. Two seats in which they were most active were Kelaniya and Mirigama. The UNP candidates in these two seats, J.R. Jayewardene and D.S. Senanayake respectively, had voiced strong opposition to *bhikkhus* involving themselves in political activity. Both of them won their seats, the latter more easily than the former.

The *bhikkhu* activists went on to claim that the substantial increase in Marxist representation in the new Parliament owed much to their own campaigns. In doing so they greatly exaggerated the importance of their role in the election campaign and the extent of their impact on the rapidly changing political scene of Sri Lanka at the transfer of power.

Senanayake's Political Legacy

Senanayake's sensitivity to the anxieties of minorities reflected a deep conviction that generous concessions to the minorities, ethnic, and religious, would ensure political stability in a plural society such as Sri Lanka's in the vital last phase in the transfer of power. An anlaysis of his response to the political implications of minority anxieties on Sri Lanka's development as an independent state needs much more space than is available in a chapter such as this. But one needs to draw attention, briefly, to at least three points of interest.

The first of these, the constitutional guarantees incorporated in the Soulbury Constitution, against discriminatory legislation likely to affect minorities, guarantees borrowed from provisions in the Ministers' Draft Constitution of 1944 which had been introduced on D.S. Senanayake's initiative, have been dealt with in Chapter IX. Secondly there was the initiative he took in forming the United National Party (UNP) in 1946. This was designed to make a fresh start in politics in the direction of a consensus of moderate opinion in national politics; it was to be a political party necessarily representative of the majority community, but at the same time acceptable to the minorities. The Ceylon National Congress was jettisoned because it had lost the support of the minorities, and seemed most unlikely to regain it.[17] His own standing in the country was sufficient guarantee of its being acceptable to a majority of the people, but its position among the Sinhalese was strengthened considerably by S.W.R.D. Bandaranaike's decision to bring in his Sinhala Maha Sabha. From the beginning it had the enthusiastic approval of the influential Christian minority, and the Muslims, who had in the past followed the lead of the Tamils in their political activity, at last broke away and sought association with the new party.[18] Within a year of the grant of independence in 1948 the

UNP consolidated its position with the entry of G.G. Ponnambalam and the bulk of the Tamil Congress members into the government. When the Tamil Congress crossed over to the new government in 1948 the equilibrium of political forces which D.S. Senanayake had sought to establish was stabilized at a level which he found acceptable, even though the Tamil Congress did not lose its separate identity and despite the fact that a section broke away from it into a stubborn, but at that time, seemingly futile opposition as the Federal Party. Indeed the entry of the Tamil Congress into the new government helped convert it into very much a consensus of moderate political opinion in the country.

The demarcation of constituencies to the new Parliament reflected these same trends. The electoral balance was heavily weighted in favor of the rural areas, which generally were more conservative in outlook. Because of the area weightage, the voting strength in constituencies varied from province to province and within provinces too, to the point where the principle of one man/one vote itself seemed vitiated. This had, at the same time, the great advantage of conveniently providing weightage in representation to the minority groups, the Tamils and Muslims in the Northern and Eastern provinces.

While the Soulbury Commission adopted the proposals in the Ministers' Draft Constitution on representation, it made one important recommendation on its own initiative, the creation of multi-member constituencies. This was in response to a suggestion made to the Commission that

"minority representation would be strengthened by the creation of multi-member constituencies on the ground that the only chance of representation for small communities depended on their concentrating all their strength on candidates of their own choice in a multi-member constituency."

The first Delimitation Commission under the new constitution decided in favor of 86 single-member constituencies, three constituencies returning two members each and one returning three members. The Delimitation Commission's powers under section 41(5) of the then Constitution were generally unfettered. They could not increase the number of members to be returned for a province; but in other respects they could do as they please and did so.

The Soulbury Commission computed the probable results of this system in terms of the communal factor, compared with the proportionate figure calculated on an all-island basis, thus:[19]

	Proportionate	Probable
Low-Country Sinhalese	41	32
Kandyan Sinhalese	25	36
Sri Lanka Tamils	12	13 or 14
Indians	10	7 or 8
Muslims	6	4

As it was, the results of the elections held in 1947 showed that the Low Country Sinhalese did relatively better than anticipated, and the Indians marginally worse. But the principle of weightage had proved to be effective both in regard to giving Sri Lanka Tamils a slightly higher proportion of seats than on a strict population basis, and of course the Kandyans were the main beneficiaries. It must be noted that the system of delimiting constituencies survived the supercession of the Soulbury Constitution in 1972, passing almost unchanged into the new constitutional structure of the first Republic (1972-1978).

Thirdly, he stood firm against mounting pressure to abandon the concept of a secular state and the principle of the religious neutrality of state and government. Thus while he recognized the need to afford some protection and assistance to Buddhism and indeed for a special obligation to foster Buddhism, all this fell far short of the demands made on him and the government by Buddhist activists. He was always an outspoken critic of *bhikkhus* engaging in politics, and the political *bhikkhus* had reciprocated by making him the prime target for their attacks. They and other Buddhist activists were kept at bay so successfully that at independence and for a few years thereafter that despite some Buddhist displeasure over the continued prestige and influence enjoyed by the Christians, there seemed little or no evidence of the religious turmoil and linguistic conflict which were to burst to the surface in 1956.

As Prime Minister and under a Cabinet system he had much greater influence and authority in resisting policies that he objected to than under the Donoughmore system. To illustrate this one turns to the fate of Kannangara's education reforms which became law in 1947. Their implementation was effected under the new constitutional structure in which the Education Ministers of the UNP government were not only more pragmatic in education policy than Kannangara had been but were also more sensitive to the interests of the Christian missions and in particular the Roman Catholics. The pace at which the education reforms initiated by the Kannangara were introduced by them was decidedly slower than it was likely to have been under him.

One one issue however he shared all prejudices of the Sinhalese politicians (except the Marxists of this period): on the Indian question. Relations between him and the new independence government on the one hand, and the leadership of the Ceylon Workers Congress, the political arm of the Indian community, had deteriorated steadily in the years 1946 and 1947. The election campaign of 1947 saw them on opposite sides of the political struggle.

One of the first political initiatives of Senanayake's government after independence was a unilateral initiative on the Indian question: *The Ceylon Citizenship Act No. 18 of 1948* restricted the status of a national of Sri Lanka to those who could claim it by descent or registration. The application of these conditions to Indians in Sri Lanka was defined in *The Indian and Pakistani Residents (Citizenship) Act No. 3 of 1949*. The requirements were much the same that Senanayake had offered Nehru in 1947. A third piece of legislation, *The Ceylon (Parliamentary Elections) Amendment Act (No. 48 of 1949)*, removed the voters of Indian origin from the electoral rolls.[20]

Under the second of these Acts applicants were required to produce documentary evidence in support of their claims to Sri Lankan citizenship. Such evidence was hard to come by, but the difficulties involved in this were compounded by the initial refusal of the Ceylon Indian Congress (later the Ceylon Workers Congress) to co-operate in the implementation of this legislation. By the time they changed their minds, it was too late for most potential applicants for Sri Lanka citizenship to stake their claims.

The new citizenship legislation not only served to assuage the fears and suspicions of the Sinhalese in general and the Kandyans in particular, but also to demolish a potentially powerful prop of the left-wing groups. The immediate effect of this was to distort the electoral balance even more markedly than before and to make the Sinhalese rural voter the arbiter of the country's politics. With each fresh delimitation of constituencies thereafter that distortion became more pronounced. This new electoral balance gave the UNP and its allies a decisive advantage in the general elections of 1952, and the left-wing parties were greatly handicapped.

Retrospect

The political settlement established by D.S. Senanayake was less stable than it appeared to be. The forces that sought to upset it were as insidious as they were truly formidable. And to grasp the significance of these we need to turn to the nature of nationalism in Sri Lanka. There was always a tendency on the part of the Sinhalese to equate their own ethnic nationalism with a wider all-island one, to assume that these — Sinhalese nationalism and Sri Lanka nationalism — were one and the same. In support of this they advanced arguments based on history and immemorial tradition. But this was a short-sighted and unrealistic attitude. The Tamils, the most numerous and articulate group among the minorities, passionately rejected this identification of the sectional interests of the majority with the wider all-island focus of Sri Lanka nationalism. The Christians (among the Sinhalese and Tamils), and more particularly the Roman Catholics, were equally apprehensive and resentful of the common tendency to equate Sinhalese nationalism with Buddhism. The Tamils for their part, developed an inward-looking ethnic nationalism of their own, though this, like its Sinhalese counterpart, lacked cohesiveness and even a touch of authenticity till language became, after independence, the basis of these rival nationalisms. The other form of nationalism, a Ceylon or Sri Lanka nationalism, emphasized the common interests of the island's several ethnic and religious groups. Its *raison d'etre* was the acceptance of the plural nature of the Sri Lanka polity; its fundamental political principle was an attempt to reconcile the legitimate interests of the majority and minorities.

Its most influential advocate at the time of the transfer of power was D.S. Senanayake. In 1948, this latter version of nationalism seemed to be a viable alternative to the narrower sectionalisms described above, and held the prospect of peace and stability in the formative first years of the new state. It was based on a double compromise: the softening of Sinhalese dominance by the establishment of an equilibrium of political forces whose keynote was moderation, and an emphasis on secularism, a refusal to mix state power and politics with religion, even though the concept of a special responsibility for Buddhism was tacitly accepted.

This Sri Lanka or Ceylonese nationalism had however a crucial flaw. It was basically elitist in conception, and it did not have much substantial popular support extending beyond the political establishment. It required D.S. Senanayake's enormous personal prestige, and consummate statecraft to make it viable.

The immediate effect of D.S. Senanayake's death in March 1952 was to give it another lease of life. The massive electoral victory which his son and successor Dudley Senanayake won in 1952 was in many ways a ringing endorsement given by the electorate to the life's work of D.S. Senanayake. The election itself had taken place in an emotional atmosphere following upon the death of the elder Senanayake. The equilibrium of forces he had established was seemingly stabilized by the resounding support received by his successor from the electorate.

And yet the first major challenge to this system had appeared when S.W.R.D. Bandaranaike crossed over to the opposition in July 1951 with a small group of his supporters. In September 1951 the Sri Lanka Freedom Party was inaugurated as a centrist political force which deliberately sought to become the focal point of all interest groups dissatisfied with the UNP which were, at the same time, opposed to Marxist solutions to the country's problems. The nucleus of a democratic alternative to the UNP had emerged.

Its populist program was directed at the large protest vote that went to the Marxist parties for want of an alternative, and to the rural areas which formed the basis of the UNP's hold on political power in the country. The Marxist left had failed to make much of an impact on the rural areas, and their perennial ideological disputes, their shifts and rifts and re-alignments, incomprehensible to the bulk of the electorate, carried no meaning to all save the true believers. More important the left was just as unsympathetic as the UNP leadership to the aspirations of the Buddhist activists with regard to religion, language and culture.

Ironically, however, neither of the protagonists — the UNP government nor its left-wing critics — showed much understanding of the sense of outrage and indignation of the Buddhists at what they regarded as the historic injustices suffered by their religion under western rule. The affront was to culture no less than to religion, and the resentment was felt even more strongly by the *ayurvedic* physician, the Sinhalese school master and the notary than by the *bhikkhus*. And as regards religion, it was the withdrawal of the traditional patronage and consequent precedence and prestige that was resented and it was to these groups, with their deep sense of grievance, social and economic discontent, and bitterness at the neglect by both the UNP and its left-wing critics, that the SLFP turned. Beneath the surface these religious, cultural and linguistic issues had been gathering momentum and developing into a force too powerful for the existing social and political set-up to accommodate or absorb. They were to tear the country apart within a decade of 1948 and accomplish the discomfiture of both the UNP and its left-wing critics.

References

[1] *Soulbury Report*, Chapter VIII, pp. 41-50; see particularly p. 50, paras 177-8.

[2] *Soulbury Report*, Chapter XIII, pp. 68-71.

[3] See, Jane Russell 'The Dance of the Turkey-Cock — The Jaffna Boycott of 1931' in *CJHSS* n.s. VIII(1) pp. 47-67; see also S. Kadiragamar, 'The Jaffna Youth Congress' in *Handy Perimpanayagam — A Memorial Volume* (Jaffna, 1980) pp. 1-112, see particularly pp. 71-82.

[4] *Hansard* [State Council] 1945 Vol. II, columns 7009-13 for Jayah's speech, and 7059-66 for Razik's speech.

[5] Chapter XI, pp. 60-64; see also Chapter X, particularly pp. 56-60.

[6] J.R. Jayewardene to Jawaharlal Nehru, 20 October 1945, printed in Roberts, *Documents*, IV, p. 2741.

[7] C.O..54/986/file 55541/5, Monck-Mason-Moore to C.E.J. Gent, Private and confidential letter of 20 November 1945.

[8] At the conclusion of the debate he took great delight in informing the house that 89% of the full membership of the house, and 94% of those present in the debate had voted in favor.

[9] Printed in Roberts, *Documents*, IV, pp. 2743-4. Though this letter was signed by the Congress President of this period, George E. de Silva, the draft was prepared by J.R. Jayewardene.

[10] The reference was to *The Discovery of India*, published in 1942.

[11] Hugh Tinker, *The Banyan Tree: Overseas Emigrants from India, Pakistan and Bangladesh* (Oxford, 1977) p. 38-39; also his *Separate and Unequal: India and Indians in the British Commonwealth, 1920-1950* (London, 1976) p. 181.

[12] Hugh Tinker, *The Banyan Tree, op. cit.*, p. 40; and *Separate and Unequal, op. cit.*, pp. 198-199.

[13] *Ibid.*

[14] Tinker contradicts himself on this question in his two books: in *Banyan Tree* p. 48, he argues that this would have allowed more Indians to qualify than under the 1941 formula; in *Separate and Unequal*, p. 339, he argues that the terms were less favorable.

[15] In *Banyan Tree*, p. 40, and *Separate and Unequal*, p. 339.

[16] See, Walpola Rahula, *The Heritage of the Bhikkhu*, (Grove Press, 1974) p. 134.

[17] In December 1943 he had masterminded the election of A. Mahadeva as Minister of Home Affairs thus bringing to an end the controversial device of a 'Pan Sinhalese' ministry elected in 1936 in the hope of presenting a cohesive program of constitutional reform to Whitehall without the inconvenience of dissident voices in the Board of Ministers. Mahadeva, incidentally, was the first Tamil to become a Minister under the Donoughmore reforms. Perianan Sunderam, an Indian, had been a Minister in the first State Council.

[18] The All Ceylon Muslim League, and the All Ceylon Moors' Association supported the new party. A.R.A. Razik became one of its founder joint Treasurers (the other being J.R. Jayewardene).

[19] *The Soulbury Report*, p. 42.

[20] Hugh Tinker, *The Banyan Tree, op.cit.*, p. 40, *Separate and Unequal, op.cit.*, p. 338-340.

PART III

The Triumph of
Linguistic Nationalism
c 1951 - 1972

Part III

The Triumph of Linguistic Nationalism
c 1951 - 1972

Introduction

Linguistic Nationalism

In the years after independence one of the major preoccupations of the government was with the need to establish a sense of Sri Lankan nationalism on territorial lines, and under D.S. Senanayake's leadership political leaders aimed at subordinating communal differences to the common goal of strengthening the foundations of nationhood. The primary aim was the establishment of a stable equilibrium of ethnic forces within a poly-ethnic polity.

Their vision of the goal of political endeavor was of a territorial nationalism without any special, much less, exclusive association with any ethnic group, or any section of an ethnic group. In this as well as in the emphasis on the concept of a poly-ethnic polity they were at one with their Marxist critics. Indeed the Marxist version was much more comprehensive because it encompassed the Indian plantation workers as well, a group which not even the most liberal of the mainstream politicians were willing to regard as an integral element of a Sri Lanka polity. Sri Lanka was to be a secular state. In this too they and their Marxist critics saw eye to eye. For many years it seemed as though these policies had succeeded, but beneath the surface powerful forces were at work to upset the equilibrium; ideals of reconciliation and harmony gave way before the stresses released by the divisive forces of language and religion, the central feature of Part III of this volume. This shift was consistent with the essence of party politics in which, given a common basis of agreement, the numerically larger group could peacefully alter the power structure. Thus the Sinhalese-Buddhist majority, long dormant, began to assert its national dominance. The first casualties were the concepts of a poly-ethnic polity, of a Sri Lankan nationalism, and of a secular state.

By mid-1950s the UNP's position in the country was being undermined, even though its hold on Parliament appeared to be as strong as ever. The economy was faltering, after a period of prosperity, and an attempt to reduce the budgetary allocation for food subsidies provoked violent opposition, organized by the left-wing parties, in August 1953. Besides, religious, cultural and linguistic issues were gathering momentum and in combination developed into a force too powerful for the existing social and political set-up to accommodate or absorb. Its left-wing opponents were just as unresponsive, and indeed generally more so than the government, to expressions of outrage and indignation of the Buddhists at what they regarded as the historic injustices suffered by their religion under Western rule.

Bandaranaike successfully channelled this discontent into an election campaign which swept the UNP out of office in 1956. His decisive victory was a significant turning point in Sri Lanka's history, for it represented the rejection of the concept of a Sri Lanka nationalism, based on pluralism, which Senanayake had striven to nurture, and the substitution of a more democratic and populist nationalism which was at the same time fundamentally divisive in its impact on the country because it was unabashedly Sinhalese and Buddhist in content. Against the background of the worldwide celebration in 1956 of the 2,500th anniversary of the death of the Buddha, an intense religious fervor became the catalyst of a populist nationalism whose explosive effect was derived from its inter-connection with language. Language became the basis of nationalism and this metamorphosis of nationalism affected both the Sinhalese and Tamil populations.

> "For a man to speak one language rather than another," the anthropologist Edmund Leach reminds us, "is a ritual act; it is a statement about one's personal status; to speak the same language as one's neighbours expresses solidarity with these neighbours, to speak a different language from one's neighbours expresses social distance or even hostility."[1]

Leach made these comments with highland Burma in mind, but they were equally valid for contemporary Sri Lanka or India.

As we shall see in Chapter XI, all the major Sri Lankan political parties of the day were baffled by this novel political phenomenon of linguistic nationalism. Yet the imperatives of their calling compelled each in turn to define their attitude to it. Most of them eventually succumbed to the blandishments of linguistic nationalism. None understood the perils involved.

In a brilliant essay, Lewis Namier has spelled out the dangers inherent in the Mazzinian precept that "The nation is the universality of the citizens speaking the same tongue."[2] "Territorial nationality," Namier explained,

> "is essentially conservative, for it is the product of a long historical development; nationalisms which place the emphasis on language almost invariably seek change, since no existing satiated community singles out one principle for its basis..."[3]

Namier spoke of the explosive impact of linguistic nationalism on mid-nineteenth century Central and East-Central Europe

> "— the demand that the state should be coextensive with linguistic nationality was an internationally revolutionary postulate which, seeing that nations are seldom linguistically segregated, proved destructive both of constitutional growth and of international peace."[4]

Illustrating this by reference to Germany he wrote of the 'double contradictory answer' given to the question 'what is the German's Fatherland?': 'Whatever speaks German shall become German': 'Whatever is German shall remain German.'[5]

A century later the same phenomenon had a near-revolutionary impact on the politics of South Asia. It compelled a skeptical Nehru to yield to pressures which re-drew the map of India, internally, on the basis of linguistic states; it eventually proved to be a stronger force than religion as its disruptive effects on the old Pakistan of two separate wings showed; and in Sri Lanka it helped destroy the civil peace for a decade or more. Sinhalese politicians who sought power through championing linguistic nationalism confronted the fearful prospect of a rival linguistic nationalism of the Tamils, and all its attendant risks and dangers both internal and external.

The consequences of the transformation may be outlined as follows: Firstly, the concept of a poly-ethnic polity ceased to be politically viable any longer. In Sinhalese the words for nation, 'race' and people are practically synonymous, and a multi-ethnic or multi-communal nation or state is incomprehensible to the popular mind. The emphasis on Sri Lanka as the land of the Sinhalese carried an emotional popular appeal compared with which the concept of a multi-ethnic polity was a meaningless abstraction.

Secondly, the abandonment of the concept of a poly-ethnic polity was justified by laying stress on the western concept of a democratic sanction deriving its validity from the clear numerical superiority of the Sinhalese-speaking group. At the same time the focus continued to be an all-island one, and Sinhalese nationalism was consciously or unconsciously treated as being identical with a Sri Lanka nationalism. The minorities, and in particular the Sri Lanka Tamils, refused to endorse the assumption that Sinhalese nationalism was interchangeable with the larger Sri Lanka nationalism. As a result 1956 marked a major turning point in Sri Lanka's recent history, and heralded the commencement of an era of ethnic tensions erupting occasionally into "race" riots and religious confrontation.

Similarly the association of Buddhism with the state, and the simultaneous reduction of Christian influence especially after 1960, were integral features of the abandonment of the concept of a polyethnic polity. There was mounting pressure for the declaration of Buddhism as the state religion, but this the political leaderships in both the major parties, the S.L.F.P. and the U.N.P., were able to resist. However, with the adoption of a republican constitution in 1972 the position changed. Chapter II of the Constitution laid it down that: "The Republic of Sri Lanka shall give to Buddhism the foremost place and accordingly it shall be the duty of the state to protect and foster Buddhism while assuring to all religions the rights granted by Section 18(1) (d)." The formula first devised by Governors Sir William Gregory and Sir Arthur Gordon in the late 19th century was still viable, but with the constitution of 1972 it had been stretched to its utmost limits. Sri Lanka had ceased to be a secular state pure and simple, even if it had not become a theocratic state which Buddhist pressure groups would have liked it to be.

Thirdly, linguistic nationalism was a populist nationalism, in contrast to the elitist constitutionalism of the early years after independence. The masses — and more especially the rural masses — had entered the political arena, and no longer could political activity be confined to the elite. This linguistic nationalism, despite its seeming novelty at the time it first appeared in the mid-1950s, had its roots in the recent past, and especially in the temperance movement of the early years of the twentieth century when a similar mixture of religious fervor and commitment to national culture had captured the imagination of the Sinhalese people, particularly in the rural areas of the low country, and in the towns in all parts of the island save the Tamil areas. In the 1950s the scale was wider, and the appeal deeper.

One of the notable consequences of this emergence of Sinhalese Buddhist populism was the setback it gave the Marxist movement.

With independence and the first elections to the House of Representatives in 1947, they had emerged as the most potent challenge to the government of the day, if not yet a credible alternative to it. To this status of the alternative government they always aspired, and it was this aspiration which was thwarted by the emergence of linguistic nationalism and the populist form it took in the mid-1950s. With the emergence of the language movement, they watched the gains of the past disappear, and the prospects of the future become much more limited. They found to their dismay and discomfiture that linguistic nationalism had an appeal which cut across class interests, and that it evoked as deep a response from the Sinhalese working class as it did among the peasantry and the Sinhalese educated elite. The cosmopolitan outlook of the Marxists and their enlightened advocacy of a multi-ethnic secular polity proved to be profoundly disadvantageous, and they were compelled to compromise on these issues, without, however, any substantial political benefits. From the position of the alternative government they were reduced in time to the status of an appendage of the populist Sri Lanka Freedom Party.

Though the Buddhist movement was generally hostile to Marxist ideology, it had no strong opposition to the adoption of a socialist program. Since plantation enterprise, nascent industry and the island's trade were dominated by foreign capitalists, and the minorities seemed to be disproportionately influential within the indigenous capitalist class, Buddhist pressure groups viewed socialism as a means of redressing the balance in favour of the majority group. Every extension of state control over trade and industry could be justified on the ground that it helped curtail the influence of foreigners and the minorities. The Sinhalese Buddhist section of the capitalist class was not averse to socialism so long as its own economic interests were not affected. The result was that the populist Sri Lanka Freedom Party has been able to reconcile a commitment to a hazy socialism with an advocacy of the interests of a section of the indigenous capitalist class — the Sinhalese Buddhist segment of it.

Population Growth

In Sri Lanka's highly politicized society the state provides or regulates a variety of goods and services. Indeed its economy is state-dominated to a much greater extent than India's. Besides people have regular opportunities, through the processes of democratic elections, for expressing their concern about the way in which these goods and services are provided. And at these elections ethnic and religious differences — and more particularly the former — have often been focal points of political contention.

The inequality of development between the various ethnic and religious groups in the country excascerbates the tensions that result from this competition and especially so in the context of an economy which remained stagnant for much of the period since the late 1950s. Such inequalities are universal. They are also unpalatable to those who regard themselves as disadvantaged and chose to use their access to political power — especially if they are a majority group — to eliminate them. How these inequalities are distributed among the various groups in the country and how these latter view these inequalities remain hardy perennials in the politics of Sri Lanka. The passions they generate are often attributed exclusively to the competition between elite groups for administrative and political power and for employment. To do so is to discount, unrealistically, the role of the masses in ethnic conflict, and the play of powerful forces such as population growth.

As early as 1949 Sir Ivor Jennings, the Vice Chancellor of the University of Ceylon and constitutional adviser to the Prime Minister of the country, commenting on the island's affairs, warned of the economic implications of the island's astonishing rate of population increase, which had reached 3.0 percent per annum in that year, and he asserted with uncharacteristic exaggeration, that this was "the fundamental problem of [Sri Lanka's] economy." If it was not quite that, it was because at that stage, the increase in population was not concentrated in the under-25 group, but spread through all age groups. In the period 1950 to 1960 the rate of growth of the under-25 age group did not pose any insuperable problems, because the economy was expanding and could cope with an addition to the labor force of around 54,000 per annum as it did from the late 1940s to the mid-1950s. Thus the political system was not much disturbed by population pressure. Nevertheless, this rapid growth of population had the immediate effect of pushing up private and public consumption needs and reducing the surplus available for investment.

The full force of population growth over the period 1946 to 1960 hit the labor market in the 1960s. Those between 15 and 65 years of age, roughly the working population, increased from 5.25 million to over

7.5 million in that decade. More important was the increase in the number of those aged 25 years and less; while their proportion of the total population did not show any significant rise, they had nearly doubled in numbers in 22 years, from 3.8 million in 1946 to 4.9 million in 1955, 6.5 million in 1965 and 7.2 million in mid-1968. In the period 1960 to 1970 the growth in the number of those seeking employment far outran the demand for labor generated by the country's stagnant economy. Estimated open unemployment climbed from 370,000 in 1959 to 550,000 in 1969-70, about 14% of the work force or one-twentieth of the island's popultion.

After 1960-1 primary and secondary education became, for all practical puposes, a state monopoly. University education had always been entirely state-financed, and so for that matter were most areas of technical education. State expenditure on primary and secondary education is one of the highest in Asia. The literacy rate, if the 0-4 age group is excluded, is as high as 85% of the total population. But as a result of its long standing commitment to free — in the sense of free tuition — education at all levels, primary, secondary and tertiary, Sri Lanka from the 1960s became an outstanding example of the global phenomenon of educated unemployment.

For the governments of the 1960s and 1970s the political implications of this were ominous. Sri Lanka was one of the first countries in the world to lower its voting age to 18. Although this was done in 1959, the elections of 1960 were contested on the previous system of votes at 21, but at the general election of 1965 the 18-21 year-voters had cast their ballots for the first time. Their impact on the electorate was immediately felt in the contribution they made to the defeat of the government in power. This happened twice thereafter, in 1970 and 1977. But above all there were the events of 1971 when the age-old conflict of generations was transformed into a mini-civil war.

Population growth has abated somewhat from the mid and late 1970s but its pressure is still felt, a pressure which accounts for the intensity of the competition for employment. This competition which occurs at all levels and not merely at that of the elite has poisoned ethnic relations in the country.

Constitutional Reform

The third significant feature of this period was constitutional reform and the emergence of devolution of power as a major political issue. The survival of the Soulbury constitution, without any fundamental changes during the first two decades after independence, was more a matter of convenience than conviction. Two governments of these years, the UNP regime of 1952-56, and Bandaranaike's coalition of 1956-59, had either the requisite two-thirds majority or wide parliamentary support to effect constitutional reform. The former was not interested in constitutional reform. The left-wing both within and outside Parliament persisted in its opposition to the constitution but its power base was not strong enough or wide enough to make this opposition anything more than symbolic or ritualistic. The emergence to political prominence of the SLFP did not, initially, strengthen the forces of constitutional reform for the new party was not as dogmatically opposed to the Soulbury constitution as were the left-wing groups.

The survival of the Soulbury constitution, without fundamental change over these two decades, may be explained on a different basis as well. The comparative flexibility of the constitution, and the lack of a bill of fundamental rights in it enabled the political system to accommodate itself to a series of far-reaching changes most if not all of it asserting or re-asserting Sinhalese-Buddhist dominance of the Sri Lanka polity and most if not all adversely affecting the ethnic and religious minorities. It was evident that the constitutional obstacle of Section 29 (2) (b) would not operate so long as legislation was framed to ensure that while there might indeed be a restriction in fact but not in legal form, and the restriction was made applicable to all sections of the community and not to a specific group. Equally important, nationalization of local and foreign business ventures was facilitated by the fact that there was no provision in the constitution for just and expeditious payment of compensation. Thus there was no constitutional protection for special economic interests and property rights in general.

The salience of the complex problems of decentralization in Sri Lanka's contemporary politics begins in this period. The post-independence political structure of Sri Lanka was a highly centralized one — indeed, an over-centralized one. The process of centralization encouraged and deliberately pursued by the British in the nineteenth century have proved to be a formidably stable legacy. The early proponents of decentralization were Sinhalese: Bandaranaike, himself, argued in favor of federalism in 1926, and for a form of Provincial

Councils in the 1940s and the early years of independence; representatives of Kandyan opinion argued in favor of a three-unit federal structure for Sri Lanka in their representations to the Donoughmore and Soulbury Commissions. After independence the main, if not the sole, demand for devolution of power through federalism or a regional councils scheme has been the Federal Party. This demand and agitation provokes strong opposition from Sinhalese both in the mainstream political parties, as well as pressure groups representing Sinhalese Buddhist interests: all of them viewed the Tamils' demand for a federal state as nothing less than the thin end of the wedge of a separatist movement.

References

[1]   Edmund Leach, *The Political Systems of Highland Burma* (London, 1954) p. 59.

[2]   Quoted in Sir Lewis Namier 'Nationality and Liberty' in his *Vanished Supremacies* (London, 1962 edition) p. 46.

[3]   Namier, 'Nationality and Liberty' *op. cit.*, p. 46.

[4]   *Ibid*, pp. 46-47.

[5]   *Ibid*, p. 64.

Chapter XI

From Parity of Status
To 'Sinhala Only'
c 1952-56

Gradualism And Its Critics

While the *swabasha* movement had made steady if somewhat slow progress in the pre-independence period, there was a noticeable slackening in its pace in the first few years after independence. The first Cabinet of independent Sri Lanka included J.R. Jayewardene, Dudley Senanayake and S.W.R.D. Bandaranaike, all of whom had been prominent campaigners for *swabasha* in the early 1940s. They did not enjoy, as Cabinet Ministers, the independence from collective responsibility and the opportunities for individual initiatives on issues of national importance that their counterparts of the Donoughmore system revelled in. Cabinet policies were more often than not in the nature of a consensus, and the Prime Minister, D.S. Senanayake, who had been noticeably unenthusiastic on issues such as language and religion when these came up in the early 1940s, was now a more powerful influence on the making of policy. He applied the brakes whenever he thought he needed to do so. None chafed under these restraints more than Bandaranaike, an aspirant to the succession, and by now a very vocal advocate of an accelerated program on *swabasha* who made little effort to conceal his disappointment that *swabasha* did not rank at the very top in the priorities Senanayake set for Sri Lanka's first post-independence government. Not that there was any positive attempt to repudiate *swabasha*, but only that with Senanayake the emphasis was on caution because he perceived it to be an issue that could upset the balance of political forces he had constructed as the foundation of the post-independence Sri Lanka polity. To illustrate these trends: the introduction of the national languages in primary and secondary education proceeded along on the time-table set for it by the government; and, no less important, a National Language Commission was established on 23 May 1951, and it proceeded with it's work for two years, that is to say, reporting on the procedure to be followed in adopting Sinhalese and Tamil as the national languages.[1]

But change was in the air. In mid-1951 Bandaranaike crossed over to the opposition and proceeded shortly thereafter to establish the Sri Lanka Freedom Party, the successor to, and indeed the lineal descendant of his Sinhala Maha Sabha. Among the reasons he gave for his resignation from the government was the delay in implementing the *swabasha* policy decided upon in the mid-1940s. From 1951 onwards Bandaranaike pledged himself to campaigning for a full-blooded policy of *swabasha*, speedily implemented, a reversal of the policy of cautious advance he had publicly advocated when the new official language policy was adopted in 1944 on the initiative of J.R. Jayewardene. This was one of the main planks of the platform his party presented at the elections of 1952. The UNP under Dudley Sena-nayake, too stood for *swabasha*, but was committed also to a policy of gradualism. Bandaranaike, at this stage, had not yet begun espousing the elevation of Sinhalese to the status of the sole national language in place of English; he was, till early 1955 at least, ready to uphold the settlement on language reached in 1944.

However in the country at large, there was evidence, that a powerful and vocal section among the Sinhalese Buddhists was ready to repudiate that settlement and to call for the replacement of English by Sinhalese only. There were, by 1953, glimpses of this policy at an official level. Thus Sir Arthur Wijewardene, one time Chief Justice, as chairman of the Official Language Commission, issued a rider to the final report of the Commission[2] in which he came out in favor of English being replaced by one and not two official languages, that is to say, by Sinhalese. "In my opinion, " Wijewardene asserted,

> "the replacement of English by *swabasha* would have been very much
> easier if instead of two *swabasha* languages as Official Languages one
> alone had been accepted in terms of the motion introduced by Mr. J.R.
> Jayewardene in the State Council on 22 June 1943."[3]

The terms of reference of the Commission of which he was chairman clearly referred to Sinhalese and Tamil as the two official languages. He had been chosen by the government of the day to head this prestigious Commission of Inquiry on a politically sensitive issue in the hope that he would rise above the partisan passions of his times; he ended by succumbing to those as easily as lesser mortals who were presumed to be less detached. The following year Wijewardene repeated this opinion even more emphatically in a rider to a report of the Commission on the National Languages in Higher Education.[4] Wijewardene was giving quasi-legal recognition to the mounting 'Sinhala-only' agitation in the country led by a very vocal combination of concerned *bhikkhus*, and the leadership of the Buddhist Theosophical Society and the Young Men's Buddhist Association. Still, as late as mid-1954 none of the major political parties in the country had thought fit to modify their language policy to suit this new situation.[5]

The mid-1950s mark a critically important watershed in the recent history of the island. For one thing there was the religious fervor associated with the *Buddha Jayanthi* — a theme to which we shall turn later in this chapter — and its explosive effect derived from its connection with language. Buddhism and Sinhalese were so closely intertwined that it was impossible to treat either in isolation. The crucial significance of the renewed link between language and religion was that Buddhist activism, which had been directed so far against the privileged position enjoyed by Christianity and Christians in Sri Lanka, shifted its attention to the Tamil minority as well. Buddhist activists and the Sinhalese educated intelligentsia had seldom, in the recent past, exerted influence on a national scale, and they felt that they had been unjustly excluded by the English-educated elite from a share of power commensurate with their numbers, and that rewarding careers were closed to them by the pervasive dominance of English as the language of administration. Concentrating their attention on the superior educational advantages enjoyed by the Tamil minority, they set their sights on the demolition of the language settlement arrived at in 1944-45 — that Sinhalese and Tamil should eventually replace English as the national languages — and insisted instead on "Sinhala only", the slogan which became the main plank of the coalition of parties set up by Bandaranaike in anticipation of the general election of 1956 (Bandaranaike himself had strongly endorsed the language-settlement of 1944-45). For the Tamils the implications of the change in language policy were starkly clear. It meant that they would be at a great disadvantage in future in employment, in the administration of the country, and eventually in the professions as well. But more importantly once language became the determinant of national consciousness, there were fears that the Tamils' identity as a distinct ethnic group would be eroded through a policy of assimilation. As we shall see in a later chapter this transformation of nationalism affected them as well — language became the focal point of a new ethnic consciousness, of two rival nationalisms.

The 'Sinhala-only' campaign brought together a formidable array of forces which had hitherto been unable if not unwilling to unite in support of a common program: the Sinhalese school teachers, *Ayurvedic* physicians, Sinhalese writers, and the *bhikkhus*. On 4 September 1954 a meeting convened by the Sinhalese teachers association — the Lanka Jatika Guru Sangamaya —brought these groups together in a federation of five associations (including representatives of peasants) which came to be called the Pancha Maha Bala Mandalaya.

Certainly the then Prime Minister, Sir John Kotelawala (1953-56) was singularly ill-equipped to handle the political problems emerging from the metamorphosis in nationalism that came about at this time. He had no feeling for language, culture and religion, and his lifestyle gave great offense to the burgeoning Buddhist movement. More to the point his maladroit handling of these diametrically opposed pressures — of the strident voices associated with the Pancha Maha Bala Mandalaya clamoring for and increasingly insistent on the imposition of Sinhalese as the sole official language, and the fears of the Tamils that such a change would be a severe handicap in, and for, years to come — converted the language controversy into a highly inflammable public issue. Thus while on an official visit to the Tamil areas in the north of the island late in 1954, he made a public announcement that he would introduce constitutional provisions for parity of status for the two languages.[6] That pronouncement was as ill-advised as it was inopportune and needlessly provocative. The government could not have mustered the special majority required for such a constitutional amendment. As it was, the offer to introduce it provoked a massive expression of opposition from among the Sinhalese.

The thunderstorm of protests against the Prime Minister's declared intention to elevate the language settlement of 1944 to the status of a constitutional provision took every section of opinion by surprise. The Pancha Maha Bala Mandalaya formed to intensify pressure on the government on behalf of a policy of Sinhala only, led the protest movement.

But the full force of its fury first fell on the two Marxist parties, the Lanka Sama Samaja Party and the Communist Party which at this time were firm supporters of a policy of parity of status for the Sinhalese and Tamil as national languages. These two parties had introduced a motion in Parliament calling for a declaration on these lines. They then organized two public meetings at the Colombo Town Hall, on 12 October 1955 by the Communist Party and on 16 October 1955 by the Lanka Sama Samja Party to explain their stand to the public. Both meetings were broken up by 'Sinhala-only' activists led by *bhikkhus*. In a bid to mobilize even wider support for the cause of Sinhalese as the sole national language, the Pancha Maha Bala Mandalaya organized an oath taking ceremony at Anuradhapura on 29 October 1955. A motorcade that left from Colombo proved to be a triumphant procession, and the ceremony presided over by *bhikkhu* attracted an enormous crowd.

The Buddha Jayanthi

In the meantime a committee of inquiry appointed by the All Ceylon Buddhist Congress was preparing a major report on the state of Buddhism in the country. Its membership was composed of prominent Buddhist laymen, many of whom were associated with the agitation for 'Sinhala-only', and a number of eminent *bhikkhus*. The committee visited 37 urban centers on the island, and was greeted everywhere with processions and largely attended public meetings at which the presumed parlous plight of the Buddhist religion was the main theme of speakers from the area in which the meeting was held, as well as of course, the members of the committee themselves.

The committee issued a path-breaking report on 4 February 1956. It contained a detailed exposition of the disadvantageous position of Buddhism in the mid-20th century, and blamed this on the cumulative effect of several centuries of foreign rule and on the neglect of post-independence governments of Sri Lanka as well. The report made it abundantly clear that the redress of Buddhist grievances was a matter of the utmost urgency, and that this could only be achieved through the political process. The fact that the report was presented to the "People of Lanka" and not to the government signified that in the committee's view, the solutions lay with the former. An English version of the report bearing the title *The Betrayal of Buddhism* was also issued.[7]

For nearly a decade after 1947 the issues which the Buddhist activists of the 1940s, and the Vidyalankara *bhikkhus* had raised lay dormant, but not extinct. It would be fair to say that the lamps that they had lit in their day were not entirely extinguished. When the time came and the fuel of religious enthusiasm was added once more, the flames roared back into fervent life. This happened by the mid-1950s, in the messianic atmosphere of the *Buddha Jayanthi*, the world-wide commemoration due to be celebrated in May 1956, of the 2500th anniversary of the death of Buddha.

This revival of religious enthusiasm found the Vidyalankara *bhikkhus* sharing the leadership in activism with others. Those others were not by any means the traditional, conventional *bhikkhus* who would renounce the world, but men who were just as intent on reform as the Vidyalankara *bhikkhus*, whose inspiration however, was not Marxism or even socialism. Their inspiration was at best a vague populism, mixed with a deep and abiding nationalist fervor. They were, in brief, another breed of political *bhikkhu*, a breed whose activity was less vulnerable to the criticisms directed at the Marxist *bhikkhus* because it was rooted in tradition, and because they worked in tandem with the lay Buddhist leadership. They also worked with the Vidyalankara *bhikkhus*. Many of these new activists were members of Bandaranaike's SLFP, some of them holding positions of influence in its executive committee. Among them were *bhikkhu* Mapitigama Buddharakkhita the *viharadhipathi* (the chief *bhikkhu*) of the Kelaniya temple, and an *alumnus* of the Vidyalankara *pirivena*.

The *Buddha Jayanthi* offered Buddhist activists the opportunity to appeal over the heads of the government and the political establishment of the day, to the people, for a restoration of the traditional convergence of nation, religion and ethnicity — Sri Lanka, Sinhalese and Buddhist. The problem that confronted the government and its critics alike was that the advantages of this convergence in sustaining a national identity and self-confidence were all too often negated by the vocal dissent of minority groups who rejected this facile identification of sectional — although they were those of an overwhelming majority — with national interests. This was the classic dilemma of majoritarian rule in a plural society.

Buddhism and Buddhist interests had suffered, and in the perception of Buddhist activists, still suffered from the decline in status and prestige that had occured under colonial rule, and the drive by the Buddhist leadership to secure a restoration of a balance of influence in national life in favor of their co-religionists, had as its fundamental principle the grant of special concessions to Buddhists. Under British rule the various indigenous religious groups had sought to protect their own interests in the context of the government's avowed formal neutrality in religious affairs that had prevailed since the last quarter of the nineteenth century. Through the efforts of organizations such as the Buddhist Theosophical Society. Buddhists had made substantial progress in winning back many of their lost rights but at independence, and in the first decade after independence, the advances made only served to emphasize the gap between aspiration and reality.

In education, for instance, Christian schools continued to hold sway despite the education reforms of the 1940s, and retained much of the prestige they had enjoyed in the days of British rule, while the preponderance of Christians and other minorities in public life especially in the higher bureaucracy, in the professions and in business, remained intact although under greater pressure than in the past, while Buddhists remained under-represented in public life in proportion to their numbers in the population. The balance, however, was inevitably shifting in favor of the Sinhalese Buddhists, but this process was also inevitably slow and in measured stages. Buddhist activists were not only thoroughly dissatisfied with the pace at which the balance was shifting but they also attributed the survival of Christian and minority privilege to the fact that competition between the two groups had been, and continued to be, heavily biased against the Buddhists. The most notable exposition of this line of argument came in documents such as the report of the Buddhist Committee of Inquiry (1956) referred to earlier in this chapter, and D.C. Vijayawardena's book *Revolt in the Temple*. The remedy they advocated was active state intervention in favor of Buddhism. In taking this stand they were moving away, consciously perhaps, from the line of policy adhered to consistently by men like Olcott and his associates who

> "were entirely willing to accept the challenges of competition and who were primarily concerned with building voluntary and autonomous organizations among Buddhists which would be strong enough to compete with the Christian ones ..."[9]

The crux of the problem was that while the political system had accommodated itself since 1931 to the fact of Buddhist-Sinhalese predominance, other areas of public life lagged far behind in adjusting to that same demographic reality. What happened in the mid-1950s was that a concern for the enhancement of the status of Buddhism became, in the messianic atmosphere of the *Buddha Jayanthi*, the prime determinant of a process of change whose main thrust was the extension of the predominance established by Sinhalese Buddhists in the political sphere into all other areas of activity.

The proposal that the *Buddha Jayanthi* be celebrated as a major national event under the auspicies of the government had come from Dudley Senanayake, then a backbench MP in semi-retirement from politics. It was readily accepted by the Kotalawela government, which proceeded to establish the Lanka Bauddha Mandalaya in October 1954 to organize and direct the *Buddha Jayanthi* activities. That body initiated an ambitious and costly program of work continuing into the Jayanthi year 1956-57 as well as beyond it. The active initiative of the government and the extent of its participation in these celebrations no doubt marked a "departure from the principles of separation of politics and religion and the formal religious neutrality of the government"[10] but no Prime Minister of the day, not even one as masterful as D.S. Senanayake, could have entirely refrained from lending the support of the state to this unique religious event.

By extending state support to Buddhism, Kotelawala was seeking to gain legitimacy for his government and popularity both for it and himself. But to no avail. To the Buddhist activists the Prime Minister was both an anachronism and a philistine and they made it their aim to replace him by a more acceptable national figure. It is often forgotten that their first choice, significantly enough, was Dudley Senanayake. But he declined their offer, first because his health was still troubling him and secondly because he saw the political implications of the program he was being called upon to champion, and these disturbed him. It was at this point that they turned to Bandaranaike, who had fewer compunctions and little hesitation about accepting their program, because he had been advocating much the same policies for many years. The potentially disruptive effect of the program did not deter him from adopting it with enthusiasm because he was confident of his ability to ride the storm and to control the turbulent forces he was being asked to lead.

The Election Of April 1956

The decision to hold the general election in 1956 offended Buddhist activists who were anxious to keep the year free of political agitation and partisan politics for the *Buddha Jayanthi* celebrations. They urged the Prime Minister to postpone the elections till after these celebrations were over, but this he refused to do. Instead he aggravated the offense by initiating the first phase of the *Buddha Jayanthi* celebrations before the elections, a move which the most articulate sections of the *sangha* — a majority in fact —regarded as a blatantly cynical exploitation of religious sentiment by a man who, they believed, had neither a sense of occasion nor any genuine love for Buddhism.

The opposition parties were now better prepared than ever before for their encounter with the UNP. This time the forces ranged against the UNP were altogether more formidable, because they were united — on the basis of an electoral agreement — unlike in 1952 or 1947. Bandaranaike's SLFP was recognized as the most viable alternative to the UNP and was, on that account, given all possible support in the prime objective of defeating the UNP. Bandaranaike, having protected his left flank by arranging a no-contest pact with the two leading Marxist parties, the LSSP and CP in September-October 1955, joined forces with more congenial allies in the shape of a section of the LSSP (under Philip Gunawardane) and two smaller Sinhalese parties, in the Mahajana Eksath Peramuna (the Peoples United Front). In its election manifesto issued on 7 March 1956 the MEP pledged itself to make Sinhalese the official language of the country, to foster *Ayurveda*, to accept the recommendations of the Buddhist Committee of Inquiry, and to reorganize the system of education in accordance with the requirements of a national — that is to say, Buddhist — cultural renaissance.

How the two major parties, the UNP and the SLFP, both hurriedly changed their language policy to one of Sinhalese only has been dealt with in detail in many monographs[11] and it is not intended to survey that familiar territory here. The SLFP's change of policy came at its annual conference held on 17 December 1955 at Nittambuva in S.W.R.D. Bandaranaike's own electorate. The UNP's *volte-face* on language was less principled than that of its main rival. It came at its annual conference on 18 February 1956. But the patent insincerity of the conversion discredited both the Prime Minister and the UNP. They lost the support of the Tamils, and as events were to demonstrate so dramatically, made not the slightest headway among the Sinhalese.

Sir John Kotelawala completely misread the trends of the day in believing that this last minute *volte-face* on language would enable him to return to power at the next general elections. Scheduled for 1957, these were now advanced to April 1956 in the hope that the UNP could profit by its change of front on language at a time when the left-wing parties were apparently handicapped by their continued adherence to parity of status for Sinhalese and Tamil as national languages.

The MEP coalition scored a decisive victory,[12] but found the implementation of their policies a matter of the utmost difficulty. This was especially so with regard to language. The government sought to reconcile its commitment to make Sinhalese the sole national language, with the political and, indeed, practical necessity to make some concession to the Tamils as regards the use of their language. Extremists on both sides made this reconciliation almost impossible to achieve. Every concession to the Tamils was fought bitterly by forces within the SLFP, led by *bhikkhus*, as well as by opponents of the government such as the UNP. Thus the years 1956-58 were years of turmoil and violence, of 'race'-riots and long periods of rule under emergency regulations as the armed services and police sought to restore law and order.

References

1   The implementation of national language policy, except with regard to education, was placed under the direction of the Minister of Finance. J.R. Jayewardene held that position for the period 1947-53.

2   That commission issued five interim reports: *S.P.* XXI of 1951; *S.P.* III of 1952; *S.P.* IV of 1952; *S.P.* VIII of 1953 and *S.P.* XVIII of 1953. Its final report was *S.P.* XXII of 1953.

3   This rider was at the foot of p. 26 of *S.P.* XXII of 1953.

4   *S.P.* XXI of 1954 "Interim Report of the Commission on Higher Education in the National Languages..." Wijewardene's rider dated 23 August 1954 was on page 6.

5   In its issue of 15 April 1954 the *Lankadipa*, a Sinhalese newspaper of the Times of Ceylon group, reported a speech by S.W.R.D. Bandaranaike in which he had reiterated his stand on Sinhalese *and* Tamil as the two national languages of the country.

6   See the report of his speech in *The Times of Ceylon* 30 September 1954 and his speech in the House of Representatives, *Hansard* (House of Representatives) 1954 Vol. 21 Columns 485-486.

7   The English version was an abridgement of the original Sinhalese document.

8   Published in Colombo in 1953. The sub-title of the volume was "Composed to Commemorate 2500 years of the Land, the Race and the Faith."

9   K. Malalgoda, 'Buddhism in Post-Independence Sri Lanka' in *CJHSS*, n.s. IV (1 & 2) 1974, p. 96.

10   Malalgoda, *op.cit.* p. 95

11   The most comprehensive and perceptive account is W. Howard Wriggins, *Ceylon: Dilemmas of a New Nation* (Princeton: 1960). See also D.E. Smith (ed) *South Asian Religion and Politics* (Princeton: 1966) especially pp. 453-488.

12   Wriggins, *Ceylon: Dilemmas of a New Nation, op.cit.*

Chapter XII

Dilemmas of Decentralization 1956-1972

Bandaranaike And Federalism

While Bandaranaike had ridden to office on a massive wave of Sinhalese-Buddhist emotion, the sobering realities of political power compelled him to impose restraints. The riots that broke out in the wake of his *Official Language Act No. 33 of 1956* (the 'Sinhala-Only' bill as it came to be known popularly) introduced very early in the life of the new administration, underlined the combustible nature of linguistic nationalism in a plural society.

The most notable feature of the *Official Language Act* of 1956 was its stark brevity; a brevity which reflected a failure and a refusal to come to grips with the complex issues involved in introducing this change in language policy, and in implementing it. Bandaranaike had coined the popular slogan 'Sinhala Only, and in twenty-four hours', and in his hour of victory he was compelled to admit that it would take considerably longer than that to implement that policy. In retrospect it would appear that his main interest was in establishing the principle of one national language rather than two. That done, the process of implementation could be on a step by step basis. Thus an important feature of the *Official Language Act*, introduced and successfully piloted through the Legislature in 1956, was that its implementation would be stretched out over a period of five years, till 31 December 1960, a period which Bandaranaike expected to use to devise or negotiate modifications and adjustments to make the change in language policy palatable to the Tamils.

In August 1956, in the meantime, the Federal Party at a convention held in Trincomalee, set out a list of demands on behalf of the Tamils. The first among these was autonomy for the Northern and Eastern

Provinces under a federal constitution; next came parity of status for Sinhalese and Tamil as official languages; and a satisfactory settlement of the citizenship rights of the Indian plantation workers in the island.

Bandaranaike for his part responded with two gestures of conciliation: the draft *Regional Councils Bill* published in July 1957, and the *Tamil Language (Special Provisions) Act* No. 28 of 1958. The latter, important concession though it was, and introduced to assuage the feelings of the Tamils, was not enough to mollify them after the trauma of the 'race' riots of 1956 and 1958. The regulations required for the effective implementation of this act were not submitted for parliamentary approval till 1966. Bandaranaike's assassination in September 1959 and the political instability that followed it explains some part of this delay, but not all of it. Indeed the regulations were passed by Parliament early in 1966, and that too by a UNP-led coalition, and in the teeth of opposition from the SLFP.

The *Regional Councils Bill* proved to be a major turning point in the history of Bandaranaike's administration. It served to alienate him from a powerful and very vocal section of the Buddhist movement. Secondly, it offered the UNP a convenient point of opposition to Bandaranaike, and one which greatly embarrassed him with his sources of political support. Thirdly, the eventual failure to introduce it disappointed the Tamils, who as we shall see, were persuaded to support it — with modifications introduced in response to their requests — as part of a political arrangement designed to effect an accommodation between the government and the main Tamil political party. Indeed, the failure to implement it eroded his credibility as a leader and eventually contributed powerfully to undermining the strength of his administration.

The fact, however, was that many of Bandaranaike's problems at this time stemmed from causes he had espoused in the past, policies he had advocated, issues he had raised, and the contradictions that flowed from them all after he had achieved his ambition of becoming Prime Minister. He was to find that the past — his own past, in particular —was often a hostage to the future and *vice-versa*. Thus, as we have seen, Bandaranaike's eminence in politics came, in part, from his commitment to the Buddhist movement, and from his eloquent advocacy of the cause of Sinhalese nationalism as distinct from a Ceylonese or Sri Lankan nationalism. Indeed, he and his Sinhala Maha Sabha had denied the authenticity of a Ceylonese or Sri Lankan nationalism, and its validity as a political concept. Instead he advocated 'a pluralist and pyramidal' structure:

> "We [i.e., the Sinhala Maha Sabha] saw differences amongst our own people — caste distinctions, up-country low-country distinctions, religious distinctions, and various other distinctions — and we felt therefore that we should achieve unity, which is the goal of us all. Surely the best method was to start from the lower rung; firstly, unity among the Sinhalese; and secondly, whilst uniting the Sinhalese, to work for the higher unity, the unity of all communities."[1]

This argument was disingenuous, and in any case, the last of these aspirations — "the higher unity, the unity of all communities" was in total contradiction of the *raison d'etre* of the Sinhala Maha Sabha. As Prime Minister in the mid-1950s he had achieved a personal political triumph and master-minded the triumph of Sinhalese nationalism. He turned now to the higher unity, but found it well beyond his grasp; when he preached the virtues of that higher unity, his voice did not carry conviction. There were, and had been, far too many twists and turns and inconsistencies.

After all he had begun his political career in the 1920s as an advocate of a federal political structure for Sri Lanka, as a means — so he argued — of bringing about better understanding among the island's several ethnic groups. The federal system he espoused was to be based on the existing provincial system of nine units, and was more elaborate than the three regions of the federal polity the Kandyans advocated when they appeared before the Donoughmore Commission. Federalism had been, for a time, the main plank of the political platform of the youthful — and not very influential — political group, the Progressive Nationalist Party which he established in the mid-1920s. The narrowing of Bandaranaike's political vision is seen in the change in nomenclature of the parties he led: from the Progressive Nationalist Party to the Sinhala Maha Sabha. The more influential political leaders of the day, Sinhalese as well as Tamil, were not at all receptive to the appeal for a federal political structure from whatever source the demand for it came.

Bandaranaike's ardor for federalism had cooled over the years —in the 1930s and 1940s he turned from federalism to decentralization of administration — and it was a grim irony that during his years as Prime Minister, the moments of his greatest political triumphs, he should have been called upon to articulate the strong opposition of the Sinhalese to any attempt to establish a federal political structure.

The Donoughmore Commissioners had seen democratization and

expansion of local government institutions as the remedy to the prevailing overcentralization of administration. This emphasis on the development of local government institutions as the path to decentralization was part of the British political tradition. As Minister of Local Government in the days of the second State Council (1936-47) Bandaranaike had been the principal advocate of a system of provincial councils (avowedly modeled on the British County Councils) as the apex of the island's modern local government system. These projected provincial councils were intended to give more formal institutional shape to decentralization and democratization at the provincial level. The point of departure, we need to repeat, was the Donoughmore Report. In July 1940, R.S.S. Gunawardene, a close associate of Bandaranaike's, introduced a motion in the State Council urging the establishment of provincial councils;[2] a report of the Executive Committee of the State Council on Local Government set out in outline the powers of these councils — executive, advisory and supervisory. The State Council's approval of the principle of establishing provincial councils, reflected the existence of a national consensus on a scheme of decentralization of administration. The legislation required for the purpose of establishing these councils was never presented for consideration by the Legislature. It was never prepared, and so an excellent opportunity was missed.

Bandaranaike's failure in this regard was in striking contrast to the success of his Ministerial colleague, C.W.W. Kannangara, in education where his persistence prevailed over the powerful vested interests arrayed against him at the Ministerial, legislative and wider national level. There is the contrast also with J.R. Jayewardene, who as a backbencher and a newcomer to the legislature, piloted the landmark language reforms through the Legislature in 1943-44. Bandaranaike's task was simpler than theirs for neither in the Legislature nor in the country was there any opposition at all on the question of the regional councils.

His commitment to regional councils continued after independence, but as a Cabinet Minister he faced two interlocking obstacles, one institutional and the other personal. The establishment of these councils inevitably called for a reduction of the powers of Ministries under the control of his Cabinet colleagues. None of them showed much willingness to accept a dimunition of their own political and administrative authority. This factor has proved to be a perennial one in Sri Lanka's post-independence political history: as we shall see it contributed greatly to reducing the effectiveness of the district level councils introduced in 1981. Sri Lankan Cabinet Ministers have zealously protected their authority and powers from their own Parliamentary Deputy Ministers no less than from local government and other bodies. Besides, Bandaranaike was seen to havr established a solid political base through the expansion and revitalization of local government. The extension of this system through powerful regional councils was perceived as a calculated attempt to consolidate his political base. Because he was the Prime Minister's main political rival within the government these regional councils were viewed as institutions which were likely to confer an overwhelming political advantage on him in the coming struggle for the succession to D.S. Senanayake. There was a third factor as well: the first post-independence government faced new and more urgent concerns, and decentralization of administration was given very low priority in its program of action. Besides, the political consensus on provincial councils proved to be very shortlived. It evaporated rapidly with the emergence of the Federal Party as the principal ethnic political party of the Sri Lanka Tamils.

Bandaranaike always argued — i.e., before independence and after — that the provincial councils and the concept of regional autonomy these councils embodied were ideally suited for the purpose of coping with the Sinhalese-Tamil rivalries and reducing resulting tensions. Once he became Prime Minister in 1956 he was at last able to take the initiative in introducing his provincial councils scheme. He did so at a time when the Sinhalese suspected any reduction of the authority of the central government as an unwarranted concession to Tamil pressure for a federal state. To make matters worse for him, when he modified his scheme to accommodate the Federal Party, the worst suspicions of his Sinhalese critics and political opponents appeared to be confirmed.

Tamil politicians in the forefront of this agitation for a federal state were vague, deliberately or unconsciously, in the terminology used in their arguments, and the distinction between provincial autonomy, states' rights in a federal union, and a separate state was blurred by a fog of verbiage, a point to which we shall return in a later chapter. The fact is that the Sinhalese, although an overwhelming majority of the population of the island, nevertheless have a minority complex *vis-a-vis* the Tamils. They feel encircled by the more than fifty million Tamil speaking people in present day Tamilnadu and in Sri Lanka. Within Sri

Lanka the Sinhalese outnumber the Tamils by more than four to one; but they in turn are outnumbered by more than five to one by the Tamil speaking people of South Asia. And the Federal Party's agitation aroused deep-seated atavistic fears among the Sinhalese of this threat from the Tamil mass in Southern India.

Historical traditions, cultural distinctions and geographic factors separate the Tamils of Sri Lanka and Tamilnadu from each other, and in the early years of independence in Sri Lanka the Tamils of the north and the east in the island had showed little inclination to identify themselves with the Tamils of Tamilnadu. Nevertheless the Sinhalese feared this possibility, and the campaign for a federal structure aggravated these fears. There were suspicions too of the attempt of the Federal Party to make the settlement of the problem of citizenship rights of Indian plantation workers in the island a plank in its political platform. Thus the program of action outlined by the Federal Party in August 1956 as a rejoinder to the change in language policy to which Bandaranaike's government was committed was regarded as having ominous long-term implications. It was in fact a grim unfolding of the political implications of the linguistic nationalism of the Tamils with local, and more ominously, sub-continental dimensions. The demands were reiterated in mid-1957 and the Federal Party pledged itself to launch a *satyagrapha* campaign to achieve these objectives.

The Bandaranaike-Chelvanayakam Pact

It was at this stage, when the extremists in the ranks of the coalition he led could think only in terms of maintaining pressure on the Tamils through a policy of confrontation, that Bandaranaike began negotiations with the Federal Party for an accommodation between the two parties as representatives of the Sinhalese and the Tamils respectively. The terms of the settlement he negotiated were published in July 1957, and it was evident that it went well beyond the language dispute *per se*: firstly, the Tamil language was to be given the status of an official language for administrative purposes in the Northern and Eastern Provinces; secondly, Bandaranaike agreed to modify the draft *Regional Councils Bill* to accommodate some of the demands of the Federal Party; and thirdly, he agreed to place limits on the settlement of

Sinhalese "colonists" in irrigation schemes in the Northern and Eastern Provinces so that the indigenous Tamils could maintain their majority position in those areas.

The moment the terms of the settlement were made public there was a storm of protests chiefly from the die-hard language loyalists in Bandaranaike's own camp. And the UNP, looking for a means of staging a comeback, were provided with an ideal opportunity to embarrass the Prime Minister on a politically sensitive issue, and to demonstrate their commitment to the 'Sinhala only' policy to an electorate sceptical of their motives.[3]

The language loyalists argued that the concession to recognize Tamil as an official language vitiated the Sinhala Only Act. This opinion the UNP shared, but our main concern here is with the other main points in the settlement, i.e., modifications to the *Regional Councils Bill*, and the presumed threat to halt colonization in the Northern and Eastern provinces.

Under the terms of the Bandaranaike-Chevanayakam Pact dated 26 July 1957, the draft *Regional Councils Bill* was to be amended so that *inter alia* the Northern Province was to form one regional area while the Eastern Province was to be divided into two or more regional areas. If this was a concession to demographic realities, other clauses of the agreement caused more controversy: provision was to be made to permit two or more regions to amalgamate even beyond provincial boundaries; subject to ratification by Parliament, a region could divide itself into two, or presumably more, regions; and collaboration for specific purposes of common interest between two or more regions was to be permitted.

To critics and opponents of the settlement the proposed amendments conjured up visions of a calculated but secret attempt to concede the demand for a federal state, with menacing potential for eventual division of the country into two separate states. Pronouncements by the Federal Party leadership that their pact with Bandaranaike was the first step in their quest for a federal political system,[4] combined with Bandaranaike's known ambivalence on the question of a unitary political structure for Sri Lanka, to lend credence to these fears and forbodings, and accounted for the ferocity with which the pact was attacked.

The arguments used by the UNP against the amendments to the Regional Councils Bill proposed by Bandaranaike have a vitally important contemporary significance in Sri Lanka today. For one thing the UNP's principal spokesman on this occasion was none other than President J.R. Jayewardene himself, then in the political wilderness having lost his parliamentary seat in 1956, perhaps the most notable and most distinguished victim of that parliamentary debacle. Today the same debate has been revived in the course of negotiations between the government of President Jayewardene and representatives of Tamil opinion, a theme to which we shall return in later chapters of this book.

Colonization was an equally emotional issue. For the Sinhalese, colonization of the dry zone was a "national" enterprise that took them back to the roots of their civilization. D.S. Senanayake's grand passion for the restoration of irrigation schemes in the dry zone was "a search for inspiration from the pre-colonial past and traditional sources of legitimacy."[5] But the establishment of "colonies" of settlers in the dry zone had one far-reaching political consequence. The rapidly expanding frontier cut into the forests which had stood for centuries as the barrier between the Tamil and Sinhalese areas of the island. This expansion did not go far in the 1930s but nevertheless there was a consciousness — especially among those Tamils who were deeply suspicious of it — that an irreversible process had begun, and with it increasing prospect of a confrontation between the intruding colonists and the Tamil settlements in the *Vanni*, especially in the regions near the provincial boundary between the Northern and North Central Provinces.

After independence the expansion of colonization in the dry zone went on apace. One of the most notable achievements of D.S. Senanayake's government was the Gal Oya project, the first new irrigation scheme for many centuries — indeed since the days of the Sinhalese kings — and one that dwarfed even the largest such ventures of ancient times. For the Tamils of the Eastern Province in particular, however, the Gal Oya project appeared as the beginning of a drastic change in the ethnic composition of the population of that region, bringing as it did thousands of Sinhalese settlers under the sponsorship of the government.

In retrospect it would seem that the pact was doomed from the moment its contents were revealed. Confronted with mounting opposition to it the Prime Minister played for time, but the pressures against it were too strong for him to resist. Led by a group of *bhikkhus* who performed *satyagraha* on the lawn of the Prime Minister's private residence in Colombo, the extremists in his own party compelled him to abrogate the pact. Once again the tensions generated by these pressures and counter pressures erupted in 'race' riots in May 1958. Later in the year — in August — Bandaranaike secured Parliamentary approval for the *Tamil Language (Special Provisions) Act No. 28 of 1958. The Regional Councils Bill* was abandoned, along with the pact with which it came to be associated.

The Bandaranaike-Chelvanayakam Pact
Phase Two: 1960 - 1964

The general election of 1956 marked the beginning of two decades of SLFP primacy in Sri Lanka's politics. Except for a brief period — 1965-70 — it either formed the government on its own or was the dominant element in a coalition government. With the breakup in mid-1959 of the coalition formed by Bandaranaike, and Bandaranaike's assassination in 1959, there was for a few months a highly confused political situation and the first of two general elections of 1960 — held respectively in March and July — was a throwback to the pre-1956 system in that a revived UNP faced a multiplicity of warring rivals with no electoral arrangement against it. The result of the election was inconclusive. The UNP emerged as the largest single party and formed a short-lived minority government, but its recovery led to a renewal of the old combination of forces devised to keep it out of power. And within parliament a grand coalition of parties — including the Federal Party — brought down the government. In the general election of July 1960 the SLFP had the advantage of a no-contest pact with the left. This had the desired effect of bringing it back to power this time, on its own, under the leadership of Mrs. Bandaranaike, and thus the beneficiary of a huge surge of public sympathy, all the more powerful for being somewhat belated.

The Federal Party voted against the UNP on the crucial vote of confidence in March 1960, and at the July election supported the SLFP. The price of their support was a commitment to implement the abortive Bandaranaike-Chelvanayakam Pact of 1957. Negotiations between the UNP and FP had broken down on the former's reluctance to give an undertaking that the pact of 1957 would be implemented. That pledge the SLFP, under Mrs. Bandaranaike, had given, but after her election victory of July 1960 she found it impossible to honor it.

The UNP had made Mrs. Bandaranaike's commitment to the Federal Party an election issue, and although the verdict of the electorate went substantially in favor of the SLFP, its leadership nonetheless felt obliged to rethink its position on this issue under pressure from Sinhalese extremists in its ranks and outside. Within six months of Mrs. Bandaranaike's assumption of office as Prime Minister, the Federal Party was totally alienated from her government, largely because of her insistence on Sinhalese becoming the language of administration throughout the island from 1 January 1961 as envisaged in the 'Sinhala Only' Act of 1956, without any substantial modifications or adjustments as concessions to the Tamils, despite the understanding reached with the Federal Party before and during the general election of July 1960. A major issue were the regulations required to give effect to the *Tamil Language (Special Provisions) Act No. 28 of 1958.* Once more there was the familiar pattern of a civil disobedience campaign in the north and east of the island in March-April 1961, the government responding with the imposition of a state of emergency in the Northern and Eastern Provinces. Within Parliament, the Federal Party moved from responsive cooperation with the government to staunch opposition. Over the next few years it became more receptive to overtures from the UNP.

With the formation of a coalition government between the SLFP and the LSSP in 1964 prospects of a reconciliation with the Federal Party appeared to have substantially improved. The policy statement of the coalition government in 1964 promised that "A Draft Bill to implement the proposal to establish District Councils will be placed before [Parliament]..." A Cabinet subcommittee consisting of 4 SLFP Ministers and Dr. N. M. Perera, Minister of Finance and leader of the LSSP, was appointed for this purpose. Within a few weeks of this however, the coalition fell on being defeated in Parliament on a vote of confidence. With that defeat the first phase in the post 1956 struggle to introduce regional or district councils as instruments of decentralization of administration came to an end. The next phase began in 1966, but this time with the SLFP and its Marxist allies adamantly opposing a UNP-FP coalition's attempts to revive this ill-fated scheme.

District Councils:
Another Attempt at Regional Autonomy

One important point about Bandaranaike's abortive settlement with the Federal Party needs to be emphasized. Despite its abrogation in 1958, its ghostly presence has hovered around every subsequent discussion on management of the Sinhalese-Tamil problem in the island. Thus in 1965 when the UNP formed a national government of which the Federal Party was a component element, the basis for securing the support of the Federal Party was an agreement on the lines of that of 1957, and in which a version of the regional councils outlined in the draft bill of 1957 formed the central feature. In the first policy statement to Parliament by the new government in April 1965 it announced that

> "... earnest consideration will be given to the establishment of District Councils which will function under the control and direction of the Central Government."

The emphasis on the term "the control and direction of the Central Government" was designed to allay the fears of the Sinhalese about the potential divisive effects of such councils. In the "throne" speeches of 1966 and 1967 this policy statement on District Councils was repeated. By June 1968 the Cabinet had given its approval to a draft bill on District Councils. The draft was published in the form of a White Paper. In the concluding paragraph of the introduction the differences between its proposals and those of S.W.R.D. Bandaranaike's draft bill of 1957 were emphasized.[6]

> "in the present draft Bill," it delcared, "it is proposed that these Councils should function under the control and direction of the Government. The Minister in charge of the function of District Councils will be the Prime Minister himself. The Government Agent of the District will be the Chief Executive Officer and all employees of these Councils will be public servants under the control of the Government Agent, there being no District Service. These Councils will not be local authorities but would be an extension of the Central Government activities taking over some functions now performed by the Kachcheris. Such functions would be vested in these bodies by the Ministers in charge of these functions, and the Ministers will have the power to direct and control the Councils in the exercise of the powers so vested in the Councils by them.

> "The Councils will function under the Language Laws of the country. The records of the Councils throughout the Island shall be kept in the

Official Language. In the Northern and Eastern Provinces records shall be kept in Tamil also. Correspondence with the Central Government shall be in the Official Language. A Member of the Council can speak in one of the three languages, Sinhalese, Tamil or English.

"Regional Councils, as envisaged by the Hon. S.W.R.D. Bandaranaike would have been empowered to amalgamate with each other. A Regional Council in the North for instance could have expanded its area of control by amalgamation with the Council in the East. No such powers of amalgamation will be vested in the proposed District Councils.

"Regional Councils would have had the authority to select settlers for the colonization schemes in the areas under their administration, and have powers over land development and colonization. All these functions have been excluded from the subjects, which will be allocated to District Councils.

"District Councils will have no 'district services'. They will be served by public servants."

The apprehensiveness one detects in this was entirely understandable because ever since January 1966, when police firing on a mob protesting against the *Tamil Language (Special Provisions) Regulations* then being debated in Parliament accidently shot and killed a young *bhikkhu*, the government was uneasy about the public response to legislation — such as a Regional Councils Bill — which could be construed as a concession to pressure from the Federal Party. Its morale had been badly shattered in late October 1966 when it lost all three by-elections of a mini-general election. No doubt two of these were seats held by the opposition, and no doubt too that except in the government-held seat which it lost it had improved substantially on its performance in 1965. But it is the result that matters, and the opposition which had made the UNP-Federal Party agreement an issue on this occasion could justifiably argue that public opinion was with them on this. By the end of 1966 it was an open secret that there was a serious rift within the inner circles of the UNP, between the Prime Minister and his deputy J.R. Jayewardene.[7] A government divided against itself could hardly have coped with the business of implementing this bill in the face of concerted counterpressure mounted by the Opposition parties and Buddhist activists. Defections of government supporters in local government bodies, most of whom attributed their change of allegiance to misgivings about the political implications of the District Councils bill, were viewed — not least by the government itself — as incontrovertible evidence of the potency of the backlash induced by the opposition's clever exploitation of the disquiet prevailing among the Sinhalese on this question. Nor were these suspicions and fears confined to the Sinhalese. Muslim opinion was firmly opposed to these councils.[8] Indeed Muslim suspicion of schemes of devolution of power to provincial or district units has remained, since the mid-1960s, a central feature of the national debate on this issue.

The limits of concessions to the Tamils on devolution were thus demonstrated most dramatically when Dudley Sennayake was forced, in mid-1969, to abandon his government's *District Councils Bill.* Opposition parties and opponents of this bill played on the well-entrenched suspicion among the Sinhalese that devolution or decentralization would inevitably pave the way for a fully-fledged federal structure, which in turn would be the precursor of moves for a policy of separation of the Tamil units of such a federation from the Sri Lankan polity. Bandaranaike's Regional Councils had lost their political viability once the Federal Party became a force to be reckoned with, and even Dudley Senanayake's assurance that the District Councils he had in mind would be directly under the control of the government was inadequate to win any support for such a scheme from the Sinhalese. The opposition to this new initiative in decentralization was unusual in its range: it brought together a formidable combination of the SLFP in alliance with the traditional Sinhalese Buddhist pressure groups, but linked now with the Marxist left, and a significant section of Muslim opinion. It proved to be altogether too powerful for the government, and the proposed District Councils scheme too suffered a fate similar to that of its predecessor of 1957; but on this occasion there was not even the publication of a bill in draft form.

The crux of the problem is that regional autonomy, not merely regional loyalties with a potential for development into separatism, is viewed as a threat to national integrity. And in Sri Lanka, to an even greater extent than in India, the political establishment exalts the modern state and treats national identity as co-extensive with it, and has generally been unwilling to concede legitimacy to these regional loyalties or does so only with great reluctance. Faced with the overwhelmingly reality of under-development it perceives centralized authority as being of paramount importance in overcoming the handicaps of poverty. In that situation anything likely to encourage if not lead to communal fragmentation is regarded with the utmost suspicion.

The failure of these efforts at institutionalizing decentralization gave added impetus to the resort to more informal methods of achieving the same ends. Some of these are outlined below.

In the period 1965-1970 government undertook the implementation of a major agricultural program aimed at self-sufficiency in paddy and subsidiary food crops. For purposes of this program the Government Agent was appointed coordinator of the activities of all the departments involved in its implementation at the district level and was vested with powers for administration of funds and control of expenditure. Coordinating Committees were set up as the lowest rungs of an administrative structure which had as its apex a Cabinet Committee chaired by the Prime Minister himself. The implementation of the agricultural program in the late 1960s was "a major breakthrough at delegation of authority and co-ordination of activities at the district and divisional levels and the establishment of a chain of command and communication with the centre." Members of Parliament were also involved in preparing the priorities under block votes for minor irrigation, as well as other village, works.

During the early 1970s two innovative programs designed to decentralize responsibility for formulating and implementing district and village development plans and also for obtaining popular participation in the preparation and implementation of such plans were introduced by a new Government. These programs which we shall discuss in a later chapter were (a) the Divisional Development Councils (DDC) and (b) the Decentralized Budget (DCB). A third innovation, the District Political Authority (DPA), came later, in 1973.

References

[1]   S.W.R.D. Bandarnaike's speech of 21 March 1932, printed in S.W.R.D. Bandaranaike, *Towards a New Era: Selected Speeches ... made in the Legislature of Ceylon 1931-9.* (Colombo, The Government Press, 1961).

[2]   R.S.S. Gunawardene's motion that "This Council is of opinion that immediate effect should be given to the recommendation of the Donoughmore Commission with regard to the establishment of Provincial Councils." *Hansard* [State Council] 1940, columns 1357-62. After a rather perfunctory debate the motion was unanimously approved.

[3]   See the statement issued on behalf of the UNP by J.R. Jayewardene as Acting

General Secretary, published in *The Ceylon Daily News*, 19 July 1957.

4   See the speech by C. Vanniasingham, President of the Federal Party at Batticaloa on 28 July 1957. He compared the pact recently concluded between the Prime Minister and the Federal Party to the Gandhi-Irwin Pact. *Ceylon Daily News*, 29 July 1957.

5   Malalgoda, 'Buddhism in Post-Independence Sri Lanka' *op. cit.*, p. 95.

6   *Proposals for the Establishment of District Councils under the Direction and Control of the Central Government* (Colombo, Government Press, 3 June 1968).

7   This rift did not extend to the District Councils Bill. On the contrary both were associated in the drafting of the bill and in negotiations on it with the Federal Party.

8   See Chapter XV for discussion of this.

Chapter XIII

Linguistic Nationalism And Buddhist Resurgence, 1956-1972

Bandaranaike And Buddhist Reform

With the triumph of linguistic nationalism, pressure for stronger links between Buddhism and the state, and a corresponding reduction if not eradication of Christian influence in the Sri Lanka polity became almost irresistible. Against the background of the *Buddha Jayanthi* pressure mounted for the elevation of Buddhism to the status of the state religion. But language reform enjoyed a priority over this more complex issue, and with the government in the coils of the language crisis of 1956-58 there was little to do except to postpone consideration of it. The postponement was effected through the classic device of harassed politicians seeking an escape from the need for an immediate solution to uncomfortable problems: a Commission of Inquiry.

In February 1957 Bandaranaike appointed the Buddha Sasana Commission. The term *sasana* itself was one of infinite flexibility, encompassing as it did the institutions, property, including monastic lands and the rights, obligations, duties and privileges of the *bhikkhus*. The term generally covered doctrine as well but that seemed less relevant on this occasion than the other aspects mentioned above. It had something to satisfy everybody: advocates of institutional reform could regard it as a mandate for modernization; adherents of the *status quo* were encouraged to believe that there was no inherent incompatibility between their interests and those of the reformers. The task before this Commission of *bhikkhus* and prominent Buddhist laymen was the unenviable one of reconciling these obviously conflicting interests. Looked at in historical perspective it was an attempt by Buddhist activists to identify the issues and set out the solutions to the problems that emerged from the severance of the historic link between the state and the Buddhist religion which had occurred in 1840. British Governors of the colony and Sri Lankan politicians alike had come up against the impossibility of returning to the *status quo ante* 1840: for all of them the religious neutrality of the state was a major premise of their thinking; and for many of them including men like Gregory and Gordon, D.B. Jayatilaka and D.S. Senanayake, the only adjustment possible to the reality of the burdens of past history and perceptions of national destiny seen as an unfolding of Buddhism's inextricable links with the state was a pragmatic recognition of a special status for Buddhism. To recognize this officially was worrisome enough in the context of those times; to spell out a policy of action based on this was as problematic in the years 1948-1956 as it had been under British rule.

The terms of reference of the Buddha Sasana Commission included the examination of the implications of the general but vague principle of "according to Buddhism its rightful place in the country", to which the government was publicly committed. They were also asked to make recommendations for a reform of the *sangha*. The Commission spent two years in preparing and drafting its report.

Bandaranaike was all too aware of the legal and constitutional difficulties to be overcome if Buddhism was to be declared the state religion, above all the formidable hurdle of section 29(2) (c) of the constitution which laid down that no law enacted by Parliament shall:

> "confer on persons of any community or religion any privilege or advantage which is not conferred on persons of other communities or religions."

It was not at all certain that the legislature would provide the special majority required for the purpose of overcoming this constitutional obstacle.

There was a greater chance of success with regard to the quest for increasing state control over the schools, in brief, for a completion of the work begun by C.W.W. Kannangara in the 1940s. There was wider support for this from Marxists and other left-wing groups. But the Minister of Education, W. Dahanayake, was adamantly opposed to a take-over of the schools run by the Christian missions and other religious organizations. He had the support of the Prime Minister on this. It would appear that the government was not at all anxious to get embroiled in another contentious issue while coping with the political fall-out from the language crisis.

There were other ways in which it sought to identify itself with the

Buddhist cause. Thus, the two premier seats of Buddhist learning, the Vidyalankara and Vidyodaya *pirivenas* were raised to the status of universities.[1] A Ministry of Cultural Affairs and a department of Official Language Affairs were established, the latter to organize the implementation of the government's language policy, and the former to channel state patronage to literature and the arts. In the revivalist atmosphere of the mid-1950s there was a general efflorescence in the arts against the background of the militant Buddhist revivalist movement, actuated on the one hand by the millennial expectations connected with the *Buddha Jayanthi*, and on the other by the nativistic urge to guard and preserve the Sinhalese language and the Buddhist religion from the presumed "threats" of the Tamils and the Christians. The year 1956, by a remarkable coincidence with the victory of the MEP, saw several momentous achievements in the arts. Though none of these latter owed anything to the patronage of the state, the argument that the breakthrough they marked could be stabilized and consolidated only by active support from the state for literature and the arts became part of the conventional wisdom of the day. The institutional apparatus established for this purpose by the Banda-ranaike government — a Ministry of Cultural Affairs — was expected to give official patronage and financial assistance to the resuscitatory zeal then manifest in all spheres of artistic activity.

The Buddha Sasana Commission

The report of the Buddha Sasana Commission was submitted to the Prime Minister in mid-1959, and was scheduled for publication in November 1959.[2] There was the prospect that with its publication the government would turn, at last, to the intricacies of defining a policy on, and implementing one, on the "rightful place" of Buddhism, and to grasp the nettles of Buddhist institutional reform.

Meanwhile the coalition of forces in the Pancha Maha Balavegaya, which had done so much to ensure the success of Bandaranaike's own political career, was crumbling in the face of the turmoil that characterized the last two years (1958-59) of Bandaranaike's adminis-tration. *Bhikkhu* activists were divided on a number of issues, and some of the most prominent among them, most notably the *viharadhipathi* of the Kelaniya temple, Mapitigama Buddharakkhita, had become controversial because of their involvement in the ugly faction fighting within the SLFP of which they were such prominent members. Many of them were also prominent opponents of some of the key social and economic reforms initiated by the left-wing members of Bandaranaike's Cabinet. Among the most noteworthy of these acts of opposition was the agitation against the *Paddy Lands Act of 1958*. The *bhikkhu* opposition to this came principally from the two powerful and wealthy chapters of Malwatta and Asgiriya, the principal representatives of monastic landlordism.[3]

The Buddhist public were now increasingly soured by the spectacle of *bhikkhus* involving themselves in political infighting, and using pressure for financial gain — for kinsfolk if not for themselves — through influence-peddling and the manipulation of bids for contracts. Their disgust at all this turned to deep consternation, and shock when the Prime Minister was assassinated on 26 September. The chief figure in the conspiracy to murder Bandaranaike was Mapitigama Buddharakkita, and the actual shooting was done by another *bhikkhu*, a close associate of the principal conspirator. The assassination of Bandaranaike with its powerful mix of political and sordid commercial motives, not to mention other even more distressing factors, underlined as nothing else did so sharply, before or after, the perils involved in *bhikkhus* engaging in partisan politics. Never again did *bhikkhus* wield the same influence in political affairs that they did in the years from 1943 to 1959.

The assassination of Bandaranaike provided reformist groups among Buddhist activists the opportunity they so desperately needed to initiate moves for far-reaching institutional reforms among the *sangha*. But the political confusion that followed on his death prevented any such initiatives. There was nobody to provide the leadership in converting the ground-swell of support for reform of the *sangha* into a coherent program of action. In the meantime political energies were devoted to coping with the shattering impact of Bandaranaike's death, and two general elections in March and July 1960. The first was indecisive; the second brought to power Bandaranaike's widow at the head of a revived SLFP which had regrouped under her leadership having excluded or expelled all those in any way linked to the political forces within that party associated with Mapitigama Buddharakkita.

When the recommendations of the Commission were published late in 1959 they proved to be immediately controversial. Among their principal recommendations was the creation of an incorporated body with wide powers over the *sangha*, and empowered to regulate entry into the Buddhist order, the education and residence of *bhikkhus*, and regulation of their engagement in social and political activities, and in paid employment outside their temples. This body was also empowered to adjudicate disputes between *bhikkhus* especially on matters relating to succession as heads of temples, issues on which *bhikkhus* had generally sought legal remedies in the civil courts. Among the other areas of activity which would come under its purview were: the collection of funds for temples and Buddhist activity, the building of temples and also publications relating to Buddhism.

There was immediate opposition to this from the two chapters of the prestigious Siyam *nikaya*. The political *bhikkhus* were too discredited to voice any opposition to these recommendations. There was considerable irony in this for the Siyam *nikaya*, historically, has had close links with secular authorities from its inception, and generally has sought centralized control of the order of *bhikkhus* — which was more or less what the Buddha Sasana Commission report tended to recommend — while the other *nikayas* had emerged into autonomous existence partly at least because there was no central authority to regulate the affairs of the *sangha* in colonial times.[4] Despite the opposition from the more orthodox *bhikkhus* the new government could well have embarked on an implementation of a program of Buddhist institutional reform. Mrs. Bandaranaike's government had other priorities, and they turned to these. Thus a historic opportunity was missed for lack of the political will to seize it and exploit its potential for a purification of the *sangha*.

The Triumph of Buddhist Activism — The Final Phase, 1960-72

At the time of Mrs. Bandaranaike's accession to power the process of elite displacement, Christian by Buddhist, had stopped well short of the objectives set for themselves by the Buddhist activists of the mid-1950s. That considerable progress had been made towards the achievement of these objectives during this period only rendered the survival of Christian privilege all the less palatable to them. The struggle for supremacy was now resumed. Her husband, despite his anxiety to restore to Buddhism the traditional patronage accorded to it in pre-colonial times, had not been able to do much in this sphere. Furthermore he was unwilling to endorse the demand that came from

Buddhist activists for Buddhism to be raised to the status of the state religion. As the new leader of the Sri Lanka Freedom Party, she pressed ahead in seeking to satisfy some of the demands of Buddhist activists. She was intent on continuing the language policy initiated by her husband, and on doing so with as few concessions to the Tamil minority as possible and with greater rigidity on principles underlying this policy than he may have shown had he been alive. Even more important, although the times seemed hardly propitious to enlarge the area of conflict from language to religion and education as well, she embarked on this two-pronged attack on behalf of Sinhalese-Buddhist interests. At that stage she was not interested in the complicated question of the status of Buddhism in the Sri Lankan polity. It was education reform, and the completion of the changes initiated under C.W.W. Kannangara that absorbed her attention.

To move into education reform was certain to bring her into conflict with the Roman Catholics in Sri Lanka. But she calculated on support from the Marxists and other left-wing groups in Parliament and outside it, who may not have shown the same enthusiasm for moves to make Buddhism the state religion. For them state control over education was a desirable end in itself. The Buddhists however, saw it as nothing less than the restoration of a balance that had been tilted very much in favor of Christians. Indeed they looked upon the existing education system as the fountainhead of Christian privilege in Sri Lanka. There was also a more practical consideration, namely that once the schools came under greater state control, Buddhist influence on the education process at the grass-roots level would be greatly increased.

The Christian groups and most of all the Roman Catholics were the principal beneficiaries of the existing system. But other religious groups including the Buddhist Theosophical Society also had their own schools. None of them fought as hard to retain this system as the Roman Catholics did on this occasion. They were bound to be, and were, inevitably, the biggest losers. The long drawn out Buddhist agitation for state control over education had at last achieved its goal.

The passions generated by this struggle embittered the Roman Catholics against the Sri Lanka Freedom Party for a decade. They found that the constitution gave them no protection against the government on this issue. As long as a restriction was so devised that it was applicable to all sections of the community and not to a specific group the constitutional obstacle of section 29)2) (b) and (c) could be cleared. It had happened on the language issue in 1956 and now it happened again on education reform in 1960-61.

An abortive *coup d'etat* in 1962 in which the leaders were Roman Catholic and Protestant officers of the army, navy and police, further strained relations between the Roman Catholics and the government.[5] It had the effect of reviving the popularity of the government and, more important, it provided the justification for the government to support Buddhist activists in a propaganda campaign against the Roman Catholics and their continuing influence in public life.

By the end of Mrs. Bandaranaike's term of office the primacy of Buddhism and Buddhists in Sri Lanka's political system and public life had become a hard reality. But this achievement, significantly enough, was won by the lay Buddhists, both within the government and outside it. The *bhikkhus* had a very limited role in it. This was not surprising considering that the *sangha*, in general, had suffered a grievous loss of prestige after the assassination of S.W.R.D. Bandaranaike. The election campaigns of March and July 1960 had been notable for the absence of *bhikkhus* on political platforms. Things changed with the abortive *coup d'etat* of 1962. *Bhikkhu* involvement in politics was resumed but on a more modest scale and with a greater awareness of the restraints that membership of the Buddhist order imposed.

No longer were the *bhikkhus* almost entirely on the side of the SLFP and its allies. They were, increasingly, sharply divided with large numbers now backing the opposition U.N.P. Among the latter were some of the more prominent political *bhikkhus* of the mid-1950s. They were alienated from the SLFP by two developments: first, a sharp difference of opinion on the implementation of the recommendations of the Buddha Sasana Commission — the main recommendations were not implemented but an attempt was made to introduce some minor changes. The response was so hostile that even these were withdrawn. Secondly, opposition to the government's attempt to bring the national press under state control, and opposition also to the SLFP's coalition with the LSSP. Thus during the election campaign of 1965 some of the most prominent speakers on UNP platforms were *bhikkhus* like Talpavila Silavamsa, and Devamottawe Amaravamsa erstwhile supporters of the SLFP, and critics of the UNP.

The return of the UNP to power in 1965 at the head of a coalition did not see a reversal of these trends. Thus although the UNP had opposed the education reforms of 1960-61, there was no relaxation of the restrictive measures they had voted against, and no concessions on these to the Roman Catholics despite a pledge given to them in 1967. Besides, in a bid to prove its *bona fides* on Buddhism the government introduced the *poya* holiday scheme under which the weekly holiday was based on the phases of the moon, and the sabbath holiday was abandoned. The effect of this was to cause some discontentment among the Roman Catholics without any compensating support from the Buddhists for the UNP. At a different level there was a policy of building up the "national status" of the two *Mahanayakes* of Malwatte and Asgiriya, who were regarded as the most acceptable — to the Buddhist public, not less than to the government — and authentic representatives of Buddhist interests. Public memories of the assassi-nation of Bandaranaike were still fresh and other incidents of 'political *bhikkhus*' over-stepping the acceptable limits of political involvement and partisanship kept these alive. Thus in April 1966, a leading *bhikkhu* politician, linked with the SLFP, *bhikkhu* Henpitagedera Gnanasiha was arrested on charges of complicity in an attempted *coup d'etat*. He was indeed one of the prime suspects, and was kept in remand for three years. He was released when the charges laid against him could not be sustained at his trial. In this situation the influence and prestige of the politically-active *bhikkhus* continued to decline, and in contrast the two *Mahanayakes* of Malwatta and Asgiriya with their general non-partisan-ship rose in esteem. Thus the government's move to give some official recognition to their position as the chief representatives of Buddhist opinion, had wide acceptance. Two official residences were allocated to them in Colombo, as one of the honors befitting the highest dignitaries of the *sangha*. Then again, it became the practice for all appointees to important official positions in the government and public life to make a courtesy call on the two *Mahanayakes* in Kandy.

At the same time — 1966-67 — the two *pirivena* universities of Vidyalankara and Vidyodaya were converted into secular institutions and the *bhikkhus* who headed these two universities lost much if not all of their patronage and influence there. Ironically enough the first Vice-Chancellor of Vidyodaya under the new dispensation was none other than the Walpola Rahula himself: his appointment on this occasion, had nothing to do with his former connection with the Vidyalankara *pirivena* but to his established reputation as a Buddhist scholar.

The official recognition — and buttressing — of the orthodox *bhikkhus* did not inhibit their intervention on political issues whenever the occasion demanded it. Thus throughout the last two decades, *bhikkhus* including the two *Mahanayakes* of Malwatta and Asgiriya, have generally been forthright in their views on issues involving relations between the Sinhalese majority and the Tamil minority: in the late-1960s there was general opposition to the concessions on language made to the Tamils in January 1966. The opposition was stronger from among the political *bhikkhus* of old, than from the more orthodox *bhikkhus*. The latter's opposition to the District Councils scheme envisaged by the government in 1967-68 was more vocal, as it was with regard to concessions made at about the same time to the Indian residents in Sri Lanka in regard to their citizenship rights.

The defeat of the UNP in 1970 and the return to power of Mrs. Bandaranaike at the head of the center-left United Front coalition saw the final phase of the process of redressing Buddhist grievances we have been concerned with here. This came with the new Republican Constitution of 1972, of which Chapter II read as follows:

"The Republic of Sri Lanka shall give to Buddhism the foremost place and accordingly it shall be the duty of the state to protect and foster Buddhism while assuring to all religions the rights guaranteed by section 18 (1) (d)."

When this proposal was introduced in the Constituent Assembly, there was wide support for it from almost all parties. (The only opposition came from the representatives of Tamil opinion, notably the Federal Party). When the 1972 constitution was replaced by a new one in 1978 under a UNP regime, this same principle was incorporated in the second republic's constitutional structure. The innovation introduced in 1972 came at a time when the Roman Catholics had embarked on a change of policy themselves in their attitude to other religions, — an acceptance if not tolerance of religious pluralism. This change came with the Vatican Council of 1963-65. And all this despite there being no attempt on the part of the SLFP to make any change in education policy. The government, nonetheless, had become much more conciliatory to the Roman Catholics than before.

In July 1971, the *poya* holiday scheme was abandoned. Almost all parties supported this move, including the UNP itself. Significantly the SLFP-led coalition took the initiative in a matter in which a section of the *sangha* and some lay Buddhist activists were adamantly opposed to the abandonment of a scheme for which they had agitated for long. During the 1970s, a period of social and economic change, and political turmoil — the youth revolt in 1971, and ethnic tension of the late 1970s, the *bhikkhus* — strangely enough, remained in the background, an attitude which changed only in the early 1980s.

The political responses to the messianism of the *Buddha Jayanthi* in Sri Lanka have a remarkable similarity to cognate processes in U Nu's Burma. Indeed there was an amazing parallel in the lines of policy adopted by the Bandaranaikes, husband and wife, in Sri Lanka, and U Nu in Burma.[6] The latter's attempt to exploit this messianism through an emphasis on the Buddhist religion and the Burmese culture in a bid to impose unity on the disintegrating Burmese polity had little chance of success. On a long term basis that program was not unviable, but the time span required was decades not years. Thailand had taken a century or more to work out a similar policy of national unification of the Tai states and its hill peoples within a Thai-Buddhist polity. There the system achieved considerable success: the main, if not only resistance has been Thailand's Malay-Muslim minority. In Burma the resistance was wider, and stronger. If U. Nu's program failed to create national unity in Burma, in Sri Lanka, on the other hand, an existing unity was gravely impaired by a program similar to his, pursued over the years 1956-64 and culminating in the new constitution of 1972.

There were, nevertheless, two important differences between the politicized Buddhism of Sri Lanka and those of Burma and Thailand. The first of these lies in the provisions of the first republican constitution which accorded to Buddhism a special status. With that the pragmatic concession to political reality which Governors Gregory and Gordon had first outlined — a special obligation to Buddhism in a secular state — was stretched to its utmost limits. Sri Lanka had ceased to be a secular state pure and simple: but it had not became a Buddhist state on the Thai and Burmese model which some Buddhist activists in Sri Lanka had urged as their objective. Ironically enough had the recommendations of the Buddha Sasana Commission been accepted and implemented, that pragmatic and very workable and sagacious compromise might well have been breached and Sri Lanka may have become much more like Burma and Thailand than it is today.

Again, none of the Sri Lankan governments since independence have deliberately or consistently followed assimilationist policies such as those pursued in Burma and Thailand. The attitude to the minorities in Sri Lanka has been embodied in a mixture of policies, sometimes emphasizing national integration, and sometimes recognizing the advantages of a pluralist approach. So long as the territorial integrity of the country is not threatened in any way, and indeed today even in the face of separatist pressures, there has been no attempt to assimilate the diverse minority groups in the country to the dominant Sinhalese-Buddhist culture. Thus not only is there genuine religious tolerance —as in Thailand — but a greater acceptance of cultural pluralism than in Thailand, where cultural pluralism perceived as having strong political undertones is deemed unacceptable.

References

1   K.M. de Silva, 'The Universities and the government in Sri Lanka' in *Minerva* 16(2) pp. 251-272.

2   See Donald E. Smith, 'The Sinhalese Buddhist Revolution' Chapter 21 in (ed) Donald E. Smith, *South Asian Politics and Religion*. (Princeton, 1969) pp. 453-509, particularly pp. 500-509.

3   K.M. de Silva, 'Buddhist Revivalism, Nationalism and Politics in Modern Sri Lanka' in J.W. Bjorkman (ed.) *Fundamentalism, Revivalism and Violence in South Asia* (forthcoming).

4   On this theme see, K. Malalgoda, *Buddhism in Sinhalese Society, 1750-1900.* (California University Press, 1976); on the issue of the Sasana Commission, see his 'Buddhism in Post-Independence Sri Lanka', *op. cit.*, p. 95.

5   Donald L. Horowitz, *Coup Theories and Officers Motives: Sri Lanka in Comparative Perspective*, (Princeton, 1980).

6   One feature of this policy, the *poya* holidays scheme which U. Nu imposed on Burma was introduced to Sri Lanka by the UNP-led coalition of 1965, not by the Bandaranaikes.

Chapter XIV

Linguistic Nationalism:
The Tamil Version
1948-1972

Introductory

The present chapter and the next one deal with the contrasting responses of the two most important of Sri Lanka's ethnic minorities to the transformation of Sri Lankan politics which began in the mid-1950s. The chapter reviewing the Muslims' response, Chapter XV, straddles Parts III and IV of this volume: their response has more and stronger elements of continuity than that of the Tamils. The latter may be divided into two parts, with the year 1972, the year in which the first republican constitution of Sri Lanka was introduced, forming a convenient and natural dividing line.

We have seen how the basic issues involved in the fundamental problem of Tamil politics in Sri Lanka — their relationship with the Sinhalese within the larger Sri Lankan polity — emerged in the early 1920s and had been dramatized in the careers of two distinguished Tamil politicians who dominated the politics of the island at this time, the brothers Ponnambalam Ramanathan and Ponnambalam Aruna-chalam. We have referred to a study in contrasts which their careers provide. Here we need to point out that the issues at stake have had a continuing relevance in Tamil politics ever since, both in Aruna-chalam's commitment to a harmonious association between the Sinhalese and Tamils in nationalist politics and nation-building, for mutual trust and responsive coordination of sectional interests in the struggle for a common goal of *swaraj*, and in Ramanathan's emphasis on the virtues of a separate Tamil identity, of a Tamil nationalism to be fostered in collaboration with the British and if necessary in oppostiion to Sinhalese nationalism.

The 'fifty-fifty' campaign for instance was the *reductio ad absurdum* of the Ramanathan tradition. At its core were two important strands of thought: an emphasis on Tamil nationalism as something essentially divergent from, if not positively hostile to, Sinhalese nationalism; and the rejection tacitly or explicitly, of the concept of a poly-ethnic state, and a Ceylonese or Sri Lankan nationalism to which Arunachalam was so strongly committed.

Tamil Congress vs. Federal Party

G.G. Ponnambalam's political career is unique in embodying both these traditions of Tamil politics. Prior to independence he was in every way the political heir of Ramanathan; in the years after independence his political career illustrated the resilience and vitality of the political strand represented by Arunachalam. During the nearly six years in which he held Cabinet office he was a national political figure, a powerful influence within the government as well as an eloquent representative of Tamil interests. No Tamil political figure after independence has enjoyed a similar eminence on a national scale, and few have displayed the same combination of skills and talents: a lawyer of the highest rank, an orator *par excellence* and perhaps the finest of his times, and an enormously skilled politician.

At the general election of 1947 he had led the Tamil Congress to a landslide victory in the Jaffna district. In moving to the Jaffna seat he had inflicted a stunning defeat on the standard-bearer of the Aruna-chalam tradition, Arunachalam's own son, A Mahadeva, who had been Minister of Home Affairs since 1943 and a prominent representative of the newly formed UNP. The other standard bearer of the Aruna-chalam tradition was curiously enough, Ramanathan's son-in-law, S. Natesan, an Indian educationist who lived and worked in Jaffna. He too was a UNP candidate, and he too lost badly to a Tamil Congress candidate. Their defeat represented the bankruptcy of a political style, not the irrelevance of the tradition they represented — a patrician aloofness which earned for them the derisive sobriquet of the turbaned heads. The resilience and continued political relevance of the Arunachalam tradition was demonstrated afresh when, within a year of his overwhelming defeat of the UNP in the Jaffna district, Ponnambalam took the Tamil Congress into the government. A faction within the party repudiated him and refused to join the government. They were led by S.J.V. Chelvanayakam who organized them into the Federal Party.

Chelvanayakam like Ponnambalam was an eminent lawyer, but was unique in being a Christian, not a Hindu unlike all the main Tamil political figures of the past and of his day. A victim of Parkinson's disease, Chelvanayakam could hardly speak above a whisper, but yet in a superb triumph of character over these two major drawbacks — in religion and physical condition — he achieved an eminence in Tamil politics matched only by Ponnambalam himself. Chelvanayakam however, played only one role: that of the principal and most consistent exponent of the Ramanathan tradition. For a brief period of three years in the mid-1960s Chelvanayakam's Federal Party was a component element of Dudley Senanayake's coalition government. But he remained a MP although not a backbench MP. From 1972 onwards till his death in 1976 he represented once more and very effectively, the strength of the linguistic nationalism of the Tamils. In the asceticism of his lifestyle and his frail physical appearance he was the delight alike of the political cartoonist and political image-maker; for the latter he was a gift from the gods, an uncanny representation of all that one needed to portray the ideal leader of an ethnic group proclaiming itself an oppressed minority. But this is to anticipate events.

Between 1948 and the mid-1950s the Federal Party seemed to be no match for the Tamil Congress, just as Chelvanayakam himself was clearly overshadowed by the more dynamic Ponnambalam. Indeed, at the general election of 1952 the Tamil Congress, working in tandem with the UNP, inflicted a severe defeat on the Federal Party. Chelvanayakam himself lost his seat to a UNP candidate — the only UNP candidate in the Jaffna peninsula, S. Natesan. Yet within three years of this defeat the Federal Party was to become the principal political party of the Tamil minority, a position it has held since then either on its own, or as the solid core of a coalition of political forces.

Ponnambalam's political career reached its peak in 1952 as one of the most powerful colleagues of Dudley Senanayake in his Cabinet. His decline came with Dudley Senanayake's resignation in 1953. Ponnambalam lost his Cabinet position in the reshuffle that followed upon this, but the repudiation was seen and known to be a personal one, the antipathy to him of the new Prime Minister, Sir John Kotelawela. Ponnambalam took a back-bench seat in Parliament while his party

continued its association with the UNP. But within two years he
watched the unfolding of the language controversies of the 1950s
which eventually eroded his own personal position, and effectively
reduced his party to a minority group in Tamil politics while the
leadership went to the Federal Party.

As with the Sinhalese it was language that provided the sharp
cutting edge of a new national self-consciousness. The Federal Party's
great contribution to Tamil politics was to give the Tamils' concept of
linguistic nationalism a coherence and cohesiveness it had lacked
earlier despite their consciousness of a linguistic, religious and cultural
separateness from the Sinhalese. When, in 1951, at the first national
convention of the Federal Party it was claimed that "the Tamil
speaking people in [Sri Lanka] constituted a nation distinct from that
of the Sinhalese in every fundamental test of nationhood" — the
"separate historical past" of the Tamils and their linguistic unity and
distinctiveness — it all seemed so much misplaced rhetoric from a
voice from the wilderness. Even so they had already scored a point
over Ponnambalam in their opposition to the citizenship legislation
through which the bulk of the Indians who had voted in 1947 were
eliminated from the electoral registers. Ponnambalam had maintained
a studied, diplomatic and embarrassed silence, while C. Suntheralingam, a Tamil member of the Cabinet, had resigned in protest and the
Tamil Congress faction which eventually formed the Federal Party had
also expressed their strong opposition to it. Again while Sinhalese
politicians of all parties regarded Sri Lanka as a national state, the
Tamils have generally preferred to look upon it as a state-nation
created by western imperialism and in particular the British. This view
has been consistently emphasized by the Federal Party as well as by
other Sri Lanka Tamils in recent years, and it is the foundation of their
claim for a measure of regional autonomy (ranging from a unit or units
in a federal structure, to the current emphasis on a separate Tamil
state).

The Federal Party's Program:
Linguistic Nationalism in Action

We begin this survey with the resolution adopted when the Federal
Party was founded in 1949. It read as follows in an English translation

of the original Tamil version:

> "We believe that the present constitution of the country is unsuited to a multi-lingual country, and is inimical to the interests of the Tamils living in Sri Lanka. The basic principles which the present government has proclaimed concerning the public good are pernicious, and the system of government is not conducive to maintaining the unity of the country. We belive that the only means of ensuring that the Tamils are guaranteed their freedom and self-respect by law, and of solving their problems in a just and democratic manner is to permit them to have their own autonomous state guaranteeing self-government and self-determination for the Tamil nation in the country: and to work indefatigably to the attainment of this objective."[1]

In that resolution lay a direct challenge to the principles of Sri Lankan nationalism to which D.S. Senanayake's government was committed and which G.G. Ponnambalam was pledged to uphold when he joined the Cabinet. At the core of this resolution lay an ambiguity which has been so prominent in all expositions of the federal concept by its adherents in Sri Lanka. Ambiguity is part of the stock in trade of politicians, but few concepts have lent themselves to a deliberate ambiguity of expression and intent better than the Federal Party's concept of autonomy. Expressed in Tamil it could mean anything from regional autonomy to a separate state. And once federalism became one of the central demands of a major party Sinhalese politicians who had hitherto viewed decentralization of administeration with an indulgent eye and as merely a technical matter, began to see dangers to the integrity of the Sri Lankan state inherent in all demands for devolution of authority.

Immanent in that resolution was the concept of the "traditional homelands of the Tamils" in Sri Lanka which plays so powerful a role in Tamil politics today. Before we turn to an examination of its validity we need to consider its refinement over the years by the Federal Party, and also its links with the purposeful opposition of that party to the entry of Sinhalese into those parts of the country regarded as "traditional" Tamil areas.

Thus at the inaugural convention of the Federal Party (or Ilankai Thamil Arasi Kachchi in Tamil — ITAK) in April 1951, a resolution urged that

> "Inasmuch as the Tamil-speaking people have an inalienable right to the territories which they have been traditionally occupying, the first national convention of the ITAK condemns the deliberately planned policy of action of the Government in colonizing the land under the Gal-Oya reservoir and other such areas with purely Sinhalese people as an

> infringement of their fundamental rights and as a calculated blow aimed
> at the very existence of the Tamil-speaking nation in Ceylon."

Charges about the damaging effects of state sponsored peasant colonization were resumed in the same forthright terms after the general
election of 1956 and against the background of the language controversies of that time. Thus the fourth annual convention of the FP held
on 19 August 1956, claimed that

> "And whereas the colonization policies pursued by successive govern-
> ments since 1947 of planting Sinhalese populations in the traditional
> homeland of the Tamil-speaking people is calculated to overwhelm and
> crush the Tamil-speaking people in their own national areas ..."

A year later at a special convention of the Federal Party held at
Batticaloa on 28 July 1957 it was claimed that

> "State-aided Sinhalese colonization of the Northern and
> Eastern Provinces will be effectively stopped forthwith."

This last was aimed at reassuring its adherents, and was at the same
time an expression of hope at the possibility of achieving this objective
through the pact which the Prime Minister, S.W.R.D. Bandaranaike
had negotiated with the Federal Party leader, S.J.V. Chelvanayakam,
and signed only two days earlier. There

> "... It was agreed that in the matter of colonization schemes the
> powers of the regional councils shall include the power to select allotees
> to whom lands within their area of authority shall be alienated and also
> power to select personnel to be employed for work on such schemes. The
> position regarding the area at present administered by the Gal-Oya
> Board in this matter requires consideration."[2]

This pact, as we have seen, was never implemented, but in
compelling the then government to confront this issue, and to do so on
terms satisfactory to the FP the latter had won a major victory. A
theory of dubious historical validity had been elevated to the level of a
fundamentally important principle that should guide relations between the two disputants in the ethnic conflicts of post-independence
Sri Lanka. In less than a decade of its first enunciation this theory had
become one of the most potent and divisive myths of Sri Lankan
political life.

That the Jaffna peninsula proper had been a traditional homeland of
the Sri Lankan Tamils for many centuries is indisputable, and there
had been an independent Tamil kingdom in the north of the island
from the 13th century to the early part of the seventeenth. Its political
status had varied over this period and with that the degree of

independence it enjoyed. Its power had reached its peak in the 14th and early 15th centuries when it began to decline and for several decades it was subjugated by the rulers of Kotte. At the height of its power it had extended its influence beyond the present northern province into parts of the Sinhalese kingdom. But that had been for a short period only.[3]

To claim that the whole of the Northern Province and Eastern Province are constituent parts of the traditional homelands of the Tamils is very much in excess of what the facts of history would support. Most of the Eastern Province and the Vanni districts were sparsely populated, and at all times have had a Sinhalese population; indeed in many parts of the interior of these areas they had been a majority of the population. The eastern seaboard was part of the Kandyan kingdom. For much of the 19th century and early 20th century, the Tamil population there was concentrated in and around Trincomalee and the Batticaloa lagoon. These littoral settlements were in the nature of a thin strip and had also a large Muslim population; the interior was forest, sparsely populated, and contained Sinhalese settlements in what are called *purana* (i.e., traditional) villages. These Sinhalese settlements, although smaller in terms of population than either the Tamil or Muslim ones, and few and far between were distributed throughout the interior of the Eastern Province and its two divisions of the Trincomalee and Batticaloa districts.

The TULF's claim that state-sponsored peasant colonization schemes located in the eastern parts of the country and in the periphery of the Northern Province constitute a process of Sinhalese encroachment on areas traditionally occupied by other ethnic groups in former times is a refinement of similar charges laid by the Tamil Congress before the Soulbury Commission in 1944. We shall turn to this second aspect later on in this chapter. Here we need to examine the charge in relation to the Gal-Oya project, the first major irrigation and settlement project after independence, and the first new major scheme since the days of the Polonnaruva kings. We need to begin with C.W. Nicholas's path-breaking monograph on the *Historical Topography of Ancient and Medieval Ceylon*[4] in which specific reference is made to the Gal-Oya scheme, and shows it as occupying for the greater part the ancient and important territorial division called Dighavapi-Mandala or Dighavapi-rata. Professor Gerald Peiris, whose research on land settlement policies[5] and their impact on the demography of the Trincomalee and Batticaloa districts are the first to critically examine these in the light of the theory of the traditional homeland of the Tamils as proposed by the FP and the TULF, points out that Gal-Oya and most of the other major colonization schemes of the Eastern Province are located in areas which in 1921 — and at the time of the census of that year — were either the sites of remnant Sinhalese villages or were under the jungle tide. Indeed these settlements had survived several centuries of war and invasion, of pestilence and privation, and the ravages of nature in the forms of droughts, floods and cyclones, till they were revitalized in the years after independence as peasant "colonies," that is to say village settlements of the Gal-Oya scheme. The second point he makes is just as important as this: that contrary to claims made by the TULF, colonization schemes such as the Gal-Oya have had little effect on the older Tamil settlements of the Eastern Provinces — or the areas in which such settlements are located.

Apart from its dubious historicity the traditional homelands theory as propounded by Federal Party politicians and publicists of this period has at least four other flaws and contradictions. One of these is the assumption that the district and provincial boundaries as at the time of the transfer of power from the British are entitled to a long-term political validity if not finality. These boundaries represented a continuous process of change in response to political, economic and administrative factors and considerations. These changes made little concession to historical traditions; indeed British administrators were either ignorant of, or ignored these. They made some concession to topography, and the island's physical features. At no stage did they make an attempt to make these boundaries conform to the ethnic profile of regions; all districts and all provinces were at all times ethnically heterogenous.

Secondly, the advocates of a traditional homeland for the Tamils need to confront the demographic reality of a vital Tamil presence in other parts of the island. 29.2% of the Sri Lanka Tamils lived outside the Northern and Eastern Provinces at the census of 1971. This figure has been maintained, and indeed has increased, since then to 32.8% at the 1981 census.

Thirdly, politicians and publicists who protest against alleged Sinhalese encroachments into the so-called traditional homelands of the Tamils, have seldom shown any sensitivity to the grievances of the Kandyan Sinhalese to the massive presence of Indian — almost entirely Tamil — plantation workers, a process of demographic transformation which is historically of very recent origin, and one which transformed parts of a traditionally Sinhalese region into a poly-ethnic community; in some parts, the Indian Tamils far outnumbered the local Sinhalese population, as for example in the Nuwara Eliya district. Tamil politicians of the Federal Party and the present Tamil United Liberation Front see no contradiction in advocating the preservation of the so-called traditional homelands of the Tamils from Sinhalese encroachment while at the same time championing the cause of Indian Tamils settled in Sinhalese areas in response to the demand for labour on the plantations which the local population was unwilling or reluctant to meet. As we have seen in Chapter II of this book, population increase through immigration of Indian labor was greater than natural increase of population during some decades of the late 19th and the early 20th century. Most if not all of these immigrants moved into the Kandyan areas to the tea and rubber plantations there.

And finally, from the 1930s when the regeneration of the dry zone of the ancient *rajarata*, the core of which lies in the present North Central Province, and its peripheral region, began on a systematic basis, the Tamils who lived to the north east looked upon this process of economic development with a mixture of fear and anxiety; a fear and anxiety which found expression in the criticisms levelled at D.S. Senanayake's land policies in the evidence of the Tamil Congress and other Tamil spokesmen placed before the Soulbury Commission.[6] The ebbing of the jungle tide that had submerged this region for centuries, and the moving frontier of Sinhalese settlement represented, or were seen to represent, a potent threat to the majority status the Tamils enoyed in the north and some parts of the north east of the island. This fear and anxiety became more pronounced after independence, and formed the basis of the theory of the traditional homelands of the Tamils. The theory — and here we come to the fourth point — ignored the hard economic reality that the forests of these regions could not serve forever as a buffer between the two ethnic groups, the one — the Tamils — anxious to preserve their ethnic dominance of these regions, and the other moving in to do battle with the forests and the anopheles mosquito in a historic return to the heartland of the hydraulic civili-zations of old. Resources of land and water are scarce in all the dry zone regions and the preservation of an uninhabited no-man's land in the face of unprecedented population pressure is as unreasonable as it is inequitable. Moreover, as Professor Peiris points out, while 'state-sponsorship' has "admittedly been a vital element in land settlement schemes," this was necessarily so because such schemes "were meant for the poorest segment of the population — the landless peasantry. But neither in this nor in state responses to ... encroachment [on state lands] do we find any evidence of discrimination against the Sri Lanka Tamils."[7]

The Language Issue

The traditional homelands theory, for all the passion it generated was essentially a defensive reaction, the political expression of the self-preservative urge. The language issue was much more than merely defensive: it was at the heart of the problem of the assertion of the Tamils' ethnic identity, at the heart too of a process of integration among them whereby parochial regional ties were transcended within Sri Lanka, while links were sought with the Indian Tamils resident in the island and, in the eyes of the Sinhalese more ominous than that, with the mass of Tamils in Southern India. To the Sinhalese the linkage between language and religion was central to the assertion of ethnic identity; to the Tamils language was all and religion if not secondary at least not as organically linked with language in ethnic identity as it was in the case of Sinhalese and Buddhism. Language transcended the religious differences among the Tamils between Hindu and Christian. It is only now, in the early 1980s, that one sees the same process at work among the Sinhalese; in the period under review in this present chapter religious loyalties remained a potent divisive issue among them.

On the language issue, the Tamils started with the moral advantage accruing to an aggrieved party in the unilateral abrogation of a policy outlined and accepted only three years before the grant of independence, and which could therefore, be regarded as an integral element of the transfer of power settlement. Much of the passionate opposition of the Tamils to the fundamental change in language policy which emerged in the mid-1950s can be explained in terms of a sense of helplessness in the face of a reneging on guarantees given just before the transfer of power. The helplessness turned to despair when it was seen that the constitution itself offered little or no protection to them in regard to this.

The two protagonists in this tragic dispute became, each in their own way, the instrument of one of the most powerful forces of change in recent times — linguistic nationalism. They were each so dazzled by its power, and so eager to exploit its potential for the clarification and amplification of ethnic identity, that they failed to understand, or understanding it under-estimated, the levels of statesmanship required for controlling its explosive effect on state and society. And as one watched the clash of linguistic nationalisms work its destabilizing way through the Sri Lanka polity, one could only think of those ancient mythic expressions of mankinds's folly in tampering with destructive forces best kept in a state of stable control: releasing the genie out of the bottle, or opening Pandora's box.

The advocates of the policy of 'Sinhala only' to be imposed through an abrogation of the settlement on language reached in 1943-44 used many arguments to support their case. Our concern here is with one of these, the fears expressed about Sinhalese, a uniquely Sri Lankan language being doomed to unequal competition with Tamil, a thriving Indian language, should parity of status be conceded to Tamil as an official language. That argument was not new; it had been used during the debate on language policy in 1944. While these fears were under-standable, they tended to exaggerate the competitive edge that extra-Sri Lankan aspects of Tamil language and culture gave the Sri Lankan version of that language. Looking back on these controversies one feels that the price the country paid in the breakdown of ethnic harmony, and in the distortion of the national priorities, outweighed the undeniable benefits the emphasis on indigenous languages brought to the people at large. Had the Sinhalese political leadership that suc-ceeded D.S. Senanayake not forced the pace of language change by seeking to give Sinhalese pride of place through an abrogation of the settlement on language reached in 1943-44, had they been more patient and eschewed the path of unilateral change, they may well have ensured the primacy of their language on a much more solid basis, without the rancor and bitterness that was the price of the 'Sinhala Only' policy. Quite apart from the natural advantages accuring to Sinhalese as the language of over two-thirds of the population, there was the powerful attraction of economic necessity — the Sinhalese areas offered by far the greatest opportunities of employment and trade. As it was the objective of 'Sinhala Only' has been pursued at the cost of conceding to the Tamils all the advantages of proclaiming to a sympathetic world that they, as a minority, have suffered greatly in the change in language policy imposed on them by an unsympathetic majority. More important, 'Sinhala Only' in its starkest form has proved to be an elusive objective, an abstraction the pursuit of which has had the double effect of destroying the political careers of many who sought to give it life, and of provoking a similar passionate commitment to the defense of their language by the Tamils. At the same time, concessions on language made to the Tamils through political necessity and a realistic adjustment to life in a plural society and democratic state have all but granted parity of status to the Tamil language. And yet the political benefits of these concessions, and the anticipated propaganda advantages local and foreign have proved to be just as elusive as the quest for 'Sinhala Only.' The significance of language concessions made to the Tamils is discussed in a Chapter XVIII of this book.

The vigor with which the Tamils fought back on the language issue, and the zeal they demonstrated on it are often seen as a rearguard struggle of a privileged minority at bay. Their fears were for their future, not the immediate present, and their political campaigns on the language issue demonstrated afresh that none fight more passionately than those who have a world to lose. The crux of the problem was the sense of grievance stemming from a feeling of relative deprivation, a sense of grievance that has persisted despite all the concessions on the use of the Tamil language in public life extracted from, if not conceded by, successive governments since 1958.

But economic pressures and concerns are only part, and often not even the most important feature, of linguistic nationalism in its various manifestations in the world. Language is the essence of ethnic identity, and language as the essence of the culture linked with it and the principal means for the protection if not preservation of that culture are just as significant as the economic factor, in explaining the powerful attractions of linguistic nationalism. Behind it all there is the realization that where the integrity of language is threatened, the cultural foundation of ethnicity is also threatened with erosion, and with that the very survival of the ethnic group. The fear, then, is of assimilation. The struggle for the integrity of the Tamil language is identified with and is regarded as identical with a defence of the rights of the Tamils in a hostile environment. It is a response which has brought the Hindus and Christians, both Roman Catholic and Protestant, together in a common defense of their Tamil identity expressed through the Tamil culture.

The one internal barrier among the Tamils that survived, for the most part, the integrative pressures of linguistic nationalism was caste. For many Tamils the preservation of traditional culture implied the maintenance of their caste system in all its rigidity. Given the fact that the *vellalas* — like their *goyigama* counterparts among the Sinhalese — formed a majority of the Tamil population the breakdown of caste barriers was more difficult to achieve than it was across the Palk Straits in Tamilnadu.

When the Tamils sought to rouse public opinion (especially international opinion) against Sri Lanka's Sinhalese majority after 1956, their campaign for the rights of the Tamil minority was vitiated by the orthodox Hindu resistance to the amelioration of the conditions of the *harijans*. Sinhalese politicians and Buddhist activists diverted attention to the evils of untouchability, to the great embarrassment of the Tamils. *The Prevention of Social Disabilities Act. No. 21 of 1957* made it an offense, punishable by fine or imprisonment, to impose "any social disability on any person by virtue of such other person's caste." By opening schools teaching in Sinhalese and establishing *viharas* in harijan villages, an attempt was made to use language and religion as parts of a policy of exploiting *harijans'* grievances against the larger Tamil community. But this link between the *harijans* and the Sinhalese Buddhists proved to be tenuous at best, and attempts to sustain it were half-hearted and fitful.

Nevertheless that policy was pursued by the SLFP-dominated governments of the 1960s and 1970s. There was during this period a positive improvement in the condition of the *harijans* but this could hardly be attributed to the government's solicitude on their behalf, for that concern was neither disinterested nor consistent. Much of that improvement was due to efforts of sections of the Tamil political leadership who had initiated a movement for the removal of the disabilities suffered by the *harijans* and long before Sinhalese politicians and Buddhist activists interested themselves in the problem. Marxist groups among the Tamils always took the lead in this. The Federal Party joined in this enterprise especially after 1956 but as the mainstream political party of the Tamil minority and dependent on *vellala* votes it was much more circumspect in dealing with these issues than the Marxists. Thus it was only in 1977 that a *harijan* was first elected to Parliament, at the fifth general election after Sri Lanka regained her independence.

Cafes and restaurants in urban areas particularly have permitted entry to *harijans* and more important, despite occasional, well-publicized and impassioned efforts at resistance, one by one the large temples have opened their doors to them. The resistance to temple entry continued into the early 1970s. It was led by C. Suntheralingam, one-time Professor of Mathematics, Cabinet Minister, and the man who devised the mathematical formula in the Pan-Sinhalese Ministry of 1936-43, and more recently, an idealogue of Eelam, a Tamil state in Sri Lanka. In Suntheralingam's futile resistence to temple entry one sees the flickering embers of the Ramanathan tradition in the politics of the Tamils of Sri Lanka fanned into flames by the defenders of Hindu-orthodoxy and *vellala* privilege. It took a small scale version of the U.S. civil rights movement in the Jaffna peninsula to douse those flames for good and all.

The Tamilnadu Factor

Divergent historical traditions, subtle but significant distinctions in cultural patterns and the presumed purity and integrity of each other's version of the Tamil language, combined with a narrow and shallow stretch of sea to separate the Tamils of Sri Lanka from the Tamils of, what is today the province of, Tamilnadu. In the early years of independence the Sri Lanka Tamils of the north and the east of the island showed little inclination to identify themselves with the Tamils of Tamilnadu across the Palk Straits. Nevertheless the Sinhalese feared this possibility. These fears were intensified with the emergence of the Federal Party, and with the unfolding of its political programs, beginning with that party's advocacy of the grant of Sri Lankan citizenship rights to Indian plantation workers resident in the island. The political program outlined by the Federal Party in 1956-57 was even more significant in this regard; indeed it was a major turning point in convincing large sections of Sinhalese political opinion that the long-term implications of that program were ominous in their potential for a linkage of Tamil groups in South Asia: Tamilnadu and Sri Lanka.

The decline of the Indian National Congress as a regional force in Southern India, and its supercession by the Dravida Munetra Kazhagam (DMK), exponents of the policies of ethnicity, more conscious of the rights of Tamils, and much less restrained in giving expression to their concern on matters relating to Tamils in Sri Lanka, served to aggravate the situation. Exaggerated assessments of the influence of the DMK's political ideology on Tamil politics in Sri Lanka, and particularly on the politics of the Jaffna peninsula, were less important in this regard than the insensitivity of Tamilnadu politicians to Sri Lankan sensibilities displayed particularly in the manner in which issues relating to Sri Lanka's two Tamil minorities were raised, and the provocative terms in which they were discussed, in the Indian legislature in New Delhi, and the Tamilnadu Legislative Assembly. In the period covered in this chapter their principal concern was on the question of citizenship rights of Indian Tamil plantation workers in the island: they were soon to extend the scope of their comments and their political concerns to the Sri Lankan Tamils as well.

And then there was the lunatic fringe of Tamil politics in Southern India, groups such as Nam Tamilar ('We Tamils') who dream of a revival of the glories of the Tamil kingdoms of old with their overseas possessions in South and South East Asia, a Tamil empire stretching over peninsular India, and into northern Sri Lanka.[8] These insubstantial posturings were taken seriously enough by people inclined to harbor suspicions of Tamil ambitions, as firm evidence of intentions for the future, not as idle dreams of a past that had gone for good and all, and served to remind the Sinhalese that Sri Lanka lay all too close to the one region of the Indian Union that has illusions about restoring the glories of empires of old.

Far more serious was the presumed threat posed by the forces of Tamil separatism in south India represented by the DMK. That threat was successfully checked by the Indian government by the early 1960s, but its appeal to Sri Lanka Tamils was there, an example to be followed.

All this was inherent in the unfolding of linguistic nationalism among the Tamils of South Asia, responding to the linguistic nationalism of the Sinhalese in Sri Lanka, and the threat of a Hindi *raj* in Southern India. It served to rouse the atavistic fears, suspicions and even hatred of Southern India in the minds of the Sinhalese.

The Indian Tamils

As with the *harijans* so with the Indian Tamils resident in Sri Lanka, caste and class barriers proved too formidable for easy crossing by the integrative forces of linguistic nationalism. The Federal Party consistently sought that linkage, but just as consistently the principal representatives of Indian opinion in Sri Lanka — the Ceylon Indian Congress — rejected it because the latters' problems were of a totally different nature from the conception of Tamil rights propounded by the former, and a joining together in political activity would only cause further difficulties for the hardpressed Indian Tamils in Sri Lanka.

The citizenship legislation of 1948-49 and subsequent amendments had provided a legal definition of citizenship which excluded most of the Indian Tamils, and the suffrage was limited to citizens of Sri Lanka. The vast majority of Indians resident in Sri Lanka were classified as stateless. It was never intended that they would remain permanently in this state of limbo. If far fewer Indians than anticipated secured Sri Lankan citizenship this was due as much to the mismanagement of the campaign of opposition to this legislation led by the Ceylon Indian Congress as to the zeal with which Sri Lankan officials stuck doggedly to the letter of the law. The Ceylon Indian Congress leadership had responded to this legislation with symbolic gestures of opposition in of the Gandhian tradition, fasts in public places, *satyagrahas* and the like, all intended to use moral pressure on the Sri Lankan government and to rouse public opinion both in the island and outside it to the cause of the Indians here.[9] They had the support at all times of left-wing and Marxist opinion. Outside the country they had the moral and political support of the Indian government, and the state government of present-day Tamilnadu. The latter's support could on occasion be more enthusiastic than was diplomatically acceptable, while other political groups and individuals in Madras and other parts of the state would go well beyond the level of support extended by the state government in sustaining the cause of the Indians in Sri Lanka. Indeed when in 1952, the Ceylon Workers Congress (as the old Ceylon Indian Congress now called itself) embarked on a 100 day *satyagraha* it required considerable tact and diplomacy to prevent "volunteers" from coming over from Madras to join the campaign.[10]

But the advantages were with the Sri Lanka government. They had compelled the Indians to come to terms with the reality that citizenship would be determined on rules and regulations designed by the Sri Lanka government with very little influence on these from India. Nevertheless the Indians were physically present in Sri Lanka, and the Indian government for its part refused to accept any responsibility for repatriating any significant portion of them to India.

The issue came up for discussion once more between the two Prime Ministers in 1953 at a Commonwealth conference in London. There

D.S. Senanayake's son and successor as Prime Minister, Dudley Senanayake, faced Nehru whose single minded opposition to repatriation
was well known. The talks between the two Prime Minsiters were more
important for the formula that Dudley Senanayake introduced on that
occasion than for any great success achieved in reaching an agreement
on it. That formula, set out below, was to be the essence of all future
negotiations.

The formula recognized three categories of Indian residents in Sri
Lanka: firstly, those who qualified for Sri Lankan citizenship under the
prevailing citizenship laws; secondly, those who do not qualify for
citizenship but, subject to future review, would be granted permanent
residence status on work permits; and the third category would be
Indian citizens who would be gradually but compulsorily repatriated to
India. The figures Senanayake had in mind for each of these categories
were as follows: 400,000 for the first category, 200,000 for the second,
and 300,000 for the third. [11]

Once more, as in 1947, there was agreement in principle, but once
more the talks collapsed in regard to its implementation, and once
more the blame for the failure attaches to Nehru whose attitude on this
has been described as "both unyielding and unreal." [12] What he wanted
was a reduction of the numbers in the third category from 300,000 to
250,000 to which Senanayake was opposed. Nehru, one suspects, was
testing the staying power and tenacity of the new Prime Minister, and
would make no concessions himself. Indeed Nehru, with the fate of the
Indian minority in Burma very much in mind, was unhappy about
accepting the principle of repatriation of Indians, even those with
Indian passports. Thus one more opportunity was missed.

After Dudley Senanayake had resigned office in September 1953
and was replaced by Sir John Kotelawala, another round of talks began,
in January 1954, and on this occasion an agreement was reached,
endorsing the three-categories formula of 1953. It was the Sri Lanka
government that was now anxious to reach an agreement, and not
merely because of the physical presence of the Indians in Sri Lanka.
There was the equally important issue of the surreptitious addition to
their numbers through a process of illicit immigration from across the
Palk Straits. A promise was extracted of Indian assistance in checking
this traffic, a task which had hitherto been performed by Sri Lanka's
miniscule security forces.

One important feature of this agreement was that Indians accepted
as Sri Lanka citizens under its terms would be placed on a separate

register, and a special constituency, an 'Indian and Pakistani district' which would return up to 4 MPs. In insisting on this the Kotelawala government was safeguarding its own political base and demonstrating its interest in protecting the Kandyan constituencies from being swamped at a future date by Indian Tamils. This agreement broke down over implementation. All parties concerned, the two governments on the one hand, and the Ceylon Workers Congress on the other, were suspicious of each others motives and intentions. The Ceylon Workers Congress was hostile to the principle of a separate register and a separate communal electorate which they regarded as flagrantly discriminatory, and one has reason to believe that their opposition to this had much to do with the eventual failure to implement the agreement. S.W.R.D. Bandaranaike never had time to focus attention on this issue during his administration and by the early 1960s it had become an intractable one with neither government prepared to make concessions to the other's point of view.

An agreement eventually emerged in 1964 with Mrs. Bandaranaike as Prime Minister of Sri Lanka, and Lal Bahadur Shastri as Nehru's successor. The basis of the agreement was the three-categories formula introduced by Dudley Senanayake in 1953. Nehru's death and India's discomfiture in the border war with China had more to do with the success of these negotiations than the negotiating skills and techniques of the Sri Lankan delegation. Nehru at every stage balked at the prospect of having to accept large numbers of Indian repatriates from territories in which they had settled. His successor, Shastri, had fewer compunctions about accepting the need to concede this principle. Besides he had a more modest vision of India's position in the world than Nehru's lofty aspiration to the role of the conscience of the world, or at least of the third world.

The agreement Shastri reached with Mrs. Bandaranaike provided for: the repatriation over a 15 year period of 525,000 Indian residents in Sri Lanka to India, along with their natural increase; the absorption of 300,000 as citizens by Sri Lanka; while the future of the remaining 150,000 would be negotiated later on by the two countries. The practical benefits to all parties were quite considerable, not least to the Indians in Sri Lanka, 300,000 of whom were to become Sri Lankan citizens. But two parties — the Indian government and the Indians in Sri Lanka — had their reservations about the principle of compulsory repatriation of those who opted for and obtained Indian citizenship.

In a reversion to a line of policy originally devised by the Kotelawala government in 1954 Mrs. Bandaranaike decided to place all persons of recent Indian origin, those who had already obtained Sri Lanka citizenship, as well as those who were entitled to it under the agreement of 1964, on a separate electoral register. This move was designed to protect the political interests of the Kandyans. It antagonized all sections of Indian opinion resident in the island. They regarded the separate electoral register and a separate constituency as patently discriminatory because it established two categories of voters, one of which was distinctly inferior because its basis was ethnic identity.

The result was a remarkable change in political alignments with the Ceylon Workers Congress, the most powerful trade union *cum* political party among the plantation workers, withdrawing its support for the government and, in a surprising *volte-face*, swinging over to an alliance with its former *bete noire*, the UNP. The reconciliation was based on the understanding that the UNP would repudiate the policy of a separate register for Indians, and examine afresh the requirement that those who obtained Indian citizenship would be immediately repatriated. With the establishment of the UNP-led coalition government of 1965 these pledges were honored. Those Indians who secured Sri Lankan citizenship remained on the general electoral roll along with all others, and those who were granted Indian citizenship were permitted to remain in the island, if necessary to the end of their working days, to be repatriated thereafter, or at a time to be determined by the Sri Lankan government. The SLFP for its part did not revive the principle of a separate electoral register for Indians, but when in office in the 1970s insisted on a linkage between immediate repatriation and the conferment of Indian citizenship.

The UNP-CWC entente has been a prominent feature of Sri Lankan politics since the mid-1960s, to the advantage of both parties. On the part of the CWC it reflected a more pragmatic and less doctrinnaire approach to politics than that of the Federal Party and its successors; it also demonstrated that the linguistic nationalism of the Tamils had its own limits and could not bring all Tamils together within the Sri Lanka polity.

References

1   This resolution is published in A. Amirthalingam, 'The Path to our Destiny' in *The Silver Jubilee Souvenir of the Federal Party* (Jaffna, 1974), p. 17.

2   See Appendix below pp. 398-400.

3   For discussion of the historical background see K.M. de Silva, *A History of Sri Lanka*, pp. 81-99.

4   This monograph was published as a special issue of the *Journal of the Royal Asiatic Society (Ceylon Branch)*, n.s. VI (1963), pp. 1-232.

5   From G.H. Peiris, 'An Appraisal of the Concept of a Traditional Tamil Homeland in Sri Lanka', mimeographed paper presented at a conference on 'The Economic Consequences of Ethnic Conflict in Sri Lanka,' 8 August 1985 at Kandy, Sri Lanka.

6   Criticisms of D.S. Senanayake's agricultural policy and irrigation schemes figured prominently in the charges of discrimination laid before the Soulbury Commission. The charge then was of a diversion of funds to the Sinhalese areas of the dry zone. The Soulbury Commission reviewed these criticisms in pp. 44-47 of their report, and rejected them (see particularly paragraph 166 on p. 47).

7   G.H. Peiris, *op. cit.*, p. 34.

8   On the 'We Tamil' movement and its political ambitions see, Robert Hardgrave Jnr., *The Dravidian Movement* (Bombay, 1965) p. 50. See also S.U. Kodikara, *Indo-Ceylon Relations Since Independence*, pp. 228-233.

9   In a self-destructive mood the Ceylon Indian Congress began by actively discouraging its membership from applying for Sri Lanka citizenship under the new legislation. Just before the time limit for applications was up they changed their mind. The result was a flood of applications at the last minute or just after the prescribed time limit. Thus scrutiny of these applications was delayed and it became easier to reject many on purely technical grounds.

10 S.U. Kodikara, *Indo-Ceylon Relations Since Independence*, *op.cit.*, pp. 220-237.

11 *Ibid.* pp. 123-5.

12 H. Tinker, *The Banyan Tree, Overseas Emigrants from India, Pakistan and Bangladesh* (London, 1977) p. 42.

Chapter XV

The Muslims in Post Independence
Sri Lanka: The Politics
of Pragmatic Adaptation

The Muslims: No "Ethnic" Political Parties

The story of the Muslims in post-independence Sri Lanka is the story of how a small minority converted its intrinsic disadvantages — disadvantages we have referred to in Chapter VIII above — into positive advantages in their efforts to strengthen their position in the Sri Lanka polity. The distribution of Muslim settlements — their dispersal rather than concentration — had been a perennial problem because of its political implications in regard to representation in the national legislature. During the debate of 8 November 1945 on the adoption of the Soulbury proposals, A.R.A. Razik made pointed reference to this, and had urged that the Muslims be treated as a "down-trodden" community who had never been adequately represented in the national legislature. To "wipe off for good the grave injustice which the Moors had suffered politically" he pleaded for the provision of 12 seats for the Moors — as he persisted in calling the Muslim community.[1] The Delimitation Commission of 1946 gave the Muslims much fewer than the 12 seats Razik asked for, but what they got was a substantial improvement on the parlous position to which they had been reduced under the Donoughmore system.

In the electoral scheme devised by the Soulbury Commissioners the Muslims entitlement in parliamentary representation was assessed at six seats. It was expected that they would probably get four. In fact they got six, one of which was H.S.Ismail's uncontested election at Puttalam, and a Muslim candidate's unexpected win at Batticaloa over a multiplicity of Tamil contestants in a seat which had a Tamil majority. In 1952 six Muslim candidates were returned to Parliament, two from the three-member Colombo Central constituency. A.R.A. Razik, defeated in the Pottuvil constituency in the Eastern Province in 1947 as a UNP candidate, won in Colombo Central in 1952 as an independent.

The Muslims had two points in their favor in competitive politics in post-independence Sri Lanka, and in regard to both they provided such a strong contrast to the Tamils. To take the first of these: since 1956 the mainstream Tamil leaders have regarded their community as a separate entity, separate that is from the island's political community, and occupying as they did distinct blocs of territory in some of which they constituted a majority of the population their politics emphasized regional autonomy based on ethnic identity and this later took a separatist or secessionist form. Their politics were perceived as a threat both to the legitimacy of majority rule and the integrity of the nation. Muslim politics offered a complete contrast to this. They deferred to the will of the majority on most occasions (such as the ready acceptance of Sinhalese as the single national language) and were deferred to in turn (on education, for instance). They were helped in this quite substantially by the volatility of Sri Lanka's political system in which from 1956 onwards the ruling party was defeated on six consecutive occasions (including 1956). The result was that Muslims were offered opportunities for political bargaining which they used to the great advantage of their community.

Looking back on it one feels that the Muslims had made one funda-mentally important decision, and this too set them apart from the Tamils. They have no "ethnic" political parties of their own nominating candidates to seats. Neither the All Ceylon Muslim League, nor the All Ceylon Moors Association became Muslim political parties in the years after independence, while their contemporary, the All-Ceylon Tamil Congress continued as a Tamil political party and was indeed, the principal Tamil political organization in the island till the mid-1950s. Muslims have sought and obtained membership, and achieved positions of influence in all the major national political parties (save the Tamil parties) and in particular the UNP and SLFP. As we have seen in Chapter VIII when the UNP was formed in 1946 the Muslim League joined it, and A.R.A. Razik as the Moor leader became one of its first joint Treasurers. Thus began a link with the UNP which has given that party a majority of the Muslim vote at every election since 1947. The defeat of the UNP in 1956 presented some difficulties to the Muslims because of their strong commitment to that party. But soon the SLFP as the party in power began to attract substantial Muslim support. This owed little to the first Muslim Cabinet Minister of the SLFP, C.A.S. Marikkar. The second of them, Badi-ud-din Mahmud, was an altogether different proposition. He was — unlike Marikkar — a man of considerable influence within the party, and he skilfully demonstrated that Cabinet office was an excellent base for a leadership role in the affairs of the Muslim community. Mahmud had two spells in Parliament, 1960 to 1965, 1970-77; on both occasions he was an appointed M.P. not an elected one. On both he was a key figure in the SLFP, but in the second he sought to expand the political base he built by forming another political organization, the Islamic Socialist Front, which linked the SLFP with an articulate but numerically small group of Muslims to the left of the traditional SLFP supporters in that community. He was defeated soundly when he stood for election, for the first time, in 1977, and the Islamic Socialist Front did not survive his defeat.

The UNP has always had more Muslim MPs than the SLFP. Within the party Colombo-based Muslims have been the dominant element until very recently when the appointment of A.C.S. Hameed as Foreign Minister, and M.A. Bakeer Markar as Speaker, marked the emergence of Muslims with a provincial base — the equivalent in the UNP of B. Mahmud the school principal from Zahira College, Gampola — to positions of prominence.

Every Cabinet since 1947 has had a Muslim in it, the present one has 3. This was not true of the Tamils. The first Cabinet after independence had 2 Tamils; there was one between 1952 and 1956, but none at all for nearly 10 years thereafter, till 1965 when the Federal Party nominated M. Tiruchelvam to Dudley Senanayake's coalition government of 1965.

Even more remarkable is the ready acceptance of Muslim candidates by Sinhalese voters in electorates in which Muslims are often less than a fifth of the total voting strength. It began with C.A.S. Marikkar for the SLFP, and Abdul Jabbar for the same party. While Marikkar won easily in a double-member constituency (Kadugannava, 1952-59), Jabbar won in a single-member constituency in which Muslims formed only 4% of the voters.[2] The most remarkable performances have been by UNP Muslim candidates. Puttalam, for instance, has no Muslim majority but it has always been held by a Muslim since H.S. Ismail was returned uncontested to that seat in 1947. Or take the case of A.C.S.

Hameed, presently Foreign Minister: he has often been the first of two MPs for the Akurana (now Harispattuva) seat in which the Muslims are only 17% of the voting strength. M.H. Mohammed, another Cabinet Minister, has won Borella, an urban constituency in Colombo with less than 5% Muslim voters, and on all occasions he has faced Sinhalese opponents. And most remarkable of all is the case of M.L.M. Abusally MP for Balangoda, a seat he won against the powerful family interest of the Ratwattes, Mrs. Bandaranaike's family, in their home territory. The Muslims constituted just 2.75% of the voters there. In brief, the Muslims are regarded as being so clearly integrated into the Sri Lankan political community that Sinhalese vote for them on party grounds against Sinhalese opponents. In contrast not a single Tamil candidate has won a seat in a predominantly Sinhalese area since independence, except for the Indian Tamils winning seats in the plantation districts or in the periphery of such districts. Only one Tamil has ever won a seat outside the Northern and Eastern Provinces since 1931: this was J.G. Rajakulendran, who won the Bandarawela seat in the State Council at a by-election in 1943, and Bandarawela had a very large Indian Tamil vote.

This peculiar — and sagacious — political behavior of the Muslims in resisting the temptation to form a Muslim political party, the equivalent of the Tamil parties whether of the indigenous Tamils or the Ceylon Workers Congress and the much less important Democratic Workers Congress in the case of the Indian Tamils, was noted as early as 1974.[3] Since then a number of persons have drawn attention to it, most notably M.H. Mohammed in the course of a television interview he gave in the aftermath of the July 1983 ethnic violence in the country. He spoke of it as a positive virtue of the Muslims, and proceeded, by implication. to draw the obvious contrast to the political behavior of the Tamils.

In practice, if not theory, the Indian Tamils have taken a leaf from the Muslims' book. Thus in the local government elections of 1979, and in the elections to the District Development Councils in 1981, Indian Tamils belonging to the Ceylon Workers Congress contested on the UNP ticket. This arrangement broke down at the local government elections of 1983, but in the aftermath of the ethnic violence of July/August 1983, a small group belonging to that community have called for a return to the old arrangement for the future, and in so doing they spoke of the wisdom of emulating the political behavior of the Muslims. Indeed they urge that Indian Tamils join the major political parties in the island, and by implication that they abandon the C.W.C. and D.W.C. because of the ethnic nature of these politcal bodies.

To be sure not all Muslims are happy with this state of affairs. Indeed some have argued — especially those from the Eastern Province where the Muslims form a substantial group in the population — the case for a Muslim political party independent of the existing national parties, and pursuing the sectional interests of the Muslims with single-minded commitment to Islamic principles.[4] That argument is based on fallacious assumptions, and the pursuit of such a policy is fraught with perils for the Muslims. There is nothing that such a Muslim political party can do for the Muslims that they cannot do as members of national political parties. And above all else advocates of such a Muslim political party tend to ignore the very substantial gains that have accrued to the Muslims since independence, a theme to which we now turn.

Muslim Interests And Electoral Politics

What the Muslims have attempted to do is to safeguard, sustain and advance their distinctive cultural identity. They have sought and obtained state support for this in two distinct fields: first, the consolidation and recognition of the personal laws of the Muslims; and secondly in education. The first of these has been dealt with in Chapter VIII and here we need do no more than state that this trend has continued after independence. The provisions of the *Muslim Intestate Succession and Wakfs Ordinance of 1931* relating to Muslim charitable trusts (*Wakfs*) was superceded by the *Muslim Mosques and Charitable Trusts or Wakfs Act of 1956*, while the *Muslim Marriage and Divorce Registration Ordinance 27 of 1929* was repealed by the *Muslim Marriage and Divorce Act 13 of 1951* (operative from 1954) which enhanced the powers of the *quazis* who were given exclusive jurisdiction in respect of marriages and divorces, and the status and mutual rights and obligations of the parties concerned. The *Wakfs Act of 1956* established a separate government department with an executive board consisting of Muslims. The constitutions of the first and second republics preserved the personal law of the Muslims.

The most significant gains have been made in education and this was especially so after 1956. Special government Training Colleges have been set up for the Muslims. Arabic is taught in government schools as an optional language to Muslim pupils, and taught by *maulavis* appointed by the Ministry of Education and paid by the state. Muslim children had the right (till 1974) to pursue their studies in any one of the three language media — Sinhalese, Tamil or English — a privilege no other group in the country enjoyed. In recognition of the cultural individuality of Muslims as distinct from the Tamils whose language is the home language of large numbers of Muslims, a new category of government schools has been established. The usual practice had been to categorize schools on the basis of the language of instruction in them and the Muslims formed part of the Tamil-speaking school population. In the new 'Muslim' schools the sessions and vacations are determined by the special requirements of the Muslim population. The establishment and expansion of their schools, it must be emphasized, vitiates the principle of non-sectarian state education which has been the declared policy of all governments since 1960.

This sensitivity to the special Muslim identity in education had begun with C.W.W. Kannangara before independence[5] and was now continued with W. Dahanayake as Minister of Education (1956-59). It received greater emphasis with Badi-ud-din Mahmud who served as Minister of Education from 1960-63, and then again from 1970 to 1977. In the first period he piloted the landmark education legislation of Mrs. Bandaranaike's first government; in his second his role was more controversial especially in regard to a crucial change of policy in university admissions — and he was often seen as a special advocate of Muslim interests through his Ministry.

It would be too naive to assume that these concessions were won because of Sinhalese altruism. On the contrary one has the feeling that quite often Sinhalese politicians have used state resources to build the Muslims as a counterweight to the Tamil community in a game of checks and balances which is an intrinsic element in the process of government in a plural society.

Muslim-Tamil Rivalry

Muslim-Tamil rivalry in Sri Lanka is a political reality, and the Muslims themselves have responded with alacrity to Sinhalese overtures to back them against the Tamils. The rivalry has been most marked in relation to education where apart from the Muslims' anxiety to break away from Tamil tutelage in schools of the Tamil medium they have successfully lobbied for more Muslim schools, and more Muslim teachers. They have pursued diametrically opposed policies on the question of university admissions. The Muslims have been among the most persistent advocates of ethnic quotas in university admissions;[6] the Tamils stand for open competition and academic merit as the main criteria for admission to the universities.

In the mid-1950s some Muslims in the Eastern Province did link themselves with the Tamils in the latters' attempt to build an organization of the "Tamil-speaking peoples" of Sri Lanka on whose behalf the Tamil political leadership campaigned to preserve their language rights. Indeed some Muslims contested on the Federal Party ticket in 1956 and won election to Parliament.[7] But their loyalty to the Federal Party did not survive the bitter conflicts on language that broke out from the very first months of the third Parliament. Soon, the Muslims reconciled themselves to the new language policy introduced by the Bandaranaike government, and the fragile alliance of Tamils and some Eastern Province Muslims as "the Tamil-speaking peoples of the island" was shattered, never to be put together again. Again, the Muslims have been among the most inveterate opponents of federalism and separatism, seeing in these the conferment of advantages on the Tamils which could endanger Muslim interests to a far greater extent than the country's unitary political structure. Thus, A.R.A. Razik as Sir Razik Fareed was one of the strongest opponents of the District Councils scheme which Dudley Senanayake sought to introduce between 1966 and 1968. Similarly two Muslim members of the Presidential Commission in District Development Councils, wrote a dissent against the main recommendations of that Commission in its report published in 1980.[8]

Neither the UNP nor the SLFP can take Muslim support for granted. While each has large reserves of support among the Muslims — the UNP's support among the Muslims has traditionally been larger than the SLFP's — they were aware that the Muslim vote can tilt the balance in not less than 15 electorates in all parts of the country and often did precisely that. They have seldom hesitated to vote against a governing party if it appeared — to the Muslims — to be inconsiderate to or negligent of Muslim interests. Thus in 1965, the then governments' failure to remedy the legal deficiencies which the

Supreme Court had pointed out in regard to the *quazi* courts, was a significant factor in turning large numbers of Muslims against them in the general election of that year. Then again some of that support returned to the SLFP and its allies in 1970 as part of a national trend against the UNP which was seen to have done more for the Tamils than for the Muslims.[9] But once again in 1977 the Muslims turned against the SLFP largely as a result of outbreaks of anti-Muslim rioting in several parts of the island in the mid-1970s. Charges of favored treatment of Muslims in the sphere of education appear to have kindled anti-Muslim sentiment among the Sinhalese. There were sporadic Sinhalese-Muslim clashes in various parts of the island in 1974-75, including a fracas at Gampola in the last week of 1975 in which the Minister of Education, Badi-ud-din Mahmud, and his old school, Zahira College, were at the center of it. A more dangerous confrontation occurred in Puttalam in early 1976, the worse episode of ethnic violence directed against the Muslims since the riots of 1915. All this led to a serious erosion of Muslim support for the SLFP.

Briefly then, while the Muslims have not been reluctant to look upon themselves as a counter-weight to the Tamils in the communal rivalries that have been so prominent in political development in post-independence Sri Lanka, they have seldom hesitated to express their displeasure at signs of neglect of their interests, or hostility to them by a government — and Sri Lanka's electoral system has provided them with all the opportunities they needed to make this displeasure felt. Governments have changed with remarkable frequency in Sri Lanka, and the Muslim community, small though it is, has contributed mightily to these swings of the electoral pendulum. As we have seen, the Muslims, in striking contrast to the Tamils, have no distinct ethnic or religious political parties of their own contesting seats to Parliament in competition with, if not in opposition to the main national political parties. Instead their political organizations work in association with and as adjuncts of the latter. The result is that the Muslim community, although numerically much smaller than the Tamils, have greater bargaining powers electorally than their numbers would seem to warrant.

References

1   *Hansard* [State Council] 1945, Vol. II columns, 7063-4.

2   This was the Galagedera seat which Jabbar won in July 1960. Marikkar had won it in March 1960.

3   K.M. de Silva, 'Hinduism and Islam in Post-Independence Sri Lanka' *CJHSS*, IV n.s. (1&2) pp. 98-103.

4   N.A.M. Hussain, 'Muslims in Sri Lanka Polity', *The Muslim World League Journal*, September 1982, pp. 46-50; October 1982, pp. 53-57; November 1982, pp. 45-47; December 1982, pp. 44-48.

5   See *The Soulbury Report* p. 49 where the Commissioners commented as follows: "We are much impressed by the efforts of the Minister of Education, himself a Sinhalese and a Buddhist, to promote the educational advance of [the Muslims]."

6   See the letter by Dr. M.C.M. Kaleel on 'University Admissions' in *The Ceylon Daily News*, 2 February 1982.

7   M.S. Kariappar, Kalmunai, and M.P.M. Mustapha, Pottuvil.

8   *S.P.V.* of 1980 *Report of the Presidential Commission on Development Councils*, pp. 83-102.

9   One of the points made was that although the Muslims had voted in larger numbers for the UNP than for the SLFP, Muslim members of UNP Cabinets generally held rather unimportant portfolios such as Labor whereas Muslim Cabinet Ministers of the SLFP were entrusted with more important areas of responsibility such as Health and Education.

PART IV

Ethnic Conflict and
Political Development, 1972-1985

Part IV

Ethnic Conflict and
Political Development, 1972-1985

Introduction

The strength of the new balance of forces of which the principal feature is the Sinhalese-Buddhist dominance of the Sri Lanka polity was demonstrated afresh when Mrs. Bandaranaike returned to power in May 1970 at the head of the United Front (UF) coalition between the SLFP, LSSP and the Communist Party (Moscow wing). Together they won 120 seats in Parliament, the first Sri Lankan government since independence to command a two-thirds majority in the national legislature without the need for support of the Tamil political parties. The election of 1970 was a setback for the FP, its worst performance since the debacle of 1952; its leader came through on a mere plurality of votes, and two of its leading members including A. Amirthalingam (the present leader of the Tamil United Liberation Front) lost their seats. But as in the mid-1950s the lost ground was recovered and on this occasion much earlier than on the previous one; in both cases the recovery came from leading the opposition to governmental policies perceived as being discriminatory to the Tamils. Despite the enthusiasm with which the Marxist parties, the LSSP and CP, had succumbed to the attractions of ethnic or communal politics in opposition in the period 1965-1970, the sharp reversal of electoral fortunes which saw them now in an influential position within the government raised hopes that their presence could mark the beginning of a more constructive phase in devising policies and mechanisms for dealing with the problems of the minorities. Not only did this not happen, but there was also very little evidence that the Marxist left made a determined bid to guide the new government to a less hostile attitude to the main Tamil parties than may have been expected from a SLFP government without Marxist coalition partners. Instead the SLFP dominated coalition applied old policies of the period 1956-1964 with regard to the Tamil minority, both indigenous and immigrant Indian, and applied them with renewed fervor. If this was only an accurate reflection of the great strength of the SLFP in the government as the principal political force in the UF coalition of the years 1970-75, it also demonstrated the ineffectiveness of the Marxist Cabinet Ministers — there were four in all, 3 LSSP and 1 CP — as a brake on the communalism that was rampant within the SLFP and through it within the UF government.

Of the acts of commission of the new government two in particular were decisive in widening the breach between itself and the Sri Lanka Tamils: the new republican constitution of 1972, of which Dr. Colvin de Silva, an LSSP stalwart and Minister of Constitutional Affairs was the mastermind; and a change in the policy on admission of students to the island's universities. Relations between the government and the leadership of the Ceylon Workers Congress, the principal trade union *cum* political organization of the immigrant Indians were as hostile as the government's attitude to the Federal Party. Indeed the period of office of the UF government was singularly barren of any political initiatives directed at defusing the ethnic tensions of the 1970s. Decentralization of administration through District Councils which had figured so prominently in the discussions on structural changes to manage ethnic conflicts and political controversies of the post-1956 period lay forgotten throughout these years. It was revived only after the electoral rout suffered by the remnants of this once powerful coalition at the general election of 1977.

In retrospect it would seem that the adoption of the first republican constitution on 22 May 1972 was the critical starting point of a new phase in ethnic conflict in Sri Lanka, a dangerously destabilizing phase which saw the triumph of the linguistic nationalism of the Sinhalese consolidated through a new political and constitutional framework, but confronting the new Tamil version of it taken to its logical conclusion in the form of a separatist movement. Between May 1972 and the end of 1976 we see a momentous shift in the political aspirations of the Sri Lanka Tamils, from demands for structural changes and constitutional reform, to an assertion of the right to self-determination on the basis of a Tamil state in Sri Lanka. That this latter change marked the culmination of a process of political thinking which began with the foundation of the Federal Party in 1949 was less important than the wide range of political support it attracted from groups not identified with, or hostile to, the FP — its traditional rival, the Tamil Congress, mainly, but also for a brief period the Ceylon Workers Congress.

More ominous for the long-term future of the Marxist parties, and the concept of a political alliance between the centrist SLFP and the former, was the challenge it faced from another quarter. The pace of change and reform in the first ten months of the UF government's tenure of office was inadequate to satisfy the aspirations of the more articulate and militant young people whose political appetite had been whetted by their zeal in working to bring the government to power. By the middle of March 1971 it was evident that the government faced a deadly threat from the Janatha Vimukhthi Peramuna (JVP) an ultra-left organization dominated by educated youths, unemployed or disadvantageously employed. The insurrection that broke out in April 1971 was, from beginning to end, a revolt of youth, an unusual, if not the first, instance of tension between generations breaking out into military conflict on a national scale. The creed of generational war was linked to eradicating a colonial status which had ended two decades previously but was presumed to be still in existence. It was a movement of the new left and the ultra-left against the established parties of the Marxist left, the LSSP and CP, and the populist SLFP. The insurgents were, in general, the children of the rural poor, Sinhalese and Buddhist. The ethnic and religious minorities of Sri Lanka played no significant part in the insurrection.

In the immediate sense the 1971 emergency failed. Once the momentum of their original thrust had been absorbed and repelled the insurgents were unable to sustain their attacks although they had the numbers to do so. The insurrection was crushed, but the defeated rebels played a part, indirectly if not directly, in shaping the future. They did this through the marked influence they had on policies adopted by the UF government: in hastening proceedings begun in 1970 for an autochthonous constitution for Sri Lanka to replace the Soulbury constitution; and in the impetus the insurrection gave to radical social and economic reform in the years 1972-75, as a result of which state control was extended to every sector of the economy, from trade to industry, and to the island's efficiently run plantations, foreign-owned and locally owned (which provided over two-thirds of the island's foreign currency earnings annually). Meanwhile restrictions were placed on land-holdings of Sri Lankans and their ownership of houses; land in excess of the ceiling imposed was taken over by the state with the promise of compensation, and in the case of houses and apartments, those in excess of the limit were re-distributed, in the first instance, among tenants in occupation of them. In brief, the rebels succeeded in pushing Sri Lanka more rapidly towards being a socialist society.

However these purportedly socialist measures did very little to improve the position of the poor, and the re-structuring of the economy which the government attempted did nothing to stimulate economic growth and little to check inflation. The economy remained stagnant, while inflation reached levels never experienced before in Sri Lanka, and unemployment rose to unprecedented levels. In a tight employment market and a state-dominated economy the struggle for jobs became fiercer than ever, and contributed greatly to the aggravation of ethnic tensions between the Sinhalese and the Tamils, not to mention the Muslims.

If the UF government made no positive contribution to easing emerging ethnic tensions, it aggravated them through its policy changes in the matter of university admissions. While other issues have contributed more substantially and dramatically to the sharp deterioration of ethnic relations in Sri Lanka in the last decade, none did more in radicalizing the politics of the Tamil areas in the north, and in particular the Jaffna peninsula, than this. It assumed such importance in regard to the management of ethnic conflict in the island that the reversal of the most objectionable features of this policy became an election pledge of the UNP than seeking to win power at the 1977 general elections, and the honoring of it was one of the first policy decisions announced and implemented soon after the UNP's overwhelming victory at the polls in July 1977. How a new policy on university admissions was devised thereafter is treated in detail in Chapter XIX.

One aspect of this university admissions policy needs mention here. It was piloted through to implementation in the face of Tamil opposition by Badi-ud-din Mahmud during his second term of office as Minister of Education (1970-77). He was always conscious of the special needs and interests of the Muslims in the vitally important area of education, and many policy decisions in his tenure of office as Minister of Education reflected his concern for these special needs and interests. In so doing he sharpened the competitive instincts of the Muslims in their traditional rivalry with the Tamils in education, and just as important contributed greatly to generating tensions between the Muslims and Sinhalese.

Significantly enough the years 1970-76 were notable for sporadic clashes between Sinhalese groups and Muslims in several parts of the island. In fact these clashes constitute the worst phase in Muslim-Sinhalese rivalries, tensions and resort to violence since the 1915 riots. Fortunately these clashes were not only sporadic, but also limited to a few localities. Causes of these clashes varied from locality to locality but the single common factor was the perception that too much concern was shown for Muslim interests in educational opportunities and employment as teachers in the government service.

We need to turn, at this stage, to the politics of the Jaffna peninsula. In retrospect it does seem that the militancy among Tamil youth there, a striking feature of this period, stemmed from similar, if not the same causes that led to the JVP insurrection and that the shock waves set off by the JVP were by no means limited to the Sinhalese areas of the country. These included the bleak employment prospects that faced Tamil youth. The frustration and anger this gave rise to turned to a profound alienation because of their perception of themselves as victims of deliberately devised policies of discrimination, and above all alienation from a political system which appeared to symbolize not merely class privileges but — and here lay the divergence from the JVP — also the dominance of an unsympathetic majority community. Thus while the Sinhalese youth in the JVP insurrection rose against a system which appeared to them as the embodiment of class privileges, and social and economic stagnation, the Tamil youths' perception accomodated all these but went beyond them in the sense of an ethnic alienation which lay at the core of their agitation, and became the cutting edge of the political unrest they generated: their rejection of the existing system because it was above all a Sinhalese-dominated system.[1] This new generation of young and impatient Tamils were soon the most militant supporters of the separatist cause, and the most volatile element in Tamil society. Beginning as foot soldiers of the separatist campaign, and the vital link between the established politicians of the TULF and the Tamil people in the north and east of the country, they were soon — by the late 1970s — much more than that: they helped fashion the ideology of separatism in the emphasis they gave to radicalism and various forms of Marxism, and to influence the strategy and tactics of the campaign for separatism. By the early 1980s, the parliamentarians of the TULF seem to have ceded to them, or were compelled to cede to them, the primary leadership role in the separatist movement. They were also — and here again there was a remarkable similarity with the JVP — the catalysts of revolutionary violence. At the core of the separatist movement, and from the very outset, were terrorist groups.

The salience of revolutionary violence and of terrorism among these youthful agitators for separatism raises complex issues relating to the legitimacy of terrorist violence by non-elected groups for achieving their ends in liberal democracies. (Had the JVP insurrection not been crushed as speedily as it was these same issues would have emerged in regard to the JVP's program as well.) Apart from the moral and political ambiguities inherent in these, there is also the fundamental problem of defining what terrorism is.

The term terrorism, like ethnicity, eludes precise definition.[2] Some writers on the theme would do without a definition of terrorism at all and proceed to describe or discuss it in its many manifestations as a harsh reality in contemporary world politics. In many ways this is preferable to the comfortble but bland moral neutrality of those who argue that one man's terrorist is another man's freedom fighter, and move on from that to blur the distinction between terrorism, war and ordinary criminal acts.[3] The distinction between terrorism, on the one hand and warfare, popular resistance and merely criminal acts on the other is provided by political strategy.

In the context of the political traditions of the Sri Lankan Tamils, there is a distinction between the current resort to terrorist acts, and civil disobedience campaigns directed against Sri Lankan goverments of post-independence Sri Lanka in the past, as well as civil rights campaigns directed against the more obnoxious features of Jaffna's caste system — the agitation for temple entry, for instance. One could argue that:

> "The obvious and most essential difference between civil disobedience and terrorism is clearly the latter's unswerving commitment to violence as a means to achieving the terrorist's goal, whereas civil disobedience uncompromisingly foreswears all forms of violence. Both may require breaking the laws of a nation, but for civil disobedience the law that is broken as an act of protest must always be somewhat relevant or appropriate to the object of the protest. Terrorism has no such restraint..."[4]

The second theme that needs emphasis are the political issues inherent in the resort to terrorism in liberal democracies Indeed, as James Q. Wilson argues:

"...if terror is practiced in a society with free elections, open courts, and a legitimate opposition it is more despicable than when terrorism...occurs in a society where no alternative means of change exist..."[5]

Terrorist violence in such societies is, as Conor Cruise O'Brien reminds us "an illegitimate and unjustifiable use of force."[6] And, just as important, force used against them by a democratic state is legitimate.[7]

The election of 1977 was as significant an electoral landmark as that of 1956, marking as it did a change of regime and not merely a change of government. Under the leadership of J.R. Jayewardene a revitalized UNP government set about introducing far reaching changes in every sphere of activity. These included a Presidential form of government under a new constitution, the second republican constitution of 1978. This constitution offered the minorities a more secure position in the Sri Lanka polity than any previous one. Sweeping economic reforms have been introduced, reducing state controls and restrictions in the economy, and providing greater incentives to the private sector. The rate of economic growth has improved substantially since 1977, and this has been sustained thereafter at a uniformly high level. Improved economic conditions in the country explain, to a large extent, the government's success in the management of the 'political market', in retaining the initiative in politics, and in keeping its rivals at bay, with the significant exception of the problems posed by separatism and terrorism in the north of island. And this last, despite several measures, legislative and administrative, taken to meet some of the long-standing grievances of the Tamils, and more wide-ranging ones such as the constitutional provisions for minority rights and language in the new constitution of 1978, and also the District Development Councils successfully introduced in 1980. Its period of office has been marked by outbreaks of ethnic violence on a scale comparable only with those of the period 1956-61. And this despite the fact that, unlike the UF government, the present regime has sought, consistently, to introduce new policies or reverse old ones, in the interests of ethnic harmony. It would be true to say that the UF government sowed the wind and its successor reaped the whirlwind.

References

1   There was an element of communalism in the JVP's ideology and program. This arose from their avowed opposition to the 'Indian presence' in Sri Lanka. Whether this was directed against India as such or the Indians in Sri Lanka is not clear.

2   W. Laquer, *Terrorism* (Boston, 1977). pp. 5-7.

3   See the discussion in Austin T. Turk 'Social Dynamics of Terrorism' and Philip E. Devine and Robert J. Rafalko, 'On Terrorism' in *The Annals of the American Academy of Political and Social Science*, special issue on *International Terrorism* Vol. 463, September 1982, pp 119-128, and pp. 39-53 respectively. See also G. Wardlaw, *Political Terrorism* (Cambridge, 1982) and P. Wilkinson, *Terrorism and the Liberal State* (London, 1979).

4   Philip E. Devine and Robert J. Rafalko, 'On Terrorism' *op. cit*, p. 44.

5   James Q. Wilson, 'Thinking About Terrorism' *Commentary*, July 1981, p. 38.

6   Conor Cruise O'Brien, *Herod, Reflections on Political Violence* (London, 1978), p. 3.

7   *Ibid.*

Chapter XVI

The Constitution of 1972 and Minority Rights

A Constituent Assembly

One of the first acts of the UF government after it took office was the summoning of a Constitutent Assembly.[1] The intention was quite deliberately to provide for the establishment of a "free, sovereign and independent republic" through an authochthonous constitution. To underline the authochthonous nature of the new constitution that was to emerge from its deliberations, the Constituent Assembly consciously and consistently acted outside the framework of the Soulbury constitution; indeed the framers of the constitution claimed that in "its essential procedures and entire functioning [it was] counterposed to the [Soulbury] constitution."

The Soulbury constitution had survived without any fundamental changes since its introduction. Its comparative flexibility — and the lack of a bill of fundamental rights — enabled the political structure to accommodate itself to a series of far-reaching changes most if not all of which adversely affected ethnic and religious minorities. It could be argued that if the constitution had provided more effective checks against legislation depriving minorities of advantages if not privileges enjoyed during colonial times and continued after independence, pressure for fundamental amendments to that constitution, or for its replacement by an autochthonous one would have come earlier and would also have been impossible to resist. As it was constitutional reform received very low priority in the 1960s from the SLFP, the party which put through the reforms ensuring and consolidating the dominance of the Sinhalese Buddhists in the Sri Lanka polity. Equally important, nationalization of local and foreign business ventures was rendered easier by the lack of provisions in the constitution for just and expeditious payment of compensation. Thus there was no constitutional protection for special economic interests and property rights in general.

By the early 1960s some of the framers of the constitution of 1946-7 were expressing concern at the ineffectiveness of the constitution in protecting the rights of minorities and arguing that only a bill of rights could guarantee the minorities a measure of protection against the pervasive pressures of Sinhalese-Buddhist extremism. In a notable reversal of attitude Sir Ivor Jennings,

"candidly admitted that a comprehensive chapter of fundamental rights was very desirable in Ceylon's constitution particularly in the conditions [then] prevailing in Ceylon".[2]

In 1963 Lord Soulbury himself expressed similar views in response to the comments of Sir Charles Jeffries, a senior official at Colonial Office, who in his book *Ceylon — the Path to Independence*[3] had claimed that:

"the Soulbury Constitution...had entrenched in it all the protective provisions for minorities that the wit of man could devise."[4]

Soulbury would not endorse this view; he argued, on the contrary that

"...in the light of later happenings — I think it is a pity that the [Soulbury] Commission did not also recommend the entrenchment in the constitution of guarantees of fundamental rights, on the lines enacted in the constitutions of India, Pakistan, Malaya, Nigeria and elsewhere."[5]

In the early 1960s the SLFP was committed to the amendment of the Soulbury constitution, not its replacement by another, and its election manifesto of 1960 spelled out the desired changes:

"...a reconsideration of the position of the Senate, the definition of democratic and economic rights, and the establishment of a democratic republic..."

Its manifesto of 1965 — which had the endorsement of the LSSP and CP (Moscow Wing) — reiterated the theme of republican status and the need to revise the constitution "to suit the needs of the country". There was, in fact, a substantial similarity in attitude on this between itself and its principal rival, the UNP. That party also advocated the revision of the Soulbury constitution; in particular, that Sri Lanka should become a republic within the Commonwealth. But when in power (1965-70) it lacked the parliamentary majority (two-thirds of all members of the Lower House) necessary to amend the constitution.

During their years in opposition between 1965 and 1970 the constituent parties of the United Front coalition government had made a far-reaching re-appraisal of their stand on the question of constitutional reform: from a mere revision of the existing constitution to a new policy of establishing a Constituent Assembly deriving

"authority from the people of Sri Lanka and not from the power and authority assumed and exercised by the British Crown and Parliament in establishing the present [Soulbury] constitution...nor from the constitution they gave us."

This was no more — and no less — than the adoption by the then coalition government of the orthodox and doctrinnaire LSSP and CP attitude on an autochthonous constitution for the island. From the mid-1940s these parties, and especially the LSSP of that time, had argued that the transfer of power should be preceded by or should be followed by the convening of a Constituent Assembly which would draft a constitution for the country. They had watched this happen in India. Now, over two decades later they were instrumental in getting a similar process initiated here.

The question naturally arises as to how the SLFP came to acquiesce in, and indeed enthusiastically endorse, this line of action? The answer one suspects lies in a notable *obiter dictum* of Lord Pearce in a case — the Bribery Commissioner *versus* Ranasinghe[6] — which came up in 1964 before the Judicial Committee of the Privy Council in London. This *obiter dictum* related to section 29 (2) (b) of the Soulbury Constitution and it made the point that it [i.e., Section 29 (2) (b)]:

"entrenched religious and racial matters which shall not be the subject of legislation [and] represent[ed] the solemn balance of rights between the citizens of Ceylon, the fundamental conditions on which *inter se* they accepted the Constitution; and these are therefore unalterable under the Constitution."

He added that

"the Court has a duty to see that the Constitution is not infringed and to preserve it inviolate".

To the SLFP — the party most committed to the Sinhalese-Buddhist domination of the Sri Lanka polity — this would have been ample justification for the replacement and not merely a revision of the Soulbury Constitution, and replacement by an autochthonous constitution drafted by a Constituent Assembly. The overwhelming electoral victory of May 1970 gave the coalition the opportunity it sought to put this new policy into effect.

The process of constitution-making proved to be controversial and not merely among the Tamils. The Federal Party moved out of the Constituent Assembly in June 1971 and did not participate in its proceedings thereafter. The UNP participated in the proceedings but eventually voted against the Constitution because of the extension of the life of the Parliament elected in May 1970 by two years through this device of a Constituent Assembly.

The Constituent Assembly and the National State Assembly[7]

In June 1971 the then Constituent Assembly resolved that the national legislature under the new constitution would have a life-span of six years after the adoption of the new constitution. Since the Constituent Assembly (which was, in effect, the House of Representatives elected in May 1970) would be the first National State Assembly under the new constitution this meant that the Parliament elected in May 1970 would probably have a life of eight years. This, the then opposition urged, was a breach of faith with the people who had not been given any indication in May 1970 that they were electing a Parliament for anything more than the normal five year term provided for by the Soulbury constitution. They argued that the government had no mandate from the people for thus extending the life of Parliament.

Under strong pressure from opposition groups in the Constituent Assembly the government decided, in 1972, to reduce the term of the first National State Assembly to five years (all future National State Assemblies would go on for a term of six years). This revision which was announced in the Constituent Assembly on 8 May 1972 did not satisfy the opposition.

In defence of its position on this issue the government advanced two lines of argument. There was first the purely legalistic one from Dr. Colvin R. de Silva, the Minister of Constitutional Affairs, that:

"It is a mistaken notion that the provision in the Constitution is a device to extend the life of the House of Representatives. With the new Constitution the House of Representatives simply fades out of the picture. The members of the first National (State) Assembly are appointees of the Constitution and like the first Prime Minister are the key to initiation of the functioning of the Constitution..."

The second line of argument was the rather more pragmatic approach adopted by the Prime Minister, Mrs. Sirimavo Dias Bandaranaike. She informed the Constituent Assembly on 12 May

1972 that the reduction of the term of life of the first National State Assembly to five years had been made at her suggestion and had been decided upon after careful thought. She argued that the government needed time to implement its Five Year Plan. Because of the insurrection of 1971 one whole year had gone by without any time to devote to development. While Dr. Colvin R. de Silva saw in this the Prime Minister's "characteristic responsivness to public opinion," opposition critics could not help asking what the situation would have been if instead of a Five Year Plan, it had been a Six, Seven or even Ten Year Plan that the government had introduced in 1971. The Prime Minister also claimed that the people had given the government a clear mandate to adopt and operate a new constitution, and in so doing they had left the Constituent Assembly completely free in respect of such matters as the first National (State) Assembly. The Prime Minister's pragmatism was no more convincing than the legalistic arguments of the Minister of Constitutional Affairs. The Government used its overwhelming majority in the Constituent Assembly to give itself an extended term of life.

Looking back on it just over ten years later, the crucial point was that the government had given itself an extended term of office through the devise of a new constitution. There had been no offer then of a referendum, no attempt to test public opinion on this issue.

The Federal Party and the New Constitution

When the Constituent Assembly began its work it was widely expected that despite the recent record of political antagonism between the parties of the governing coalition and the main Tamil parties, an attempt would be made to consolidate the consensus that thad emerged on the language rights of the Tamils. The latter were anxious that the regulations introduced in 1966, and which had been so strongly opposed by the governing coalition while in opposition, would not be tampered with. No such re-assurances on that were forthcoming. However, when the government moved an official resolution to the effect that: "all laws shall be enacted in Sinhalese [and there] shall be a Tamil translation of every law so enacted" there were hopes that this re-statement of the existing position would be taken for what it was, a conciliatory gesture. The Federal Party responded with a re-statement of its main demand on language since 1956. It moved an amendment to the official resolution quoted above, an amendment to the effect that Sinhalese and Tamil shall be the official languages of Sri Lanka, the languages of the courts, and the languages in which all laws shall be published. The acrimonious debate that followed upon this stemmed from the recognition that the Federal Party's amendment was tantamount to a total rejection of the then existing position on the national language, a consensus achieved through the years since 1956, and a consensus which the Federal Party itself had come to accept. The whole question of language rights was thus re-opened but neither side was willing to make concessions to reach an agreement acceptable to both. On 28 June 1971 the Federal Party amendment was defeated by a vote of 87 to 13, upon which its members walked out of the Constituent Assembly, and did not return to participate any further in its deliberations. The UNP members voted with the government on this.

That there was a consensus on language to which the Federal Party among others had given tacit acceptance was incontrovertible.[8] At the same time it is important to remember that clause 29 (2) of the Soulbury constitution — that relating to minority rights — was an integral part in this consensus. Although the protection this clause afforded to the minorities was less comprehensive than its framers intended it to be, it nevertheless acted as a deterrent against patently discriminatory legislation. That the government was resorting to the device of a new constitution in preference to a reform of the old one, partly at least, because it wished to do away with that clause was well-known. Once this vital clause had been removed a significant element in the consensus on language had been unilaterally discarded to the detriment of the Tamil minority. Thus it was no longer possible to speak of a consensus on language which the Federal Party itself had come to accept, tacitly or otherwise.

The constitution of 1972, unlike its predecessor contained a chapter of Fundamental Rights and Freedoms, including: the equality of all persons before the law; the prohibition of discrimination in public employment on the ground of religion, race, caste or sex; freedom of thought, conscience and religion; protection of life and personal liberty; freedom of speech, of peaceful assembly and of association; and freedom of movement and residence.

In practice, however, their effect was largely nullified by the wide-ranging scope of the restrictions on these rights and freedoms incorporated in Section 18 (2) of the constitution, which read thus:

> "The exercise and operation of the fundamental rights and freedoms
> provided in this chapter shall be subject to such restrictions as the law
> prescribes in the interests of national unity and integrity, national
> security, national economy, public safety, public order, the protection of
> public health or morals or the protection of rights and freedoms of
> others or giving effect to the Principles of State Policy set out in Section
> 16".[9]

This attenuated bill of rights was hardly adequate compensation to
the minorities for the loss of clause 29 (2) of the Soulbury
Constitution.

Religion

Chapter II of the constitution laid it down that:

> "The Republic of Sri Lanka shall give to Buddhism the foremost place
> and accordingly it shall be the duty of the state to protect and foster
> Buddhism while assuring to all religions the rights granted by Section 18
> (1) (d)".

With this Sri Lanka ceased to be a secular state pure and simple, even if
it had not become the Buddhist state on the lines of Burma or Thailand
which Buddhist pressure groups would have liked it to be. The wide
support this clause had in the Constituent Assembly — the government had the support of the UNP on it — was just as notable as the
lack of opposition to it from the Christian minority.

One of the remarkable new developments of the years after 1970
was the improvement in relations between the Roman Catholics and
the SLFP. Partly this was because the Roman Catholics themselves
had come to accept the new balance of forces as a political reality. And
while the government made no attempt to change its education policy
which had been the point of divergence between the SLFP and the
Roman Catholics since 1960, it nevertheless became much more
conciliatory. Thus when Pope Paul VI made a brief stop-over in
Colombo in late 1970 in the course of an Asian tour, he had been
welcomed by the Prime Minister herself. This conciliatory gesture on
her part was at once an acknowledgement of her appreciation of the

support her party had secured from Roman Catholics in 1970, and a signal that the rigid anti-Catholicism with which she had been identified in the past, especially during the period 1960-64, had now been abandoned. In July 1971 the new government formally revoked the *poya* week-end scheme which the Roman Catholic laity, if not the heirarchy of the church, had found to be an inconvenience. That all opposition parties gave their support to this decision was less significant that the fact that it was an SLFP-dominated regime that had taken the initiative on it despite the opposition of sections of the *sangha*, and Buddhist lay organizations.

The Roman Catholics responded by seeking a constructive accommodation with linguistic nationalism and came to accept the dominance of the Sinhalese Buddhists in Sri Lanka as a political reality. The new outlook was entirely in keeping with, if indeed it did not flow from, the decisions taken at the Vatican Council of 1963-65, and the greater readiness demonstrated there, than in the past, towards acceptance of religious pluralism. This the Protestants had done a generation earlier, with some reluctance at first but with greater conviction in the years before the transfer of power and thereafter. The new realism was a striking contrast to the attitude of the Federal Party to the special status accorded to Buddhism in the new constitution. The latter condemned it as a clear act of discrimination in favor of the Sinhalese-Buddhist majority.

References

[1] For the background to this see K.M. de Silva, 'Sri Lanka (Ceylon): The New Republican Constitution' in *Verfassung und Recht in Ubersee* III (3) 1972 pp. 139-149. See also the very perceptive article by L. Wolff-Philips, 'Post Independence Constitutional Changes in the Commonwealth' in *Political Studies* XVIII (1970) I pp. 18-43, especially p. 35 where he predicted that "Some kind of constitutional innovation (most likely a new antochthonous constitution) will be necessary [in Sri Lanka] in the early 1970's."

[2] J.A.L. Cooray. *Constitutional Government and Human Rights in a Developing Society* (Colombo, 1969) p. 35.

[3] (London, 1962).

[4] Lord Soulbury's foreword to B.H. Farmer, *Ceylon, A Divided Nation* (O.U.P., 1963).

[5] *Ibid.*

[6] See, Bribery Commissioner vs. Ranasinghe [1964] in 66, *New Law Reports*, 73.

7   For discussion of this see, K.M. de Silva 'Sri Lanka (Ceylon): The New Republican
     Constitution', *op cit.*

8   The strongest evidence of this lay in the fact that the Federal Party joined the UNP-
     led coalition of 1965.

9   Section 16 of the constitution set out certain Principles of State Policy, which bore
     a strong imprint of the government's political outlook and commitments — the
     realization of the objectives of a socialist democracy. These principles were not
     justiciable, and the constitution in fact stated that they conferred no legal rights
     and were not enforceable in any court of law. The princples were set out, as in some
     constitutions, in order to guide the making of laws and the governance of the
     country.

Chapter XVII

The U.F. Government and Sri Lanka's Ethnic Problems, 1972-77: Policies and Responses

Introduction

The five years from 1972 to 1977 were a sterile phase, unproductive in initiatives and policy options on improving relations between the island's main ethnic groups. It was as though the UF government exhausted its political resources in confronting the JVP and the insurgency of 1971 and in devising a response to these. Despite the speed with which that insurrection was crushed, the government's morale never recovered from having to deal with so formidable a threat from left-wing groups. A right-wing putsch could have been handled just as easily but with much less damage to the government's morale, and without any erosion of its credibility as a socialist regime.

The new constitution was in many ways the consolidation of the linguistic nationalism that had dominated Sri Lankan politics since 1956. This was how many of its advocates preferred to see it, and the form in which its strongest opponents — the Tamils' political leadership —preferred to see it too. The latter argued that the new constitution gave validity and confirmation to the second-class status of their citizenship by consolidating the position of Sinhalese as the official language while Tamil was granted a distinctly inferior and hazy position, as well as by according to Buddhism 'the foremost place' among religions.

Opposition to the new constitution brought the two main Tamil political parties — the Federal Party and the Tamil Congress — together for the first time since 1948. Along with the leadership of the Ceylon Workers' Congress and other Tamil politicians they established the Tamil United Front (TUF). The CWC was the weakest link in this chain; its ties to the TUF were intrinsically fragile and the association between it and the two other parties was seldom as cordial as the founders of the TUF claimed it was. Nevertheless all previous attempts to bring the leadership of the Indian plantation workers to the point of coordinating their political activities with those of the indigenous Tamils failed, and so even a brief and fitful association, as this proved to be, was a considerable political achievement.

A by-product of the increasing alienation of the Tamils from the Sinhalese since the adoption of the new constitution was the conversion of a large section of the Tamils of the north to the idea of a separate Tamil state in Sri Lanka, an indication of the intensity of feeling in the Tamil areas of the country at what they regarded as a deliberate attempt to reduce them to subordinate status. The Federal Party itself was a recent, but not entirely reluctant, convert to this policy, and it's — and the TUF's — enthusiastic advocacy of a separate state for the Tamil-speaking areas of the Northern and Eastern Provinces introduced a new dimension of hostility into relations between themselves and the UF government.

The TUF: From Regional Autonomy to Separatism

On 24 May 1972, two days after the constitution of the first republic was officially adopted, the Federal Party presented a political program setting out the aspirations of the Tamils, a program which came to be known as the Six-Point Plan. The component elements of this plan were, in effect, a recapitulation of the principal demands of the Tamils over the two previous decades.

The first of these was a reiteration of the Federal Party's insistence on parity of status for Tamil with Sinhalese as an official language. The extension of rights of citizenship to all Indians who had settled in Sri Lanka but had been treated as stateless under the country's citizenship laws was the second; while the third was a formal commitment to the concept of a secular state, one in which the equality of all religions was assured and no special privileges were conferred on any one of them. The fourth demand was for a constitutional guarantee of fundamental rights and freedoms on the basis of equality of all persons in the country. The fifth item in this program, however, was specific to the special problems of the Tamil areas of the country — the abolition of untouchability and the amelioration of the condition of the *harijans* —

and was more in the nature of an affirmation of the TUF's commitment to social change, rather than a demand for governmental action. Last of all there was a demand for a decentralized structure of government as the basis of a participatory democracy.[1]

This program was advanced in the hope that it would be the basis for negotiations between the newly established TUF and the United Front government. The latter, however, seemed to be in no mood for discussions with the newly formed TUF. Partly in order to force the hands of the government, but more important, to seek a mandate from the Tamil people for the TUF program, S.J.V. Chelvanayakam, the Leader of the Federal Party, and now of the TUF, resigned his seat in the National State Assembly (as Parliament was called under the constitution of 1972-77) in order to force a by-election. His resignation came in 1972 but it was to take two years or more before the government would hold the by-election.

If the postponement of this by-election was calculated to demonstrate the government's determination not to yield to pressure from the TUF, it soon became, naturally enough, one more grievance accumulated by the Tamil community against the government. Besides it only served to strengthen the already powerful forces at work pushing the Federal Party away from the moderate program embodied in the Six Point Plan, to a full-blooded insistence on separatism.

The factors involved in this transformation are dealt with below in some detail. These include: the role of the educated unemployed; the significance of a new policy on university admissions in radicalizing politics in the Jaffna peninsula; the transformation of the security forces and the police from being the small but efficient and impartial peacekeeping force they were in the ethnic disturbances of the mid-1950s and early 1960s into paradigms of ethnic soldiers and policemen; and finally the linkage between the politics of the Jaffna peninsula and the politics of Tamilnadu. By the time the Kankesanthurai by-election was held in February 1975, the political climate of the Jaffna peninsula and the Northern Province had been transformed by the operation of these factors and their impact on the people of their region.

The Federal Party fought this by-election on its Six Point Plan elaborated in 1972; the government candidate — a member of the CP (Moscow Wing) — argued that support for Chelvanayakam would strengthen the separatist forces. The results of the 1970 election at Kankesanthurai where Chelvanayakam's previously large majority had crumbled in the face of the determined efforts of C. Sunthera-lingam to exploit the issue of Hindu orthodoxy and *vellala* privilege, had encouraged hopes that in 1975 Chelvanayakam could be restricted to a narrow majority. In 1975 he won an overwhelming victory. Addressing his constituents on this occasion, in a message clearly meant for a national rather than a local audience, he expressed his desire

> "... to announce to my [sic] people and the country that the Eelam Tamil Nation should exercise the sovereignty already vested in the Tamil people and become free."

One sees in this a shift of emphasis from a struggle for equality to an

> "assertion of freedom; from the demand for fundamental rights to the assertion of self-determination; from the acceptance of a pluralistic experiment to the surfacing of a new corporate identity."[2]

There were two other events which consolidated this shift of emphasis. The first was the resolution adopted at a convention of the TUF held at Pannakam on 14 May 1976 — the Vaddukoddai resolution as it has been subsequently named — by which vague and disconnected separatist aspirations were embodied in a more cohesive statement, a program of action, the chief feature of which was a call for the establishment of a separate Tamil state — Eelam. Significantly, by now the Tamil United Front had become the Tamil United Liberation Front (TULF); equally significantly, the Ceylon Workers' Congress was having second thoughts about its association with the TULF, for there were no advantages for the Indian Tamils in a separate Tamil state in the north and east of the island. Secondly, there was the trial-at-bar, also in 1976, where two TULF MPs and one former MP stood charged with sedition for distributing pamphlets — on independence day — advocating the establishment of a separate state.[3] On this occasion a legal challenge was made to the validity of the Republican constitution of 1972. The trial provided an opportunity

> "for a sharpening of the juridical and historical underpinnings of the new corporate identity of the Tamil people."

In support of the claim for a separate state the Vaddukodai resolution looked back to a dim memory of statehood in the distant past, and transformed this, through a misinterpretation of historical events and data, into a continuing tradition of independent statehood and unbroken national consciousness. The separate state they had in mind was of uncertain extent: the Vaddukodai resolution of May 1976, and the TULF's election manifesto of 1977 give two contradictory interpretations of the territorial boundaries of Eelam.

The Vaddukodai resolution claimed that the:

> "Sinhalese people have used their political power to the detriment of
> the Tamils by (*inter alia*) ... making serious inroads to the territories of
> the Tamil kingdom by a system of planned and state-aided colonization
> and large-scale regularization of recently encouraged Sinhalese en-
> croachments calculated to make the Tamils a minority in their own
> homeland."

The territorial dimensions of Eelam were defined as follows:

> "Whereas throughout the centuries from the dawn of history, the
> Sinhalese and Tamil nations have divided between them the possession
> of Ceylon, the Sinhalese inhabiting the interior parts of the country in
> its southern and western parts from the river Walave to that of Chilaw
> and the Tamils possessing the northern and eastern districts ..." [the
> TULF resolves that] "Tamil Eelam shall consist of the Northern and
> Eastern Provinces (of Sri Lanka)."

In its manifesto for the general election of July 1977, the TULF
elaborated further the concept of the "traditional homeland of the
Tamils." The claim now was that:

> "Even before the Christian era the entire island [of Sri Lanka] was
> ruled by Tamil kings ..."

From this claim which was, in fact, a falsification of history, the
manifesto proceeded thus:

> "From this background of alternating fortunes (of the Sinhalese and
> Tamil rulers of ancient Sri Lanka) emerged, at the beginning of the 13th
> century, a clear and stable political fact. At this time, the territory
> stretching in the western sea-board from Chilaw through Puttalam to
> Mannar and thence to the Northern Region, and in the east,
> Trincomalee and also the Batticaloa Regions that extend southwards up
> to Kumana or the northern banks of the river Kumbukkan Oya were
> firmly established as the exclusive homeland of the Tamils. This is the
> territory of Tamil Eelam."

Here clearly was a misinterpretation of history. A Tamil kingdom
did exist from the 13th century to the early part of the 17th, but except
during the brief heyday of its power it seldom controlled anything
more than the Jaffna peninsula, and some adjacent regions on the coast
and some parts of the interior. Set against a history stretching over
2500 years the independent existence of this kingdom covered a very
brief period, and even during that period its status and influence varied
so dramatically; at times a very powerful kingdom; at others a satellite
of expanding Dravidian states across the Palk Straits, and at times
subjugated by the Kotte kingdom, and generally acknowledging its

suzerainity. There is little or no evidence to support the claim made in the Vaddukoddai resolution and the TULF manifesto of 1977 that there was either an unbroken 'national' consciousness or a continuing tradition of independent statehood.

There were, besides, contradictions and ambiguities in these claims, between the claim made in the Vaddukoddai resolution of 1976 that there was possession of the northern and eastern districts of the island by the Tamils "from the dawn of history" to the more historically accurate statement in the manifesto of 1977 that a Tamil kingdom had emerged "at the beginning of the 13th century." The first defines the boundaries of Tamil Eelam in terms of people: "Tamil Eelam shall consist of the people of the Northern and Eastern Provinces"; the manifesto of 1977, as we have seen, adopts a territorial definition.

Youth, Universitites and Employment

The most militant agitators for separatism were the educated unemployed, by now a substantial element in Tamil society in the north. They provided the grass-roots contacts between the Tamil parliamentarians and the Tamil people, and they pressed the TUF on to a campaign for a separate state as an expression of their desperation at the bleak prospects of employment that faced Tamil youth. Increasing competition from the Sinhalese with the expansion of education facilities in the Sinhalese areas of the country would in any case have reduced the prospects of the Tamils in their traditional search for positions in the bureaucracy and the state's technical and educational services. The Tamils could hardly have maintained the percentage of such posts that they held in British times. With the change of government in 1956 and the new language policy adopted shortly thereafter, the number of Tamils entering the public sector began dropping and this reduction has not been reversed.[4] The teaching profession in the Jaffna peninsula is overcrowded and affords few opportunities for young graduates, especially after the take-over of the schools by the state. Similarly one of the detrimental if unintended effects of the expansion of the public sector and the pre-eminence it achieved in all areas of economic activity has been a contraction in employment prospects for the Tamils.

Even so the Tamils managed, up to 1970, to hold their own in some of the more prestigious spheres of activity such as the medical, scientific, technical and engineering fields. This is largely a reflection of the superior facilities for science education in the Jaffna peninsula which enabled the Tamils to enter the medical, science and engineering faculties of Universities in much larger numbers than their population ratio *vis-a-vis* the other ethnic groups in the island. In 1969-70 the Tamils, mainly from Jaffna and Colombo, constituted 35 percent of the intake into the science oriented courses, and over 45 percent in the engineering and medical faculties.

Entrance to the universities had been on the basis of academic achievement tested through rigorous competitive examinations. In the early 1970s B. Mahmud, as Minister of Education, succeeded in committing the UF government to a fundamental change in policy, to a system of standardization by language media at the University entrance examination.[5] The effect of this was to place the Tamil students at a great disadvantage in that they needed to obtain a higher aggregate of marks to enter the universities — in the medical, science and engineering sections — than the Sinhalese. Not only was this system maintained since 1970, but other schemes were introduced, all of them representing a departure from the practice of selecting students on the basis of actual marks obtained at an open competitive examination. Among these was the district quota system which seemingly involved a balance in favor of rural areas and backward communities. But there is no mistaking the fact that it gave a decided advantage of weightage to the Kandyans and the Muslims.

No longer did academic ability *per se* suffice to ensure entry to the university, and those who suffered most from the change were undoubtedly the Tamils of the north (although the Sinhalese in the city of Colombo and the crowded Colombo district fared badly too). They regarded this change in university entrance policy as patently and deliberately discriminatory. The Tamils have been so dependent on state employment that even a quota system which gives them a higher proportion of places than their numbers in relation to the ratio of Sri Lankan Tamils to the total population of the country, would in practice, be a hardship. The new university entrance policy of the 1970s made entry to the professions and to scientific and technical education much more difficult for the Tamils. Nothing has caused more frustration and bitterness among Tamil youth than this, for they regarded it as an iniquitous system deliberately devised to place obstacles before them.

The question of University admissions is thus a fundamentally important factor in the current breakdown in ethnic relations in the island, and in radicalizing the politics of the Tamil areas of the north and east of the island, and we need to provide a resume of the issues involved in this rather unusual problem. Prof. C.R. de Silva, who has done more than any other scholar to shed light on the complexities of the politics of Univerity admissions, points out that:

> "Education, especially university education, is a key channel of social mobility in most developing countries and hence the distribution of opportunities for higher education is often regarded as the distribution of future wealth, status and power. In countries like Sri Lanka where university education is available only to a small minority, the competition therefore becomes very intense. Further problems arise, when in the context of a plural society each ethnic and religious group tends to evaluate the ratio of university admissions obtained by its members as an index of equality of opportunity or of discrimination. University admissions thus cease to be the exclusive preserve of academics and become the concern of politicians and leaders of various groups and interests."[6]

Indeed the island's politicians have long regarded university admissions as too important a matter to be left to university teachers to handle on their own. From the mid-1960s university places (i.e., the number of students to be admitted to the universities) and the basis of admission have been settled at the highest political level — the Cabinet no less. So it was in the 1970s and so it is today.

Prof. de Silva reminds us that it was really in the 1960s when Sinhalese and Tamil replaced English as the medium of instruction in the higher classes of the secondary schools that political and sectional pressures on university education began to build up.[7] The rapid growth of secondary education resulted in intensified competition for entry to the Universities especially to the prestigious University of Ceylon at Peradeniya. Such political pressure as there was in the 1960s had been for the expansion of the universities to accommodate ever-increasing numbers of students; the procedure for admission to the universities was not yet a matter of dispute or even discussion. That came in and after 1970 with the victory of the UF coalition and when it came it was soon seen as part of the wider problem of Sinhalese-Tamil rivalry in the areas of language, employment and education. The crux of the problem was that the indigenous Tamils who constituted 11.1% of the population had for years enjoyed a position of predominance in the science-based faculties. This was facilitated by their higher rate of literacy in English and the excellent facilities for science education in the schools of the Jaffna District from which many of them entered the universities. In 1970 for instance, the Tamils had just over 35% of the admissions to the science-based faculties; in Engineering and Medicine it was as high as 45%. With the changeover to *swabasha* there were, in effect, two distinct streams of students seeking admission to the university, one educated in Sinhalese and the other in Tamil. There was also a much smaller English stream consisting of students of almost all ethnic groups. Since examiners marked in one or other of those streams and not both, it was a matter of time before the superior performance record of the Tamils would be attributed to deliberate over-marking on the part of Tamil examiners. Late in 1970 there was a rumor that the Tamils had obtained almost 60% of the admissions to the Engineering faculty of the University of Ceylon, Peradeniya, at that time the only such faculty in the country. The source of the rumor, which had appeared before the admissions list was officially announced, was never satisfactorily established but it was widely suspected that these inaccurate figures had been leaked to the student leadership at Peradeniya by some officials in the lower rungs of the administration at that university.

The consequences were truly momentous. The allegation of favoritism among Tamil examiners was investigated but there was no evidence to substantiate such a charge. Nevertheless the government decided on changing the hitherto accepted basis of admission and to introduce a lower qualifying mark for Sinhalese medium students, so that a politically acceptable proportion of Tamil-to-Sinhalese students could be admitted to the university.[7] The significance of this step was that

> "at long last the principle of choice of candidates for university education on the basis of their academic performance as reflected in the raw marks had been successfully challenged.[9]

Though the Tamil political leadership protested strongly against the

> "iniquituous nature of differential 'qualifying marks' for Sinhalese and Tamil candidates the immediate effect of the change in terms of the number of Tamil students admitted to the science-based faculties was merely marginal, a drop from 35.3% to 33.6%, an actual increase in the aggregate from 337 to 359."

But as Prof. de Silva points out

> "the real significance of the change in 1971 does not lie in these figures. It marked the ascendancy of a group of Sinhalese [officials, and advisors] in the Ministry of Education, a group which firmly believed

that some adjusting mechanism was necessary to give Sinhalese students
a chance in competing for the coveted places in science-based courses at
the University. It was this group which came up with the suggestion for
media-wise standardization for [the 1973 admissions]." [10]

'Media-wise' standardization was a device to reduce all marks to a
common scale so that in the end the number qualifying from each
language medium would be proportionate to the number sitting the
examination in that medium. It was a device to neutralize the superior
performance of the Tamil medium students in science subjects as
depicted by 'raw marks'. Those who proposed the measure argued that
the difference in performance between Sinhalese and Tamil students
must necessarily be attributed to differences in facilities, teaching or
marking and that standardization was merely a devise to check such
imbalances. The fact that differences in facilities and teaching available
to students within any one medium were often as great, if not greater,
than any overall difference between the two media was glossed over.

Once again however the immediate effect on numbers of Tamils
entering the university was marginal, and far less damaging to Tamil
interests than the acrimony the change caused would appear to
support. To quote Prof. de Silva again:

"The Sri Lankan Tamils, though they constituted just 11.1% of the
population provided about 30% of the science students in the secondary
schools and the scheme of [media-wise] standardization ensured that
this proportion of places in the university accrued to them." [11]

In the next year came 'the district quota' system, introduced, it
would seem, to satisfy two interest groups, the Kandyans, and the
Moor/Malay group. Both groups regarded themselves as educationally
backward, and both were not content with the changes in admissions
policy effected since 1970. Since the Moor/Malay group were were
educated mainly in the Tamil medium, standardization pitted them
against the Tamils in the competition for places in that medium of
instruction, and they saw the contest as an unequal one. Mahmud,
leader of the Islamic Socialist Front, was not unmindful of their
interests.

The district quota system was designed to allocate university places
in proportion to the total population resident in each district. The
scheme benefitted the Kandyan region, and the rural areas generally,
as well as the Moors/Malays. One refinement of the district quota
system devised to benefit this last group was as follows: the criterion
used in determining a student's district for purposes of this quota in

the case of Sinhalese and Tamil students was the location of the school from which they sat the examination. In the case of Moors/Malays it was the district of birth. Thus a Sinhalese or Tamil from a backward district who won a scholarship to a Colombo school and sat the examination from Colombo would form part of the Colombo quota. A Moor/Malay in the same circumstances would qualify for admission through his home district where the qualifying mark was substantially lower than for Colombo schools.

For the Tamils the district quota system was a heavy blow: the percentage of university places in the science-based disciplines held by them fell from 35.3% in 1970 to 20.9% in 1974 and 19% in 1975. In 1974 there was, for the first time, a substantial fall in the absolute number of Tamils entering the science-based courses despite a continued expansion in the total intake into those courses.

The Sinhalese, on the other hand, profitted enormously from this even if those resident in Colombo, and to a lesser extent in other urban areas, suffered a drop in the number of admissions too; in science-based courses they now constituted 75.5% in 1974; and this figure rose, even higher to 78.0% in 1975. Since they had over 86% of the places in the humanities and social sciences, Sinhalese students were now in the same privileged position in the universities as their politicians were in the national legislature in terms of seats there. The Moors/Malays saw their number of admissions to science based courses double between 1970 and 1975 even though they were still well below the magic figure of 6-7%, the ethnic quota which some of their political leaders advocated as their due.

Writing in 1975 Prof. C.R. de Silva spelled out the political consequences of the district quota system:

> "The political impact of the district quota system has been little short of disastrous. It has convinced many Sri Lanka Tamils that it was futile to expect equality of treatment with the Sinhalese majority. It has immensely strengthened separatist forces within the Tamil United Front and contributed to the acceptance of a policy campaigning for a separate state in early 1975. It has kindled resentment against the Muslims in both Tamil and Low-Country Sinhalese areas and rendered relations betwen the Kandyan and Low-Country Sinhalese more fragile than before." [12]

Thus the district quota base for admissions proved to be a double-edged weapon. For while it certainly shifted the balance in favor of the Sinhalese it also proved to be 'communally' divisive among the Sinhalese themselves, in distorting the pattern of entry between the urban and rural populations, and between the heavily populated low-country Sinhalese regions where competition for places was most acutely felt and the Kandyan areas where the minimum marks for admission to the universities were so much lower than in other parts of the country. This latter, it should be noted, was because of the presence of very poor Indian Tamil workers on the tea estates:

> "The quota allotted to many Kandyan districts were swollen by large numbers of resident plantation Tamils whose estate schools gave them but a fractional chance of a secondary education, much less of entering the University. Thus ... the Sinhalese living in the Kandyan areas ... obtain[ed] relatively easy access to the universities in 1975 by the operation of a weighted quota system. The high drop-out rate in the Kandyan provinces ... [ensured] that these places would be reserved for a relatively small group of ... students many of them from the affluent classes."[13]

Opposition to these changes came swift, vocal and strong. It came from the Tamils naturally enough, — their views were neither considered or, if considered, given little weight — but also and more effectively in terms of its potential impact on government policy from the Sinhalese of the urban areas of the low-country. The question came up for discussion before a Cabinet sub-committee — the Sectoral Committee on Social Overheads, Mass Media and Transport of the National Planning Council. The committee submitted its report early in October 1973: it recommended the abolition of media-wise standardization, and commented adversely on the district quota system and the rationale behind it so far as this rationale could be discerned in the reports and arguments of the officials who advocated it. Nevertheless the committee did not take their criticisms to their logical conclusion and recommend the abandonment of the district quota system; quite clearly the political forces that favored the district quota system were too strong for that. Eventually the committee recommended a complicated modification of the admissions system: 70% on 'raw marks' and 30% on a district basis of which half or 15% was to be reserved for what were termed educationally backward areas. When these proposals were submitted to the Cabinet only a modified district quota system was adopted — district quota places were granted to Jaffna and Colombo along with other districts but standardization on the basis of the language medium in which the examination was taken was retained.[14]

However even those modest changes were too much for a small but influential group of Sinhalese activists, the Sinhala Tharuna Sanvidhanaya, who strongly opposed them. We shall hear of them again in relation to the same problem in 1978. They had the support of a powerful group of *bhikkhus*. But their campaign failed because the government stood firm in the face of their opposition. More significantly for the future of this policy on university admissions, J.R. Jaye-wardene, as leader of the UNP, pledged his party to an abolition of standardization if it was returned to power at the next general elections.

The modifications in university admissions policy introduced in 1975 brought distinct advantages to Tamils; their share of admissions to the science-based faculties rose by 35% between 1975 and 1976. The total percentage rose to 25. To them, however, these gains seemed minor, and intrinsically illusory. Too much had happened between 1970 and 1975 to suggest that other changes would not be hastily introduced to deprive them of these gains. In brief there was no guarantee that the advantage would be secure over the next few years.

Separatism, Violence and the Security Forces

Many of the essential ingredients of separatism had now emerged: a leadership that had taken a public position advocating separatism, a band of militant agitators intent on converting the leadership's public utterances and political rhetoric — the leadership was not known for any steadfast adherence to that cause — into a policy of action to be imposed through violence if necessary, and intent on selling the legitimacy of their political cause to the masses and the world at large. Grievances of the *literati* and the rest of the elite were more than adequate as a substitute for widespread mass social and economic discontent in generating support for the separatist cause.

By the mid-1970s radicalization of politics in Jaffna was an established fact, and with radicalization came violence, including the beginnings of a terrorist campaign that was to last throughout the next decade. At the beginning the targets in these carefully chosen acts of political violence were Tamils associated with the government, culminating in the attempted murder of a pro-government Tamil MP, and the murder of the Mayor of Jaffna, Alfred Durayappah, the most prominent of the Tamil supporters of the UF government in the north. And so there was the familiar cycle of violence: political rhetoric, symbolic acts of violence, the killing of carefully chosen supporters of the government in the Jaffna peninsula, all aimed at conveying the chilling political message that opposition to and indeed deviation from the TUF's program carried fearful risks.

An important link in this chain of violence were the security forces stationed in the north of the island, and who were soon sucked into the vortex of Jaffna's increasingly turbulent politics. There had been from the early days after independence a combined service force located in the Jaffna peninsula with the twin objectives of checking illicit immigration into the island from Tamilnadu and Andrapradesh, and curbing the very profitable and highly organized — indeed, centuries old — smuggling trade through the northern ports, in particular Velvettithurai. On this smuggling trade we shall have more to say later on in this chapter. Suffice it to say here that it linked the economy of the Jaffna peninsula with that of the southernmost parts of Tamilnadu.

There had always been Sinhalese officers of all ranks in the police force in the Jaffna peninsula. For most Sinhalese police officers, service in the Jaffna peninsula was a barely tolerable hardship; not infrequently officers with a record of transgression of the disciplinary code of the police force were sent there on punishment. But Sinhalese policemen were not unwelcome in Jaffna; on the contrary in the caste-ridden society of Jaffna they were, as outsiders, impartial arbiters in conflicts which had a caste connotation.

But the attitude of the Tamils to the security forces changed in the 1960s and with it their view of the role these forces played. They were seen to be part of the state's security network devised to keep the Tamils down; and these forces themselves were often compelled to take hard decisions for perceptibly political reasons. Once the phenomenon of youth unrest and violence came to dominate the political scene in the north, the police force found that the boundary between the routine business of maintaining law and order on the one hand and political activity on the other became increasingly blurred. Tamil officers in the police force faced an impossibly difficult conflict of loyalties, between their commitment to their duties, and their own ethnic identity. The result was that more Sinhalese officers were sent to the north, for the government regarded Tamil officers as either unreliable or ineffective. Thus the police force in the north and the security forces in general became overwhelmingly Sinhalese in ethnic composition. Few were proficient in Tamil and this widened the gulf between them and the people among whom they served. But more important, once politicial violence, politically motivated armed robberies, and open intimidation of potential or actual witnesses of these crimes became a feature of life in the Jaffna peninsula, the security forces confronted a wall of silence among the people, a wall which they found impossible to penetrate. Gang robbers in Jaffna arrogantly demonstrated their immunity from arrest — because no one would dare to stand witness against them — and their nonchalance, in brash daylight incursions in which a common push bicycle was their mode of conveyance to and from the scene of their depredations.

The security forces were perceived now as a Sinhalese army of occupation, and they in their frustration at their inability to bear down effectively on the perpetrators of these robberies and acts of violence often turned violent themselves — a force perceived as an army of occupation was driven by the inexorable logic of their ambiguous position in Jaffna to behaving like one. And that in turn was a factor of great importance in the late 1970s and 1980s in the breakdown in communications and understanding between the Sinhalese and the Tamils not merely in Jaffna but in all parts of the island.

The crux of the problem was that there had been, by the beginning of the UF's tenure of power, a remarkable change in the ethnic composition of the security forces in the island. In the officer corps of the security forces and in the police, as in the higher bureaucracy of the early post-independence years, there had been an under-representation of Sinhalese Buddhists. This was less so in the rank and file. War service had contributed greatly to the *espirit de corps* and *elan* of this small security force and it had proved its worth as an impartial peace-keeping force during the ethnic disturbances of the mid-and-late 1950s, both on its own as well in support of a hard-pressed and thinly spread police force. The frequency of their use as a peace-keeping force had contributed to a growing contempt for the incompetence and cynicism of politicians, culminating in the abortive coup of 1962. Not surprisingly one consequence of the abortive coup had been a purge of the officer corps. The guiding spirit in this was religion not ethnic identity. The decades long conflict between Buddhist and Christian in Sri Lankan society had reached its denouement. The police force had seen this same crisis of identity a few years earlier — in 1958 — when Bandaranaike had quite deliberately chosen a civil servant as Inspector General of Police, overlooking the claims of all the Deputy Inspectors General, once again on grounds of religion. He had less reason for thus disturbing the normal patterns of promotion and preferment than his widow had in confronting an abortive coup. Thus by the mid-1960s the security forces and the police force reflected more accurately than in the past, the ethnic profile of Sri Lankan society. When the UNP-led coalition was in power, there was yet another abortive coup — in 1966. Ominously it was not the senior officers who were prosecuted as the conspirators but — with one exception — junior officers, and non-commissioned officers, Buddhists to a man, and intent on protecting the Sinhalese-Buddhist identity of the armed services from any possible dilution by the new government. They were by now ethnic soldiers.

The third phase in the changing composition of the armed services came in 1970 when the UF was returned to power. The commissions of a number of officers were withdrawn. This time the guiding principle was political conviction not religious affiliation. Anyone suspected of not toeing the new political line was removed, and for the first time influential political appointees were introduced into the army, at least one of whom was an active politician. The rank and file both in the police and the armed services were by now largely Sinhalese and Buddhist.

The Tamilnadu Connection

Within the Indian Union Madras, or Tamilnadu as it became later, was one of the main centers of separatist tendencies. The rise of the Dravida Kazhagam (DK) and later the Dravida Munnetra Kazhagam (DMK) in the early 1950s reflected the same powerful force of linguistic nationalism that was to transform the politics of Sri Lanka in the same period. By the early 1950s the Congress party in Madras had become more Tamil than it had been ever before, but this transformation did not prevent its being supplanted by a more authentic instrument of Tamil regional sub-nationalism, the DK and later DMK. Between 1952 and 1967 the DMK had risen from challenger to the Congress to the ruling party there.[15]

Confronted by this force of linguistic nationalism Jawaharal Nehru had responded by appointing the States Re-organization Commission. He had done so with considerable reluctance for he was appalled by the parochialism and worse still the communalism of this potentially state-destroying force. One outcome of the Commission's work was the creation of Tamilnadu state. This concession to linguistic nationalism did not save the Congress as a regional force in the new state. On the contrary it strengthened the DK and DMK and seemed, at first, to do little to dampen the forces of separatism which had been encouraged in the struggle for the creation of a linguistic state. In 1957 provocative political gestures encouraged by the DK and DMK led to the passage of the *Prevention of insults to the National Honour Act* aimed at stopping the practice of burning the national flag or the constitution. Then in March 1963 came the 16th Amendment to the Indian constitution which placed a legal ban on seccessionist parties and the advocacy of secession. By now the DK had abandoned its official goal of Dravidistan and its separatist agitation. Its official policy now was one of greater autonomy for Tamilnadu. The central government itself made a major concession in the form of a three language formula by which the Tamil language was guaranteed the status of an official regional language for Tamilnadu. By 1969 the DK had changed its name to the DMK, and the Tamilnadu unit of the Indian National Congress itself had come to terms with this regional party after it had conformed to the requirements of the 16th Amendment and changed its political goal to one of advocating a greater measure of autonomy.

For our purposes the important point is that the DK and the DMK were even more conscious of the rights of Tamils in South Asia than the Congress dominated state governments of Madras had been, but acted with much less restraint in demonstrating their concern about these, so much so that the increasingly turbulent politics of the Jaffna peninsula began to be treated as an integral part of the internal politics of Tamilnadu. The DMK, effectively checked from pursuing its separatist goal in India, took vicarious pleasure in giving encouragement and support to separatist tendencies among the Tamils of Sri Lanka. To the latter, worsening relations with the UF government tended to make ties with Tamilnadu more attractive than they had once been. The links, however, were still fitful and tentative.

Tamil politics in South Asia thus had a regional rather than a purely local impact. One important instrument of this regionalization, if not, internationalization, was the convening in 1966 of a Conference of the International Association for Tamil Research. One of the leading figures in its establishment was a Sri Lankan Tamil, Fr. Xavier Thaninayagam, a Roman Catholic priest who had been a lecturer at the University of Ceylon, Peradeniya, and moved to Kuala Lumpur as the Foundation Professor of Indian Studies at the University of Malaysia. These conferences have become a regular feature, held either in Europe, or in South and South East Asia. Whenever these were held in the South Asia they took on a political dimension and were "by no means limited to the congregation of scholars." Thus an American scholar described the Fifth International Tamil Conference held at Madurai in 1981 as a three-pronged affair, with the "research" and "public" conferences accounting for two parts, and the third "being devoted to the domain of public spectacle."[16] Seven years earlier — January 1974 — when this conference was held in Jaffna the three-pronged nature of the event was seen for the first time. The organizers had hoped that the government of Sri Lanka would either sponsor or give its official support to the conference, but neither sponsorship nor support was forthcoming and they had to rely entirely on local resources and support from the Tamil communities overseas.

From the outset organizers of the conference were under pressure to convert it into a great public event with a heavy political content, and in the end that did happen. The grand finale of the conference was scheduled for 19 January and the conference was shifted from the original venue to a more capacious one to accommodate the large crowd expected. Eventually the size of the crowd — about 50,000 by some estimates — exceeded the most sanguine expectations of the organizers. They packed the hall in which the conference was due to take place, and crowded into the vicinity of the hall and onto the roads that led to and from it. An academic conference had become a public spectacle with obvious potential for conversion into a massive political meeting.

The conference took place at a time when the state of emergency declared over the whole island in the aftermath of the JVP insurrection was still in force. Stringent restrictions were in force in regard to the holding of public meetings. The shift of venue had been approved by the police under the emergency regulations, and on the understanding that the meeting would be held inside the hall using only the public address system therein, and also that only those in the list of speakers submitted by the organizers would be entitled to speak, and that 'no political or controversial' speech would be made. The organizers agreed to comply with those requirements.

These details have been provided here as the essential background to what happened at this meeting. The meeting was an orderly one, but there was always the danger that someone would use the occasion for a provocative political speech. There was just such a person waiting in the wings, a youth leader from Tamilnadu, Janatharan by name, who was neither a delegate to the conference nor an invitee. The police regarded him as a "security risk", and as a foreigner, he was not permitted to address public meetings. He had addressed meetings in Jaffna and in nearby towns in breach of the law, and had been warned by the police against persisting with this. It was known that some youth groups in Jaffna had planned to get him to address the crowd on this present occasion. The organizers of the meeting were intent on honoring their agreement with the police, but they failed in their efforts to prevent him from appearing at this meeting. Some senior TUF politicians played a more ambiguous role: instead of supporting the organizers on this issue, at least one of them, in a gesture that was regarded by the police as a signal for a breach of the law, garlanded Janatharan. The police were intent on seeing that he did not address the meeting. When he seemed likely to do so, they moved in to prevent that from happening. In doing so they caused a stampede by the large crowd, and in the resulting melee 7 persons were killed. The police party was a small one, and although they carried arms no shots were fired, but the use of tear gas caused panic, in the course of which persons fleeing hither and thither disloged an electric wire. This live wire either fell on the crowd, or persons in the crowd trampled on it, resulting in 7 deaths.[17]

That, in brief, is an anatomy of this tragic end to what was expected to be the grand finale of this conference. The whole incident was in the nature of a tragedy waiting to happen. All the combustible items that constitute the crisis in Jaffna's volatile politics were there: a celebration of Tamil language and culture, an assertive youth element setting the pace in politicizing the event, Tamil politicians exploiting the situation for political advantage, the Tamilnadu presence in a very provocative form, and a handful of police seeking to maintain law and order and in the process triggering off a totally unintended result, in providing the separatist cause with its martyrs. The event itself, in a distorted form, is now part of the political mythology that constitutes the ideology of separatism: police brutality, a Sinhalese-dominated government which acted in total disregard of the importance of a conference that had come to mean so much to Tamils in Sri Lanka, and Tamilnadu. There was an unmistakable intensification of separatist agitation in the wake of this incident, as well as an increase in terrorist activity. The security forces found the search for actual and potential troublemakers a frustrating experience as the local population would not voluntarily help in apprehending these young men; besides when there was the slightest chance of capture, they moved across the Palk

Straits to Tamilnadu which served them as a refuge, and as a bridge-head for raids into the Jaffna peninsula.

It was at this point — the passage to and from Jaffna to the Tamilnadu coast — that the smugglers entered the picture both as transport agents for fugitives, and as sources of ready money. Also the safe houses established on both sides of the Palk Straits for the traditional smuggling trade were now put to other uses — as havens for men on the run, and for storing arms — in support of the separatist cause. Very soon the more politically conscious smugglers and the terrorist groups had joined forces. Each needed and used the other. There was the inevitable metamorphosis of the smuggler into "guerrilla" and "freedom fighter", and indeed two of the most dynamic and powerful leaders in recent times thrown up by this blending of clandestine trading activity and militant and violent political agitation were prominent smugglers.

The UF and the Indian Tamils in Sri Lanka

The other segment of the Tamil population, the Indians, confronted a combination of severe economic and political pressures. No government since independence reflected more acutely a Kandyan outlook and influence than the UF coalition led by Mrs. Bandaranaike, and this Kandyan influence lay behind much of the political pressure directed against the Indians.

Kandyan pressure had always been of prime importance in the development of policy on questions relating to the position of the immigrant Indians in Sri Lanka. As we have seen, rigid citizenship laws had eliminated the majority of the Indian plantation workers resident in the island from the voters' lists. This had had the effect of giving the Sinhalese population, and in particular, those of the Kandyan areas, a quite disproportionate share of the seats in Parliament. After the delimitation of 1959 the weightage incorporated in the structure worked even more emphatically than before in favor of the Sinhalese.[18] By 1970 the Sinhalese had 80% of the seats in Parliament though they were then 71% of the population. Significantly, the system of demarcating constituencies to the legislature was one of the features of the Soulbury constitution to be retained and incorporated in the republican constitution of 1972.

Secondly, in the 1970s the Kandyan influence has served to radicalize land policy in general, and to impose state control and ownership on the plantations. These initiatives have assumed the form of a passionate search for a redress of historic grievances. Marxist groups had always advocated the nationalization of foreign-owned plantations and a ceiling on landholdings by local landowners, but although they were now powerfully represented in the Cabinet, they could hardly have had so strong an influence on land policy on their own if their strong commitment had not coincided with that of the Kandyan interests in the Cabinet. Indeed in many ways the commitment of the latter was more passionate and consistent in its emphasis on the nationalization of plantations and on land reform.

Thirdly, Kandyan influence has been basically anti-capitalist in outlook, an understandable development given the animosity of the Kandyans toward the enterprising outsiders who have dominated economic activity in their region — whether the outsiders were Low-Country Sinhalese, Indians, Muslims or Europeans. There were very few Kandyans in the indigenous capitalist class and this no doubt has facilitated the easy reconciliation of aristocratic leadership and socialist ideology. The seemingly traditional aristocratic leadership of the SLFP did not mean a triumph of conservatism: on the contrary it was receptive to populist pressures and socialist ideology.

One of Mrs. Bandaranaike's most constructive achievements after her return to power in 1970 has been the settlement, on a permanent and amicable basis, of the vexed question of persons of Indian origin. Through negotiations with the Indian Prime Minister, Mrs. Gandhi, she brought to a successful conclusion a settlement initiated originally in 1964. The question of statelessness was to be eliminated for good and all. For the moment the more urgent requirement was an agreement on how to deal with the balance of 150,000 left over for later consideration in terms of the 1964 pact. The decision was that there would be an equal division of these into Indian and Sri Lanka citizens. Not all the stateless were covered by this 1974 agreement; there were a number, variously computed at between 50,000 to 75,000, left over for further consideration, the last of the stateless. But much more important for Mrs. Bandaranaike was that the Indian government accepted the principle that those who were recognized as Indian citizens must be repatriated to India, upon the granting of such citizenship, and that the process of repatriation itself must be expedited in order to make up for the time lost between 1965 and 1970.

From the point of view of the Indians who have obtained Sri Lanka citizenship there was the distinct advantage that no attempt was made by her to revive the scheme of a separate electoral register for them. Thus nearly half a million of them would eventually be integrated into the Sri Lanka polity, and Sri Lanka citizenship would confer on them the political legitimacy which they, as an ethnic group, have not had since 1949. But these long-term political implications of the Prime Minister's diplomacy and skilfully crafted settlement of this issue seem to have had very little effect on the thinking of some members of her own cabinet.

And relations between the leadership of the Ceylon Workers Congress and the government were as unfriendly as those of the latter with the Federal Party. It is almost inevitable that a government in which Kandyan influence is predominant would be inclined towards attitudes of apprehension and a suspicion of, if not open hositlity to, the Indian community resident in the island. And so it proved to be. It was not the Prime Minister herself, but the Minister of Agriculture and Lands, H. Kobbekaduwa, who gave expression to the traditional Kandyan hostility to the Indians through word and deed. His speeches against them were unabashedly racist in tone.[19] And he followed them up with administrative acts avowedly discriminatory in intent and effect, a policy of unconcealed hostility more vigorous and far more severe in impact than anything in the past.

He used his authority as Minister in charge of land acquisitions to take over almost all the plantations owned by political activists among the Indian residents in Sri Lanka. This was done *well before* the *Land Reform Act of 1972*, which placed a ceiling on landholdings, was introduced. Among those affected were the Ceylon Workers Congress leader S. Thondaman, and V. Annamalai, who had been an appointed M.P. in the Parliament of 1965-70. Evidently the Minister of Agriculture and Lands, if not the United Front government, was hoping to destroy the economic base which sustained the leadership of the Ceylon Workers Congress.

With the implementation of the *Land Reform Act of 1972* one was struck by the contrast in the policies adopted by the Ministry of Agriculture and Lands on the one hand and the Ministry of Plantation Industry on the other, with regard to the workers — largely Indian —on the plantations under their control. In the plantations under the Ministry of Plantation Industry there was minimal displacement of workers — and in most plantations no displacement at all — and all the rights they had previously enjoyed were confirmed and even consolidated. This included the right to trade union activity. In the plantations which came under the Ministry of Agriculture and Lands, summary dismissal of workers — in effect, expulsion from the plantations which are their homes — was quite common; workers were often deprived of their right to membership of the Employees Provident Fund;[20] and no trade union activity was tolerated except through the aegis of mushroom unions which enjoyed political patronage but not the confidence of the workers. Moreover, once the plantations were taken over, the experienced and skilled managerial and technical staff as well as the clerical staff were dismissed from their posts at short notice, and were replaced by political appointees, Sinhalese almost to a man. There was overwhelming evidence of harassment and intimidation of Ceylon Workers Congress trade unionists on these plantations. The expulsion of Indian workers from the plantations was one of the most distressing social problems in some of the towns in the plantation areas in the aftermath of the nationalization of the plantations: whole families of Indians were reduced to living on the sidewalks of the towns and bazaars, or to seeking shelter for the night in verandahs of public buildings, such as railway stations, and to eke out an existence as poorly-paid casual laborers. Fortunately this turned out to be a temporary phenomenon, but its brevity owned little to the initiative of the UF government.

The point that emerges from this discussion is that two ministries within the same government pursued diametrically opposed policies with regard to the Indian plantation workers under their control. Thus discrimination here was at a ministerial rather than cabinet or governmental level; one minister was a Kandyan, the other, a prominent left-wing politician.[21]

The immigrant plantation workers have been, since independence, the most economically depressed group in Sri Lanka, but never more so than in the early and mid-1970s. In this they were the victims of impersonal market forces, declining yields and falling prices of plantation products rather than of any policy of discrimination.

All sections of the population felt the impact of the inflationary pressures of the 1970s, the unprecedented increase in food prices accompanied by a drastic curtailment of government expenditure on food subsidies. But the effect of these on the plantation workers was devastating, a precipitous decline from a bare subsistence to grinding poverty. The grimmest, and most telling, evidence of this lies in the maternal and infant mortality rates which were considerably higher among the plantation workers than the national average.[22] Deaths by starvation were a frequent occurrence in the plantations in the 1970s, especially in late 1973 and through much of 1974. The government's lack of concern in the face of this appalling fall in living standards of the plantation workers is explicable only in terms of powerful anti-Indian sentiment so deeply rooted among influential cabinet ministers that it was proof against appeals to conscience and humanitarianism.

The situation was aggravated, no doubt, by increasing unemployment on the plantations. The plantations are in no position to provide employment to the natural increase of the estate population when the regular workers were themselves generally under-employed. The leadership of the Indian plantation workers complained that the latter had been by-passed in the provision of welfare facilities in health and education. These were usually provided by the plantations rather than directly through the state and none but the most financially stable and viable of the plantations were able to maintain their welfare facilities unimpaired much less expand them. The plantation economy was, up to the mid-1970s, in a generally depressed state.

Because most of the plantation workers are without votes they were at a great disadvantage in the search for employment outside the plantations since no politicians, other than the plantation workers leadership itself, are interested in their cause. Certainly they — even those who have a vote — do not have the same access to land on irrigation projects, much less to state-owned land in the vicinity of plantations, that the Sinhalese have. All that was available to them, apart from work on plantations, was occasional employment in the vicinity of the estates and in the bazaars and towns in the plantation districts as casual laborers.

The more enterprising of the Indians began to move out to the Northern Province to work on the farms and other ventures there, while some were squatters on government land in the Vavuniya and Mannar districts and elsewhere. The insecurity of their position was demonstrated in 1973 when about 400 displaced plantation workers, all citizens of Sri Lanka, moved into the Eastern Province with the encouragement of Tamil politicians there. The government's reaction — once more it was the Minister of Agriculture and Lands who provided the leadership in this — was swift and decisive. The full rigor of emergency legislation was used to evict the squatters.[23] This was clearly discriminatory since the Eastern Province in recent times had accommodated thousands of Sinhalese squatters whose landholdings have been regularized by the state. The penury of the plantation workers attracted wide publicity in the West when a television program focused attention on them, much to the embarrassment of the plantation and tea distributing companies with their headquarters in England — most notably firms like Brooke-Bonds and Liptons — and the Sri Lanka government as well. This adverse publicity contributed powerfully to persuading the plantation companies to accept what had hitherto been unthinkable, the nationalization — with compensation — of their plantations. The alternative, to continue in ownership but to divert revenues into massive investments in welfare facilities for their workers, was altogether more expensive.

The final phase in the nationalization of the plantations was also its major one in the sense that the estates that now came under government control were the large efficiently-run foreign-owned plantations, the source of the main part of the country's hard-currency earnings. This came in 1975 at a time when the UF coalition was in the throes of an internal political crisis which was soon to culminate in the expulsion of the LSSP from the government. The result was that this formidable exercise — the completion of the process of state control over the plantations — was presided over by the Minister of Agriculture and Lands. Thus the Indian plantation workers were to find adjustment to state ownership of the estates, which by itself was not intrinsically inimical to their interests, more difficult than it might have been under a more sympathetic and enlightened politician. Thus despite assurances that no worker would be evicted from the plantations in which they worked — in effect, their homes — evictions took place, under pressure from influential associates of powerful politicians. Where these pressures were resisted, or for that matter where there were any obvious reluctance to comply with hints that they move out, violence was used to speed them on their way. Thus in May 1977 disturbances occurred in two estates,[24] Sanquahar in Pussellawa (near Gampola) and Devon in Talawakele where the grimy workers' houses — the lines as they were called — were attacked and such property as they possessed looted. More to the point, nationalization did nothing to improve living conditions on the plantations although by 1976 tea prices showed a marked improvement, indeed the first substantial one since the mid-1950, and despite the fact that this improvement in prices was sustained over the next year as well — the last of the government's period of office.

The government's nationalization program on the plantations proceeded apace with a Luddite frenzy which appeared to suggest to one observer that "the estates will be made over to Sinhalese cooperatives, and the present Indian workers will have to search for non-existent alternative employment."[25] In April 1977 an announcement was made that about 8000 acres of the finest tea lands in the country located in the Nuwara-Eliya Maskeliya district (and electorate) would be parcelled out among the peasants of that region. The announcement provoked an unexpectedly strong opposition from an unusual combination of forces, the superintendents of the estates concerned, the trade unions representing the workers, and representatives of the clerical and other support staff.[26] The agitation succeeded in thwarting these moves but partly at least because the elections of July 1977 turned the ruling party out of power.

In concluding this review of relations between the UF regime and the Tamil minority one point needs emphasis, namely that the Marxist parties within the government contributed little or nothing to stemming the rising tide of communalism in this period. During the early 1960s both the LSSP and the CP had abandoned their original support for parity of status for Sinhalese and Tamil as official languages. As allies of the SLFP they came to adopt the SLFP's position on language, and soon this support took on a distressingly communalist form in the opposition to the language proposals announced and introduced in 1966 by Dudley Senanayake's UNP-led coalition. In that campaign there was little to choose, in regard to crude communalist agitation, between the SLFP and its two Marxist allies. Thus in the 1970s with the UF in power, the indigenous Tamils saw little difference between the Marxists and the SLFP in official policies affecting minority rights. As regards the plantation workers there was a distinct difference in attitude as seen in the Ministry of Plantation Industry under Dr. Colvin R. de Silva, who was able to spare the workers of the plantations that came within the purview of his Ministry the hardships inflicted on those who came under Kobbekaduwa's Ministry of Lands. But this, in fact, proved to be the limit of the Marxists achievement in rising above the communalism that was so rampant in the government in which they served. The Marxists in the UF coalition had been co-belligerents with the SLFP in the latter's campaigns against the indigenous Tamil minority since 1965 and thus could do and did very little, in general, as a restraint on their senior partner in the coalition during the UF's existence.

The UF and the Muslims

The UF and, in particular, the SLFP had good reason for elation at detaching a substantial section of the Muslims from their traditional links with the UNP. This was the work, mainly, of Mahmud who chose for this purpose the Islamic Socialist Front, an *ad hoc* 'umbrella' organization for Muslim supporters of the UF. In his hands the critically important post of Minister of Education became at once a political base and a fountain of patronage to be used to strengthen the ties between his community and the party to which be belonged.

Such success as he achieved in the general policy of building links between the Muslims and the UF proved to be transient. He was soon a controversial figure; his education policy, and in particular that on university admissions, was a major point of divergence between the government and the Tamils. More significantly, by 1973, anti-Muslim sentiment was kindled among the Sinhalese by charges of favored treatment of Muslims in the sphere of education. In 1974-75 there were sporadic Sinhalese-Muslim clashes in various parts of the island with a dangerous confrontation at Gampola in the last week of December 1975. The incident at Gampola was especially poignant for Mahmud, for he himself and the school he had carefully nursed through difficult times — by now a prestigious and privileged institution on which state funds had been lavished with conspicuous generosity — were at the center of the controversy. If the timely intervention of the police prevented widespread violence at Gampola the clash that occurred in in Puttalam in early 1976 was — up to that time — the worst episode of communal violence since the Sinhalese-Tamil riots in the late 1950s. Several persons, mostly Muslims, were killed in these riots, many of them by police firing on a crowd gathered in a mosque. Charges made by the Muslims of police partiality in this incident, and excesses committed against Muslims on this occasion, were disregarded by the government. Indeed the Prime Minister, Mrs. Bandaranaike, in an official statement in the National State Assembly on 6 February 1976, endorsed the version of the incidents set out by the police.[27] The policies which Mahmud was so visibly associated with had come to grief in this renewal of Sinhalese antagonism to the Muslims, and when Mahmud, for the first time in his political career[28], stood for election in July 1977, he was resoundingly defeated, and the Islamic Socialist Front did not survive his defeat.

Epilogue

This recrudescence of ethnic and religious tension seemed menacing enough on its own, but there were other events which made the last weeks of 1975 especially somber for the government. In October 1975 the political alliance between the SLFP and the LSSP, which had lasted, in opposition and government, since 1964, came to an end. A rift within the ruling coalition became public knowledge in mid-August. A sharp difference of opinion over the mechanics of the nationalization of foreign-owned plantations in the island resulted in acrimonious bickering between these two major component units of the UF. All attempts to heal the rift proved futile, and the LSSP was expelled from the government.

The political consequences of this were not immediately evident. On the contrary, the government sought to stabilize its position by exploiting the political advantages expected from staging the Non-Aligned Nations Conference in Colombo in August 1976, in the hope that the prestige likely to accrue to the Prime Minister from the international publicity for the conference, and from her position as its President, could buttress its position at home.

Indeed, as if to give credence to this theory, the government retained a parliamentary seat at a by-election in August 1976, its first such success since 1972. However, instead of boosting the morale of the government before the general elections due in mid-1977, this victory actually encouraged moves, begun during the period of the conference, to secure a further postponement of the general elections originally due in 1975, by an amendment of the Constitution. Despite the losses sustained by the departure of the LSSP, the government had the support of nearly two-thirds of the National State Assembly and thus a constitutional amendment was within its reach if just two or three opposition MPs could be won over, if necessary by offers of ministerial appointments. Though the Prime Minister herself did not publicly support these moves, significantly, she did not repudiate them either.

This campaign received an unexpected but serious setback when, in early October 1976, all six Communist Party MPs (including their representative in the Cabinet) and five SLFP cabinet ministers declared themselves opposed to any move to postpone the elections. This was clear evidence of a split in the Cabinet over the issue, and of a sharp difference of opinion between the two remaining coalition partners, the SLFP and CP.

Nevertheless, the move was not immediately abandoned, only the tactics were changed and took the form of SLFP negotiations with the TULF through its President, S.J.V. Chelvanayakam, in a serious bid to seek a resolution of differences between them and the government. For this purpose the government had hastily abandoned its original plans to appeal a decision against it at the trial-at-bar of three prominent TULF politicians, two of whom were MPs. The negotiations began in late 1976 and continued into the first quarter of 1977. Among the benefits the SLFP negotiators hoped for in their discussions with the TULF was the latter's support to extend the life of Parliament.

With the failure of this attempt at a last-minute reconciliation with the Tamil United Liberation Front (TULF), the government at last woke up to the reality of isolation in its bid to postpone the elections. Worse still, the coalition was disintegrating; left-wing members of the SLFP left the party, and this was followed later by a breach between the SLFP and CP. By the end of February 1977 the UF coalition had been dissolved and what remained was a dispirited and demoralized SLFP government confronting Sri Lanka's worst wave of strikes for 20 years, which had been engineered by its erstwhile coalition partners. The political situation in the country became even more unsettled with the death, at the end of April 1977, of S.J.V. Chelvanayakam, leader of the TULF, for this brought an end to the discussions between the TULF and the SLFP.

At the general elections of July 1977, there was no electoral pact against the UNP between the SLFP and the left, for the first time since March 1960. The constituent parties of the coalition that had triumphed in May 1970 were in direct competition with each other, and the alignment of forces at the general election of July 1977 was thus totally different from that of May 1970.

References

[1]   N. Tiruchelvam, 'The Making and Unmaking of Constitutions: Some Reflections on the Process', in *CJHSS* n.s. VII(2) pp. 18-24, see particularly pp. 19-20.

[2]   N. Tiruchelvam, *op.cit.*, p. 21.

[3]   *Ibid.*

[4]   For discussion of this see S.W.R. de A. Samarasinghe, 'Ethnic Representation in

Central Government Employment and Sinhala-Tamil Relations in Sri Lanka, 1948-1981' in (eds) R.B. Goldman and A.J. Wilson, *From Statehood to Independence* (London, 1984) pp. 173-184.

5   On this issue see, C.R. de Silva: 'Weightage in University Admissions: Standardization and District Quotas in Sri Lanka, 1970-75': *Modern Ceylon Studies* V(2) pp. 152-178; 'The Politics of University Admissions: A Review of Some Aspects of University Admissions Policy in Sri Lanka, 1971-1978', *The Sri Lanka Journal of Social Sciences*; 1(2) pp. 85-123.

6   C.R. de Silva, 'The Politics of University Admissions: A Review of Some Aspects of the Admissions in Sri Lanka, 1972-1978', p. 85.

7   *Ibid.*

8   For example, the qualifying mark for admission to the Medical Faculties was 250 (out of 400) for Tamil students, and 229 for Sinhalese students. The same differential qualifying marks applied in the case of Sinhalese and Tamil students who sat the examination in the English medium: in this instance students sitting the examination in the same medium had two different qualifying marks to enter the medical faculties.

9   C.R. de Silva, *op. cit.*, p. 87.

10   C.R. de Silva, *op. cit.*, p. 89-90.

11   C.R. de Silva, *op. cit.*, p. 90.

12   C.R. de Silva, 'Weightage in University Admissions: Standardization and District Quotas in Sri Lanka', *Modern Ceylon Studies* V(2), p. 166.

13   *Ibid.*

14   C.R. de Silva, 'The Politics of University Admissions', *op. cit.*, pp. 93-97.

15   On the politics of Tamilnadu during this period see, Lloyd Rudoph "Urban Life and Populist Radicalism: the Dravidian Movement in Madras". *Journal of Asian Studies* XX (1961) pp. 283-297; and Robert L. Hardgrave, Jr., "The DMK and the Politics of Tamil Nationalism", *Pacific Affairs* XXXVII (1964-65) pp. 396-411, and "Riots in Tamilnadu: Problems and Prospects of India's Language Crisis." *Asian Survey* V (1965), pp. 399-407.

16   Norman Cutler, 'The Fish-eyed Goddess Meets the Movie Star: An Eyewitness Account of the Fifth International Tamil Conference.' *Pacific Affairs* LVI(2) (1983) pp. 270-287. The quotation is from page 277.

17   For an impartial assessment of the incidents relating to the deaths caused on this occasion, see *S.P.* VII of 1980, *Report of the Presidential Commission on the Inquiry into Incidents which took place between 13 August and 15 September 1977.* (The Commissioner was M.C. Sansoni, former Chief Justice, and a Burgher), pp. 66-70. The Commissioner supported the findings of the magisterial inquiry held in 1974, at which it was established that the deaths had been caused by electrocution when some electric wires were accidentally dislodged. It was "unreservedly held that not a single rifle bullet was fired [by the police on that occasion].

18   The demarcation of constituencies effected in 1959 worked on the principle of counting the total population of a province in computing the number of seats to which it was entitled without regard to the fact that most of the Indian workers resident in the plantation districts had been excluded from the franchise. As a result the Kandyans, with just over a quarter of the island's population, had 44% of the seats in Parliament. See *S.P.* XV of 1959, *The Report of the Delimitation Com-*

mission.

19 A good example is a speech reported in *The Ceylon Daily News*, 1 August 1973.

20 At its inception the title Employees' Provident Fund was deliberately chosen in preference to National Provident Fund to enable the plantation workers of all categories to benefit from membership in it. The decision was made by S.W.R.D. Bandaranaike himself.

21 Dr. Colvin R. de Silva, one of the leading criminal lawyers in the country, historian, and national political figure (a member of the LSSP). He held this post till 3 September 1975.

22 Dr. B. Seneviratne, *The Health of the Plantation Workers*, Coordinating Secretariat for Plantation Areas, Kandy, Sri Lanka, Bulletin No. 4. (1975).

23 For the regulations referred to in the text see *The Government Gazette*, 647 of 19 June 1973 and 65/9 of June 1973.

24 See, M.H. Gunaratne, *The Plantation Raj* (Colombo, 1980) for an interesting and authentic account of these developments.

25 H. Tinker, *The Banyan Tree, Overseas Emigrants from India, Pakistan and Bangladesh*. (O.U.P., 1977). This pessimistic prediction was not fulfilled.

26 M.H. Gunaratne, *The Plantation Raj, op. cit.*

27 *Hansard* (National State Assembly) Vol. XVIII, Columns 467-9.

28 During his parliamentary career Mahmud had always been a nominated MP, one of the six such MPs. The system of nominated MPs was abolished under the 1972 constitution but MPs nominated in 1970 were permitted to retain their seats till Parliament was dissolved.

Chapter XVIII

The Constitution of 1978 and Minority Rights

The Election of 1977 and Its Aftermath

The general election of July 1977 transformed the political landscape of the country. The second landmark general election since independence it swept the UNP to power and reduced the SLFP temporarily, at least, to parliamentary insignificance, to a mere 8 seats from 90 in the previous parliament, while the Marxist left disappeared from the parliamentary scene when all its MPs were defeated, many of them quite decisively. All the prominent SLFP politicians who entered Parliament with the electoral victories of the Bandaranaikes in 1956 and 1960 lost their seats, with the exception of Mrs. Bandaranaike and the Deputy Leader of the SLFP who retained his seat by a very narrow margin. One sensed the working of some massive collective will sitting in judgment over those who had set the pace in politics since 1956, finding them wanting, and sternly dismissing them.[1]

The island's electoral system as it then existed was such that when a major shift of political power occurred through the ballot a new regime was returned to power with a far higher proportion of seats in the legislature than was warranted by the vote it received. For the first time the winning party at a Sri Lankan general election obtained a clear majority — 50.9% — of the popular vote but this was enough to give the UNP 140 out of 168 seats, and absolute majorities in 126 of these. Since 1959-60 the distortions of the electoral system had worked to the disadvantage of the UNP but in 1977 the SLFP found itself with only 4.8% of the seats although it had obtained 29% of the vote. More extraordinary still as a result of the peculiar demographic profile of the island, with a concentration of Tamils in the north, and to a lesser extent, the east of the island, the TULF with about one fifth of the popular vote secured by the SLFP had more than double the number of seats, i.e., 18 as against 8 for the SLFP. For the first time since independence a Tamil, A. Amirthalingam, Leader of the TULF, became Leader of the Opposition.

This distortion of the electoral process would by itself have given an unusually sharp focus to minority rights over the life of the new parliament, but minds of politicians and the intelligentsia alike were concentrated on these issues much earlier and more urgently than would normally have happened when a fracas in Jaffna town — a clash between the police and a section of the people there — precipitated a ferocious outbreak of communal violence between the Sinhalese and Tamils, in mid-August 1977, which spread to many parts of the island and bore comparison with the ethnic disturbances of the mid-1950s. Over 100 persons were killed and over 25,000, both Tamil and Sinhalese, rendered homeless.[2]

These incidents were the direct result of causes whose roots lay in the atmosphere of communal distrust stemming from the political attitudes and policies of the SLFP-dominated UF regime of the early and mid-1970s. At the heart of this crisis of confidence in ethnic relations was the position of the security forces in Jaffna, and the police in particular who, trapped in a cross-fire of contending factions, found themselves, willing or not, a crucially important factor in the troubled politics of the peninsula.

The new government stopped the conflagration with a mixture of firmness and restraint, and more significantly, without resort to emergency rule. At the height of the disturbances it announced that a Commission of Inquiry would be appointed to examine the circumstances that had led to the outbreak of violence, and M.C. Sansoni, a former Chief Justice, was subsequently appointed a one-man Commission.

The riots were a setback to what appeared to be a promising beginning of a policy of reconciliation.

In its election manifesto the UNP had spelled out its policy in regard to the problems of the indigenous Tamils. There were three main items in this. First of all, there was a reference to minority rights in the section on constitutional reforms. It read as follows:

"We will ensure in the constitution that every citizen, whether he
belongs to a majority or minority, racial, religious or caste group, enjoys
equal and basic human rights and opportunities. The decisions of an All
Party Conference which will be summoned to consider the problem of
non-Sinhala people will be included in the constitution".

Secondly, there was a reference to decentralization of administration down to the village level, to "make the people partners in the
planning, organization and implementation of policy". There was
reference also to the administrative machinery to be established for
this purpose, at the apex of which were to be District Development
Councils headed by a District Minister, and consisting of MPs of the
District, elected heads of local bodies, and government officials. This
was clearly intended as a concession to the Tamil minority though,
naturally enough, it was not specifically referred to as such.

Third, and most significant of all, a whole section of the manifesto
was devoted to 'Problems of the Tamil-speaking People' under that
sub-heading. The two paragraphs of this section are quoted below:

"The United National Party accepts the position that there are
numerous problems confronting the Tamil-speaking people. The lack of
a solution to their problems has made the Tamil-speaking people even
support a movement for the creation of a separate state. In the interests
of national integration and unity so necessary for the economic
development of the whole country, the Party feels such problems should
be solved without loss of time. The Party, when it comes to power, will
take all possible steps to remedy their grievances in such fields as:
(1) Education   (2) Colonisation   (3) The use of the
Tamil Language   (4) Employment in the public [sector]
and semi-public corporations.
We will summon an All-Party Conference as stated earlier and
implement its decision."

In setting out its proposals in such detail the new leadership of the
UNP was reaching out for a new beginning in the management of Sri
Lanka's ethnic tensions and rivalries.

By the beginning of 1977 the TULF was in the unusual position of
being wooed by the SLFP during its feverish bid for support of an
amendment of the constitution to extend the life of Parliament beyond
May 1977. One TULF MP had spoken up on supporting the SLFP in
this enterprise provided the basic demands of the Tamils were granted.
And the SLFP's offer on this was examined at a meeting between the
leadership of the two parties. Although these negotiations did not bear
fruit, there had been influential TULF politicians, who during the
discussion, had indicated their preference for the SLFP as against its

challenger, the UNP. With Chelvanayakam's death these negotiations had come to a halt. Now, after the elections the UNP faced an untested and insecure leadership within the TULF.

Not since the year 1930 when Ramanathan died had there been so huge a void in the Tamil political leadership in the country. On that occasion it took five years or more for a new and youthful leadership to fill that void, and for G.G. Ponnambalam to secure a dominance in Tamil politics that lasted till the mid-1950s. There was thus an amazing parallel between the late 1970s and the early 1930s except that in the course of 1976 and 1977 the Sri Lanka Tamils had lost not one but three outstanding leaders: S.J.V. Chelvanayakam, leader of the Federal Party since 1948 and of the TUF (later, TULF) from its inception, very much the father figure of Tamil politics; the silver-tongued G.G. Ponnambalam who had led the Tamil campaigns up to 1956, when Chelvanayakam established his supremacy, and was the latter's main rival; and M. Tiruchelvam, the only TULF politician with any recent experience of Cabinet office. All of them were distinguished senior lawyers at the very top of their profession, capable of negotiating on equal terms with the Prime Minister of the day and — this was particularly true of Chelvanayakam and Ponnambalam — of securing acceptance of an agreement by the Tamil electorate.

The present TULF leadership thus faced an enormous challenge in taking over from these senior politicians. Their task was rendered all the more formidable by the volatility of Jaffna's politics since the early 1970s. The transition of the present leadership from the second rung to the top of the ladder may have been easier in less troubled times. The result was a change in political style, from a charismatic leadership, to a more low-key one. The change could be summarized thus: the Tamil masses in Jaffna held Chelvanayakam in awe as a father figure, and indeed they referred to him as *Periayar* or the great leader; his successor, Amirthalingam, was referred to as an elder brother, suggesting thereby the head in a collective leadership, a chairman of a board rather than an unchallenged single leader. Besides, there were the TULF's links with Tamil youth groups — intent on radicalizing the politics of the north and east of the island, and intent also on holding the new leadership to the objective of a separate Tamil state in Sri Lanka, Eelam, on which it had secured so resounding a mandate in the Jaffna peninsula and the Northern Province if not in the Eastern Province. Thus there was another amazing parallel between the early 1930s and the late 1970s in the politics of Jaffna, and the Northern

Province — the pace-setters were youth groups. In 1931, as we have seen, a group of youthful enthusiasts succeeded in cajoling the Tamil politicians of the day into a boycott of elections to the State Council.[3] Within a few months of this, it was evident that they had driven their seniors, reluctantly or not, into a *cul de sac* and it was to take two years or more before the politicians re-established their hold on the electorate in the Jaffna peninsula.[4] It would take their counterparts of the present day much longer than that to establish anything approaching a similar independence of action.

Soon after its election victory the new government had given positive evidence of a more accommodating policy in regard to the grievances of the Tamil minority. Thus in its statement of policy in the National State Assembly on 4 August 1977 the government pledged itself to introducing far-reaching changes in the status accorded to the Tamil language. Again, and once more before the riots of mid-August broke out, a major concession was made in regard to a grievance of more recent vintage — a declaration that standardization of marks for admission to universities would be abandoned with immediate effect was made almost immediately after the new government took office.

The TULF's response was rigidly doctrinnaire. An amendment to the government's statement of policy of 4 August 1977, moved by the TULF on 18 August, after the outbreak of communal rioting, was both tendentious and provocative — an insistence on proclaiming the TULF's commitment to the establishment of a separate Tamil state in Sri Lanka. The amendment itself could hardly have been more ill-timed for this re-iteration of the TULF's advocacy of the dismember-ment of the Sri Lanka polity literally fanned the flames of Sinhalese communal feeling. An extravagant exercise in rhetoric, part of the ritual of parliamentary politics, was seen as the launching of a major political campaign directed from the office of the Leader of the Opposition and all the more dangerous and sinister for that. The Sinhalese had hardly had time to get accustomed to the idea of a Tamil in the role of Leader of the Opposition when this ill-advised amendment to the government's policy statement appeared to suggest that conciliatory moves were so many sops to a particularly intransi-gent Cerberus.

In the circumstances the TULF leadership's failure to reciprocate these gestures by holding back its separatist demands for a few months, at least, till the new regime had time to convert the proposals for a settlement of the problems of the indigenous Tamils, outlined first of all in its election manifesto and now repeated in the policy statement presented to the national legislature, into a program of legislative and administrative action, contributed not a little to the spread of communal disturbances to parts of the island that had been spared the worst of the ethnic violence of the mid-1950s.

Constitutional Reform

If these ethnic conflicts deflected the government's attention from more pressing issues this was not for very long. High on its priorities was a fresh and searching look at Sri Lanka's constitutional framework. The constitutional changes it had in mind had been outlined as early as 1971 when they had been moved as alternative proposals to the then government's constitutional reforms during the debates of the Constituent Assembly. Subsequently, they had been incorporated in the election manifesto of the UNP for the 1977 general elections thus:

"Executive power will be vested in a President elected from time to time by the people...The constitution will also preserve the parliamentary system we are used to for the Prime Minister will be chosen by the President from the Party that commands a majority in Parliament and the Ministers of the Cabinet will also be elected Members of Parliament".

Constitutions and constitutional reform were among the main points of debate in the election campaign of 1977. The SLFP for its part placed the constitution of 1972 as the first item of its manifesto, an assertion of pride in what it regarded as a major achievement, and an indication of the need to protect the principles it embodied. It also provided, quite deliberately, a point of departure from which to attack the UNP's own proposals for constitutional reform. The focus of attention was the concept of an Executive Presidency, which drew fire from all the component elements of the UF coalition of old, and not merely from the SLFP alone. There was thus a notable difference between the election campaigns of 1970 and 1977; in 1977, unlike in 1970, it was a central issue. Thus the UNP was able to treat its overwhelming victory at the polls as an unmistakably positive endorsement by the electorate of its proposals for constitutional change.

The first steps in the implementation of these changes came in August-September 1977 in the appointment of a parliamentary select committee on constitutional reform, and the adoption by the National State Assembly of a constitutional amendment establishing a presidential system of government. Under the terms of this amendment the Prime Minister, J.R. Jayewardene, assumed office as the first elected executive President of the country on February 4, 1978. The result of the committee's deliberations, however, was not an amendment of the constitution of 1972 but its replacement by another, the second major overhaul of the island's constitutional system since independence.[4]

The constitution of the first republic (1972-78) despite strengthening the armory of executive power, kept the Westminster model, formulated for the island in 1946-8, almost unchanged. The second republic of 1978 initiated a distinct change in structure and form by establishing a presidential system which brings into operation new political styles. The new constitution is a unique blend of some of the functional aspects of Sri Lanka's previous constitutions and features of the American, French and British systems of government — a presidential system designed to meet Sri Lanka's own special requirements in the light of past experience in the working of previous constitutions. The new political style included referendal democracy, an extensive charter of fundamental rights (more substantial than that incorporated in the previous constitution), proportional representation on the list system in place of the 'first-past-the-post' principle of representation based on the British model and consultative advisory committees to Cabinet ministers.

Other and equally prominent features of the new constitution provided evidence of continuity in the island's constitutional structure: the retention of Prime Ministerial and Cabinet government, the role of the legislature as an important factor in decision making; and the whole structure bore the imprint of a commitment to, and renewal of faith in the concept of a Sri Lankan nationalism, and was in that sense a perpetuation of a political philosophy which underlay the structure of the system introduced in 1946-47.

The resort to a Select Committee of the National State Assembly for the purpose of drafting a new constitution provoked controversy. The repudiation of the government's election promise of an all-party conference meant that political parties not represented in the Assembly could not participate directly in the process of drafting the constitution. The traditional left, not represented in Parliament rejected the new constitution as an exercise in Bournapartism. None of its representative parties chose to give evidence before the Select

Committee. This the SLFP did, but its MPs walked out of parliament during the debate on the constitution in protest against the process of constitution-making adopted by the government and against some of the salient features of the new constitution, especially the executive Presidency and proportional representation. Again although no previous constitution, not even that of 1947, offered the minorities a more secure position within the Sri Lanka polity than the present one, the TULF refused to participate in the Select Committee proceedings. In this sense the present constitution like its predecessor has been rejected by all major opposition groups, in brief by large and very vocal sections of the political nation.

Our concern in this present chapter is with the attitude of the TULF. The conceptual basis for the TULF's refusal to participate in the process of constitution making was set out by its leader, A. Amirthalingam thus:

> "The Republican Constitution of 1972 sought to sever the legal and constitutional link with the past. Once there is such a break in legal continuity, the sovereignty of the inhabitants of the Island, until then under eclipse (during a period of foreign domination or externally designed constitutional rule), resurfaced. Hence the sovereignty of the Tamil nation, which was ethnically, geographically and linguistically separate, identifiable and distinct, revived. The United National Party had a clear, unequivocal mandate to assert the sovereignty of the Sinhala nation and enact a new constitution. The mandate of the majority of the Tamil nation pointed to a different duty".[5]

This statement reiterated the major conceptual transformation in Tamil aspirations from 1972-77, the assertion of a corporate identity by the Tamil people shaped by their perception of a distinct history, language and culture. That this identity was inherently incompatible with and antagonistic to the corporate and collective identity of the Sinhalese people is the basis of the current crisis in Sinhalese-Tamil relations.

Fundamental Rights

The fundamental rights incorporated in the new constitution are altogether more substantial than those in the constitution of 1972, a point of considerable importance so far as the minorities and in particular the Tamils are concerned. For, as Mark Fernando, one of the legal experts involved in drafting the new constitution points out:

"A right or freedom does not become 'fundamental' merely by reason of its enumeration in the constitution or even by its inclusion in a chapter headed 'Fundamental Rights'. It becomes fundamental only if it is placed at the foundation of the constitution, becoming an essential part of it, which no persons can violate or infringe with impunity; the quality of being fundamental depends on the extent of recognition, entrenchment and protection".[6]

The fundamental rights of the new constitution, he adds,

"go beyond a mere matter of legal provisions in a few Articles of the constitution...They provide for a genuine and effective recognition, entrenchment and protection of Fundamental Rights — all three elements are necessary; recognition without entrenchment is an illusion; recognition and entrenchment without protection are a mere deception..."[7]

The Fundamental Rights of the 1978 constitution are more strongly and genuinely entrenched and afford greater protection, quite apart from being more detailed and precisely formulated and being more in number, than those of the constitution of 1972. Moreover, provision is made for protection through and by the Supreme Court against the infringement or even imminent infringement of such rights by either executive or administrative action. Again the constitution provided for the creation of a post of Parliamentary Commissioner for Administration (Ombudsman) with powers to investigate and report on allegations of infringement of fundamental rights.

All eight Fundamental Rights enumerated in Article 14(1) are extended by Article 14(2) to a large category of non-citizens — the stateless Indian Tamil minority. In the constitution of 1972 only citizens were entitled to the rights enumerated in section 18(1) (c), (d), (e), (f), (g), and (i). They have now been extended to all the permanent and legitimate residents of Sri Lanka for a period of ten years from 1978 long enough, hopefully, to resolve the vexed question of the citizenship rights of these persons.

Most of the Fundamental Rights incorporated in the new constitution are free of any restriction, and even those that are not, are far less circumscribed than those of the previous constitution were by provisions such as section 18(2) of that constitution. There are some however, Article 12(1) for instance, which are not so well protected. The provisions of this article which states that

"no citizen shall be discriminated against on the grounds only of race, religion, caste, sex, political opinion or place of birth" are qualified by those of 15(7) which spells out the nature and extent of the limits imposed;

> "in the interests of national security, public order, and the protection of public health and morality or for the purpose of securing due recognition and respect for the rights and freedoms of others or of meeting the just requirements of the general welfare of a democratic society".

Article 15(7) similarly restricts freedoms from arbitrary arrest, and detention incorporated in Article 13 (1) and (2) as well as freedom of speech, of assembly, of association, of public worship and of movement.

Language Rights

Language — the "pedigree of nations" in Dr. Johnson's felicitous words — had been the rallying point of Sinhalese and Tamil ethnic identity and assertiveness since the mid-1950s. Although language had lost some of its virulence as a factor in Sri Lanka's ethnic tensions and rivalries by the 1970s, the framers of the constitution of 1978 sought an accomodation on language and gave it very high priority. The terms of that accomodation incorporated in the new constitution are, at the very least, a consolidation of the *modus vivendi* on language rights that had emerged after two decades of strife. They are, in fact, much more than that, as would be clear by comparing the provisions of the constitution of 1978 relating to language rights with those of its immediate predecessor.

The constitution of 1972 had unequivocally consolidated the 'Sinhalese only' policy of the 1950s and emphasized the essentially subordinate role of the Tamil language: thus while the use of the Tamil language was recognized and permitted within the limits set out in the *Tamil Language (Special Provisions) Act No. 28 of 1958*, regulations drafted under the provisions of this act were "deemed subordinate legislation". The reference was quite deliberately directed at the *Tamil Language (Special Provisions) Regulations* adopted by Parliament in 1966. The constituent parties of the UF had opposed the adoption of these regulations within Parliament, and had organized extra-parliamentary agitation against it as well.

In contrast, Chapter IV of the 1978 Constitution, while maintaining the status of Sinhalese as *the* official language (Article 18) recognizes Tamil as a national language (Article 19), a significant modification of the 'Sinhala Only' policy. A contemporary observer, a prominent Tamil lawyer, assessed the significance of this change thus:

"...for the first time in the political history of this country the new constitution recognizes the existence of the Tamil community as a distinct nationality with a separate language and Section 19 provides that the national languages of Sri Lanka shall be Sinhala and Tamil. This is a step which previous governments have been unable or unwilling to take and the status afforded to Tamil as a national language in the new Constitution is by itself a significant step forward in the attempt to bring about a unity of purpose amongst the members of the Sinhala and Tamil communities in this country and thereby foster the growth of a truly national awareness and consciousness."[8]

A similar assessment of the significance of the language provisions of the 1978 constitution was spelled out in pertinacious detail and clarity in 1980 by two prominent Muslims.[9] The relevant extract from a long memorandum submitted by them read as follows:

"...The constitutional background today relating to the Tamil language, which proceeds from the base of one Country and one Nation, are contained in Articles 19 to 24 of the Constitution. They are too lengthy to reproduce here but their following broad effect may be noted —

(i)   While Sinhala is made the official language of the Republic, Sinhala and Tamil are declared to be the National Languages of Sri Lanka.

(ii)   A Tamil will be entitled to be educated through the medium of the Tamil language.[10]

(iii)   The Tamil language is also to be used as the language of administration for the maintenance of public records and the transaction of all business by public institutions in the Northern and Eastern Provinces.[11]

(iv)   A Tamil in any part of the country shall be entitled to receive communications from and to communicate and transact business with any official in his official capacity, in Tamil.[12]

(v)   A Tamil in any part of the country shall be entitled to certified copies of public documents in Tamil or if the original is in any other language a Tamil translation.

(vi)   Any local authority conducting its affairs in Tamil will be entitled to receive communications from and to communicate with any official in any part of the country in Tamil.

(vii)   A Tamil candidate for public or judicial office or office in the Local Government Service will be entitled to be examined through the medium of the Tamil language subject to the condition that he may be required to acquire a sufficient knowledge of the Sinhala Language and provided that a person may be required to have a knowledge of Sinhala as a condition of admission to any public office if the duties of such office cannot be discharged without sufficient knowledge of Sinhala.[12]

(viii)   All laws and subordinate legislation have to be enacted, made and published in both Sinhala and Tamil.[13]

(ix)   All existing written laws have to be published in both Sinhala and Tamil as expeditiously as possible after the adoption of the Constitution.

(x)   While Sinhala is made the language of the courts throughout Sri Lanka, the language of courts exercising original jurisdiction in the Northern and Eastern Provinces shall also be Tamil.

(xi)   Any party or any attorney representing a party is entitled in any court in the Island to submit pleadings and other documents and participate in proceedings in either Sinhala or Tamil.

(xii)   Any judge or juror or applicant or attorney if he is a Tamil and not conversant with the Sinhala language in a court where Sinhala is the only language of the court would be entitled to a translation to Tamil provided by the state."

The document from which this extract was derived was a note of dissent submitted by two Muslim members of the Presidential Commission on Development Councils in 1980. Their summary of the language provisions of the 1978 constitution was both fair and accurate.

Chapter IV of the constitution is an elaboration of Articles 14(1)(f) and 27(6) which, respectively, guarantee the freedom to use one's own language, and lays down as a principle of State Policy "that no citizen shall suffer any disability by reason of language." Moreover, all the rights enjoyed by the Tamil-speaking people of the island under the *Tamil Language (Special Provisions) Act No. 28 of 1958* was incorporated in the constitution and cannot therefore be changed except by way of a Constitutional amendment.

Most of the language rights set out in Chapter IV had been in existence in the past, derived from the language legislation of the 1950s and regulations connected with it such as those approved by Parliament in 1966, or from legislation relating to education, public administration and justice, to mention only the most important areas of public interest relevant to the use of the Tamil language. Yet in theory, if not in practice, ordinary legislation could override them, and although this had seldom happened, the more important point was that no real remedy was available against their denial through regulations or even administrative decisions. The language provisions of the 1978 constitution changed all that.

There were, and still are, gaps between language rights provided by law and indeed incorporated in the constitution, and their practical effectiveness. The fact that article 25 of the 1978 constitution casts a responsibility on the state to provide adequate facilities for the use of the national languages as specified in the constitution makes the gaps between promise and fulfillment seem more the result of a lack of concern at the top, rather than lethargy at the bureaucratic level, and especially at the clerical rather than executive level at that, where the problem actually lies.

Nevertheless gaps and all the language rights the Tamil minority in Sri Lanka enjoy are on par with those of the French in Canada, substantially better than those of the English-speaking minority in Quebec, and immeasurably superior to those of the Tamils of Malaysia who form an overwhelming majority of the Indian community in their country. A more appropriate comparison is with the language rights of the minorities in the cantons of Switzerland. The comparison is appropriate because Switzerland is often cited by Tamil critics of Sri Lanka's language policy, as the most important success story of modern pluralist democracy, and they identify Switzerland's language policy as one of the keys to this success.[12] Such critics focus attention on article 116 of the Swiss constitution which lays down that

"...in direct dealings between the citizen and the confederation, and *vice versa*, the federal government must adapt to the language of the individual within the limits of the official language."[13]

The official languages of the confederation are German, French and Italian. While Sri Lanka has, in theory, only one official language, in practice Tamil has as important a position — it is now recognized as a national language — as, for instance, Italian does in Switzerland. But more important than this, there are two principles in operation in Swiss language policy: the principle of personality at the federal level, and the principle of territoriality at the cantonal level, and it is at the cantonal level that the more relevant comparison lies. These cantons are not only remarkably homogeneous, but also persons "moving to a new canton are obliged to use its local languages for the transaction of official business."[14] Indeed

"...the canton (in accordance with the principle of territoriality) determines the official cantonal language (or in a few cases, languages). The cantonal language is the medium of instruction in the public schools. In addition, all cantonal laws and regulations are issued only in the official language(s). While compromises are made in practice, the cantons have no legal obligation to provide translations or deal with citizens in languages other than their own."[15]

Thus the practical realities of Swiss language policy show the language policy of Sri Lanka in a more favorable light, and the comparision would be even more favorable if one were to focus attention on education. Sri Lanka's Tamil minorities — indigenous and Indian and Tamil-speaking Muslims — have always enjoyed the right to an education through the medium of the Tamil language in whatever part of the country they live. This right extends to university and technical education as well. Thus apart from the University of Jaffna which teaches in Tamil and English, the University of Peradeniya is unique in providing instruction through three languages, Sinhalese, Tamil and English. The University of Colombo provides instruction in Tamil in some of its departments of study, in addition of course to instruction in Sinhalese and English.[16] So far as education is concerned the Tamil minorities of Sri Lanka have enjoyed advantages which minorities in the Swiss cantons do not enjoy, or have seldom enjoyed.

The Electoral System

Just as important for its implications for ethnic relations in the island is the new system of direct election of the executive President of the country (Article 30(2)). The election is on the basis of a single transferable vote system under which if no candidate secures 50% of the votes, all other than the first and second in terms of the votes polled are eliminated and the second or third preferences of the votes polled by them will go to the first two in the list. The minorities could determine the fate of the rival Sinhalese parties far more decisively — especially where the two parties are fairly evenly divided in terms of votes — than under the Westminster system of single member constituencies electing members on the first-past-the-post basis. It had become increasingly evident in general elections since the mid-1950s that there was little or no disadvantage in a subtle or even blatant anti-Tamil campaign in the Sinhalese areas; indeed elections were won or lost in the Sinhalese areas of the country. The situation is very different today as was evident during the Presidential campaign of 1983, the first to be held under the new constitution. No party or individual aiming at the Presidency could afford to alienate the minorities. The speed with which all major political parties approved of the recognition of Tamil as one of two national languages is evidence of this. In other words, the system of direct Presidential elections could bring the Tamils into the political scene as a balancing element, especially where the two chief contenders are more evenly balanced in terms of electoral support than they were in 1983.

The distribution of seats in the legislature is a more complex issue. The system that prevailed between 1948 and 1978, was based on population and area: one seat per thousand square miles and one per 75,000 persons. The population component was incresed to 90,000 in 1976. The area provision aimed at giving weightage to rural areas and backward regions; it had the advantage of helping the minorities too because they were concentrated in the relatively sparsely populated Northern and Eastern Provinces. These latter provinces had eight of the twenty-five 'area' seats, the balance being divided among the other seven provinces. Thus over the period 1947-1960 26.3% of the 95 seats were allotted on an area basis, and 8.4% of the total number of seats went to these two provinces even before population was considered. With the increase in population this advantage diminished: by 1970 —when there were 151 seats — the 'area' seats were 16.6% of the total and the Northern and Eastern Provinces still had the same proportion, i.e., 8 out of 25 or 5.3% of all the seats. By 1977, with the Second Amendment to the 1972 constitution, the population quota was raised to 90,000. The percentage of seats reserved for these two provinces had declined to 4.8%. Thus the old system gave the Tamils of the North and East a significant if gradually declining weightage on an area basis. These two provinces had 13% of the population, and 32% of the seats allocated on the area basis.

With the 1978 constitution there came a change in the system of allocating seats on an area basis: each of the nine provinces now received four seats. Thus the share of the two provinces, in terms of 'area' seats, fell from 32% to 22%, and in the new legislature they would start with only 4.1% of the seats before the voters lists are considered. Nevertheless because of a vital change in the basis of determining the voting strength of electoral districts, from "popu-lation" to "registered electors", the advantages hitherto enjoyed by the Sinhalese rural voter since the general election of 1952 are substantially reduced. No longer are the stateless Indian Tamils and those who have opted for Indian citizenship counted as part of the population for the demarcation of electoral districts. Under this system the Northern and Eastern Provinces with 13.2% of the registered voters would have a total of 35 seats out of 196 or 17.9%, as against the 26 seats they had at the 1977 general election, i.e., 26 out of 168 or

15.5%.

The advantages of proportional representation are likely to be much greater for the Tamils in the plantation districts and these around Colombo. For the first time since the parliament of 1947-52, the Indian Tamils elected a representative to Parliament in 1977; significantly it was in a three member constituency. Under the new system an Indian Tamil is almost certain to be elected to Parliament in the Nuwara Eliya district, and one is likely to win in Badulla as well. Besides all major parties are likely to place a Tamil high on their list for Colombo in the hope of attracting the Tamil vote there. The great advantage in proportional representation as far as the Tamils living in the Sinhalese majority areas are concerned is that it enables Tamils to secure representation in the Legislature without the acrimony inherent in a direct electoral competition with Sinhalese candidates.

There are other advantages stemming from the operation of the proportional representation in the Legislature. A repetition of the enormous majorities gained by the victorious parties at the general elections of 1970 and 1977, lopsided victories which deprived the Tamils of any prospect of acting as a balancing force in Parliament will almost certainly not be repeated under the new system. Proportional representation will eliminate distortions of this sort, and it is much more likely that the minorities would be in a strong bargaining position in the Legislature in the future. Besides it would take political skills of a very high order to organize a coalition within the Legislature which could command the two-thirds majority required to amend the constitution. Thus proportional representation is potentially a more effective safeguard against the amendment of the constitution without due regard being paid to the interests of the minorities. Given the country's multiparty political structure, ideology and ethnicity are likely to pose formidable, if not insurmountable, obstacles in any search for common ground in amending the constitution.

The new constitution, then, is a purposeful attempt to alleviate some of the grievances of the Tamil minority. A constitution, by itself, cannot assuage the discontent of the indigenous Tamils in regard to education, employment and economic development of the north and east of the island. Besides entrenched clauses in the constitution ensure the inviolability of the unitary nature of the Sri Lankan state (Article 2) while Buddhism is elevated to the "foremost" place among the island's religions (Article 9). Thus the new constitution, like its immediate predecessor, makes no concession to federalism, nor does it make provision for the decentralization of power. Sinhalese remains the sole official language, and no concession is made to the demand of the TULF for equality of all religions within the Sri Lankan polity. But as against this the pressure to elevate Buddhism to the status of the state religion, and to restrict the Presidency, by law, to a Sinhalese Buddhist made no headway at all. Besides, the criticisms raised by opposition groups against the new constitution did not, significantly enough, extend to attacks on the concessions made to the Tamil minority under it. The new constitution, in fact, is by far the most notable and resolute initiative in ethnic reconciliation taken in the recent political history of the island.

References

[1] On the general election of 1977 see Vijaya Samaraweera, 'Sri Lanka's 1977 General Election: the Resurgence of the UNP'. *Asian Survey*, December 1977, XVII (12) pp. 1195-1206. Jane Russell'Sri Lanka's Election Turning Point' in *The Journal of Commonwealth and Comparative Studies.* XVI(1) 1978. pp. 79-97.

[2] On the riots of this period see, *S.P.* VII of 1980, *Report of the Presidential Commission on the Inquiry into incidents which took place between 12 August and 15 September 1977.*

[3] Jane Russell, "The Dance of the Turkey-Cock — The Jaffna Boycott of 1931.' *CJHSS* n.s. VIII(1) pp. 47-67.

[4] The constitution of 1978 is reviewed in R. Coomaraswamy, *Sri Lanka: The Crisis of the Anglo-American Constitutional Traditions in a Developing Society* (New Delhi, 1984), A.J. Wilson, *The Gaullist System in Asia — the Sri Lanka Constitution of 1978* (London, 1980). See also C.R. de Silva, 'The Constitution of the Second Republic of Sri Lanka (1978) and its Significance', *The Journal of Commonwealth and Comparative Politics*, XVII (2) 1979, pp. 192-209. See also *CJHSS* n.s. VII(2), a special issue on 'The Constitution of 1978.'

[5] Cited in N. Tiruchelvam, 'The Making and Unmaking of Constitutions — Some Reflections on the Process', in *CJHSS* n.s. VII(2), p. 19.

[6] Mark Fernando, 'Fundamental Rights and the Constitution' in *CJHSS* VII(2), p. 53.

[7] *Ibid*, p. 59.

[8] N. Satyendra, 'Language in the New Constitution', *The Ceylon Daily News*, 4 October 1978.

[9] *S.P. V* of 1980, *Report of Presidential Commission on Development Councils*, pp. 86-7.

[10] Article 21(1) of the Constitution.

[11] Sections iv to xii in this extract are a summary of Articles 22 to 24 of the Constitution.

[12] See, for example, S. Nadesan, 'Ceylon's Language Problem' in *The Ceylon Daily News*, 12, 13, 14 and 15 October 1955.

[13] Carol L. Schmid, *Conflict and Consensus in Switzerland* (University of California Press, Berkeley, 1981) p. 21.

[14] Cynthia H. Enloe, *Ethnic Conflict and Political Development* (Boston, 1973) p. 97. On the homogeneous nature of Switzerland's territorial units and sub-units see also, Kenneth D. McRae, *Switzerland: Example of Cultural Coexistence* (Toronto, 1964).

[15] Carol L. Schmid, *Conflict and Consensus in Switzerland*, p. 21.

[16] These rights are consolidated and incorporated through Articles 21(2) and 21(2) of the 1978 Constitution.

Chapter XIX

Policies of Reconciliation, 1977-1983

Introduction

The new constitution was expected to mark the beginnings of a breakthrough to a new phase in ethnic harmony in the island. It did not do so. Despite a conciliatory policy adopted by the government towards the Tamil minority, the TULF — unlike the leadership of the Indian Tamils — held back from responding on a similar note. This was principally because they were unwilling or unable to abjure the separatist program on which they had campaigned during the general election of 1977. In addition the wounds caused by the communal riots of August 1977 took long to heal, and besides the political activities of tightly organized groups of youthful Tamil agitators — and their terrorist tactics — kept these wounds from healing. Coupled with a propaganda campaign in some western countries directed by groups of expatriate Tamils, their defiant rejection of a policy of reconciliation kept ethnic relations, brittle at best since the riots of August 1977, strained and tense. Together — and this is the third point — they provided Sinhalese extremists within and outside the government with invaluable material for their own propaganda campaigns and weakened considerably the resolve of moderates and liberals in the ranks of the Sinhalese to back conciliatory initiatives of the government with enthusiasm when they backed these at all. We shall deal with this in detail in Chapter XX of this book.

University Admissions Policy[1]

The first of these conciliatory gestures concerned a reversal of the UF government's university admissions policy. As we have seen this was announced on 4 August 1977 just after the new government took office. Given all that had happened on this issue between 1970-77, it was a bold political decision even for a government that had inflicted a stunning defeat on its opponents and now commanded an overwhelming majority in parliament.

To announce the abolition of standardization was one thing: to evolve a new and viable university admissions policy — viable both politically and academically — was another. Before it could set about this complicated business, a time-consuming one at the best of times, the government had to cope with the communal riots that erupted unexpectedly in August 1977. At the time admissions to the universities for 1977 were processed the country had hardly recovered from the communal riots and it was necessary therefore, to step warily through the minefields of "university admissions". The following quotation from Prof. C.R. de Silva neatly summarizes the main features of the problem that confronted the government.

> "When the marks were processed it became clear that if district quotas and standardization were not applied, the Tamils would considerably outnumber the Sinhalese in the much sought after faculties of Medicine and Engineering. Some inkling of this situation reached the members of Sinhalese nationalist groups. Assertions were made by them that Tamil examiners had inflated marks. A one-day strike by all Sinhalese secondary school children in protest against government policy was planned [in February 1978] and indeed, this was only averted by the closure of all government schools for the day and by taking into custody several of the alleged organizers.[2]

Among the latter were a few of the leading lights of the Sinhala Tharuna Sanvidhanaya who, in a previous year, helped organize opposition to the UF government's decision to move away from the rigid district quota scheme that had prevailed from 1975.

While the government stood firm on its decision to abandon standardization some significant concessions were made in other areas: in a move that could be described only as one of those rare, successful attempts to pursue two diametrically opposed policies at the same time without damaging its own interests, the government decided that although standardization was being abandoned, all students who would have gained admission to the universities had there been standardization should be admitted. Secondly, special consideration was to be given to students from districts which were under-privileged in terms of educational facilities. The 3700 students originally admitted on the basis of raw marks were now joined by nearly 900 others, many of them Sinhalese. Subsequently, more than 250 students were admitted on a 'district' basis.

This remarkable exercise in pragmatism brought advantages to everyone. As we have seen the government refused to give way on the issue of standardization, and so the Tamil political leadership tacitly accepted the compromise that had emerged. They had good reason for satisfaction, for the number of Tamil entrants to the medical and engineering faculties rose by over *250 percent* compared to the previous year. Indeed on the basis of the change, the proportion of Tamil students entering science-based courses equalled or exceeded the 35%-40% they had obtained under the system of open competition in 1969-70 and 1970-71.[3] Third, those who had been agitating for an increase in the total intake to the universities had reason to be satisfied: admissions were up by 25%. Fourth, there was also an increase in the number of Sinhalese entering the universities, especially from the rural areas.

The changes, however, were not regarded as permanent or even long term: by mid-1978 the whole question of university admissions became once more a matter of acute political controversy because many Sinhalese supporters of standardization , distinctly unhappy with the 1978 compromise scheme, were intent on upsetting it. Their contention was that the Sri Lankan Tamil minority of 11% could consistently obtain such good results — 35%-40% of medical and engineering entrants to universities — only by unfair means. They proceeded to back up their charges with allegations that examiners in the Tamil medium had been partial in their grading of examination scripts at the national examination through which entrance to the universities was determined, and in particular the examination held at the end of 1977.

In persisting with these criticisms the proponents of standardization were bent on doing much more than embarassing the government. They were intent on persuading the government to reconsider the change in policy recently adopted, and they soon had a champion of their cause within the Cabinet itself — the then Minister for Industries and Scientific Affairs, Cyril Mathew, beginning his controversial role as the outspoken champion of Sinhalese-Buddhist interests, and the most vociferous critic of the TULF. At an emotion-charged parliamentary session he proceeded to produce some answer scripts extracted from those submitted at the 1977 General Certificate of Education (Advanced Level) examination and charged that these provided evidence of Tamil examiners deliberately and consistently giving Tamil students higher marks than they were entitled to. In making these accusations Mathew touched a raw nerve; the evidence he produced was inadequate to substantiate his charge of widespread partiality in grading of answer scripts but enough to confirm the suspicions of those who were inclined to entertain doubts about the impartiality of Tamil examiners.

Shortly afterwards the Minister was associated at a press conference on the theme of university admissions, with the Vice-Chancellor of the University of Sri Lanka. (This was at the tail-end of a short-lived experiment begun under the UF regime under which all universities in the island were converted to units of a monolithic university with its headquarters in Colombo, and with a single Vice-Chancellor for this university). It was part of a publicity drive on behalf of a new and allegedly fool-proof mechanism for university admissions: ethnic quotas based on population ratios. To hear the advocates of this scheme one would think it was a simple painless solution for a complex problem: on the face of it, there were advantages in it for all groups with one exception. The exception, needless to say, were the Sri Lankan Tamils. There was no official support for this policy from the government as a whole, but it is significant that many Sinhalese Buddhist activists have urged its adoption, and it has been taken up enthusiastically by the Moor/Malay group who would benefit most if such quots are introduced. They, in fact, are its most consistent and persistent advocates.

When the Vice-Chancellor of the University of Sri Lanka, and a battery of highly placed officials — Sinhalese, all — associated themselves with Minister Mathew's charges, confidence in this examination was seriously undermined. Then, again, the same issues were raised before the Sansoni Commission appointed to investigate the communal disturbances of 1977. The two groups involved in this prolonged and acrimonious discussion before the Commission had different motives. The Tamils were clearly on the defensive; the Sinhalese who raised the issues hoped thereby to embarass both the Tamils and the new government, the latter for initiating the abandonment of standardization, the former for alleged manipulation of examination procedure to the benefit of students in the Tamil medium.

A new institutional framework for higher education adopted in 1979/80 helped to stabilize the formula adopted in 1978, that combination of a new national merit quota, regional merit quotas, and a special allocation for educationally backward districts, all based on aggregates of marks, referred to in technical language as 'raw' marks. The establishment of a University Grants Commission (UGC) and Ministry of Higher Education, and above all the placing of these directly under the President of the republic, helped guarantee this stability, and protected university admissions policy from a repetition of the series of *ad hoc* changes that had been among its principal — and most pernicious — features under the UF government.

The Commission had a membership of five till 1985 when it was increased to seven. It consisted in its first phase of 3 Sinhalese, one Tamil and one Muslim. The establishment of this Commission did lead to relative stability in the system of admissions; changes were much less frequent than they had been in the early 1970s. More important, there was relative stability also in the ethnic proportions in university admissions; the Tamil share has been consistently higher than the proportion of Sri Lanka Tamils in the population and much higher in regard to the science-based disciplines, especially medicine and engineering. They have never been lower than 35% in these disciplines since 1978. The smaller minorities had yet to gain their 'ethnic quotas' in university admissions, but there was a distinct improvement in the position of the Moor/Malay group.

It was evident that the formula adopted in 1978 needed to be kept in constant review. Once more a committee was appointed for that purpose. Among the problems that attracted attention was the special allocation of 15% of places to the so-called educationally disadvantaged districts. Twelve of these districs constituted half of the island's twenty-four administrative districts.[4] The number was subsequently raised to thirteen during 1980. The minimum mark for admission in some of these districts was lower than that for Colombo and Jaffna where the competition was keenest, by as much as 100 out of a total 400. In a situation where a single mark could make the crucial difference between admission to medicine and engineering on the one hand, rather than agriculture or science, this differential was seen to be grossly unfair. There were other disadvantages as well, especially the growing clamour from politicians in other rural districts to partake of the largesse distributed to the fortunate thirteen districts, an agitation based on the argument that by any standard of assessment their districts were only slightly better off in terms of schools, equipment, and teachers than the thirteen that benefitted from the existing quota system for disadvantaged areas.

In late 1981 a new formula was announced for 1982-83. The merit quota was to be increased to 40%; the district merit quota to 60% and the 15% special allocation eliminated. The abolition of the 15% allocation was received with a sigh of relief by those convinced that the pendulum had swung too far toward the so-called underprivileged districts. Representatives from the latter group put up a spirited defense of a special vested interest and succeeded in preventing implementation of the new scheme. 1982-83 were election years, and the government preferred to let the existing system continue rather than persist with a change which had brought together an amazing coalition of forces —Sinhalese from rural areas, Tamils from the districts of Mannar, Mullaitivu, Vavuniya, Batticoloa, Trincomalee and Amparai; and Muslims as a whole — together in defense of the 15% allocation. In 1984 another official committee was appointed to review the whole question, and one outcome of its deliberations was a recommendation for a reduction in the number of underprivileged districts to five; and the percentage of places available to them to 5 rather than the previous 15. No change was made in the merit quota of 30%, but the district quota went up to 65%. This time the resistance to change was not as effective in yielding results as it did in 1982. The new formula would be operative from 1985-86.[5]

Despite the gains that accrued to the Sri Lank Tamils by way of a higher percentage of places in the science-based faculties after 1977 there is naught for their comfort. They cannot hope, by the very nature of things in such a sensitive area of ethnic competition, to retain their present advantageous position for long. Their percentage of places can only go down and not up, and this has nothing or little to do with any policy of discrimination. For as education facilities improve in the Sinhalese areas of the country, and this process is an inevitable one even if somewhat slow and uneven, the advantages the Tamils have had will diminish rapidly in the face of the fierce competition they will face. Nor are the Sinhalese the only rivals of the indigenous Tamils. Within the Tamil-medium itself they will face increasing pressure from the Moor/Malay group — who at present have less than 5% of the places in the universities although they form 7% of the population; and secondly over the next decade they will also be challenged for places by the Indian Tamils who could, quite conceivably, be also the beneficiaries of a Sri Lankan version of affirmative action. Besides, among the indigenous Tamils themselves, those in the Jaffna peninsula and Colombo will face the competitive zeal of their fellow Tamils in the presently educationally backward areas such as Mannar, Mullaitivu and Vavuniya in the Northern Province, and Batticaloa and Trincomalee in the Eastern Province. Nor is there any guarantee that either the present formula for admissions or the examination procedure will remain unchanged. Changes are likely in both even if there is no return to standardization. Admission on a district basis, introduced originally as an avowedly temporary device, has survived into the 1980s. Indeed, in Sri Lanka seemingly temporary devices often enjoy a longevity denied to measures and institutions designed to last long. The anguish the Tamils feel on this issue stems mainly from a sense of relative deprivation, the feeling — indeed, the knowledge — that the halcyon days of the late 1960s when Tamils dominated the science-based faculties of the universities are not likely to return and that the present gains are temporary ones. Even if standardization and the district quota system had not been adopted from the early 1970s a reduction in the percentage of places gained by the Tamils in the science-based faculties would have come, gradually at first, but with much greater speed by the end of the decade and in the 1980s as the Sinhalese areas caught up with the Jaffna peninsula in terms of well-equipped schools and eventually overtook it. By stepping in to force the pace of this inevitable development and doing so in an obviously discriminatory manner the UF government of the 1970s caused enormous harm to ethnic relations and converted the university admissions issue from a controversial educational problem to a complex and emotion-charged political issue, the consequences of which confront the country even today.

Education

In the field of general education the government initiated a move, in mid-1979, to redress a grievance of the Christians, especially the

Roman Catholics, which went back to the days of the nationalization of schools in 1960-61 and the administrative mechanisms for this.[6] Some schools — largely Roman Catholic — remained outside the system but were not permitted to levy fees. It was now decided to grant financial assistance to all non-fee-levying private schools, and to a lesser extent to fee-levying private schools as well. The major beneficiaries of this move were the Roman Catholics, but Protestant groups, and the Muslims and Hindus benefitted as well. Such assistance — though on a somewhat more modest scale — had been promised to the Roman Catholics in 1966-67 but after some hesitation and much vascillation the then government had not honoured the pledge for fear of political consequences in the shape of opposition from Buddhist activists. J.R. Jayewardene, as the second-in-command in Dudley Senanayake's coalition government of 1965-70, had been primarily responsible for negotiating a settlement of this issue with the Roman Catholic heirarchy at that time. Now as executive President of the Republic, he redeemed the pledge and helped thereby to remove a long-standing grievance. The Roman Catholic Archbishop of Colombo, the Most Revd. Nicholas Marcus Fernando, described this move as "a long-awaited relief from a heavy and unjust burden [the Roman Catholics] had to shoulder for the past eighteen years."[7]

This bold initiative aroused surprisingly little opposition. The apparent equanimity with which Buddhist activists accepted this decision is as remarkable as their continued opposition to modifications introduced in university admissions policy in 1977-78. It is evidence of changed priorities in their demands and their perception of potential harm to the interests of Buddhists and Sinhalese. The Roman Catholics, it would appear, have ceased to be regarded as a threat to Buddhist interests; this was rendered all the easier by the Roman Catholics' acceptance of the political reality of a Buddhist dominance in Sri Lanka. As for the Tamils, on the other hand, the separatist policies advocated by the TULF, and the expatriate Tamil pressure groups in Western countries, in combination with the activities of terrorist groups in Jaffna seemed to underline a persistent threat to the territorial integrity of the Sri Lanka polity, and to the interests of the Sinhalese as an ethnic group.

Decentralization — District Development Councils, 1979-1985

The centerpiece of the government's policy of reconciliation were the District Development Councils to which it had committed itself in its manifesto for the elections of July 1977. That document, as we have seen in Chapter XVIII, made reference to the need to decentralize administration down to the village level, to "make the people partners in the planning, organization and implementation of policy." There was reference also to the administrative machinery to be established for that purpose. At the apex were to be District Development Councils headed by a District Minister, and consisting of MPs of the district, elected heads of local bodies, and government officials. In its statement of policy in the National State Assembly on 4 August 1977 the pledge was renewed. But the outbreak of communal violence in August 1977 proved to be a setback to the implementation of this program. While the riots brought the problem of relations between the two main ethnic groups in the island to the attention of the politicians, they also delayed the initiatives planned by the government on the basis of its election manifesto and its statement of policy on 4 August 1977.

It was only in the middle of 1979 and against the background of an imminent eruption of ethnic hostilities that the government turned its attention to the problem of decentralization of administration which the Tamil leadership had for long regarded as an essential feature in any political settlement.[8] On 10 August 1979 a 10-member Presidential Commission was appointed to report on the decentralization of administration through the device of District Development Councils. A TULF representative was appointed to serve on the Commission.

The appointment of this Commission was a reaffirmation of the government's commitment to a policy of decentralization of administration or, more accurately, to depart from the policy of concentrating administrative and political authorities in Colombo which had been a feature of government policy since independence, itself a continuation of a trend which began in the earlier phases of British rule. With the appointment of this Commission the TULF's separatist agitation was, if not called off, at least put into cold-storage. There was at one stage the hope that the composition of the Commission would be on an all-party basis, and given the renewed United Left Front's return to the traditional support its component parties had given to minority rights and provincial autonomy, and the JVP's advocacy of much the same line of policy, there were great potential advantages from such a composition. But this was soon abandoned in favor of a more limited exercise of a Commission in which all the parties represented in Parliament would have a nominee or nominees. This too was later narrowed down to a Presidential Commission of 10 persons of whom two were directly representative of party interests, the UNP and the TULF. The SLFP declined to nominate a member to serve on the Commission. In terms of its ethnic composition there were apart from the Chairman who was a Kandyan Sinhalese, three Sinhalese, three Muslims and three Tamils.

Perhaps the most notable feature of this Commission's work was the limited nature of its assignment. Its terms of reference limited it to filling in the details of a policy that had already been laid down, and which stemmed from the UNP's election platform of 1977. It was expected that this Commission would complete its work within three months of its appointment and considering its terms of reference this was not as unrealistic as it may sound. But it was mid-February 1980 by the time its report was ready.

The core of its recommendations were contained in the seventh chapter, entitled 'District Ministers and Development Councils'.[9] "The District Minister and Development Councils," the report stated

"are the pivots of the scheme of decentralization of administration we have recommended..." "The scheme has two objectives. First, the decentralization of the administration by placing an Executive Minister in each District, who is charged with the development of the District, and the co-ordination of Central Government activity there. Secondly, the scheme has the objective of enabling the participation of the local people in the planning and implementation of the development projects in each District through Development Councils."

"... In our view," the Commission's report added

"a Development Council composed as it would normally be by persons holding a variety of political opinions and drawn from a diversity of social groups within a district will be the collective voice of the District, and ensure that due heed is paid to the needs and aspirations of the local people in the planning and implementation of development projects. The District Minister system will be strengthened by this institution of a Development Council for it makes it possible to ensure popular participation in the development of each District."

By the time the Commission's report was presented to President Jayewardene there had indeed been a noticeable improvement in relations between the government and the TULF. There was evidence too of distinct improvement in the law and order situation in the Jaffna peninsula and certainly political violence was less apparent than it had been for several years. Thus the measures taken in July-August 1979 appear to have succeeded in creating a more promising atmosphere for political initiatives designed to restore communal harmony in the island. The most notable of these was the *Development Councils Act* which parliament approved on 21 August 1980.

In a remarkable reversal of the normal practice this Act went beyond the recommendations of the Commission upon whose report it was ostensibly based. Partly this is explained by the brevity — to the point of being skeletal — of the Commission's recommendations in regard to some of the crucial features of these Councils and the relationship of the Council to the District Minister; the Commission's terms of reference were as we have seen, narrower than usual, and in themselves limited it to filling out the details of a scheme whose outlines had already been decided upon. There was also the urgency attached to the preparation of its report in view of the brittle nature of ethnic peace in the island at the time it was appointed. Thus, with every week's delay beyond the period of two months for which it was appointed the need for the government to prepare legislation in anticipation of this report became more compelling. The outlines of legislation were ready by the last quarter of 1979 and once the report was published all that was necessary was to use this draft legislation as the basis of the bill to be presented before parliament. The bill, in fact, gave flesh and blood to the skeletal recommendations of the Commission. If this procedure was unusual, the problem that confronted the government was too urgent and too complex to be dealt with at a slower pace. Indeed, even so there were complaints that too much time was taken over all this.

In retrospect it would appear that the swift passage of the bill through parliament, and the wide support it received within the UNP constituted a major political achievement. Twice before, once in 1957-58 and again in 1966-68, political initiatives for decentralization of administration had been abandoned in the face of extra-parliamentary agitation and internal bickering within the ranks of the ruling party. On this present occasion not only was the political will[10] to pursue with this bill to its eventual enactment altogether greater, the opposition was also altogether weaker and less organized. The SLFP opposed the bill but walked out of parliament before the vote on the bill was taken.

As for the left-wing opposition, in all its diversity, the commitment to decentralization of administration was much more thoroughgoing, so far as one can judge from public pronouncements, than anything proposed by the government.

Elections were held for seats in these councils in the 24 districts in the island on 4 June 1981. They were, as elections in Sri Lanka generally are, orderly and peaceful — except in Jaffna on this occasion where the violence initiated by a terrorist attack on the police was unprecedented in Sri Lanka's long electoral history. Fortunately, the violence was contained within the Jaffna peninsula and did not spread to other parts of the island. This violence which disrupted the polling in Jaffna, plus the SLFP's boycott of the elections and the very low poll reflecting voter apathy, all contributed to making an inauspicious start for these councils.

Nevertheless, in the initial stages the councils did very well in the areas that mattered: in Jaffna and the other Tamil regions. They appeared to have blunted the edges of the separatist agitation, and indeed, helped to give the restive Jaffna peninsula a brief period of peace. The council at Trincomalee, one of the critical areas in the inter-action between the island's main ethnic groups, was a pronounced success. In other parts of the country there was a noticeable lack of enthusiasm for the councils, but the abler chairmen and executive committees did convert these bodies into effective instruments of local level development. From the outset, however, there were complaints about the inadequacy of the financial base of these councils for the work they were intended to do. The other main complaint was that even where the money was available the councils lacked the power to embark on any important development projects on their own initiative. Needless to say most of the criticisms came from the TULF especially from Jaffna and the Northern Province where expectations about these councils were greatest and where, naturally, the sense of disappointment was also very great when the aspirations of those who agitated for them seemed far away from speedy fulfilment.

These were teething troubles of a new institutional framework, not unmistakeable evidence that the councils were doomed to failure *ab initio*. While the TULF critics of the system had some support from others in the rest of the system — i.e., in the Sinhalese areas — in regard to inadequacy of funds for these councils, there was none at all in regard to pressure for expansion of the powers of the councils. Nevertheless, in the early part of 1983 a committee of senior officials was appointed by President Jayewardene to examine the working of this system and to determine what measures should be taken to make the councils more effective.

The committee identified three

> "constraints that inhibited the proper implementation of the Development Councils scheme..."

namely the delegation of powers to the districts; inadequacies in the budgetary process and the development fund, and in the district administrative service.[11]

It had taken over a year for the delegation of powers, duties and functions to District Ministers by Cabinet Ministers. That delegation was formally made in late September 1982, but as late as May 1983 it was still ineffective at a practical level because district officials of line Ministers and departments had

> "not yet been informed as to the manner in which they should carry out their duties in respect of the delegated functions."

These delays were compounded by legal and constitutional difficulties. Thus, although the District Ministers had

> "in turn delegated the functions which had been delegated to them by the Ministers, to the Executive Committee of the Development Councils ... the Attorney-General [had] questioned the legality of this further delegation ..."[12]

Besides, the funds appurtenant to the functions delegated to the District Ministers had not been passed down to the district. Also, the Development Fund of the districts had not been provided with the monies envisaged under section 19 of the Act. As for the district administrative service, no schemes of recruitment of qualified personnel for the district service were yet ready.

Many of these delays were inherent in the introduction of a new institutional framework and its administrative structures, as well as fresh evidence of the traditional reluctance of Sri Lankan Cabinet Ministers to countenance any reduction of their powers. The fact that 1982 became, quite unexpectedly, an election year when the Presidential election due in 1983 was advanced by six months or so also aggravated the problem: political and administrative energies were concentrated on the presidential election, to the neglect of other issues. Thus, the delegation of power to District Ministers by Cabinet Ministers was made on 23 September 1982[13] only a month before the Presidential election, and the second phase, the delegation, in turn, of these powers by the District Ministers to Executive Committees of

Development Councils took place only on 27 December 1982[14], two months after the Presidential election. Besides, general budget cuts and other financial restraints imposed by the Treasury in 1982-83 to keep inflation in check also adversely affected the financial position of the new Councils. Nevertheless the problems identified by the Committees were not insuperable ones, and remedies for these, also identified by it, presented few difficulties in adoption and implementation.

Positive Responses: The Muslims and the Indian Tamils

The Muslims' response to the political pressures of the 1970s and early 1980s has been dealt with in Chapter XV. Suffice it to say here that memories of the Sinhalese-Muslim rivalries and tensions of the 1970s have faded away, and while trade rivalries still persisted these seldom if ever erupted to the surface in the form of violent reactions. As a community with a penchant for trade and commerce, the Muslims have found the economic policies of the post-1977 era much more congenial than the restrictive and stagnant economy of the early 1970s.

Their political demands and pressures have been very limited: they are among the most persistent advocates of a policy of ethnic quotas in university admissions[15] and public employment. They were joined in this by influential Sinhalese groups, but neither singly nor together have they been able to persuade the government to adopt such quotas in these two areas. The constitutional and practical difficulties have been too great to be easily overcome. Above all, this agitation for ethnic quotas brought to the surface once more the long-standing rivalry between the Muslims and the Tamils. That rivalry was seen in its sharpest form in the strong opposition of the Muslims to all forms of devolution of power.

A glimpse of the complications arising from their opposition to any departure from the prevailing unitary structure of the country is provided in the dissent referred to in Chapter XVIII, written by two Muslim members of the Presidential Commission on Development Councils of 1980.[16] The burden of their argument was that the concessions made to the Tamils in the 1978 constitution were generous enough on their own, and adequate to meet all reasonable demands of the Tamils. The dissent does not merely confine itself to expressions of concern at the potentially harmful consequences of such Development Councils for the Muslims. The contention of the authors of this dissent was that any further concessions to the Tamils beyond those provided in the new Constitution, such as the Development Councils recommended by the Commission, would inevitably "have an impact on the unitary state of the country" and would thus require a constitutional amendment as well as "the approval of the people at a Referendum under Article 83" of the constitution.

That dissent was evidence, if new evidence was at all necessary, that solutions to the minority problems of Sri Lanka are always caught up in the jostling among the minorities themselves as they jockey for positions of advantage in the race for political and economic gains. If the Development Councils Bill was seen as primarily a response to Tamil pressures, the balance was adjusted, in the first week of December 1980, by the creation of a Department of Muslim Religious and Cultural Affairs placed under the senior Muslim member of the Cabinet, as good an example of a political establishment engaged in callibrating the machinery of democracy to secure a tolerable balance of interests, as we are ever likely to find in any plural society.

The political pragmatism of the Muslims was matched by that of the Indian Tamils of Sri Lanka. About the latter there had been no direct mention in the UNP manifesto of 1977. The ties between the UNP and the Ceylon Workers Congress had been strengthened ever since J.R. Jayewardene took over the leadership of the party in 1974, and these had been reinforced by participation in a common struggle against the UF and the SLFP core of that coalition in the years 1975-77. The links were augmented by the electoral support given by the Indians to the UNP at the general election of 1977. They survived the attacks on the Indians by Sinhalese mobs during the ethnic disturbances of 1977.

The CWC leader joined the Parliamentary Select Committee on the constitution, and used his influence there to extract two major concessions. One of these, the extension of all eight Fundamental Rights enumerated in Article 14(1) to the stateless Indian Tamils resident in the island, has been mentioned in the previous chapter. The second was the elimination of one of the long-standing grievances of the Indians in the island, the distinction between citizens by descent, and citizens by registration. Article 26 of the Constitution abolished this distinction, and thus, removed the presumed stigma of second class citizenship attaching to the Indians who had obtained it through registration under the terms of the Indo-Sri Lanka agreements of 1964 and 1974. The third concession had come in December 1977 through an administrative decision rather than legislative amendment or constitutional provision. This was the removal of the bar placed 40 years earlier on plantation workers resident on estates from voting in local government elections. Together these conferred on Indian Tamils in Sri Lanka, in the main plantation workers, a distinct improvement in legal status, and underlined their equality with Sri Lankan citizens by descent. When the CWC leader S. Thondaman joined the Cabinet in September 1978 it completed the process of bringing the Indian Tamils within Sri Lanka's 'political nation' for the first time since the 1930s, and consolidated the improved status of the Indian community within the Sri Lankan polity since July 1977.

For the Indian Tamils, political life and life on the plantations are inextricably linked. In recognition of this, the new government made a deeply significant gesture of reconciliation in August 1977 when a representative of the Ceylon Workers Congress was appointed to the directorate of each of the two giant state corportions controlling the management of the nationalized plantations. These appointments had more than symbolic significance for the workers representatives now had a direct and influential voice in policy-making for the plantations. Their initiatives have contributed greatly to improving living conditions — especially housing — and welfare facilities on the plantations, while wages on plantations have improved substantially above what they were prior to mid-1977.[17] A long-standing demand for equalization of wages for women engaged in the same work as men on the plantations was conceded by the government in 1984. Above all the woefully inadequate "schools" in the plantations have been taken over and integrated into the national education system far more systematically than in the past, and much more is spent now by the state on education of children of the plantation workers[18] through the Ministry of Education and through the two State Plantation Corporations. (Indeed, it is estimated that over a tenth of the gross earnings of the plantations is now diverted to welfare facilities including education). By mid-1980 the last of the "registered" plantation schools were absorbed into the national educational network. These relics of the past, symbolic of the peripheral nature of 'education' and schools as a welfare measure in the plantations, have been swept away; with their disappearance there is now greater hope for the future, in the sense that education will have the same liberating effects as it has had on the poorer segments of other ethnic groups in the island. The CWC has raised the question of affirmative action for this educationally deprived ethnic group and, like the Muslims, have advocated ethnic quotas in higher education.

References

[1] This discussion of this theme here is based on my chapter 'University Admissions and Ethnic Tension in Sri Lanka, 1977-83' in R.B. Goldman and A.J. Wilson (eds) *From Independence to Statehood: Managing Ethnic Conflict in Five African and Asian States*, (London, 1984) pp. 97-110.

[2] C.R. de Silva, 'The Politics of University Admissions', *op. cit.*, p. 99.

[3] *Ibid*, pp. 100-101.

[4] These were: Anuradhapura, Badulla, Batticaloa, Hambantota, Moneragala, Mullaitivu, Nuwara Eliya, Polonnaruwa, Mannar, Vavuniya, Amparai and Trincomalee. Of these, Batticaloa, Mullaitivu, Mannar and Vavuniya were Tamil majority areas, while Trincomalee had a sizeable Tamil population. The Muslims are a significant group in Amparai, Batticaloa, Trincomalee and Mannar.

   The Puttalam district was added to this list in 1980. It was largely Sinhalese in ethnic composition, but has a substantial Muslim minority.

[5] *Report of the Committee Appointed to Review University Admissions Policy*, (UGC, Colombo, 1984). The five districts retained are Amparai, Mannar, Mullaitivu, Hambantota and Badulla.

[6] See *The Ceylon Daily News*, 30 June 1979; *The Catholic Messenger*, 1 July 1979.

[7] *The Ceylon Daily News*, 30 June 1979.

[8] See, N. Tiruchelvam, 'The Politics of Decentralization and Devolution: Competing Conceptions of District Development Councils in Sri Lanka', in R.B. Goldman and A.J. Wilson (eds) *From Independence to Statehood, op. cit.*, pp. 196-209.

[9] *S.P. V* of 1980, *Report of the Presidential Commission on Development Councils*, pp. 37-46.

[10] For discussion of this see Chapter XX.

[11] *Interim Report of the Committee on Implementation of the Scheme of Development Councils*, 24 June 1983.

[12] *Ibid.*

[13] See the *Government Gazette Extraordinary*, 211/16 of 23 September 1982.

[14] *Government Gazette Extraordinary*, 225/4 of 27 December 1982.

[15] See the letter of Dr. M.C.M. Kaleel, President of the All-Ceylon Muslim League — and a Vice President of the UNP — to the editor of *The Ceylon Daily News*, 2 February 1982, entitled 'University Admissions'.

16 *S.P. V* of 1980, pp. 83-102.

17 See S.W.R. de A. Samarasinghe, "The Indian Tamils of Sri Lanka: an immigrant community in search of an identity". Unpublished mimeographed paper, presented at the Asian Regional Workshop on Ethnic Minorities in Buddhist Polities; Bangkok, Thailand, 25-28 June 1985.

18 G.A. Gnanamuttu, *The Child in the Plantations*, (The Church of Ceylon, Diocesan Committee for Social Study and Action, Colombo, 1979.

Chapter XX

Separatism and
Political Violence:
Challenge and Response, 1977-1983

Introduction

The advocacy of separatism by the principal Tamil party in the country was something new in Sri Lanka's politics. Its emergence has been reviewed in Chapter XVII of this present work. Our main concern here is with the evolution of goverment's policy on separatism and on the terrorism that came to be associated with Tamil separatism.

Where an ethnic (or religious) minority is concentrated in a particular region of a country, and where in addition, it constitutes the overwhelming majority of the population in that region, which is the case with the Tamils of the Jaffna peninsula and district (and to a lesser extent in the other component districts of the Northern Province) geography and demography combine to provide an ideal breeding ground for a separatist movement. Ethic cohesion and a heightened sense of ethnic identity, important ingredients for the emergence of separatist sentiment had existed there since the mid-1950s; indeed some would add that these had been in existence since the 1940s in the period of the '50-50' campaign. But the extension of separatist sentiment into a separatist movement depends on other factors: for example, as in the case of the Sri Lanka Tamils, a perceived threat to ethnic identity from political, economic and cultural policies; per-ceived grievances of a political or economic nature or both; and a sense of relative deprivation at the loss of, or the imminent loss of, an advantageous or privileged position.

These factors operating in combination have helped generate Tamil separatism in Sri Lanka. The threat it poses to the Sri Lanka polity is all the greater because of the operation of another factor — once more a potent combination of geography and demography — the existence of a great reservoir of Tamil separatist sentiment and a powerful sense of Tamil ethnic identity just across the narrow and shallow seas that separate Jaffna from Tamilnadu on the Indian sub-continent. Once a separatist movement emerged among the Tamils of Sri Lanka it was fostered, nurtured and protected in Tamilnadu, as a surrogate for the Tamil state which the Tamils of Tamilnadu had been compelled — through a constitutional amendment as the first line of the Indian government's armory of attack — to abjure in their own country.

Separatist agitation, whether in Sri Lanka or in the Basque country in Spain, in Corsica, or nearer home, in the Indian Punjab, leads to radicalization of the political process in the affected region or regions. Inevitably too this radicalization spawns terrorist groups at the fringes of such movements, and as was the case in Sri Lanka from the beginning, at the core.

We have seen how separatism and politically motivated violence associated with it erupted to the surface in the mid-1970s. The UF government, which had earlier crushed the JVP insurrection, was now confronted with a political challenge of a more complex nature — how to respond, politically, to an open advocacy of separatism by the principal ethnic party of the Tamils, especially when there were doubts about the seriousness of the purpose behind the move. Was it a deadly threat to the integrity of the Sri Lanka polity, or was it as so many suspected at the beginning, another exercise in political rhetoric to consolidate the TULF's hold on the electorate? One political decision was taken early in 1976 — the decision to prosecute three prominent TULF politicians, two of whom were MPs, on charges of sedition for distributing pamphlets, on independence day, advocating the establishment of a separate Tamil state. For the TULF, this prosecution was a longed for opportunity, a much desired *cause celebre*. They used trial at bar to challenge the legality of the 1972 constitution. The court limited its scrutiny to the narrower issues of the case, and to the technicalities of the law and exonerated the accused. Both parties were dissatisfied with the verdict. The government declared its intention to appeal against it to a higher court; the TULF was chagrined that the wider issue was not adjudicated upon. But as we have seen in Chapter

XVII the appeal was not proceeded with because the government —
now very much a SLFP government — was soon engaged in
negotiations with the TULF for support for a further extension of the
life of the national legislature elected in 1970. The price demanded by
the TULF for this support was political concessions within the
framework of their six point program adumbrated in 1972. These
negotiations ended in failure, not however without an erosion of the
political credibility of both groups.

The UF government adopted a two-tier policy: the prosecution of
TULF politicians for the advocacy of separatism; the prosecution of
others for politically motivated acts of violence, on a case by case basis,
and under the emergency regulations imposed through the state of
emergency originally clamped down in April 1971. While the use of
these emergency regulations gave the prosecution great advantages in
making arrests, retaining suspects and gaining access to information,
they had their own serious shortcomings. These were seen when the
national legislature was prorogued on May 1977. The state of
emergency lapsed with that. The suspects were all released. No charges
had been filed against them in the courts. They now returned to their
previous pursuits, a combination of clandestine trade and political
violence.

The Search for a Policy on
Separatism and Terrorism — August 1977 to July 1983

With the outbreak of communal violence in mid-August 1977 the
new government confronted, very early in its tenure of office, the
political fall-out of policies pursued by its predecessor. The communal
riots of August 1977, the first of three major outbreaks of ethnic
violence during its period of rule, bore comparison with the last major
ethnic disturbance in Sri Lanka, the riots of 1958. Like the latter it was
a 'race' riot pure and simple and was seen by the government in that
light. As we have seen in Chapter XVIII the government brought the
situation under control very quickly. One important point in its
handling of this outbreak of communal violence needs specific
mention; it was done without resort to the proclamation of a state of
emergency. In August 1977 this policy reflected the new government's
doubts about the willingness of the police and the armed services —

and especially the rank and file in those services — to serve as an impartial law enforcement agency, given the fact that in the previous seven years (1970-77) recruitment had been on a political basis. The rank and file of the police force and the armed services, and to a lesser extent, the officer corps, had become overwhelmingly Sinhalese and Buddhist. And besides, memories of the abortive *coup d'etat* of 1966 were still fresh in the minds of the UNP leadership. To impose a state of emergency and to unfold the full range of emergency regulations available for use in such situations was to confer almost unlimited power on the police and armed services, and this the government was unwilling to do.

Over the next five years — till the first quarter of 1983 — the UNP government persisted with this policy of dealing with eruptions of ethnic violence under the normal laws of the country and without resort to emergency powers and the wide range of regulations available under the latter. Curfews would be imposed in trouble spots, but there would be no declaration of a state of emergency. This policy was seen to be very effective in keeping the peace, but it had its critics.

The criticisms came from two opposite ends of the ethnic spectrum. The Tamils, especially the TULF, believed that despite the justified fears of potential abuse of power by the security forces under emergency rule, the regulations which took effect when a state of emergency was enforced acted as a powerful deterrent on potential lawbreakers. These also afforded potential victims of mob violence greater protection than was possible under the normal laws of the country. On the other hand, there were Sinhalese critics of this policy who felt that once the threat of separatism appears as an objective fact of politics, the choice before the government was often the stark one, of a tolerance of cultural traditions associated with ethnic identity — indeed permitting the full expression of such cultural traditions — and the suppression of secessionist demands, by armed force where necessary, if there were signs that secessionist aspirations were striving for fulfillment. To do that one would need to resort to occasional periods of rule under a state of emergency.

The TULF's criticisms of this policy did not evoke much sympathy from the government, and none at all from representatives of Sinhalese-Buddhist opinion. The TULF had campaigned vigorously on a separatist program in July 1977, and had won convincing if not overwhelming victories in the constituencies of the Jaffna peninsula. In general the TULF's performance in other parts of the Northern

Province fell well below that of its record in the Jaffna peninsula, and in the Eastern Province it was overtaken by the UNP, but even so it could claim, with justice, that the Tamils of the north and east had endorsed their program. Having won on this separatist platform the TULF was now the main opposition party in the national legislature, and its leader was elevated to the position of Leader of the Opposition. There was no precedent in the history of the parliamentary democracies of the Commonwealth for the position of the Leader of the Opposition being held by the head of a party committed to a separatist program, and thus to the dismemberment of the polity. Naturally questions were raised about the TULF's links, both at the leadership level and the constituency level, with militant youth groups who had spearheaded the campaign for separatism and were now intent on holding the TULF to that program.[1]   When these militant groups continued their program of terrorist activities in the north of the island, the ambiguity of the TULF's position within the country's political system was emphasized with every violent incident.

Unlike the JVP insurrection political violence in Jaffna was not an open confrontation with the state. It consisted of sporadic and more often than not carefully orchestrated symbolic acts of violence against persons and state property. Like the JVP the various militant youth groups and factions, and their terrorist units were Marxists of the far left as far as the leadership was concerned, but unlike the JVP there was a wider range of non-Marxist elements represented at the leadership level, and much more so in the rank and file.

One — almost natural and predictable — effect of the ethnic disturbances of 1977 was to strengthen the extremist youth groups in the Jaffna peninsula — the Liberation Tigers of Thamil Eelam as they came to be called — by gaining wider support for them among the Tamil people, if indeed these events did not confer a greater degree of respectability on their separatist aspirations than in the past. They were thus able to indulge in a career of violence, murder and robbery with little risk of identification by witnesses; the violence and killings were directed quite calculatedly at Tamil police officers and actual or potential defectors from the ranks of the TULF parliamentary group, and also against suspected informants. From one spectacular incident to another they moved with conspicuous impunity demonstrating that they had public support (or at least were able to extract it by threats of reprisals) and, more to the point, that the police were quite unable to cope with this threat to law and order, and potential risk to the peace of the island. Moreover, if there was the slightest prospect of falling into the hands of the security forces they moved across the Palk Straits to Tamilnadu where they had sympathizers and supporters.

The government, for its part, faced an extraordinarily difficult situation. The normal legal machinery and police procedure were ineffective in meeting the challenge to the state posed by the Liberation Tigers and their activities. The ease with which this extremist group got away unscathed with daring daylight robberies and, physical violence, extending with increasing frequency to killings of carefully chosen victims including, on occasion, Sinhalese police officers stationed in the north of the island, was doubly provocative: first through an inevitable undermining of the morale of the police who were already chafing under the restraints imposed by established legal procedures in coping with these politically-motivated acts of violence and defiance of authority; and secondly the indignation felt in the Sinhalese areas that the government seemed powerless to act in the face of a deadly threat to its authority. Both could provoke a backlash, the police by retaliating with greater force than was prudent — their patience worn thin by the constant challenges to their authority — and among the Sinhalese through a recrudescence of ethnic violence directed against Tamils living in their midst. Thus whenever Sinhalese policemen were killed by terrorist activity in the north of the island and their bodies were brought to their homes in the Sinhalese areas the government was compelled to take extraordinary precautions to prevent communal outbreaks in those localities.

And so on 22 May 1978 Parliament approved 'a bill to proscribe the Liberation Tigers of Tamil Eelam and other similar organizations'. It was introduced because of the spate of crimes of politically motivated violence in the Northern Province and the breakdown of law and order there. The new law was intended to last for one year after which the situation was to be reviewed.

This new law did not yield the results anticipated by the government. On the contrary the politically-motivated violence and robberies persisted, culminating in the most spectacular incident up to that time, and one which conveyed an unmistakable message of political symbolism, that of 7 September 1978 when an Avro aircraft flying between Colombo and Jaffna, and belonging to Air Ceylon, the national airline was blown up on the runway at the Ratmalana airport in the suburbs of Colombo during the celebrations that followed the introduction of the new constitution. Fortunately, the aircraft was empty at the time, and was still on the tarmac. There were no casualities, but the explosive device had been timed to go off when the plane was airborne and flying over the city of Colombo.

The TULF for its part also confronted great difficulties in evolving a coherent and credible response to the problems created by the Liberation Tigers. They denied that there were any political links with this latter group, and also often issued statements repudiating the violence associated with them. Yet, so far as their Sinhalese critics were concerned, this denial did not carry conviction; the TULF leadership's association with these groups in the early and mid 1970s was well-known. Perceptive observers of the politics of Jaffna realized that the TULF was in no position to place too great a distance between itself and militant youth groups operating in Jaffna, because the links between them forged in the heat of the political struggles against the UF government could not be easily severed. And in fact they made no attempt to sever such links. As a result relations between the TULF and the government were noticeably strained.

In the early part of 1979 this estrangement was exacerbated by the activities of groups of Tamil expatriates in a number of Western countries intent on internationalizing Sri Lanka's ethnic conflict. Internationalization had begun with the Tamilnadu link, and through it, a wider Indian one, and has been dealt with in earlier chapters of this book; references will be made to it later in this chapter and in the next. Internationalization proper began in the early and mid-1970s in Britain, and spread later on to Western Europe and Scandinavia through the well orchestrated, and very effective, efforts of groups of Tamil expatriates protesting against the policies of the UF government, and indulging in a propaganda campaign intended to demonstrate that the Tamils were victims of a deliberately planned policy of discrimination. Quite often their aims were clearly self-serving; in many instances the objective was to obtain the right to convert their status as temporary residents to permanent resident status, or indeed to full citizenship rights on the basis that they qualified for this as "refugees" from a harsh regime. But there were more immediate and less personal objectives as well: to get the media to focus attention on the problems of Sri Lanka's Tamil minority, and to use the unfavorable publicity this generated against the Sri Lankan government, to put pressure on it, hopefully through political action and official diplomatic channels by the governments of the countries in which these Tamil expatriates most resided.[2]

If the UF government's policies provided the Tamil expatriates with the data for their propaganda campaigns, and gave their propaganda the element of authenticity it needed to win support from sympathetic sections of the media, the riots of August/September 1977 gave the campaign even greater credibility. The campaign spread across the continent of Europe, in the western democracies, but Britain continued to be the main center.

The change of government in 1977, and the reversal of the UF's policies which had been the focal points of the expatriate Tamils' campaign, the changes introduced through the new constitution of 1978 made not the slightest difference to the campaign. By now the expatriate Tamil groups were the most vocal advocates of a separatist state for the Tamils of Sri Lanka — the state of Eelam. And more sigificantly, the campaign spread to the more prosperous Tamil expatriate community in the United States, and Boston because one of the main centers of Eelamist propaganda there. The Boston group achieved their most notable success when the lower house of Massachusetts legislature was persuaded to adopt a series of resolutions

"...memorializing the President [of the U.S.A.] and the Congress to utilize the powers of their offices to rectify the gross injustices which have been inhumanly inflicted on the Tamils of Sri Lanka."

The date of passage of this resolution was 9 May 1979:[3] the Governor of Massachusetts declared 22 May 1979 "Eelam Tamils' Day" and handed over a copy of the resolution to M. Sivasithamparam, Amirthalingam's deputy, and President of the TULF in 1979. Sivasithamparam — G.G. Ponnambalam's erstwhile deputy — was at that time in the U.S. on a political mission in support for the cause of the Sri Lankan Tamils. Moreover, A. Amirthalingam as Leader of the Opposition, lent his support to such campaigns during his visits abroad, in breach of the convention of political neutrality of the Leader of Opposition whenever he went outside the country.

The activities of the advocates of separatism thus brought the country, by mid-1979, to the brink of another round of communal violence. As in August 1977 when it confronted the communal disturbances of that month, so now in mid-1979, the government adopted a blend of firmness and conciliation in dealing with a potentially dangerous situation. First of all the legal apparatus of the state was revamped and strengthened. There were two steps in this. The law proscribing the Liberation Tigers and similar organizations, originally intended to last just one year, was extended in May 1979 for another year. The second step was the more significant one, and more controversial too: on 19 July Parliament approved the second reading of the *Prevention of Terrorism (Temporary Provisions)* bill avowedly modelled on the British *Prevention of Terrorism Act* devised as a response to the situation in Northern Ireland and terrorism unleashed by the Irish Republican Army both in Northern Ireland and England itself. Opposition critics of the *Prevention of Terrorism (Temporary Provisions)* bill argued that many of the rigorous regulations generally imposed through the declaration of a state of emergency were now being incorporated as part of the legal framework of the country. Civil libertarians expressed concern about the potential dangers in this new legislation to the fundamental rights incorporated in the new constitution.[4] Government spokesmen responded to this latter criticism by arguing that in Sri Lanka as in other liberal democracies where separatism challenged the integrity of the state and where terrorism posed dangers to public security special legislation of this sort was a regrettable but inevitable part of the price the country was called upon to pay in resisting these threats and repelling them.

Simultaneously a state of emergency was declared in the north of the island, and a military commander appointed to co-ordinate security arrangements in Jaffna, and with instructions to stamp out terrorism there. Once more a state of emergency had become part of the armory of the state in dealing with politically inspired violence. But on this occasion its operation was restricted to one part of the island, and for a limited period of time. The state of emergency was to lapse on 31 December 1979, and it was not extended beyond that date. By this time the army had become an integral part of the peacekeeping force in the restive Jaffna peninsula and other parts of the Northern Province. The pressures mounted by terrorist groups were much too great for the small and scattered police force, the normal instruments for the maintenance of law and order, to deal with.

These vigorous measures served some at least of the purposes they were intended for — an impending crisis was averted in 1979. The measures of conciliation pursued simultaneously with them have been reviewed in Chapter XIX. All we need to do here is to provide a summary of those, beginning with the appointment of a 10 member Presidential Commission, in August 1979, to report on the establishment of district-level Development Councils as a means of decentralization in the country.

The appointment of this Commission marked the beginning of a period of improved relations between the government and the TULF. We have seen how the Commission completed its work in February 1980, and how Parliament approved legislation establishing these District Development Councils on 21 August of that year. The government and the TULF both demonstrated a willingness to take political risks on this issue, one on which two previous governments had to confess defeat. The TULF, for its part, took the bold decision to put its separatist objectives and program in cold storage as a *quid pro quo* for the establishment of these councils. The draft legislation had been scrutinized by the TULF and the powers of the Councils had been enlarged well beyond those recommended by the Commission, in response to criticisms and suggestions offered by the TULF. More important the government had withstood pressure from the Buddhist activists and influential representatives of the *sangha* to postpone implementation of the scheme; and just as important, it resisted pressure from a group of 15 MPs who made a last minute bid to have the draft bill amended before it was submitted for debate in Parliament.[6]

Reference has been made in the previous chapter to the elections held throughout the island for seats in these Councils on 4 June 1981. The election campaign was peaceful and orderly except in Jaffna,[7] where terrorist groups directing their attack on groups desirous of constructive change, first assassinated the leader of the UNP campaign in Jaffna, and killed others prominently associated in that campaign. Extremist groups were demonstrating their opposition to the concept of District Development Councils as part of the process of decentralizing administration; more important they were expressing their determination to prevent the UNP from establishing an electoral foothold in the Jaffna peninsula. To meet this mounting violence the police force was strengthened by a large contingent of policemen and police reservists. The stage was set for a tragic sequence of events. These reinforcements checked the violence temporarily, but became themselves the target of violence. On the eve of the elections a terrorist group shot and killed four policemen who were on election duty. This incident provoked just the response the terrorists had anticipated and desired: unfocused anger of the police in one of the worst incidents of police reprisals in the encounter between them and the young militants and terrorists in Jaffna. The violence was inflicted on property not persons, culminating in a mindless act of barbarism, the burning of the Jaffna Municipal Library. This violence and police reprisals compelled the postponement of the election in the Jaffna district. Fortunately the violence was contained within the Jaffna district, and did not spread, on this occasion to other parts of the country. 1981 had seen sporadic but localized outbursts of ethnic violence, and in one of the most serious of these outbreaks victims of mob violence included the Indian Tamils who had nothing at all to do with separatist agitation and violence. It was evidence of the brittle nature of the calm that seemed to settle on the country in the wake of the emerging detente between the government and the TULF.

The elections to the District Development Council in Jaffna, postponed because of the violence we have referred to earlier, were held shortly afterwards, and the result was an overwhelming victory for the TULF who won every seat on that Council, a difficult enough achievement under a system of single member constituencies, but remarkable for an election held under proportional representation. That victory helped consolidate the improvement in relations between them and the government which had begun somewhat tentatively in the last quarter of 1979.

One important feature of this period were the regular meetings between the government — cabinet ministers and officials — and the TULF MPs and their advisers held with President Jayewardene in the chair. At these informal meetings issues relating to the management of ethnic tensions were discussed, solutions suggested and proposals that emerged from the discussions were often implemented, and if not implemented on any regular basis, at least tested out for their impact. Certainly by the middle of 1982 it seemed as though the establishment of the District Development Councils had yielded the political results expected from them, namely to give the Jaffna peninsula a respite from turbulent political agitation. But it was not a durable peace, for terrorist violence continued to take its toll either in clashes between terrorist groups and the police and security forces, or in the fratricidal conflicts among the fragmented terrorist groups themselves. And there were also those other victims of terrorist violence — men and women suspected of being police "informers", as well as the so-called "social parasites" small time thieves and hoodlums who had been of use to the militants and terrorists, but were now an embarrassment and were dispatched as ruthlessly as the informers. For them as for the informers the usual punishment was a shot through the head, the body left near a lamp-post, or hanging from one, with a placard attached announcing to the world why this summary punishment had been meted out.[8]

There was little the police and the security forces could do to check these killings, and the robberies associated with the militants and terrorists. All they could see was that the newly established cordiality between the government and the TULF had done little to check these either. On the contrary it seemed to them that these cordial relations between the government and the TULF were a positive hindrance in the struggle against the Tamil militants and their terrorist groups. Worse still, the failure to stem the tide of terrorism was being attributed to a political factor, the influence of the TULF with the highest levels of government, rather than to the inadequacies in the police and security forces' intelligence gathering exercises.

Electoral Politics and
Their Impact on Ethnic Relations 1982-83

With a presidential election scheduled for late 1983, and parliamentary elections in mid-1984, there was naturally an intensification of political activity in 1982 as a prelude to these. But when the government took the country and the opposition parties by surprise by calling for a presidential election in October 1982, the assumptions on which the electoral system of the new constitution was based, namely that it would compel candidates to widen their appeal beyond the solid Sinhalese-Buddhist core of the electorate to the minorities, was put to the test. This chapter will not attempt an analysis of the national election campaigns of 1982-83, four in all, and the issues that dominated these in any great detail. Our interest is in those salient features relevant to the theme of the management of ethnic conflict in the country.

The framers of the constitution had reason for satisfaction with the zest with which the candidates of the national parties sought to bring the minorities within the scope of their electoral appeal. President Jayewardene addressed campaign meetings in the troubled north of the island, as did his main opponent, the SLFP candidate, H. Kobbekaduva. The latter, in fact, made a strong bid for Tamil votes in that part of the country, by pledging that he and his party would repeal the *Prevention of Terrorism (Temporary Provisions) Act* if returned to power; and promised a system of price supports — through restrictions on imports — for agricultural products of that region. During the campaign the TULF maintained a stance of neutrality as between President Jayewardene and his opponents.

By winning that election J.R. Jayewardene became the first Sri Lankan head of government to win two consecutive terms of office. It was also the first time since 1952 that a government in Sri Lanka had been returned to power at a general election. The winner secured a majority in all but one of the island's 24 districts — the exception was the Jaffna district where the SLFP did better than the UNP.[9]

Parliamentary elections were due any time up to the last quarter of 1983. Once more President Jayewardene surprised the opposition and the country, this time by calling a referendum in December 1982 to ask voters in Sri Lanka whether they wished to vote at the general election due in 1983 or whether, by a single direct vote, they would give his government another six year term of office. This move had both legal and constitutional validity, but was nevertheless quite controversial.[10]

The arguments advanced by the government to substitute a referendum for a parliamentary election were, first, that such an election could lead to serious outbreaks of violence, especially — and this was the second point — in the context of an immediate danger of "Naxalite"-type threats from disgruntled left-wingers of the defeated SLFP. The third reason had direct relevance to the theme of this chapter, that a strong hand was needed to deal with the Tamil separatist movement and its terrorist wing.

In regard to this third reason, the central issue was that while a simple parliamentary majority was adequate to impose a state of emergency in the event of a serious threat to security from an outbreak of ethnic violence, a two-thirds majority in Parliament was required to continue such a state of emergency beyond three months. Without a two-thirds majority the government would be at the mercy of the fractious parliamentary opposition in securing an extension of a state of emergency beyond three months.

Ironically enough it was the first two rather than the third that the government emphasized in making its case, in Parliament and in the country for the substitution of a referendum for a parliamentary election. In fact it was this third point that was to have greater cogency in justification of such a referendum, in the context of the ethnic violence that broke out in July 1983. Assuming that the government could have converted the majority secured at the Presidential election of October 1982 into a landslide victory at a parliamentary election, it would still have been very difficult to secure two-thirds of the seats in Parliament under a system of proportional representation.

As it was, the opposition was not merely taken by surprise but some parties within it, notably the SLFP, were seriously embarrassed by this call for a referendum to extend the life of the Parliament elected in July 1977. The SLFP was split on this issue, with one faction supporting the call for a referendum both within Parliament when the matter came up for debate there, and in the election campaign that followed. The embarrassment stemmed from events that had taken place in 1972 in regard to the introduction of the first republican constitution. The TULF opposed the referendum because it was being deprived of an opportunity to test public opinion in the north and east of the island for its policies and a fresh endorsement of the support it had won in 1977 in those regions.

Although the electorate supported the referendum by a large majority thus effectively guaranteeing the UNP its huge majority in parliament till 1989, the government fared badly in most parts of the north and the east where the TULF led the opposition to the referendum. Threats of violence prevented any serious campaign in favor of the referendum in the troubled north of the island. The vote against the referendum in the Jaffna district was a resounding 91% where, moreover, in striking contrast to most other parts of the island there was a substantially larger turn out of voters on this occasion than at the presidential election.

Immediately after the referendum the government perhaps sensing a mood of disenchantment at the postponement of parliamentary elections for six years — for that was the effect of the electorate's approval of the referendum — called for by-elections in 18 parliamentary constituencies in which it had fared badly at both the presidential election and the referendum. The TULF was chagrined that these by-elections were held only in the Sinhalese areas, while no by-elections were held in the north and the east in seats in which the government's performance at the presidential election and the referendum had been considerably worse than in other parts of the country.

These by-elections were held on 18 May 1983 and the UNP won 14 of them. This was accompanied by a notable success at the local government elections held on the same date and on 20 May. The UNP won all but five of these local bodies in the Sinhalese areas. Violence organized by terrorists groups marred the elections in the Jaffna peninsula. The TULF won these elections in a very low poll, but in other parts of the northern and eastern regions it won comfortably in a normal poll.

Once again UNP candidates in the Jaffna peninsula faced death threats — some of them were killed — and were generally intimidated into withdrawing from the fray. But even more significant was the humiliation in public of the TULF leadership, including the TULF leader, A. Amirthalingam by terrorist groups who compelled him on one occasion to abandon an election meeting he had organized and at which he presided.

A state of emergency was imposed in May 1983 to combat mounting tension. It had the support of the TULF.

Two consequences flowed from all this. First, the cordial relations between the government and the TULF broke down over these disagreements on electoral policies. Secondly, and more important, the terrorist threat in the north of the country was causing great concern both in the government and among the Sinhalese in general, and in both a dissatisfaction with current policies on dealing with the terrorists, the growing feeling that the regular bi-lateral discussions at a political level between the government and the TULF had done little to keep the terrorists in check.

The Riots of July 1983[11]

The period from around August 1982 to the end of May 1983 had been one of intense political activity: first, the Presidential election of October 1982, followed by the referendum of December 1982, and followed in turn by 18 by-elections in the Sinhalese areas of the country and local government elections in municipalities and urban councils all over the island. This prolonged period of political campaigning, and the unusual frequency of electoral contests kept political passions and rivalries inflamed and overheated throughout these months. Inevitably too communal tensions were aggravated by all this, especially because in the early months of 1983 terrorist violence eruped with greater frequency.

Yet, there were signs of conciliatory moves afoot. A committee of high-ranking officials had been appointed to make recommendations on strengthening and indeed revitalizing the District Development Councils. Above all moves were afoot to summon an All Party

Conference for the resolution of outstanding ethnic issues. this was explicitly intended to move beyond the stage of bilateral talks, between the government and the TULF which had been a feature of the years 1981 and 1982 but which had ended in an impasse, to a wider national forum. A round table conference for this purpose was announced for the end of July 1983. One of the principal groups invited, the TULF, was in one of their frequent moods of introspection, unable to decide whether to participate or not (or least put up a show of doubt to satisfy their own electorate) aggrieved at the lack of an opportunity to test their electoral popularity through parliamentary elections. They were scheduled to meet at their annual conference in the third week of July where policies for the immediate future were to be determined.

While the TULF's convention was in progress at Mannar, a terrorist ambush which killed 13 soldiers in Jaffna on 23 July, led, first to army reprisals there and subsequently to the worst outbreak of ethnic violence since 1958. These riots were quite widespread, although not as widespread as those of 1958. Unlike in the riots of 1958 the worst affected area was the city of Colombo and its suburbs. The riots were an urban rather than a rural phenomenon.

The symbolism of the terrorist attack was not missed. It was timed to coincide with the TULF convention, to upstage the latter, and to serve as a warning that a conciliatory response to the government's proposals would be quite misplaced in the current mood of youth opinion in the north; 23 July was also the sixth anniversary of the UNP's return to power in 1977. Thus in one decisive move, the terrorists had once again attacked the principal advocates of constructive change in the troubled ethnic scene of Sri Lanka.

Sinhalese mobs did not distinguish between Sri Lankan Tamils and Indian Tamils in their ferocious, vengeful and diffused outburst of indignation against terrorism in the north. In fact the victims of these assaults had shown no outward sympathy for the terrorists or indeed for the TULF. Tamils living in the Sinhalese areas had voted in large numbers for the government. Yet they faced the rage of the mobs. Colombo city was the scene of a wave of arson and destruction with the middle class residential areas facing the brunt of the mob's fury. Much of the violence reflected a ferocious mood of disapproval of the government's handling of the terrorist threat. There was a self-destructive aspect too, most evident in the senseless burning of factories and shops owned by Tamils but providing employment for large numbers of Sinhalese.

What marked off the riots of July 1983 from those of 1958 was the role of the security forces. The breakdown in law enforcement in the early days of the riots had no precedent in past; it took the government nearly a week to re-establish its authority and quell the violence. The security forces were either generally indifferent to or they ignored their peace-keeping role, repeatedly refusing to intervene when their intervention could have saved lives and property. The machinery of law and order had almost totally collapsed. There are two parallels for this in recent itmes, the Malaysian riots of May 1969,[12] and the Delhi riots of 1984 in the aftermath of the assassination of Prime Minister Indira Gandhi. A *New York Times* report on the attacks on the Sikhs in November 1984 would serve as an amazingly accurate account of what happened in Colombo and its suburbs in that dreadful week of July, 1983:

> "The first is the repeated failure of the police to intervene against acts of terror and killing. The second, based on mounting evidence from witnesses, is the apparent organization behind the attacking gangs, strangers who arrive in trucks and disappear when the deed is done."[13]

The "apparent organization" referred to in this extract were code words for the local units of the Indira Congress in Delhi and some important political figures in it. The situation in the Sri Lankan riots was much more complex. Despite the comments of some contemporary observers of these incidents suggesting a link between the mobs and influential government politicians no firm evidence has yet emerged to support that contention. The fact is that the mobs that roamed the streets of Colombo, and the other towns of Sri Lanka on that fateful week were composed of people professing a wide range of political views and included supporters of the UNP. Anyone who saw them at work would have sensed the operation of something like a mass of visceral antagonisms, a frightening force fed on a diet of rumors, tensions, fears and paranoia, and a fearsome rage directed against the Tamils — any Tamil for that matter — on the assumption that they were all communally responsible for the terrorist outbreaks in the north, and in fact for the incident that sparked off this vengeful fury.[14] The country's political structure was shaken to its foundation.

A state of emergency had been in force since the middle of May 1983. Now in the aftermath of the riots curfews were imposed under the emergency regulations. For a few days the curfews were ignored both by the mobs and the security forces. It took a few days before the security forces began the business of restoring order, tardily and hesitantly at first, but within a week with professional competence; soon curfews and emergency regulations became vigorous instruments of peacekeeping. But not before the government had made an important concession to Sinhalese opinion, an admission on state television by the President of the republic, that the policy of conciliating the TULF and separatist forces was a mistaken one, and a promise was made of firm and effective steps to curb separatism.

Thus one important change of policy flowed from the riots of July 1983. In August 1983 Parliament approved the sixth amendment to the constitution, imposing a ban on political parties that advocated separatist policies and penalties too on individuals that advocated separatism. Twenty years earlier India had introduced a similar ban through the 16th amendment to the Indian constitution. An important and inevitable consequence of this was that all TULF MPs forfeited their right to sit in the national legislature unless they took an oath abjuring the advocacy of separatism. None of them have chosen to take such an oath.

References

[1] The close links that developed between the TULF leadership, especially the present TULF leadership, and militant youth groups emerge very clearly through the evidence given before, and gathered by the Sansoni Commission, S.P. VII of 1980, and in the report itself.

[2] Among the groups that began to take an interest in the problems of Sri Lanka's Tamil minority from the early and mid-1970s were, the London-based Minority Rights Group, Amnesty International and the Geneva-based International Commission of Jurists.

[3] The complete text of the resolution was published in *The Ceylon Daily News*, 30 May 1979.

[4] For this viewpoint see Virginia Leary, *Ethnic Conflict and Violence in Sri Lanka* (Geneva, Switzerland, International Commission of Jurists, 1981) pp. 43-55.

[5] See, *The Ceylon Daily News*, 21 August and 27 August 1980, for an official communique issued by the Presidential Secretariat on 20 August 1980 on discussions held between President Jayewardene and a delegation of *bhikkhus* and laymen on the District Development Councils bill; and a statement issued by spokesmen for their delegation setting out their objections to the bill and these councils.

[6] Minutes of the Government Parliamentary Group meeting held on 21 August 1980. The letter from the 15 MPs was dated 8 August 1980.

[7] On this see Bruce Mathews, 'The Situation in Jaffna — and how it came about.' *The Round Table* (1984) 290, pp. 188-204.

8   Civil libertarians both Sri Lankan and foreign (including Amnesty International and the International Commission of Jurists) have shown little or no concern for the victims of the terrorists, an evasion of responsibilities which must undermine the objectivity of their reporting on alleged civil rights violations in Sri Lanka.

9   On these elections see, C.R. de Silva, "Plebiscitary Democracy or Creepng Authoritarianism? The Presidential Election and Referendum of 1982", and M.P. Moore, "The 1982 Elections and the new Gaullist — Bonapartist State in Sri Lanka," in (ed) James Manor, *Sri Lanka in Change and Crisis* (London, 1984), pp. 35-50, and 51-75 respectively.

10   See, my article 'Extending the life of Parliament by Referendum in Sri Lanka,' in *The Parliamentarian*, the Journal of the Parliaments of the Commonwealth, LXVI (3) July 1985, pp. 134-137.

11   On the riots of 1983, see, ed. James Manor, *Sri Lanka in Change in Crisis;* T.D.S.A. Dissanayake, *The Agony of Sri Lanka* (Colombo, 1983.)

12   On the Malaysian riots of May 1969, see, Karl von Vorys, *Democracy without Consensus:* Communalism and Political Stability in Malaysia (Princeton, 1975) pp. 308-338.

13   *The New York Times*, 4 November 1984, p. 10, a report under the title "Mobs' Wrath Brings Death to Sikh Area" by Barbara Crossette.

14   For a detailed account of these events see, T.D.S.A. Dissanayake, *The Agony of Sri Lanka.*

Chapter XXI

The Aftermath: 1983-1985

Those who watched the city of Colombo burn that fateful last week of July 1983 may have been forgiven for believing that recovery from the shattering effects of these riots would be glacially slow, and that in any case one of the main casualties would be Sri Lanka's democratic political system. The recovery began much sooner than seemed possible that week, and the democratic system survived without any considerable damage.

Recovery and reconstruction took place against the background of the internationalization of Sri Lanka's ethnic conflict. This internationalization had two aspects, the first of which was the shock and dismay in the European democracies and the United States at this demonstration of the failure of Sri Lanka's democratic political system in the management of her ethnic problems, and it represented also a genuine, humanitarian concern at the plight of Sri Lanka's Tamil minorities. The other aspect is a central theme in this chapter, the intensification of Indian pressure on Sri Lanka on behalf of the Tamils.

The Indian Factor

The return of Indira Gandhi to power in India in 1980 had marked a decisive change in the relations between the two neighbors, a sharp change from the very cordial relations that had prevailed under Moraji Desai and the Janatha government. Indeed India's relations with all her neighbors had never been better than they were with Desai as Prime Minister. When the Sri Lankan riots of August 1977 broke

AFTERMATH   343

out there was much agitation in Tamilnadu and Pondicherry, and the
Indian Prime Minister had been under considerable pressure to send
an official delegation or Cabinet Minister to Colombo to see the situation there first-hand. Interested parties in Tamilnadu, particularly,
had been quick to paint these incidents in Sri Lanka in the worst
possible colors, as being in part at least anti-Indian. Instead an
emissary of the Indian Prime Minister was sent to the island. This
emissary, S.A. Chidambaram, was acceptable to the Sri Lankan government and indeed the invitation to him to visit the island had come from
the then Sri Lankan Prime Minister J.R. Jayewardene.

After a brief stay in Colombo, Chidambaram returned to Madras on
31 August and went on to New Delhi on 1 September to report to the
Prime Minister. Chidambaram's report served to reassure the Indian
Prime Minister that the riots were entirely an internal matter and
reflected nothing hostile to India or Indians. He proceeded thereafter
to Madras where he gave the same reassuring picture to the Chief
Minister, M.G. Ramachandran, having previously met the Chief
Minister of Pondicherry, M. Ramaswami.

Mischief makers in Southern India got little encouragement from
the center, or from Chief Ministers M.G. Ramachandran and M.
Ramaswami. Earlier *hartals* and anti-Sri Lanka processions and demonstrations had been staged in Madras and Pondicherry. Now the two
state governments actively discouraged these. Desai, for his part,
assured the Sri Lanka Prime Minister that he appreciated the difficulties he faced and that he had India's good wishes and sympathetic
understanding in the hard steps he had taken to bring the situation
under control.

With Mrs. Gandhi in power after 1980 the cordiality between the
two governments was rapidly eroded by the frequency with which Mrs.
Gandhi took it upon herself to comment on Sri Lanka's internal
politics, in matters totally unconnected with the island's Indian
minority or with the problems of the Tamil minority. The Sri Lankan
government either completely ignored her tactless public remarks, or
on occasion, a demi-official response was delegated quite pointedly to
one of the younger Sri Lankan Cabinet Ministers.

Given this background the Indian government's response to the
riots of July 1983 was predictable: public statements of concern, a
concern which in Mrs. Gandhi's case was more than a little self-
serving. With general elections due in 1984 and her electoral base
eroding in many parts of India, including some of her strongholds in

Southern India, she was anxious to mollify Tamilnadu and retain if not consolidate her — and the Congress Party's — base there. Thus in July 1983, Mrs. Gandhi did what Moraji Desai refused to do in August 1977 — she sent a Cabinet Minister, Narashimha Rao, the Foreign Minister, to Colombo on 27 July, and later on with the consent of the Sri Lanka government, a mediator, G. Parathasarathy, an experienced diplomat.

In Tamilnadu there were demands for Indian "intervention" (a euphemism for invasion) and the strong possibility of "volunteers" moving in across the Palk Straits from Tamilnadu. The parallel quoted was Bangladesh and the Indian intervention in 1971 — a theme to which we shall return later in this chapter — and the entry of about 35,000 refugees from Jaffna who had crossed the seas to Tamilnadu, was used to bolster the case of those who advocated a similar line of action for the Sri Lankan situation.

There was also a significant change in the basis of India's declared interest, during times of ethnic tension, in the affairs of Sri Lanka. Generally on previous occasions the main concern had been with the "stateless" Indians resident in the island, and with Indian citizens here, both categories being largely plantation workers. This, by any standard of assessment, was a legitimate interest, although the presence of plantation workers with Indian citizenship in the island was due to a concession made to the CWC — with the knowledge and approval of the Indian government — by the UNP whereby they were granted the concession of remaining in the island for the duration of their working lives. (Under Mrs. Bandaranaike's government such persons were required to leave the island once their status changed from stateless to Indian citizen.) In the late 1970s and early 1980s Indian interest in the affairs of Sri Lanka was not limited to these categories of persons, but extended to all Tamils, an expansion of dubious rectitude which India defended on the grounds that Sri Lankan affairs relating to its Tamil minority affected the politics of Tamilnadu, either indirectly through raising tensions there or directly through the entry of refugees. The Indian government, although to a much lesser degree than the Tamilnadu politicians, found themselves empathizing with, if not identifying with, the Sri Lanka Tamil minorities. In the aftermath of the communal riots of 1983, India was a source of reassurance to the TULF at a moment of acute distress to that political group.

Despite this, however, India's role during this crisis was more constructive than many Sri Lankan political observers believed it would be. It acted as a restraint on Tamilnadu; and the Indian initiative was partly responsible for the commencement of negotiations between the TULF and the Sri Lanka government in the last quarter of 1983. These talks continued into and through 1984, with the Indian diplomat, G. Parathasarathy, in the role of mediator.

The riots of 1983 gave the TULF the opportunity to revive the debate on the devolution of power, an opportunity which they eagerly seized in the negotiations referred to above, to formally withdraw their support for the District Development Councils, arguing that these were inadequate in meeting the needs of the Tamil minority as they perceived it in the changed situation. They turned now to a more comprehensive devolution of power, on the lines, in fact, of the councils envisaged in the abortive agreement of 1957 between S.W.R.D. Bandaranaike and S.J.V. Chelvanayakam: a scheme of Provincial Councils, and with over-arching Regional Councils linking these Provincial Councils. Their main objective now as in 1957 was in the creation of a large regional unit encompassing the Northern and Eastern Provinces in which the Tamils would be a dominant if not overwhelming majority.

That, indeed, was the principal objective of the TULF in its decision to participate in the All Party Conference which began in January 1984. Such a conference had been an important item in the UNP's election manifesto and for the general election of 1977, but once in office it had preferred bilateral negotiations between itself and the TULF, and on occasion with the CWC linked with the government, in these talks. The decision to move ahead with an All Party Conference was an admission that these bilateral talks between the government and the TULF had not yielded the results anticipated by both sides.

The crucial issue before the Conference was the question of devolution, and in regard to this the Indian government committed itself to a support of the TULF's standpoint. The rationale for this support was that something with wider power and more extensive territorial limits than the District Development Councils was required to get the more moderate sections of Tamil opinion — by which it meant the TULF mainly — to move away from supporting separatism as a desirable goal. While the presence of TULF delegates at this Conference gave the discussions a significance and meaning they would not otherwise have had, the conference's claim to represent the full spectrum of political opinion in the island received a serious setback when the SLFP, after giving the concept of such a conference some support initially, stayed away eventually. However, other Sri Lankan political parties and groups, as well as representatives of religious organizations including groups of the *sangha*, participated in the discussions.

India's own manoeuverability in its diplomatic intervention in the search for a settlement of Sri Lanka's ethnic problems was much more limited than the Indian government and the Indian mediators realized. The diplomatic and political pressure for concessions on devolution from the Sri Lankan government and the Sinhalese in general confronted greater resistance at a multi-lateral discussion such as the All Party Conference, than they may have if the discussions were bilateral — between the government and the TULF. And yet both governments were anxious that the talks be multi-lateral rather than bilateral; the Indian government because it aspired to the role of an honest broker and this was an exceedingly difficult one in bilateral negotiations given the TULF's public posture of an Indian protege; the Sri Lankan government because it enabled the representation of a much wider and generally more 'hard-line' range of opinion inimical to any loosening of the island's unitary political and administrative structures, a backdrop against which the government's commitment to the District Development Councils scheme appeared less limited and restrictive than it seemed to advocates of a more thoroughgoing exercise in regional autonomy.

Even more harmful to India's presumed role of an honest broker than the TULF's less than adroit performance at the negotiating table was the existence of military training camps, if not bases, for Sri Lanka Tamil separatists in Tamilnadu, from which they made regular forays into the island. These had been in existence for some time and the Tamilnadu government generally had turned a blind eye to the activities in these.

These guerilla training camps and facilities could not be wished away by embarrassed Indian diplomats and Cabinet-level politicians. Reports on these training camps and 'bases' appeared in western newspapers[1], with enterprising journalists publishing accounts of activities there in graphic detail. These accounts found confirmation in the comprehensive coverage of the camps and bases in a prestigious Indian journal.[2] And if more solid evidence was required of the use of Indian soil by Sri Lankan guerrillas and terrorists, this was forthcoming when a section of the Madras International Airport was accidently blown up by bombs due for transfer to Sri Lanka for the destruction of aircraft of the Sri Lanka national airline at Colombo's International Airport[3]: the explosion killed over two dozen Sri Lankan passengers in the transit lounge of the Madras airport on this occasion. Although the identity of the perpetrators of this terrorist outrage was known, no action has yet been taken by the appropriate Indian authorities to prosecute them. Moreover, the Indian government has refused to acknowledge the existence of training camps and facilities for Sri Lanka Tamil guerrillas and terrorist groups on Indian soil. They have sought to divert attention from Sri Lankan charges and protests on these with counter-charges of human rights violations in Sri Lanka, attributing these quite explicitly to the lack of discipline among the Sri Lanka security forces. In so doing they met an embarrassing fact with a half truth. For just as it is true that army reprisals against civilians in Jaffna and elsewhere in the north and east in the island during clashes with terrorists have been frequent, and the resulting death toll high — the record, in fact, is both deplorable and grim — Indian and other critics of Sri Lanka's small and ill-equipped armed services seldom mentioned the strong disciplinary measures — generally on a collective basis — taken against offending regiments and platoons. But more important, as Sri Lanka's army, used for decades as a "parade ground" force for ceremonial purposes, becomes more battle-hardened, it has also become better disciplined. The improvement in this regard since July 1983 has been significant if not remarkable. Yet the original image of the Sri Lankan armed forces as being in the main groups of ill-disciplined 'ethnic' soldiers, persists. This greater maturity in response to terrorist attacks far more destructive of life than those of July 1983 was even more pronounced among the civil population of the Sinhalese areas. We shall have more to say about the role of the armed services in the Sri Lanka polity later on in this chapter.

On the other hand, Sri Lankan Tamil guerrillas and terrorists operate in Tamilnadu with a freedom and publicity for which the only parallel is the PLO and its various factions in the Arab world. Quite apart from the public support they enjoy in such large measure in Tamilnadu, they engage in fund-raising drives at public meetings in other parts of India as well. This double standard on separatism and terrorism — to crush separatism ruthlessly when it is seen to pose a palpable threat to the Indian polity as was done in 1984 in the Punjab through Operation Blue Star, to protest vigorously at the tolerance accorded to Indian extremists and terrorist groups operating in the western world (the Sikhs in Britain, Canada and the United States for instance) and yet to feign ignorance of the existence of training camps and 'bases' for Tamil guerrillas and terrorist groups on Indian soil has been and continues to be one of the great stumbling blocks to cordial relations between India and Sri Lanka. And despite greatly improved relations between the two countries after Rajiv Gandhi succeeded to the Prime Ministership of India on his mother's assassination, and especially after his convincing victory at the general election that followed, there is no evidence of any serious efforts being made by the Indian government to prevent the use of Indian territory by guerrillas and terrorists for attacks on a friendly neighbor, much less to close down these facilities and camps.

The fact is that even Rajiv Gandhi, so much less dependent on the Southern Indian political base than his mother, and intent on taking a more even-handed approach then her to the problems posed by Sri Lanka's ethnic conflicts, finds his options more limited than he would like them to be. And the constraint lies in the ethnic politics of Tamilnadu and the public support the Sri Lankan Tamils enjoy there. Rajiv Gandhi learned to his cost the perils involved in taking a strong line against the leadership of the Sri Lankan Tamil separatist groups operating in Tamilnadu, when he was compelled to go back on his decision to deport three of these men from India to Britain and the United States.

Thus a recognition of the limits of political initiatives available to the Gandhis, mother and son, have restricted them to a mediatory role, in persuading the TULF — in the case of Indira Gandhi — to join the negotiating process at the All Party Conference of 1984, and to expand the scope of the Indian initiative — under Rajiv Gandhi — to persuade the Sri Lanka government to begin discussions and later on nego- tiations with the various Tamil separatist and guerrilla groups. Up to the end of 1984 the Sri Lankan government had steadfastly refused to consider discussions, much less negotiations, with such groups. In both instances an Indian mediator was the go-between, G. Paratha- sarathy under Mrs. Gandhi, and Romesh Bhandari, secretary to the Ministry of Foreign Affairs of the Indian government, under Rajiv Gandhi. The first of these initiatives failed by the end of 1984. The second took place away from Sri Lanka, in Bhutan, and at the end of 1985 there were few signs that it would be any more successful than the first. At the core of the discussions and negotiations in both instances was that hardy perennial of Sri Lankan politics, and its most feared nettle —decentralization of administration.

Decentralization, 1984-85:
Back to the Drawing Boards

Despite the government's reservations about the proposal for the establishment of Provincial Councils, and even stronger reservations about the concept of Regional Councils linking these, it nevertheless placed it for discussion at the All Party Conference. If the proposal attracted any support at all it came from left-wing parties and fringe groups. All other groups and parties — other than the TULF, of course —expressed strong opposition to it, and among those most strongly opposed were the Muslims who saw little advantage — on the contrary, very great disadvantages — in a Regional Council which linked the Northern and Eastern Provinces and left the Muslims facing a dominant Tamil majority there. And, of course, Buddhist opinion, lay and *sangha* represented at the conference, reiterated their traditional opposition to schemes of devolution of authority to regional units of administration. The *sangha* representatives did show some flexibility and realism in their attitude when they came out, at last, in support of the existing system of District Development Councils, and even agreed to a widening of their powers and a strengthening of their financial resources. However when a draft ordinance incorporating a system of revitalized district councils, empowered to link together where necessary on a wider provincial basis, was tabled for discussion at the All Party Conference on 30 September 1984, critics focused their opposition on this latter feature and declined to support the draft bills. The TULF itself declared its opposition to it, as did the SLFP (which had refused to participate in the discussions of the conference) the one because it did not go far enough in the direction of autonomy, the other because it seemed to go too far in undermining the country's unitary structure.

Despite this setback discussions continued within the All Party Conference, and outside it, on the framework of a political settlement which would incorporate an effective system of decentralization of power. To accommodate the wishes of the TULF, two draft bills were placed before the Conference, one of which was a draft district and provincial council bill.[4] This too was rejected by the TULF, and with that the government itself withdrew its support of the proposal, relieved no doubt to jettison a scheme which has had so little political support in the country, and which on the contrary had such ominous potential for arousing fear and suspicion among the Sinhalese, as well as the Muslim minority.

One significant advantage emerged fom all this — a consensus of Sinhalese Buddhist opinion in favor of retaining and strengthening the District Development Councils introduced in 1980-81. Up to 1983 there had been an apathy about these which no amount of propaganda on them by the government could overcome. To that extent the crisis of 1983 had consolidated the gains made in 1980 through the introduction of the District Development Councils, even if the TULF were no longer satisfied with them. That legislation remained in the statute book, and all it requires are some administrative changes —and where necessary amending legislation — to make them more viable instruments of devolution of power than they were in the early months. Had that legislation not been approved in 1980, its introduction in the current state of ethnic relations in the island would have been faced with much greater, and perhaps more politically effective, resistance than it did on that previous occasion.

All this has substantial significance at the present moment when the debate on forms of devolution of authority, and the unit of devolution, continues between the Sri Lanka government and representatives of Tamil opinion with the Indian government still serving as mediator. Tamil organizations continue to insist on a regional linkage between the Northern and Eastern Provinces, but the government is equally adamant — as is the SLFP, its main rival as a national political party — in its refusal to accept a linkage which cuts across provincial borders. For its part the government has made a major concession in deciding to accept a scheme of Provincial Councils in place of the present district level councils. For in conceding this, the government will need to give the moribund provincial structure a new lease of life, and the provincial system which emerged under British rule would thus be perpetuated despite their boundaries being artificial ones largely devised for administrative convenience in British times, and despite the province having ceased to be a unit of administration since the early 1960s. Over the last twenty-five years the district had replaced the province as the largest unit of regional administration. If such councils are established it would mean that Bandaranaike's Provincial Councils would, at last, come into existence, nearly fifty years after he

first mooted them — in response to the suggestions of the Donoughmore Commission — but without the national consensus in support of
them that existed in the 1940s.

Pressure from the Militants

These discussions on the mechanics of devolution took place against
the backdrop of an increasing frequency of guerrilla attacks and
terrorist incidents in the north of the island, and the extension of these
into the eastern seaboard. The guerrilla forces were now much larger,
much better trained, and much better equipped than they were before.
This training and equipping of guerrilla forces had begun well before
the riots of July 1983, but there is no mistaking the intensification of
these processes as a result of the violence inflicted on the Tamils in
July 1983. Tamilnadu had always been a ready haven for these guerrilla forces, but now the support they received was strengthened
immeasurably, as was the extent of the protection they enjoyed. Their
morale was stronger, and their motivation keener after these riots than
before, and by the end of 1983 they demonstrated a greater willingness
to take risks, and greater resourcefulness and daring in their attacks on
the security forces and on carefully chosen targets. Till about the end
of 1985 they were, in many ways, better equipped than the small
security services stationed in the north of the island.

The size of these guerrilla forces has been variously estimated, and
the range is from 1500 to 3000. Considering that the Sri Lanka armed
services never mustered more than 20,000[5] up to the end of 1984, the
guerrilla groups were large enough to pose a threat to the Sri Lanka
security forces. The finances involved in equipping and maintaining
such a force are formidable even taking into account the resources
available either voluntarily or otherwise from the Tamils of the north
and east of the island, and of course the resources made available to
them in Tamilnadu both at the state level and from private citizens.
This was quite apart from the bank robberies and other thefts
organized by these guerrilla groups. Before these guerrilla forces
became as large and well-equipped as they were by 1984, the question
of finances to maintain and equip them was not as exacting a problem
as it is today. The expatriate Tamil communities in the west are a
source of financial assistance, especially its United States component

with its groups of wealthy medical professionals; the expatriate communities in Britain and Europe are in no position to match the U.S. group in the extent of financial support rendered. Thus reliance has to be placed on other sources of money, and there is strong evidence that as with many guerrilla groups in other parts of Asia, the Tamil guerrillas of Sri Lanka have turned to the narcotics trade. This is not so much through the control and direction of local sources of supply as is the case with the Karens of Burma, or the Afghan guerrillas fighting the Russians, but as couriers, as part of a link in the wider narcotics trade of the golden crescent of North-West Asia, to Europe. And as so often happens, the smugglers are the main suppliers to the couriers. Thus Europe's junkies become, unwittingly, an important source of funds for Sri Lanka's Tamil guerrillas.[6]

By the end of 1983 the Sri Lanka government faced a purposeful challenge from the Tamil separatist guerrillas, and with their attacks becoming more daring in scope and powerful in impact, the government responded with a new institutional structure, and new policies. Of the former, the most significant was the establishment of a Ministry of National Security in March 1984, to coordinate the activities of the security forces and the police in organizing counter-insurgency and counter-terrorist activities. Of the policies adopted three are of significance: the attempt to check the easy flow of men and arms to and from Jaffna and Tamilnadu by establishing a surveillance zone; a new policy on peasant settlements in the border between the Tamil areas and the Anuradhapura and Polonnaruva districts; and a marked increase in the expenditure on the armed services. All three produced controversy, the first two more than the third, and in the case of the first of these the anticipated advantages were not forthcoming. On the contrary the consequences of the move eventually caused more difficulties for the government in regard to its relations with Tamilnadu and India.

The concept of a surveillance zone covering most of the north and north-western coastal region seemed simple enough, and there was an awareness that in implementing it the civil population of the littoral would face serious difficulties especially in the crowded Jaffna peninsula. The implementation of the policy began in the last week of November 1984. The fundamental objective was to control the traffic across the seas from the Jaffna peninsula to the Indian coast, and to check what had hitherto been the free movement of guerrillas to and from Jaffna through their use of fishing craft, and speedier vessels (generally those of smugglers). The first to feel the pressure of these restrictions were the smugglers and fisherfolk, but the latter had no resources to fall back on when their livelihood was seriously affected by the ban placed on fishing in the area. Both had become associated with transport of guerrillas and terrorists, the smugglers with greater enthusiasm than the former, and with a stronger sense of commitment.

One unexpected result of this move was a new wave of refugees to Tamilnadu — the first had been in the aftermath of the July 1983 riots — an altogether poorer group than in 1983, generally fisherfolk who had lost their livelihood. The numbers were much smaller than in 1983, but the fact that people got across to Tamilnadu in this way showed that the surveillance zone was more porous, less efficacious than it was intended to be and above all not as rigorously enforced as might have been. It was evident that much greater resources in naval craft and trained personnel than Sri Lanka's diminutive navy possessed were called for to make this policy really effective.

This latest phase in the influx of refugees to Tamilnadu was, in its initial stages, voluntary, but soon pressure was used on the fishing population in the surveillance zone to flee to Tamilnadu in large numbers to aggravate the refugee situation there. In this campaign the TULF and the militants worked together. The TULF leadership had been living in exile in Tamilnadu as guests of the state government since the outbreak of ethnic violence in July 1983. With the collapse of the All Party Conference they appeared to be more receptive than before to the presumed attractions of Indian intervention on behalf of the Tamils of the north, on the Bangladesh model (others thought of the Cyprus situation as a more appropriate model.)[7]

Despite its uniqueness — the one single recent example in international affairs of a successful separatist campaign — the Bangladesh experience figured most frequently in the plans and calculations of the Tamil separatists in urging Indian intervention — that is to say — invasion on behalf of the Tamils of Sri Lanka.

The refugee problem in its later manifestation, but greatly exaggerated both in regard to the numbers involved, hardships faced by the fisherfolk and the alleged harrassment they suffered at the hands of the security forces, was used by the TULF and the various Tamil militant groups as well as their allies in Tamilinadu to argue the case for Indian intervention. The argument was that the conditions in the north of Sri Lanka were exactly the same as the situation in East Pakistan prior to the decisive Indian intervention there which led to the creation of Bangladesh.

Between the Bengali Muslims of the old Pakistan, and the Tamils of Sri Lanka there is a world of a difference: the former were a clear majority of the population in the whole of the old Pakistan, while the latter are a small minority of the island's population, just over a tenth on their own and less than a fifth even if the island's Indian Tamils are grouped together with them. True the Sri Lanka Tamils are an overwhelming majority of the population in the Jaffna peninsula and a clear majority in other parts of Sri Lanka's Northern Province. But even if the Tamils of the three districts of the Eastern Province are included in the calculation, the Tamils are not the overwhelming majority of a clearly marked and cohesive territorial unit that the Muslims of East Bengal were. Besides there was no parallel among the Muslims of East Bengal for the large numbers of Sri Lanka Tamils — 29.2% in 1971 and 32.8% in 1981 — living and working in predominantly Sinhalese areas. All these differences were scarcely considered as separatist Tamils concentrated attention on the combination of factors which successfully created Bangladesh or, to see it differently, dismembered the old Pakistan. That combination consisted of Indian intervention —through its armed forces — and widespread popular resistance to the West Pakistani (largely, Punjabi) presence in East Bengal.

This pressure for Indian intervention received little encouragement from New Delhi. The firm assurances to Sri Lanka that India contemplated no such intervention did not dampen the enthusiasm of Tamil separatist groups who kept up a steady barrage of propaganda on the need for Indian intervention.

The establishment of a surveillance zone did not bring about any significant reduction in guerrilla attacks within Sri Lanka: on the contrary these attacks assumed a new dimension of terror directed now, and for the first time, against Sinhalese peasants living in the Vanni regions of the Northern Province. In November and December 1984 two such attacks on unarmed civilians, one consisting of new settlers in Mullaitivu, and the other on a traditional Sinhalese fishing village (the villagers were mainly Roman Catholics)[8] on the north east coast were designed to cause panic in those regions, to get Sinhalese people there to flee to other parts of the country. These massacres were among the most horrifying in the long record of clashes between Sinhalese and Tamils in Sri Lanka. Their purpose was not merely to terrorize, but to spell out a political message, an attempt to underline imperatives of the traditional homelands theory and in its most brutal form; in regard to this the Tamil militants were using terrorism to enforce what the TULF had preached for so long, the exclusive right of the Tamils to the resources of these areas.

These two attacks raised the level of violence in clashes between the Sinhalese and Tamils to a more diabolical plane.[9] And here one needs to draw a distinction between mob violence and deaths caused by such violence in a period of communal rage, ferocious and terrible though that is in its own way, and the cold-blooded massacre of whole families by armed young men using machine gun fire on civilians, or herding captives into a building which is then blown up with the victims inside. Similar techniques were adopted in attacks on Sinhalese peasants in the Trincomalee district in the early part of 1985 and towards the end of the year. But by far the most chilling incident of all was the Anuradhapura massacre of 14 May 1985[10] when a group of Tamil terrorists dressed in army uniforms seized a bus, drove into the bus station of the town of Anuradhapura and used automatic weapons to kill everybody in sight there, and moved across then to the site of the sacred bo-tree[11] — one of the oldest and holiest Buddhist sites in Sri Lanka — and killed pilgrims, a *bhikkhu* and some nuns and people in trade stalls near the shrine.

One new feature of the ethnic conflicts of this phase was the bloody clashes between Tamils and Muslims in the Eastern Province in April 1985. The clashes had begun, in fact, in Mannar in the Northern Province, with the killing of some Muslims by Tamil guerrillas on suspicion of providing information on the latter's activities to the security forces. The violence spread later on to the Batticoloa and Amparai districts of the Eastern Province and resulted in a large number of deaths on both sides. The Muslims were resisting the spread of separatist agitation and the violence and extraction of resources linked with it, to their villages.

Much of the violence associated with the Tamil guerrillas and terrorists during this period was in the Mannar, Mullaitivu, Kilinochchi and Vavuniya districts of the Northern Province. These are, and generally always have been, sparsely populated and with a mixed population, although the Tamils were a majority in the more settled parts.

In the early part of 1985 the government announced a policy decision to organize a settlement of the Vanni regions under its aegis, a shift of population there intended to create a buffer zone in the form of peasant settlements moving upwards to the borders of the Jaffna district. This was a response to the threat posed by Tamil guerrillas using this region as a base of operations, the announcement that new settlements were envisaged, and new settlements under state control, provoked strong opposition from a wide range of Tamil opinion.

Since the mid-1970s there had been a shift of population there largely by Indian Tamils displaced from their homes as a result of the nationalization of the plantations in the hill country in the Central Province, in 1972-75, and more recently as a result of the 1977 riots. More important, others were attracted there by the prospect of the availability of land for homesteads. Most of these people were squatters on state land and their settlement there was encouraged and supported by Tamils from the north associated with the TULF and also by radical youth groups, who looked upon these settlements as the nucleus of a Tamil buffer zone, against prospective Sinhalese settlers moving in.

This was one issue on which Thondaman's CWC and the TULF have a common outlook. For the ethnic disturbances of the 1970s and 1980s had reinforced the need for a refuge from violence or the threat of violence. For the Sri Lankan Tamils the Jaffna peninsula had served this purpose since the mid and late 1950s. The Indian Tamils saw similar advantages in the Vanni regions adjacent to Jaffna, where they would in addition have the advantage of freedom from the rigors of Jaffna's caste-oriented society. Thus even those like Thondaman's CWC who had no truck with separatism were conscious of the need for at least one area of the island serving a similar purpose for them and were conscious of the need to protect the ethnic identity of these regions from any possibility of serious dilution by colonization in its periphery or within it by new settlers.

Thus two diamterically opposed concepts of a buffer zone emerged: one in which the CWC no less than the TULF and those to the far left of the TULF seek to preserve these areas as an exclusively Tamil region; and the other asserts the rights of all Sri Lankans to the land and economic resources of the region.

We turn next to the third policy initiative taken by the government. It too was controversial but for a different reason. Sri Lanka, traditionally, had taken pride in the welfare state it had developed over the last five decades. The price it paid was the neglect of its security services. In 1978, the expenditure on defense was only $40 million, or 1.5% of its GNP. An American observer of Sri Lanka's welfare policies points out that Sri Lanka "unlike its South Asian neighbors or even most other countries of the Third World,... is virtually demilitarized."[12] In that sense Sri Lanka is much like that other sturdy democracy, Costa Rica, except that Costa Rica has only a police force. Now as a result of the threat posed by Tamil guerrillas and terrorists, there has been a policy of diverting larger sums of money to the expansion and modernization of its armed services. By 1985 expenditure on the armed services rose to $200 million or 3.5% of t‍ e GNP, and it is anticipated that this level of expenditure would have to be sustained over the next few years, thus diverting to defense money which would normally have gone to the maintenance and expansion of her welfare state, or the rapidly expanding irrigation system. The choice is a hard, or even a harsh one, but no longer can Sri Lanka take shelter — as she has done over the last two decades or so — under the Indian defense umbrella. For that umbrella, like the proverbial banker's umbrella, has not been available when one needs it most, in this instance to protect the coasts of Sri Lanka from intrusion by guerrillas based in Tamilnadu, or from a smuggling trade which has graduated from the traditional exchange of scarce and desirable commercial goods to weapons, armed men, and narcotics.

References

1   See *The Sunday Times* (London) 1 April 1984, and Reuter reports on these bases published in Sri Lanka in the *Sun* of 23 May 1984 and the *Island* of 25 May 1984. See also the London based journal *South:* the Third World Magazine, March 1985, pp. 14-15.

2   *India Today*, 31 March 1984, pp. 88-94, see particularly the essay in investigative reporting entitled "Sri Lanka Rebels' An Ominous Presence in Tamilnadu."

3   The incident occurred on 26 July 1984. See *The Economist* (London) 11 August 1984, and *The Philadelphia Inquirer*, 4 August 1984. There were 31 deaths in all, of whom at least 25 were Sri Lankan passengers in the transit lounge of the airport.

4   This included an imaginative but complex three-tier structure of District Councils, Provincial Councils and a Council of State (a second chamber for the Sri Lankan legislature).

5   This included reserves. The force stations in the Jaffna Peninsula and the Northern Province seldom exceeded 2500 men in all.

6   See *The Guardian* (Manchester, England) *Weekly*, August 11, 1985, p. 11, an article by Laurent Crellsamer, "Tamil Emigrants could be Europe's major source of heroin." The Article made the point that: 'Frightening quantities of heroin are being smuggled into Europe from a completely new source — Colombo, the capital

of Sri Lanka. Last year alone some 1500 kilos of heroin were smuggled into Western Europe from this source. The men running the traffic have in a few months become the main targets of Europe's police forces, and the quantity of heroin transiting via the Sri Lanka route is on the way to overtaking all other competitors in the field." See also *The Asian Wall Street Journal*, 9 September 1985 article entitled "Drugs, Guns and Tamil Terrorism." Extracts from this article were published in *The Island* (Colombo) 11 September 1985.

7   A pointed reference was made to this by G.K. Reddy, an influential Indian journalist, in an article entitled "No Question of Taking India for a Ride," in *Frontline* 23 March-5 April 1985, pp. 75-76, published by *The Hindu* (Madras, India).

8   The two attacks took place on 30 November 1984 and 19 December 1984 respectively.

9   The terrorists turned their guns also on the TULF. Two former TULF MPs were assassinated on or around 1 September 1985 — their bodies were found on 3 September. They were V. Dharmalingam and M. Alalasunderam, both of whom lived in Jaffna unlike most of their colleagues who moved to Madras. Dharmalin-had been in Parliament since 1956.

10   On this attack see *The New York Times*, 15 May 1985; and The *Sun*, 15 May 1985, *The Island*, 17 May 1985; the dead numbered 146, including 25 women, 6 children, one *bhikkhu* and 4 Buddhist nuns.

11   The bo-tree *(ficus religiosa)* is believed to be a branch of the sacred bo tree under which the Buddha attained enlightenment at Buddh Gaya in India. It was sent to Sri Lanka in the 3rd Century B.C. by the Indian Emperor, Asoka.

12   J.W. Bjorkman, "Health Policy and Politics in Sri Lanka," *Asian Survey* XXV(5) May 1985, p. 547.

PART V

Conclusion

Chapter XXII

Conclusion

Sri Lankan politics in the 100 years covered in this survey present an intriguing enigma: in one dimension of it, the history of that period would appear to provide a classic example of the failure of ethnic integration in a poly-ethnic state, through the application of inappropriate if not misguided policies and practices; the second dimension points to an unusual example of the remarkable resilience, indeed the sturdy survival, of conditions that foster stable and effective democracy in the face of acutely divisive linguistic and religious differences and an unpromising economic base. Despite flawed policies and short-sighted decisions there is a creditable record of innovative and imaginative attempts to accommodate the minorities, and just as important, assimilation was never regarded as a practical policy option in determining relations between the Sinhalese-Buddhists and the minorities.

A Conflict of Minorities?

We need to begin this concluding chapter with a review of some of the salient points in the current crisis in Sri Lanka politics, the conflict between the Sinhalese majority and the Sri Lankan Tamil minority. It would be clear to readers of this book that this conflict is not a simple straightforward confrontation between an aggrieved and cohesive Tamil minority and an insensitive and powerful Sinhalese majority. Would it be more accurate to describe it as a conflict between two minorities?

Ethnic conflict between the Sinhalese and Tamils is a twentieth century manifestation of an age-old rivalry between two peoples who have shared the island of Sri Lanka for at least two thousand years. One needs to keep in mind the historical dimension of the rivalries, a palimpsest with layer upon layer of troubled historical memories where the events of several centuries ago assume the immediacy of the previous weekend, and those of a thousand years, that of the last year. The country is haunted by a history which is agonizing to recall but hazardous to forget.

As we have seen, the Sinhalese outnumber the Tamils 6 to 1 within Sri Lanka, and yet far from this overwhelming majority status giving them a sense of security they regard themselves as a historically beleagured minority facing an ancient antagonist whose main stronghold lies across the seas in Tamilnadu in South India. The Tamils of South Asia — of Tamilnadu and Sri Lanka — outnumber the Sinhalese by more than 4 to 1. We confront the powerful influence of the Sinhalese sense of historical destiny, of a small and embattled people who have preserved Theravada Buddhism when it was obliterated in southern India under a Hindu revivalist tide, and whose language, despite its roots in classical Indian languages, is uniquely Sri Lankan. And along with it there is the perception of the Tamils as the traditional national enemy against whom their ancestors fought at various times in the past. There is, above all, the perception of southern India as the source from which scores of invasions of the heartland of ancient Sri Lanka were launched.

These historical memories reinforce the present sense of Sinhalese insecurity in dealing with the Tamils, and reinforce too their belief that they are a minority. Yet to accept the Sinhalese perception of themselves as a minority facing a massive and implacable Tamil phalanx is to ignore several facts of Sri Lankan politics. First of all, the Sri Lankan Tamils living outside the Tamil areas of the north and east of the island have distinct political outlooks of their own, and if these were occasionally distinct from the outlooks of the Sinhalese majority, just as often they were distinct also from those of the Tamils of the Jaffna peninsula. Secondly, within Sri Lanka, the Indian Tamils have strong political links with the present governing party, the UNP, in a political alliance that has withstood the vicissitudes of Sri Lanka's changing political system for twenty years since 1964; and at present the leader of the Indian Tamils is a member of the Cabinet.

Nor, can the Jaffna Tamils be described as a harassed minority, the victims of ruthless acts of violence — though violence admittedly has been frequent enough in recent times — and calculated policies of discrimination directed at them. They are, in fact, an achievement-oriented, industrious people who enjoy high status in society, considerable influence in the economy and the bureaucracy, and a prominent if no longer a privileged position in the education system at all levels, primary, secondary and tertiary. There are two Sri Lanka Tamils in the present Cabinet, the present Chief Justice of the island and the Attorney General are Tamils, while the Inspector General of Police — the head of the police — was till very recently, a Tamil. Most of the Tamil fears and their own sense of insecurity stem from the knowledge that they would lose, if they have not already lost, the advantageous position they once enjoyed or presently enjoy in many areas of public life in the country, in brief a classic case of a sense of relative deprivation spurring a people on to a dogged resistance to policies of and proposals for change.

As we have seen they were the beneficiaries of a remarkable educational effort by the missionary movement of nineteenth century Sri Lanka. These efforts were generally concentrated not diffused; the region in and around Colombo was an obvious location, but one area of activity was surprising, the Jaffna peninsula, isolated from the rest of the island, a region with a hard dry climate and lack of natural resources but with an industrious people. There the missionary enterprise had a powerful impact on a very receptive people. In that region of the island alone American missionaries (their headquarters were in Boston) were permitted to operate, but not the American missionaries alone. The historical legacy of their endeavors was the creation of a superb network of schools and the production of generations of educated Tamils who were being equipped primarily for service in the lower rungs of the British administrative system and in the commercial houses in Colombo. There they earned a well-deserved reputation for diligence and competence and for a tolerance of the tedium that this sort of work involved.

The Jaffna peninsula did not have the resources to retain and support this population. It began to export 'labor' in the form of literate and educated youths to the more prosperous southern parts of the island. They did not meet much competition from the Sinhalese until well into the 20th century; their main competitors were the Burghers. In time Jaffna began to export its educated 'labor' also to the British colonies emerging in what is now Malaysia and in much smaller numbers to the East African colonies. This emigration came to a halt in the 1920s and the movement to Colombo and the Sinhalese areas was strengthened. Just as it was said of 18th century Scotland that the most pleasing prospect there was the road that led to London, it could be truly said that the most pleasing prospect in Jaffna was the road — and later the railway — that led to Colombo.

By the 1930s Tamils, disproportionately represented in the public sector, as clerks, teachers, and technicians, were well established in the professional services as doctors and engineers as well. More significantly, they now faced Sinhalese competition, and their advantageous position in government employment became a point of contention and division in politics. The Soulbury Commissioners reported in 1945 that appointment to the public services

> "... provides a common source of dissension between majority and minority communities ... [The] Ceylon Tamils appear, at any rate as late as 1938, to have occupied a disproportionate number of posts in the Public Services... That they have won for themselves a much larger share is a consequence of the higher standard of literacy and education which this community has so long enjoyed, and of its energy and efficiency. For similar reasons the Burghers have achieved an even more remarkable position."[1]

The Commission viewed

> "... the Sinhalese challenge to the predominant position of the Tamils in public appointments ... [as] the natural effect of the spread of education and of the efforts being made to bring other portions of the island up to the intellectual level of one portion of it ..."[2]

Having identified the problem they turned to the British experience to reassure the Tamils:

> "In this connection, we cannot help recalling a period in our own history when, as the result of the superior educational facilities and better teaching prevalent in Scotland, a minority was enabled to secure a larger share of administrative and executive posts in the United Kingdom than could have been justified on any proportional allocation. Since then the English have made strenuous and not altogether unsuccessful endeavours to redress the deficiencies of their past."[3]

Thus at the time of the transfer of power the Tamil minority was warned in the clearest possible terms — even though the style chosen for their warning was understatement rather than exaggeration — that hard times lay ahead of them as educational standards improved among the Sinhalese. Unlike some achievement-oriented minorities in other parts of the world, the Chinese in Malaysia for instance, the Sri

Lanka Tamils grew accustomed to state employment. Their stake in commerce and industry and plantation agriculture did not match their stake in their chosen field of activity, and the determining factor was a quest — almost a passion — for security and a steady income, a reflection of their awareness of the limited opportunities for employment available to them in the Jaffna peninsula. This made them exceptionally vulnerable and exceptionally sensitive to changes in language policy, to educational reform, and changes in the mechanisms for determining admission to tertiary education in a country in which expansion in university education lagged far behind the expansion of secondary and primary education. Over the next twenty-five years they would be overtaken in almost every sector of state employment and in the professions by the Sinhalese, overtaken but far from being overwhelmed. They retained their advantageous position in some of the professions — medicine, law and engineering. This represented the intellectual capital of the past, carefully gathered, and protected and augmented but, in their eyes, not expanding rapidly enough to overcome what they saw as the disadvantages of the new policy changes which would adversely effect the next generation of Tamils.

Suffice it to say that depending on the sector of the economy and specific areas within these, the position of the Tamils now varies from one of continuing but precarious superiority in some, to others in which they are at a disadvantage. It is a complex situation of pluses and minuses, and where moreover change, sometimes rapid, sometimes slow, is the order of the day.[4]

In one sector of the economy, however, the Tamils are now clearly at a disadvantage, or to put it differently and perhaps more fairly, they have lost the privileged position they enjoyed prior to independence and even at the time of the transfer of power. This is in regard to employment in the government service. A distinction is drawn here between government employment and state sector employment because the nationalization of the plantations has converted the Indian plantation workers into state sector employees and this distorts the picture as regards ethnic identity as a factor in state employment. Our comments here and in the next two paragraphs are restricted to government service proper. There the prominent position presently enjoyed by some Tamils in the higher bureaucracy, in the Police and the Judiciary, is as much evidence that there is no policy of discrimination directed against Tamils, as it is a reflection of the advantages they enjoyed in the past, advantages which are rapidly eroding in the face of competition from Sinhalese.

On this important subject studies in depth have only just commenced. Dr. S.W.R. de A. Samarasinghe's recent study of "Ethnic Representation in Government Employment in Sri Lanka 1948-1981"[5] is the most notable of these. It takes off from Professor S.J. Tambiah's oft-quoted and still to be superseded article on "Ethnic Representation in Ceylon's Higher Administrative Service, 1870-1946".[6] Samarasinghe points out that:

"The Tamils have already lost the relative position in Central government employment that was enjoyed in the past.[7]

"Apart from the obvious economic loss this entails," he adds, "there is the psychological adjustment that many Jaffna Tamil families must make in the wake of this change. There is the fact that government jobs are no longer as easily obtained as they were a generation or two ago. The Sinhalese, on the other hand, are bound to view the change as a natural and inevitable adjustment which bestows on them their 'due' share. Clearly, there are two different perceptions of the same phenomenon. The result is, the Tamils have begun to feel they are 'discriminated' against and the Sinhalese feel recent changes have simply reversed the 'discrimination' they had been subjected to in the past."[8]

The passions these rivalries generated are often attributed exclusively to the competition between elite groups for administrative and political power and for employment. To do so is to discount, unrealistically, the role of the masses in ethnic conflict, and the play of powerful forces such as population growth. We have reviewed this latter theme in earlier chapters of this book. Here we need to reiterate the point that while population growth has abated somewhat from the mid and late 1970s its pressure is still felt, a pressure which accounts for the intensity of the competition for employment. This competition which occurs at all levels and not merely at that of the elite has poisoned ethnic relations in the country, cutting across class issues, class loyalties and class consciousness with an ease which bewilders left-wing academics and politicians alike. The latter — the academics much more so than the politicians — are emotionally and ideologically unprepared to confront the realities of the role of the masses in ethnic conflict, where:

"Given a choice, people prefer to hate others because of their religion, or race, caste or tribe, rather than because of their wealth. The wealthy in one's own community are a source of vicarious pride. The status (and accomplishment) of members of one's own community provides self-esteem to all members of the community. For this reason it is not easy to create class cleavages and class parties in a multi-ethnic society except where class and ethnic cleavages coincide."[9]

If the Sinhalese were — and are — insecure because of the burden of history and memories of the past, the Tamils are insecure because of fears for their future. And just as the Sinhalese sense of insecurity lies behind the misguided policies intent on forcing the pace of change, when change in their favor was inevitable if somewhat slower than they wished it to be, the Tamils sought to protect their interests and to redress the balance which was now shifting markedly against them by making exaggerated claims to a special status in the Sri Lanka polity, claims asserted in a number of forms and at various times, all of which made the management of ethnic tensions harder than it might have been without them.

And here we need to make the point that the unusual prominence the Sri Lanka Tamils have had in Sri Lankan public life in the early twentieth century has left an indelible mark on their political attitudes. Thus, in 1918, a document presented by the Jaffna Association to the Colonial Office made the point that:

"... The Tamils of Ceylon have hitherto, in spite of their inferiority in numbers, maintained a position of equality with their Sinhalese brethren, whether in official or unofficial life."[10]

This special position they owed to a number of exceptional circumstances, but one of them undoubtedly was the political dexterity of the two brothers, Ponnambalam Ramanathan and Ponnambalam Arunachalam.

Up to the early 1920s the Tamils did not regard themselves as a minority, nor were they regarded as a minority. At that time the term "minorities" had a much more restricted meaning in the Sri Lankan context than it has today: it included the Europeans, Burghers and Muslims but not always the Christians or the Tamils. In fact, the political thinking of that period accepted the concept of *two* majority communities, the Sinhalese and the Tamils. The situation changed in the 1920s: instead of two majority communities there was now one majority community, the Sinhalese and several minorities which now included the Tamils. Ramanathan gloried in the role of a minority spokesman, or rather the spokesman for the minorities, but even so old assumptions died hard, for we have that shrewd observer of the Sri Lankan scene, Governor Sir Hugh Clifford, commenting in November 1926 that:

"... the Sinhalese resent the reluctance of the Tamils to accord
themselves merely a minority section of an united Ceylonese nation
..."[11]

Thus we see the emergence of a duality in the Tamil political
attitudes, an assertion of minority rights, but the search for a wider and
larger role. In Ramanathan's time this duality took the form of a
leadership of a phalanx of minorities, with the Tamils in the lead. This
duality inevitably led to confusion about the nature of the Tamils' role
or position in the Sri Lankan polity, and this confusion has continued
to affect the political vision of the Tamils' leadership ever since. The
'50-50' campaign can only be explained as an attempt to perpetuate this
duality. The sharp terms in which it was rejected by both Sir Andrew
Caldecott, who as Governor of the island confronted the political
pressures that emerged from that agitation, and by the Soulbury
Commissioners, sprang from their clear grasp of its implications in the
management of ethnic tensions in Sri Lanka. The latter viewed the '50-
50' campaign as an "inequitable" and "artificial means to convert a
majority into a minority."[12]

Traces of this duality linger on in contemporary Tamil politics in Sri
Lanka. It takes various forms. It appears in the concept of the "Tamil-
speaking peoples of Sri Lanka" with its assumption of tutelage over the
Muslims; it is immanent in the insistence on federalism; and it lies at
the heart of the campaign for separatism.

Thus the present conflict betweeen the Sinhalese and the Tamils
takes on an unusual complexity. It is much more than a conflict
between a majority and minority, or indeed a conflict between two
minorities. The conflict is between a majority with a minority complex,
and a minority with a yearning for majority status, a minority with a
majority complex.

Compromises, Adjustments and Accommodations

We turn now to the second level of assessment referred to in the
first paragraph of this chapter. With regard to this the most significant
point is that many of the critical issues that divided the people of the
country over the last fifty years or more have been sorted out, not on a
permanent basis or with a winner-take-all attitude with the demands of
the Sinhalese and Buddhists being conceded in their entirety. Instead
there has been all too often a refreshing practicality and pragmatism

moderating the outcome of conflicts such as those on religion and language.

Religious strife in the form of tensions and conflicts between Buddhists and Christians — in particular the Buddhists and Roman Catholics — was one of the most divisive factors in Sri Lankan public life for about 80 years or so beginning in the last quarter of the 19th century. These religious tensions — largely among the Sinhalese — had been, at times, so sharp that they gave every impression of remaining an abiding factor of division in Sri Lankan public life. Yet they have ceased to be a contentious issue in politics since the early 1970s.

Many of these tensions had been linked to controversies over state control over election. By the end of the 1960s the Roman Catholics had reconciled themselves to a more limited role in education, and in Sri Lankan public life. Within the church there were groups who argued that it needed to move away from its traditional attitudes on education of its flock. There was, in addition, a steady decline in the percentage of Christians in the Sri Lankan population, down from 9.1% at the census of 1946 to about 7% at present. Some part of that decline may be attributed to the emigration of the Burghers who were a Christian community, but the Burghers were always an almost miniscule element of the population, and a drop of two percentage points needs to be explained on a more realistic basis. The evidence would appear to suggest that many Christians are abandoning their religion, some of them moving to Buddhism. It would also appear that most of the lapsed Christians are Protestants. The Roman Catholics are not unaffected by these trends, but they are making converts among the Indian plantation workers. (It is estimated that 15% of Indian plantation workers are now Roman Catholic). The Church itself is less cohesive and monolithic than it was during much of the period of its rivalry and confrontation with the Buddhists. Today ethnic identity divides the Roman Catholics into two groups, the one Sinhalese and the other Tamil, each somewhat suspicious of the other, divisions which work themselves up through the hierarchy of a once self-confident and assertive priesthood.[13]

Secondly, language, the focal point of Sinhalese and Tamil ethnicity — has lost some if not much of its capacity to generate ethnic tensions. In theory Sinhalese has been the sole national language since 1956, but adjustments and modifications made to the original 'Sinhala Only' policy between 1958 and 1978 have all but conceded the parity of status for the two languages, Sinhalese and Tamils, which Tamil critics and opponents of the change of language policy introduced in 1956 have insisted upon.

A comparison with the language policies of Switzerland and India shows the Tamil language enjoying a surprisingly advantageous position in Sri Lanka. Thus, because the language rights guaranteed to the Tamils are operative in all parts of the island, and not merely in the north and the east, their practical value is at least on par with, if not superior to language rights available to the minority population groups in the cantons of Switzerland. The great majority of such cantons are "officially unilingual."[14] Indeed while "...Switzerland maintains more than one official language, the languages are spoken in clearly defined territorial areas."[15] Or again there is the comparison with the status of Tamil in India. Article 343(1) of the Indian Constitution is quite explicit on the question of the official language: "the official language of the Union shall be Hindi in the Devanagiri script." While English enjoys the status of a national language — as a "transitional" measure — Tamil is recognized as a regional language, in Tamilnadu. Like all other states in the Indian Union Tamilnadu is enjoined by the constitution to communicate with the central goverment and with other states, in Hindi. This is laid down in Article 346 of the constitution. Sri Lanka, by a curious irony, is the only sovereign state in which Tamil is recognized as a national language.

Above all there is a greater awareness in Sri Lanka today of the perils of the current situation where language divides the main ethnic groups just as conspicuously as, and with far more harmful effects politically than, the dominance of English which once separated the elite from the vernacular-speaking masses. The current Tamil discontent in the Jaffna peninsula and the north of the island adds a powerful political motivation to the cultural attractions of the resurgent Tamil linguistic nationalism across the Palk Straits. The new generation in the Jaffna peninsula and the north of the island no longer look in the direction of the south of the island as their parents and their grandparents did. They turn naturally enough to the stronger and more self-confident, if not more mature, culture of Tamilnadu. Linkages built through student life in Tamilnadu universities and colleges are strengthened by personal and political contacts in that state. Thus the division into two language streams causes a fissure in the Sri Lanka polity which is sufficiently damaging on its own to the stability of the country, but also becomes all the more threatening because of the powerful link the

Tamil language provides between one part of the Sri Lanka polity and Tamilnadu.

How to bridge this linguistic gulf between the Sinhalese and the Tamils exercises the minds of educationists and politicians alike. Two policy options have been considered: the use of English as a link language; and a policy of national bilingualism based on Sinhalese and Tamil. Both have their advantages and their flaws. Bilingualism — as the Canadian experience has shown — is not particularly well suited to situations where there are territorial concentrations of linguistic groups, and where the majority group is overwhelmingly superior in numbers. Sri Lanka, in addition, has other disadvantages. The two languages have each a distinctive script so that bilingualism in Sri Lanka confronts greater problems than one in a situation in which the two languages are based on a common script. In Canada the two languages involved are both major world languages; in Sri Lanka the Sinhalese majority see few personal advantages — especially economic advantages — in learning Tamil, a local and regional language, when a similar effort directed at learning English or any other world language would be of greater personal benefit. English, as a link language, has obvious advantages; apart from anything else it has served that purpose in Sri Lanka in the past, in helping to bridge the gap between the Sinhalese and Tamil elites. Yet it carries a disadvantage that it was, in the past, a symbol of the elite status against which the *swabasha* movement was directed, and memories of that elitism and the struggle against it still survive. Perhaps the only practical solution would be a three language formula with Sinhalese as the official language, and Tamil and English as national languages; trilingualism, would overcome the disadvantages of bilingualism in the Sri Lankan context.

Thirdly, a settlement has been devised on the status of Indian Tamils in Sri Lanka, and the terms of this settlement made between 1964 and 1974 as well the elaboration of this made since July 1977, constitute a major political accomplishment considering the passions and fears that this question has aroused since the late 1920s. Once agreement was reached on the number of Indians on whom Sri Lanka citizenship was to be granted, their inclusion within the "political nation" was accomplished over a twenty year period. Moreover, the number of Indians eventually admitted to Sri Lanka citizenship has proved to be larger than that agreed to in 1964 and 1974[16], and besides whenever the UNP has been in power during this period Indian plantation workers admitted to Indian citizenship have been permitted to remain in the island for the duration of their working lives through, what in effect was, an informal system of work permits.

The import of migrant workers from India — and to a lesser extent from China — to the British colonies in the nineteenth century and early decades of the twentieth was regarded as a short term solution to an urgent immediate problem, a shortage of labor in plantation agriculture and quite often in mining, in the docks, in sanitation, and in general the hard unpleasant work which the local population spurned. But whether these workers came in as indentured labor (to the British West Indies, Mauritius or Fiji), migratory workers from southern India to Sri Lanka, or as citizens of the British *raj* moving from one part of it to one of its newer units as was the case in Burma, all these host societies confronted enormous difficulties — political, economic and social — in absorbing these immigrants and migrants as nationals when the colonies became independent status. The policies adopted to cope with these problems, and the terms on which these migrant communities were granted the status of nationals of these new states, varied sharply, but on any comparative basis the treatment of the Indian minority in Sri Lanka is much more generous and humane than that in many other host societies. One does not need to use Uganda as an obvious contrast, for there are other and more appropriate contrasts closer at hand, and none more appropriate and closer than Burma. Or again there is the case of Fiji where Indians admitted to Fijian citizenship face restrictions on the right to hold land, and confront a political system that gives the Fijians — by now a minority of the population — a dominant position if not the status of a permanent majority.[17]

The British followed a quite different policy in Malaysia where the issue of citizenship rights of immigrant groups was settled *before* the transfer of power, and settled on terms more favorable to these groups than was the case in Sri Lanka and many other colonial societies. Of that decision itself one could say that it was one more example of British pragmatism at work, a concession to political realities; a Sri Lankan type of settlement of the citizenship issue in Malaysia was impossible at that time when the British still confronted a dire threat posed by insurgent forces. And again while the Indian Tamils in Sri Lanka constituted just over a tenth of the population, the immigrant community in Malaysia, Chinese and Indian was very nearly half the population. The Indians themselves were more than a tenth of the population. But the Indians, like the Chinese, in Malaysia have had to accept, as the central feature of the political system of present day Malaysia, the *bhumiputra* concept with constitutional provision made for a special superior status in the Malaysian polity for the Malays, and where this status is placed beyond politicial challenge, or even political or academic debate.

The fourth point is the accommodation reached in 1980 on decentralization of power. There the great difficulty had been Sinhalese — and Muslim — fears of the political implications to the Sri Lankan polity of any scheme of decentralization. Yet the principle was conceded in 1980, and embrodied in legislation and institutional form. There marked a remarkable determination to extend the scope available for creative political initiatives in an area that had hitherto been limited by a lack of political will. The Tamil commitment to decentralization is almost an obsession: it stems from a mixture of insecurity, and the urge to preserve their cultural identity from dilution or erosion in regions in which they are a majority or a substantial element of the population. It sets off pressures which stretch the limits of political action available to Sri Lankan politicians to the breaking point, where the alternatives that loom ahead are either electoral disaster for themselves, or major political breakdown.

The capacity of devolution of authority to regional units, be they districts or provinces or something larger than provinces, to reduce ethnic conflict is more limited than enthusiastic advocates of it are willing to concede. The great success stories often cited range from Switzerland, to India and contemporary Nigeria. In the first and third of these the dominance of the polities by the larger ethnic group, the German Swiss and the Hausa respectively is softened by the multiplicity of territorial units, provinces or states, all of which have some role to play in the control and exploitation of national resources. The states of the Indian Union are more or less equal in size and power, and none dominates the polity, or could seriously threaten secession without facing the political consequences which separatism invites when the acceptable and tolerable limits of its expression are exceded. Indeed

> "the conflict regulation potential of territorial autonomy [is limited]...
> when territorial units...make extravagent and even incompatible de-
> mands...which the polity cannot accomodate, thus escalating rather
> than regulating conflict."[18]

as was demonstrated by recent events in the Punjab.

The successful operation of the system of decentralization for Sri

Lanka envisaged in the *District Development Councils Act of 1980* calls for political skills of a high order, and also great patience. Pressure for decentralization of administration is limited to the Tamils, and to the north and east of the island in which the Tamils are either a majority or form a substantial minority. There is no pressure — on the contrary strong opposition to it — from all other ethnic groups and all other parts of the island. Quite apart from the fears of the Sinhalese majority, these are the fears of the Muslim minority especially those living in the Eastern Province whose pent up hostility to the Tamils there erupted with fearful ferocity in a major outbreak of communal violence, Muslim against Tamil, and *vice-versa*, in April 1985. In other words devolution of power to units larger than a district or a province is perceived as threatening the smaller minority — the Muslims — in areas in which a larger minority — the Tamils — would be likely to dominate the affairs of a large territorial unit, a province or a regional unit linking provinces. But most important of all the close proximity of the Jaffna region to Tamilnadu in southern India complicates the problem of conceding any great measure of autonomy to the districts or as the Tamils now demand, to provincial or regional councils, for fear that this would act as a spur to separatist pressures rather than serving as an effective check on them. The close links that were established in relations between Tamil political groups, ranging from the TULF to various separatist groups, and the government and opposition in the Southern Indian state of Tamilnadu have naturally aggravated the situation, and more so the establishment of training camps for terrorist groups and guerrillas who make raids into the northern and eastern coastal regions of Sri Lanka from these. And thus decentralization which was, and should be, a purely Sri Lankan matter has taken on a cross-national dimension of which India's role as mediator in the current political negotiations between the Sri Lankan government and representatives of Tamil opinion is the most conspicuous feature.

One unfortunate consequence of concentrating attention on district and provincial units — and, if Tamil opinion would have its way, even larger regional units — has been a neglect of one of the less controversial and more viable forms of decentralization — local government institutions at the municipal and urban council levels and village council levels. Over the last thirty years very little has been done to strengthen the financial bases of these councils, or their powers to initiate local development projects. On the contrary there has been an ever-increasing control over these bodies by the central government, in the name, generally, of efficiency and co-ordination of services and economic development, but in fact in the pursuit of political objectives designed to benefit the party in power. This tendency reached its peak in the period 1970-77. The result was that an important range of institutions which could be used for a genuine devolution of power through participatory democracy and local initiatives lost a great deal of their vitality. Moreover, in its anxiety to reach *some* agreement on the structure and functions of District Development Councils, the Presidential Commission of 1980 decided to abolish Village Councils and to transfer the functions of these bodies to local level units of the District Development Councils, and to informal (i.e., non-political) village organizations. That decision was based on a mixture of idealism and realism: that, the political divisions of a highly politicized society should not affect village organizations; and secondly, that the administrative costs of running these village councils had kept increasing to the point where very little money was left for development programs and such programs were of a distinctly *ad hoc* nature. After five years of this decision it is now clear that mechanisms and informal institutions substituted for Village Councils have not provided either the administrative efficiency or the responsiveness to local needs anticipated when they were instituted.

The fifth point is just as important as the other four, perhaps even more so in demonstrating a sensitivity to minority rights. None of the Sri Lankan governments since independence have deliberately or consistently pursued the assimilationist policies which some Asian countries — Burma, Indonesia and Thailand to name just three — impose on their minorities. The attitude to the minorities in Sri Lanka has been embodied in a number of policies seeking to reconcile a concern for national integration with a commitment to pluralism. This ranges from the concessions made to the Muslim minority in regard to their schools, to the recognition of the special needs of each religious group in the unrestricted practice of their religion, and the recognition through law of the traditional practices of the Muslims and Hindus in regard to marriage, divorce, inheritance and rights to property. It is also seen in the use of the Tamil language in the national insignia, coins and currency, in road signs, and official documents — many if not most of these documents appear in both Sinhalese and Tamil, or in Sinhalese, Tamil and English versions. Few countries in the world have as many national holidays — that is, apart from the week-end holidays — as Sri Lanka and at least a fourth of these are holidays of the ethnic and religious minorities. Not even in the face of the threat to national integrity from separatist demands has there been any attempt to reverse this policy, and to seek to assimilate the diverse minority groups in the country to the dominant Sinhalese-Buddhist culture.

Retrospect

In the decade after independence, there was every prospect that the country would have, and could have, developed a homogenous political culture. The tensions caused by linguistc nationalism put paid to that. Nevertheless, despite such tensions the island's political culture has not been fragmented to the point of rendering her democratic structure totally unstable. Divisions in Sri Lanka's poly-ethnic society are not mutually reinforcing points of divergence: thus while language is the essence of ethnic identity, the religious differences have so far been within the Sinhalese community, and the conflict between the Sinhalese and Tamils is not a clash of religions so much as one between two versions of linguistic nationalism even though the proportion of Christians to Hindus in the two Tamil minorities is much larger than the proportion of Christians to Buddhists among the Sinhalese. The proportions are around 15% each among the Tamils and around 5% among the Sinhalese, or one in every twenty Sinhalese is a Christian while one in every seven Tamils is a Christian.

In some of the smaller European democracies — Austria, Belgium and the Netherlands spring to mind as examples — where religious and or linguistic divisions have deep historical roots, political stability has been insured — since the second world war — by a deliberate lowering of expectations on both sides of the divide through the device of coalitions between communal parties. This same process has kept the Malaysian political system viable and stable since independence, and has helped to withstand the political tremors set off by the ethnic riots of May 1969. It was also effective as a stabilizing force in Sri Lankan politics in the years 1947-1955, and 1965-8. The major political premise of this accomodative policy is an explicit recognition of the cleavages — religious ethnic or linguistic — reflected by the political parties in the coalition. Although the process of government is then often reduced to a prosaic and humdrum search for areas of agreement between the contending factions, it has the great advantage of ensuring sensitivity to minority rights in the formulation and application of government policies.

Or again there is the example of another democracy with a deeply divided society, Canada, where the practice is one of proportionate representation of all politically-important elements of the Canadian people in the Cabinet whatever their contribution to the governing party's electoral victory. This was the prevailing practice in Sri Lanka under the UNP in the first decade after independence and there has been a return to it since 1977 when two Muslims, (there are 3 Muslims in the Cabinet now) two Tamils and an Indian Tamil have been appointed to the Cabinet which also has three Roman Catholics (one of whom is a Tamil): thus about a fourth of the places in the present Cabinet has gone to representatives of ethnic and religious minorities.

All these devices and strategies are directed at one crucially important issue, the inappropriateness of purely 'majoritarian' decision-making in severely divided societies. Where such cleavages exist, are both sharp and highly politicized, political stability is ensured, if not guaranteed, by devising institutional arrangements for effective access to decision-making to the minorities, and in so doing affording them a sense of security and the power of self-protection. Sri Lanka's record in this regard has been more constructive and imaginative than its recent history of the persistence of ethnic tensions and frequent eruptions of violence would lead us to believe. Except in regard to the period after July 1977 it would be true to say that ethnic tensions have generally occurred whenever governments have stressed majoritarian principles to the point of denying the legitimacy of cultural pluralism.

The capacity of the Sri Lankan political system to adjust, to compromise, to accomodate is one of the redeeming features of the recent history of the country especially of her history since independence. It is in the pragmatic strand in Sri Lankan politics that the hope lies for the eventual peaceful management of the ethnic issue in its present form, in the search for practical resolution of controversial issues, in the resort to makeshift and expediency, and in abjuring abstract theorizing and ideological intensity.

References

1   *The Soulbury Report*, p. 49.

2   *Ibid*, p. 50.

3   *Ibid*.

4   The debate on this issue is conveniently summarized in pp. 21-41, *Sri Lanka: The Ethnic Conflict, Myths, Realities and Perspectives* (new Delhi, 1984, for the Committee on Rational Development, Colombo); see also *Inter-racial Equity and National Unity in Sri Lanka* (Marga Institute, Colombo, 1984).

5   S.W.R. de A. Samarasinghe, 'Ethnic Representation in Central Government Employment in Sri Lanka, 1948-1981' (eds) Robert B. Goldmann and A. Jeyaratnam Wilson *From Independence to Statehood: Managing Ethnic Conflict in Five African and Asian States* (London, 1984) pp. 173-184.

6   In the *University of Ceylon Review*, Vol. XIII (1955) pp. 113-134.

7   Samarasinghe, *op. cit.*, pp. 179-180.

8   *Ibid*.

9   Myron Weiner, *Sons of the Soil: Migration and Ethnic Conflict in India* (Princeton, 1978) p. 173.

10   Memorial of the Jaffna Association to W.H. Long. Secretary of State for the Colonies, 2 January 1918. It was enclosed in a dispatch from Governor Sir John Anderson, to Long, 81 of 8 April 1918 in C.O54/854.

11   C.O.537/697, Sir Hugh Clifford's secret dispatch to L.S. Amery of 20 November 1926.

12   *The Soulbury Report*, p. 70.

13   For an insightful analysis of the current problems of the Roman Catholic Church in Sri Lanka see R.L. Stirrat, "The Riots [of 1983] and the Roman Catholic Church in Historical Perspective" in (ed) James Manor, *Sir Lanka in Change and Crisis* (London, 1984), pp. 196-213.

14   Carol L. Schmid, *Conflict and Consensus in Switzerland* (Berkeley, 1981) p. 20.

15   *Ibid*.

16   One of the more fruitful results of the abortive All Party Conference of 1984 was the decision that 94,000 stateless persons — Indian plantation workers — should be granted Sri Lankan citizenship. This recommendation was accepted by the government, and implemented in January 1986. There will be no more "stateless" persons resident in the island. The plantation workers would fall into two clear categories: Sri Lankan citizens, and those with Indian citizenship but resident in the island for the duration of their working lives.

In terms of the Indo-Sri Lankan agreements of 1964 and 1974, 600,000 persons plus their natural increase were to be granted Indian citizenship. Up to the end of 1984 only 419,943 plus a natural increase of 168,606 had been granted such citizenship. 335,980 had left for India along with 123,823 children of such persons.

17   There is also the case of Guyana where a complex electoral system has been devised to the disadvantage of the 'East' Indian community.

18   Milton T. Esman, 'The Management of Communal Conflct' in *Public Policy* XXI, Winter 1972, pp. 49-78. The quotation is from p. 64.

BIBLIOGRAPHY

I
Sri Lanka — General

The following is a list of short introductory surveys of the island's history and politics.

S. Arasaratnam   *Ceylon* (Englewood Cliffs, 1964).

K.M. de Silva   'Historical Survey' in K.M. de Silva (ed.) *Sri Lanka, A Survey*, (London, 1977), pp. 31-85.

B.H. Farmer   *Ceylon, A Divided Nation*, (London, 1963).

E. Meyer   *Ceylon (Sri Lanka)*, (Paris, 1977), (in French).

S.A. Pakeman   *Ceylon*, (London, 1964).

U. Phadhnis   *Sri Lanka*, (Delhi, 1973).

Books and Monographs on Sri Lanka — History and Politics

R. Coomaraswamy, *Sri Lanka: The Crisis of the Anglo-American Constitutional Traditions in a Developing Society*, (Delhi, 1984).

J.A.L. Cooray, *Constitutional and Administrative Law of Sri Lanka (Ceylon)*, (Colombo, 1973).
Constitutional Government and Human Rights in a Developing Society, (Colombo, 1969).

K.M. de Silva, *A History of Sri Lanka*, (London, 1981).
(ed.) The University of Ceylon, *History of Ceylon*, Vol. III, (Colombo, 1973).
(ed) *Sri Lanka, A Survey*, (London, 1977).

Social Policy and Missionary Organizations in Ceylon, 1840-1855, (London, 1965).
(ed) *Universal Suffrage, 1931-1981: The Sri Lankan Experience* (Colombo, 1981).

T.D.S.A. Dissanayake, *The Agony of Sri Lanka: An In-depth Account of the Racial Riots of July 1983*, (Colombo, 1983).

T. Fernando and R.N. Kearney, *Modern Sri Lanka: A Society in Transition*, (Syracuse, 1978).

Martin E. Gold, *Law and Social Change. A Study of Land Reform in Sri Lanka*, (New York, 1977).

F. Houtart, *Religion and Ideology in Sri Lanka*, (Colombo, 1974).

Inter-racial Equity and National Unity in Sri Lanka, Colombo, The Marga Institute, 1984).

V.K. Jayawardena, *The Rise of the Labour Movement in Ceylon*, (Durham, North Carolina, 1972).

Sir Charles Jeffries, *Ceylon, The Path to Independence*, (London, 1962).

Sir Ivor Jennings, *The Constitution of Ceylon*, (3rd ed. London, 1953).
The Economy of Ceylon, (2nd ed. London, 1951).
and H.W. Tambiah, *The Dominion of Ceylon*, (London, 1952).

J. Jiggins, *Caste and Family in the Politics of the Sinhalese 1947-1976*, (Cambridge, 1979).

J. Jupp, *Sri Lanka, Third World Democracy*, (London, 1978).

H.N.S. Karunatilake, *Economic Development in Ceylon*, (New York, 1971).

R.N. Kearney, *Communalism and Language in the Politics of Ceylon*, (Durham, North Carolina, 1967).
The Politics of Ceylon (Sri Lanka), (Ithaca, N.Y. 1973).
Trade Unions and Politics in Ceylon, (Berkeley, 1971).

S.U. Kodikara, Indo-Ceylon Relations since Independence, (Colombo, 1965).

E.R. Leach (ed.), *Aspects of Caste in South India, Ceylon and North-West Pakistan*, (Cambridge, 1960).

G.R.T. Leitan, *Local Government and Decentralized Administration in Sri Lanka, (Colombo, 1979)*.

G. Lerski, Origins of Trotskyism in Ceylon, (Stanford, 1968).

E.F.C. Ludowyk, *The Modern History of Ceylon*, (London, 1966).

K. Malagoda, *Buddhism in Sinhalese Society, 1750-1900*, (Berkeley, 1976).

James Manor (ed.), *Sri Lanka in Change and Crisis*, (London, 1984).

S. Namasivayam, *The Legislatures of Ceylon*, (London, 1951).

R.F. Nyrop, *et. al.* (eds.), *An Area Handbook for Ceylon*, (Washington, D.C., 1974).

B. Pfaffenberger, *Caste in Tamil Culture: The Religious Foundations of Sudra Domination in Tamil Sri Lanka*, (Syracuse, 1982).

Satchi Ponnambalam, *Sri Lanka, the National Question and the Tamil Liberation Struggle*, (London, 1983).

Bhikkhu Rahula, *The Heritage of the Bhikkhu*, (N.Y., 1974).

M.W. Roberts, *Caste Conflict and Elite Formation. The Rise of a Karava Elite in Sri Lanka, 1500-1931*, Cambridge, 1982).
(ed.), *Documents of the Ceylon National Congress and Nationalist Politics in Ceylon, 1929-1950*, 4 Vols. (Colombo, 1978).
(ed.) *Collective Identities, Nationalism and Protest in Sri Lanka during the Modern Era*, (Colombo, 1978).

Jane Russell, *Communal Politics under the Donoughmore Constitution, 1931-1947*, (Colombo, 1983).

Carol L. Schmid, *Conflict and Consensus in Switzerland* (Berkeley, 1982).

Marshall R. Singer, *The Emerging Elite: A Study of Political Leadership in Ceylon*, (Cambridge, Mass., 1964).

D.E. Smith (ed.), *South Asian Politics and Religion*, (Princeton, N.Y., 1966).

D.R. Snodgrass, *Ceylon: An Export Economy in Transition*, (Homewood, Illinois, 1966).

Sri Lanka: The Ethnic Conflict. Myths, Realities and Perspectives, (New Delhi, 1983) (for Committee for Rational Development, Colombo).

D.C. Vijayavardhana, *The Revolt in the Temple*, (Colombo, 1953).

W.A. Wisva Warnapala and L. Dias Hewagama, *Recent Politics in Sri Lanka*, (New Delhi, 1983).

I.D.S. Weerawardene, *Government and Politics in Ceylon 1931-1946*, (Colombo, 1951).

A.J. Wilson, *Electoral Politics in an Emergent State: The Ceylon General Election of May 1970*, (Cambridge, 1975).
Politics in Sri Lanka, 1947-1979, (London, 1979).
The Gaullist System in Asia, The Sri Lanka, Constitution of 1978, (London, 1980).

Calvin Woodward, *Growth of a Party System in Ceylon*, (Providence, Rhode Island, 1969).

W. Howard Wriggins, *Ceylon: Dilemmas of a New Nation*, (Princeton, N.J., 1960).

III

Unpublished Theses Consulted

K.N.O. Dharmadasa, "The Rise of Sinhalese Language Nationalism: A Study in the Sociology of Language" (Ph.D. Monash, 1979).

A. Sivaraja, "The Strategy of an Ethnic Minority Party in Government and in Opposition: The Tamil Federal Party of Sri Lanka (1956-1970)". MA (Political Science) University of New Brunswick, 1978.

IV

Bibliographies

H.A.I. Goonetileke, *A Bibliography of Ceylon: A Systematic Guide to the Literature on the Land, People, History and Culture Published in the Western Languages from the Sixteenth Century to the Present day.* 5 Volumes. (Zug, Switzerland, 1970-1983).

Daya and C.R. de Silva, *Sri Lanka (Ceylon) Since Independence (1948-1976)* (Hamburg, 1978).

V

General Works on Ethnicity and Politics

B. Anderson, *Imagined Communities*, (London, 1983).

Marguerite R. Barnett, *The Politics of Cultural Nationalism in South India*, (Princeton, N.J. 1976).

F. Barth (ed.), *Ethnic Groups and Boundaries*, (London, 1969).

Paul R. Brass, *Language, Religion and Politics in North India*, (Cambridge, 1974).

J. Das Gupta, *Language Conflict and National Development*, (Berkeley, 1970).

K. Deutsch, *Nationalism and its Alternatives*, (Knopf, 1969).
Nationalism and Social Communication, (Cambridge, Mass., 1953).

G. de Vos and L. Romanucci-Ross (eds), *Ethnic Identity, Cultural Continuities and Change*, (Palo-Alto, 1976).

R. Emerson, *From Empire to Nation*, (Boston, 1960).

Cynthia Enloe, *Ethnic Conflict and Political Development*, (Boston, 1973).
Ethnic Soldiers, (Harmondsworth, 1982).

Joshua A. Fishman, *Language and Nationalism*, (Newbury House, Rowley, Mass., 1971).

Joshua A. Fishman, C. Ferguson and J. Das Gupta (eds), *Language Problems of Developing Nations* (N.Y., 1968).

N. P. Gist and A.G. Dworkin (eds)., *The Blending of Races*, (N.Y., 1972).

N. Glazer and D.P. Moynihan, *Beyond the Melting Pot*, (Cambridge, Mass., 1970).
(eds), *Ethnicity, Theory and Experience*, (Cambridge, Mass., 1975).

R.B. Goldmann and A. Jeyaratnam Wilson (eds), *From Independence to Statehood: Managing Ethnic Conflict in Five African and Asian States*, (London, 1983).

G. Gunatilleke, N. Tiruchelvam and R. Coomaraswamy (eds), *Ethical Dilemmas of Development in Asia*, (Lexington, 1983).

T.S. Kang (ed), *Nationalism and the Crisis of Ethnic Minorities in Asia*, (Westport, Greenwood Press, 1979).

E. Kedourie (ed.), *Nationalism in Asia and Africa*, (London, 1970).

A. Lijphart, *Democracy in Plural Societies*, (Yale, 1977).
The Politics of Accomodation: Pluralism and Democracy in the Netherlands, (Berkeley, 1968).

K. McRae (ed.), *Consociational Democracy: Political Accomodation in Segmented Societies*, (Toronto, 1974).

Mahathir bin Mohamad, *The Malay Dilemma*, (Kuala Lumpur, 1970).

Baldev Raj Nayar, *National Communication and Language Policy in India*, (N.Y., 1969).

E. Nordlinger, *Conflict Regulation in Divided Societies*, (Cambridge, Mass., 1972).

A. Rabushka and K.A. Shepsie, *Politics in Plural societies: A Theory of Democratic Instability*, (N.Y., 1972).

William R. Roff, *The Origins of Malay Nationalism*, (London, 1967).

Donald Rothschild and V.A. Olorunsola, *State Versus Ethnic Claims: African Policy Dilemmas*, (Boulder, Colorado, 1983).

Joseph Rothschild, *Ethnopolitics: A Conceptual Framework*, (New York, 1981).

Anil Seal, *The Emergence of Indian Nationalism*, (Cambridge, 1971).

A.D. Smith, *State and Nation in the Third World*, (London, 1983).
The Ethnic Revival in the Modern World, (London, 1981).
Theories of Nationalism, 2nd ed. (London, 1982).

H. Tinker, *A New System of Slavery: The Export of Indian Labour Overseas, 1830-1920*, (London, 1974).
Separate and Unequal: India and the Indians in the British Commonwealth, 1920-1950, (London, 1976).
The Banyan Tree: Overseas Emigrants from India, Pakistan and Bangladesh, (Oxford, 1977).

K. von Vorys, *Democracy Without Consensus: Communalism and Political Stability in Malasia*, (Princeton, 1975).

M. Weiner, *Sons of the Soil: Migration and Ethnic Conflict in India*, (Princeton, N.J. 1978).

A. Jeyaratnam Wilson and Dennis Dalton (eds), *The States of South Asia: The Problems of National Integration*, (London, 1982).

C. Young, *The Politics of Cultural Pluralism*, (Madison, Wisconsin, 1976).

VI

Articles & Pamphlets — Sri Lanka

S. Arasaratnam, 'Nationalism, Communalism and National Unity in Ceylon,' in (ed) P. Mason, *India and Ceylon: Unity and Diversity*, (Oxford, 1967), pp. 260-278.

M. Banks, 'Caste in Jaffna' in E.R. Leach (ed.), *Aspects of Caste in South India, Ceylon and North West Pakistan*, pp. 61-77.

H. Bechert, 'Sangha, State, Society, Nation. Persistence of Tradition in 'Post-Traditional' Buddhist Societies'. *Daedalus*, Winter 1973, pp. 85-95.

The Betrayal of Buddhism. Report of the Unofficial Buddhist Committee of Inquiry, (Balangoda, Sri Lanka, 1956).

J. W. Bjorkman, 'Health Policy and Politics in Sri Lanka. Developments in the South Asian Welfare State.' *Asian Survey* XXV(5) May 1985, pp. 537-552.

Companion to the Buddhist Commission Report: A Commentary, (The Catholic Union of Ceylon, Colombo, 1957).

J.A.L. Cooray, *'The Revision of the Constitution'*, The Sir James Pieris Centenary Lecture, (Colombo, 1957).

Fr. P. Casperz, S.J. 'The Role of Sri Lanka Christians in a Buddhist Majority System' in *The Ceylon Journal of Historical & Social Studies*, (hereafter *CJHSS)* n.s. IV (1 & 2) pp. 104-110.

K.N.O. Dharmadasa, 'Language and Sinhalese Nationalism: The career of Munidasa Cumaranatunga,' *Modern Ceylon Studies*, III (2), pp. 125-143.

C.R. de Silva, 'The Constitution of the Second Republic of Sri Lanka (1978) and its Significance'. *The Journal of Commonwealth and Comparative Politics*, XVII (2) pp. 192-209.
'The Politics of University Admissions: A review of some aspects of the admissions policy in Sri Lanka 1971-1978', *Sri Lanka Journal of Social Sciences*, I (2) pp. 85-132.
'The Representational System' *CJHSS*, VII (2), 25-35.
'Weightage in University Admissions. Standardization and District quotas in Sri Lanka'. *Modern Ceylon Studies*, V (2) pp. 152-178.

K.M. de Silva, 'A Tale of Three Constitutions: 1946-48, 1972 and 1978', *CJHSS*, n.s. VII (2), pp. 1-17.
'Discrimination in Sri Lanka' W.A. Veenhoven (ed) in *Case Studies on Human Rights and Fundamental Freedoms: A World Survey*, 5 Vols. (The Hague, 1975-77), Vol. III, pp. 71-110.
'Nationalism and Its Impact' in *CJHSS*, n.s. IV (1 & 2), pp. 62-72.
'The Transfer of Power in Sri Lanka: British Perspectives. *ibid*, pp. 8-19.

M. Fernando, 'Fundamental Rights and the Constitution', *CJHSS*, n.s. VII (2), pp. 51-60.

T. Fernando, 'Elite Politics in the New States. The case of post-independence Sri Lanka', *Pacific Affairs*, XLVI (3), pp. 361-383.

G. Gunatilleke, N. Tiruchelvam and R. Coomaraswamy, 'Violence and Development in Sri Lanka: Conceptual Issues', in G. Gunatilleke *et al* (eds), *Ethical Dilemmas of Development in Asia*, 1983, pp. 129-178.

F. Halliday, 'The Ceylonese insurrection' in *New Left Review*, in October 1971, reprinted in (ed.) R. Blackburn, *Explosion in a Sub-Continent*, (Harmondsworth, 1975), pp. 151-220.

R. Jayaraman, 'Indian Emigration to Ceylon: Some Aspects of the Historical and Social Background of the Emigrants. *The Indian Economic and Social History Review*, IV (4) 1967, pp. 319-359.

Sir Ivor Jennings, 'Nationalism and Political Development in Ceylon' *Ceylon Historical Journal*, III (1-4) pp. 62-85, 99-114, 197-206.
'Politics in Ceylon since 1951,' *Pacific Affairs*, XXVIII (4) pp. 338-353.
'The Making of a Dominion Constitution' *The Law Quarterly Review*, (October, 1949), pp. 456-79.

R.N. Kearney, 'Educational Expansion and political volatility in Sri Lanka', *Asian Survey*, XV (9), pp. 727-44.
'Ethnic Conflict and the Tamil Separatist Movement in Sri Lanka.' *Asian Survey*, XXV (9) pp. 898-917.
'Sinhalese nationalism and social conflict in Ceylon', *Pacific Affairs*, XXXVII, pp. 125-136.

R.N. Kearney, and J. Jiggins, 'The Ceylon Insurrection of 1971'. *The Journal of Commonwealth and Comparative Politics*, XIII (1) pp. 40-64.

E.R. Leach, 'Buddhism in the post-colonial order in Burma and Ceylon' *Daedalus*, (Winter, 1973).

K. Malalgoda, "Buddhism in post-independence Sri Lanka', *CJHSS*, XX (2), pp. 93-97.
'The Buddhist-Christian Confrontation in Ceylon 1800-1880', *Social Compass*, XX (2) pp. 171-200.
'Millenialilsm in Relation to Buddhism', *Comparative Studies in Society and History*, XII (4), pp. 421-41.

S. Nadesan, *Ceylon's Language Problem*, (Colombo, 1956).

R. Oberst, 'Democracy and the Persistance of Westernized Elite Dominance in Sri Lanka,' *Asian Survey* XXV (7) pp. 760-772.

G. Obeysekere, 'Religious Symbolism and Political Change in Ceylon' *Modern Ceylon Studies*, 1 (1), pp. 43-63.
'The Sinhalese-Buddhist identity' in G. de Vos and L. Roma-nucci-Ross (eds), *Ethnic Identity, Cultural Continuities and Change*, (Palo Alto, 1976.)
'The Origins and Institutionalisation of Political Violence' in James Manor (ed.) *Sri Lanka in Change and Crisis*, 1984, pp. 153-174.

R.S. Perinbanayagam and Maya Chadda, 'Strategy of internal relations: An examination of the conflict in Ceylon' in Tai S. Kang (ed.), *Nationalism and the Crises of Ethnic Minorities in Asia*, Westport, Connecticut, Greenwood Press, 1979, pp. 132-138.

B. Pfaffenberger, 'The Cultural Dimension of Tamil Separatism in Sri Lanka', *Asian Survey*, XXI (12), pp. 1145-57.

Michael Roberts, 'Elites, Nationalism, and The Nationalist Movement in Ceylon' pp. xxix to ccxxii, introduction to Michael Roberts (ed), *Documents of the Ceylon National Congress*, Vol. I.
'Ethnic Conflict in Sri Lanka and Sinhalese Perspectives: Barriers to Accomodation', *Modern Asian Studies*, VII (3) pp. 353-376.
''Problems of Social Stratification and the Demarcation of National and Local Elites in British Ceylon,' *Journal of Asian Studies*, XXXIII (4), pp. 549-577.

J.E.M. Russell, 'The Dance of the Turkey-Cock — The Jaffna Boycott of 1931' in *CJHSS*, VIII (1), pp. 47-67.
'Sri Lanka's Election Turning Point' (The General Election of 1977), *The Journal of Commonwealth and Comparative Politics*, XVI (1) pp. 79-97.

S.W.R. de A. Samarasinghe, 'Ethnic Representation in Central Government Employment and Sinhala-Tamil relations in Sri Lanka, 1948-81' in R.B. Goldmann and A. Jeyaratnam Wilson (eds) *From Independence to Statehood*, pp. 86-108.

V. Samaraweera, 'The Evolution of a Plural Society' in K.M. de Silva (ed.) *Sri Lanka, A Survey*, pp. 86-108.
'Sri Lanka's 1977 General Election: The Resurgence of the UNP' *Asian Survey*, XVIII (12), pp. 1195-1206.

W. Schwarz, *The Tamils of Sri Lanka*, Minority Rights Group Report No. 25, (London, revised ed. 1979).

Donald E. Smith, 'The political monks and monastic reform' in Donald
    E. Smith (ed.) *South Asian Politics and Religion*, pp. 489-501.
    'The Sinhalese-Buddhist revolution', *ibid.*, pp. 453-88.

R.L. Stiratt, 'The Riots and the Roman Catholic Church in Historical
    Perspective', in James Manor (ed.) *Sri Lanka in Change and
    Crisis*, 1984, pp. 196-213.

S.J. Tambiah, 'Ethnic Representation in Ceylon's Higher Admini-
    strative Services, 1870-1946' *University of Ceylon Review*, XIII (2
    & 3) pp. 113-34.
    'The Politics of Language in India and Ceylon' *Modern Asian
    Studies*, 1 (3) pp. 215-40.

N. Tiruchelvam, 'The Making and Unmaking of Constitutions —Some
    Reflections on the Process', *CJHSS*, VII (2) pp. 18-24.

Xavier S. Thaninayagam, 'Language rights in Ceylon', *Tamil Culture*, V
    (3) pp. 217-230.

L.A. Wickremaratne, 'Kandyans and Nationalism: Some Reflections',
    CJHSS, n.s. V (1 & 2) pp. 49-68.

A.J. Wilson, 'Ethnicity, national development and the political process
    in Ceylon' in B. Grossman (ed.) *South East Asia in the Modern
    World* (Hamburg, 1972), pp. 151-164.
    'Minority Safeguards in the Ceylon Constitution', *CJHSS*, 1 (1)
    1958, pp. 73-95.
    'Oppositional politics in Ceylon 1948-1968', *Government and
    Opposition* IV (1), pp. 54-69; reprinted in *The Opposition in the
    New States* (ed.) Rodney Barker, (London, 1972).
    'The Tamil Federal Party in Ceylon Politics', *The Journal of
    Commonwealth Political Studies*, IV (2) pp. 117-139.
    "Sri Lanka and its Future: Sinhalese versus Tamils", in A.J.
    Wilson and D. Dalton (eds), *The States of South Asia*, 1982, pp.
    295-312.

W. Howard Wriggins, 'Impediments to unity in new nations. The case
    of Ceylon'. *The American Political Science Review*, LV (2) pp. 313-
    21.

VII

Articles and Pamphlets — General

A. H. Birch, 'Minority Nationalist Movements and Theories of Political
    Integration' *World Politics*, Vol. 33, 1978, pp. 325-344.

Walker Connor, "Nation-Building or Nation-Destroying?" *World Politics*, Vol. 24, 1972, pp. 319-55.
'The Politics of Ethnonationalism' *Journal of International Affairs*, Vol. 27, 1973, pp. 1-21.
'A Nation is a Nation, is a State, is an Ethnic Group, is a...' *Ethnic and Racial Studies*, Vol. 1 (4) 1978, pp. 377-400.

J. Das Gupta, 'Ethnicity, Language Demands and National Development in India', in Glazer and Moynihan (eds) *Ethnicity: Theory and Experience*, pp. 29-52.

Milton J. Esman, "The Management of Communal Conflict" in *Public Policy*, Vol. 21 (1) 1973, pp. 49-78.

Joshua A. Fishman, 'Nationality-Nationalism' in Joshua A. Fishman *et al* (eds) *Language Problems of Developing Nations*, pp. 39-51.

C. Geertz, 'The Integrative Revolution' in C. Geertz (ed.) *Old Societies and New States: The Quest for Modernity in Africa and Asia*, (New york, 1963) pp. 105-57.

A.H. Halsey, 'Ethnicity: a primordial social bond' *Ethnic and Racial Studies*, 1 (1) 1978, pp. 124-8.

M. Hechter, 'The Political Economy of Ethnic Change' *The American Journal of Sociology*, 79 (5) 1973, pp. 1151-1178.

Donald L. Horowitz, 'Ethnic Identity' in Glazer and Moynihan (eds) *Ethnicity: Theory and Experience*, pp. 111-140.

N. Rosh White, 'Ethnicity, Culture and Cultural Pluralism'. *Ethnic and Racial Studies*, Vol. (2) 1978, pp. 139-53.

V. Selvaratnam, 'Intercommunal Relations and Problems of Socio-Economic Development: The Malaysian Dilemma', in G. Gunatilleke *et al* (eds) *Ethical Dilemmas of Development in Asia*, 1982, pp. 97-128.

A.D. Smith, 'The Diffusion of Nationalism', *British Journal of Sociology*, Vol. 29, 1978, pp. 234-48.

A.J. Stockwell, 'British Imperial Policy and Decolonization in Malaya, 1942-52', *The Journal of Imperial and Commonwealth History*, XIII (1) October 1984, pp. 68-87.
"The White Man's Burden and Brown Humanity: Colonialism and Ethnicity in British Malaya", in *The Southeast Asian Journal of Social Science*, Vol. 10 1982, pp. 44-68.

J. Stone, 'Introduction: Internal Colonialism in Comparative Perspective", *Ethnic and Racial Studies*, Vol. 2 (3) 1979, pp. 255-9.

R.H. Taylor, 'Perceptions of Ethnicity in the Politics of Burma', in *The Southeast Asian Journal of Social Science*, Vol. 10 (1) 1982, pp. 7-22.

C.J. Thomas and C.H. Williams, 'Language and Nationalism in Wales: a case study', *Ethnic and Racial Studies* (Vol. 1 (2) 1978, pp. 235-58.

M. Yapp, 'Language, religion and political identity: a general framework' in D. Taylor & M. Yapp (eds) *Political Identity in South Asia*, London, 1979, pp. 1-34.

APPENDICES

DOCUMENTS

I

from The Ministers' Draft Constitution of 1944, Sessional Paper XIV of 1944

7.   Parliament may make laws for the peace, order and good government of Ceylon.

8.   In the exercise of its power under Article 7 Parliament shall not make any law —

(a)   to prohibit or restrict the free exercise of any religion; or

(b)   to make persons of any community or religion liable to disabilities or restrictions to which persons of other communities or religions are not made liable; or

(c)   to confer on persons of any community or religion any privileges or advantages which are not conferred on persons of other communities or religions; or

(d)   to alter the constitution of any religious body except with the approval of the governing authority of that religious body.

II

The Ceylon (Constitution) Order-in-Council, 1946

29.   (1)   Subject to the provisions of this Order, Parliament shall have power to make laws for the peace, order and good government of the Island.

(2)   No such law shall —

(a)   prohibit or restrict the free exercise of any religion; or

(b)   make persons or any community or religion liable to disabilities or restrictions to which persons of other communities or religions are not made liable; or

(c)   confer on persons of any community or religion any privilege or advantage which is not conferred on persons of other communities or religions; or

(d)   alter the constitution of any religious body except with the consent of the governing authority of that body:

Provided that, in any case where a religious body is incorporated by law, no such alteration shall be made except at the request of the governing authority of that body.

(3)   Any law made in contravention of subsection (2) of this section shall, to the extent of such contravention, be void.

(4)   In the exercise of its powers under this section, Parliament may amend or repeal any of the provisions of this Order, or of any other Order of His Majesty in Council in its application to the Island:

Provided that no Bill for the amendment or repeal of any of the provisions of this Order shall be presented for the Royal Assent unless it has endorsed on it a certificate under the hand of the Speaker that the number of votes cast in favour thereof in the House of Representatives amounted to not less than two-thirds of the whole number of members of the House (including those not present).

Every certificate of the Speaker under this subsection shall be conclusive for all purposes and shall not be questioned in any court of law.

III

The Official Language Act,
No. 33 of 1956

An Act to prescribe the Sinhala Language as the One Official Language of Ceylon and to enable certain transitory provisions to be made.

(Date of Assent: July 7, 1956)

Be it enacted by the Queen's Most Excellent Majesty by and with the advice and consent of the Senate and the House of Represeratives of Ceylon in this present Parliament assembled, and by the authority of the same, as follows: —

Short Title

1.   This Act may be cited as the Official Language Act, No. 33 of 1956.

Sinhala Language to be the one official language

2.   The Sinhala language shall be the one official language of Ceylon:

Provided that where the Minister considers it impracticable to commence the use of only the Sinhala language for any official purpose immediately on the coming into force of this Act, the language or languages hitherto used for that purpose may be continued to be so used until the necessary change is effected as early as possible before the expiry of the thirty-first of December, 1960, and, if such change cannot be effected by administrative order, regulations may be made under this Act to effect such change.

Regulations

3.   (1)   The Minister may make regulations in respect of all matters for which regulations are authorized by this Act to be made and generally for the purpose of giving effect to the principles and provisions of this Act.

(2)   No regulation made under sub-section (1) shall have effect until it is approved by the Senate and the House of Representatives and notification of such approval is published in the Gazette.

IV

The Tamil Language (Special Provisions) Act, No. 28 of 1958

An Act to make provision for the use of the Tamil language and to provide for matters connected therewith or incidental thereto.

(Date of Assent: September 4, 1958)

Whereas the Sinhala language has been declared by the Official Language Act, No. 33 of 1956, to be the one official language of Ceylon:

And whereas it is expedient to make provision for the use of the Tamil language without conflicting with the provisions of the aforesaid Act:

Be it enacted by the Queen's Most Excellent Majesty, by and with the advice and consent of the Senate and the House of Representatives of Ceylon in this present Parliament assembled, and by the authority of the same, as follows:

Short Title

1.   This act may be cited as the Tamil Language (Special Provisions) Act, No. 28 of 1958.

Tamil language as a medium of instruction.

2.   (1) A Tamil pupil in a Government school or an Assisted school shall be entitled to be instructed through the medium of the Tamil language in accordance with such regulations under the Education Ordinance, No. 31 of 1939, relating to the medium of instruction as are in force or may hereafter be brought into force.

(2)   When the Sinhala language is made a medium of instruction in the University of Ceylon, the Tamil language shall, in accordance with the provisions of the Ceylon University Ordinance, No. 20 of 1942, and of the Statutes, Acts and Regulations made thereunder, be made a medium of instruction in such University for students who prior to their admission to such University, have been educated through the medium of the Tamil Language.

Tamil Language as a medium of examination for admission to the Public Service

3.   A person educated through the medium of the Tamil language shall be entitled to be examined through such medium at any examination for the admission of persons to the Public Service, subject to the condition that he shall, according as regulations made under this act on that behalf may require, —

(a)   have a sufficient knowledge of the official language of Ceylon, or

(b)   Acquire such knowledge within a specified time after admission to the Public Service:

Provided that, when the Government is satisfied that there are sufficient facilities for the teaching of the Sinhala language in schools in which the Tamil language is a medium of instruction and that the annulment of clause (b) of the preceding provisions of this section will not cause undue hardship, provision may be made by regulation, made under this Act that such clause shall cease to be in force.

Use of the Tamil language for correspondence.

4.   Correspondence between persons, other than officials in their official capacity, educated through the medium of the Tamil language and any official in his official capacity or between any local authority in the Northern or Eastern Province and any official in his official capacity may, as prescribed, be in the Tamil language.

Use of the Tamil language for prescribed administrative purposes in the Northern and Eastern Provinces

5.   In the Northern and Eastern Provinces the Tamil language may be used for prescribed administrative purposes, in addition to the purposes for which that language may be used in accordance with the other provisions of this Act, without prejudice to the use of the official language of Ceylon in respect of those prescribed administrative purposes.

Regulations

6.   (1) The Minister may make regulations to give effect to the principles and provisions of this Act.

(2)   No regulation made under sub-section (1) shall have effect until it is

approved by the Senate and the House of Representatives and notification of such approval is published in the Gazette.

This Act to be subject to measures adopted or to be adopted under the proviso to section 2 of Act No. 33 of 1956.

7.   This Act shall have effect subject to such measures as may have been or may be adopted under the proviso to section 2 of the Official Language Act, No. 33, of 1956, during the period ending on the thirty-first day of December, 1960.

Interpretation

8.   In this Act unless the context otherwise requires "Assisted school" and "Government school" shall have the same meaning as in the Education Ordinance, No. 31 of 1939;

"local authority" means any Municipal Council, Urban Council, Town Council or Village Committee;

"official" means the Governor General, or any Minister, Parliamentary Secretary or officer or the Public Service; and "prescribed" means prescribed by regulation made under this Act.

V

RESOLUTIONS PASSED

At the 5th (special) National Convention of
the Federal Party held on 28 July 1957 at
Batticaloa

Resolution-No. 1

"This special session of the National Convention of the Ilankai Tamil Arasu Kadchi assembled at the Town Hall Batticaloa on the 28th of July 1957 having considered the agreement reached between the representatives of the Federal Party on the one hand and the Prime Minister on the other and having reviewed the report of the negotiations submitted to it by its representatives reiterates its unalterable determination to achieve

(1)   An Autonomous Tamil linguistic state or states within the framework of a Federal Union of Ceylon,

(2)   Parity of status for the Tamil language with Sinhalese throughout Ceylon and,

(3)   The revision and reorientation of the present unnatural and undemocratic ctiizenship laws of Ceylon to ensure the recognition of the right of every Tamil speaking individual who has made Ceylon his home to full citizenship.

"This convention having regard to the fact that by the agreement *inter alia*,

(a)   state-aided Sinhalese colonisation of the Northern and Eastern provinces will be effectively stopped forthwith.

(b)   that the Tamil language is given official recognition as the language of a National Minority,

(c)   That Tamil shall be the language of administration of the Northern and Eastern provinces,

(d)   that the right of every Tamil speaking person in every part of the country to transact all affairs with government in KTamil and to educate and nurture his children in the Tamil language and culture is secured,

(e)   and further in consideration of the large measure of regional self government granted to the people under the proposed Regional Councils Act.

"Resolves to accept the agreement as an interim adjustment and hereby ratifies the decision to withdraw the Satyagraha which was scheduled to commence on the 20th August 1957.

"This convention further calls upon the Government to implement expeditiously the terms of the agreement reached between the Prime Minister and the Federal Party expeditiously [sic] in good faith and in the spirit in which it was entered into."

Resolution - No. 2

This special session of the National Convention of the Ilankai Tamil Arasu Kadchi calls upon the Tamil speaking people who are struggling for the attainment of full freedom and self respect solemnly to resolve to work for the regeneration and unification of the Tamil speaking people by undertaking immediate action for the removal of all forms of social inequalities and injustices, in particular that of untouchability which still exists among a section of the people and towards this end to organize a campaign of self purification if necessary by Ahimsa and Satyagraha for the achievement of this goal without which the Tamil speaking Nation in Ceylon cannot and never will realise its fundamental object of attaining Political and Cultural freedom for the Tamil speaking people of Ceylon by the establishment of a Tamil linguistic state or states within the frame work of the Federal Union of Ceylon.

VI

The "Bandaranaike-Chelvanayakam Pact," July 26, 1957

Text of Joint Statements by Prime Minister and Representatives of the Federal Party

The following are the two joint statements issued by the Prime Minister and Representatives of the Federal Party on July 26:

Statement on the general principles of the Agreement between the Prime Minister and the Federal Party

"Representatives of the Federal Party have had a series of discussions with the Prime Minister in an effort to resolve the differences of opinion that had been growing and creating tension.

"At an early stage of these conversations it became evident that it was not possible for the Prime Minister to accede to some of the demands of the Federal Party.

"The Prime Minister stated that from the point of view of the Government he was not in a position to discuss the setting up of a federal constitution or regional autonomy or any step which would abrogate the Official Language Act. The question then arose whether it was possible to explore the possibility of an adjustment without the Federal Party abandoning or surrendering any of its fundamental principles and objectives.

"At this stage the Prime Minister suggested an examination of the Government's draft Regional Councils Bill to see whether provision could be made under it to meet reasonably some of the matters in this regard which the Federal Party had in view.

"The agreements so reached are embodied in a separate document.

"Regarding the language issue the Federal Party reiterated its stand for parity, but in view of the position of the Prime Minister in this matter they came to an agreement by way of an adjustment. They pointed out that it was important for them that there should be a recognition of Tamil as a national language and that the administration in the Northern and Eastern Provinces should be done in Tamil.

"The Prime Minister stated that as mentioned by him earlier it was not possible for him to take any step which would abrogate The Official Language Act.

[Use of Tamil] "After discussions it was agreed that the proposed legislation should contain recognition of Tamil as the language of a national minority of Ceylon, and that the four points mentioned by the Prime Minister should include provision that, without infringing on the position of the Official Language Act, the language of administration in the Northern and Eastern Provinces should be Tamil and that any necessary provision be made for the non-Tamil speaking minorities in the Northern and Eastern Provinces.

"Regarding the question of Ceylon citizenship for people of Indian descent and revision of the Citizenship act, the representatives of the Federal Party put forward their views to the Prime Minister and pressed for an early settlement.

"The Prime Minister indicated that this problem would receive early consideration.

"In view of these conclusions the Federal Party stated that they were withdrawing their proposed satyagraha."

Joint Statement by the Prime Minister and Representatives of the Federal Party on Regional Councils.

"(A)   Regional areas to be defined in the Bill itself by embodying them in a schedule thereto.

"(B)   That the Northern Province is to form one Regional area whilst the Eastern Province is to be divided into two or more Regional areas.

"(C)   Provision is to be made in the Bill to enable two or more regions to amalgamate even beyond provincial limits; and for one region to divide itself subject to ratification by Parliament. Further provision is to be made in the Bill for two or more regions to collaborate for specific purposes of common interest.

Direct Election]   "(D)   Provision is to be made for direct election of regional councillors. Provision is to be made for a delimitation Commission or Commissions for carving out electorates. The question of M.P.'s representing districts falling within regional areas to be eligible to function as chairman is to to be considered. The question of Government Agents being Regional Commissioners is to be considered. The question of supervisory functions over larger towns, strategic towns and municipalities is to be looked into.

Special Powers] "(E) Parliament is to delegate powers and to specify them in the Act. It was agreed that Regional Councils should have powers over specified subjects including agriculture, co-operatives, land and land develop- ment, colonisation, education, health, industries and fisheries, housing and social services, electricity, water schemes and roads. Requisite definition of powers will be made in the Bill.

Colonisation Schemes] "(F) It was agreed that in the matter of colonisation schemes the powers of the Regional Councils shall include the power to select allottees to whom lands within their area of authority shall be alienated and also power to select personnel to be employed for work on such schemes. The position regarding the area at present administered by the Gal Oya Board in this matter required consideration.

Taxation, Borrowing] "(G) The powers in regard to the Regional Coun- cils vested in the Minister of Local Government in the draft Bill to be revised with a view to vesting control in Parliament wherever necessary.

"(H) The Central Government will provide block grants to the Regional Councils. The principles on which the grants will be computed will be gone into. The Regional Councils shall have powers of taxation and borrowing."

VII

A statement containing the minimum demands submitted to the Leaders of the U.N.P. and the S.L.F.P. on 30.3 1960 by Mr. S.J.V. Chelvanayakam on behalf of the Federal Party when both parties failed to get an absolute majority in Parliament after the 1960 March General Election and sought the support of the Federal Party to form a Government

The results of the General Election have demonstrated emphatically that the Tamil speaking peoples of Ceylon have endorsed in overwhelming numbers their acceptance of the policy and objectives of my Party, which can be briefly stated as follows: —

(1) The replacement of the present unitary Constitution by a Federal Constitution which recognizes the autonomy of the Tamil-speaking areas.
(2) The restoration of the Tamil language to its rightful place enjoying parity with Sinhala as an official language of the country.
(3) The granting of Citizenship rights to Tamil persons of Indian origin who are settled in Ceylon.
(4) The cessation of planned colonization of the traditionally Tamil areas with Sinhalese people.

However, since we have been asked for an indication of the minimum points on which agreement can be effected between ourselves with a view to my Parliamentary Group supporting your party to form the Government we are setting down briefly four points which I think should be acceptable, but by my making these suggestions we should not be understood to be surrendering or abandoning any of our fundamental objectives.

Acceptance of the matters on which agreement is effected between our-selves should be indicated by reference in the Throne Speech and thereafter implemented by legislative action which should be completed within a period of three months.

(1) Granting of regional autonomy for the Northern and Eastern Provinces by the creation of one regional body for the Northern Province and one or more regional bodies for the Eastern Province with the right of these bodies to amalgamate. Powers to be delegated or conferred on such regional bodies for specific subjects including agriculture, co-operatives, land and land development, land alienation and colonisation, irrigation, education, health, industries and fisheries, housing and social services, electricity, water schemes and roads.

Pending the establishment of the regional bodies state-aided colonization referred to above is to be suspended.

(2) Tamil to be recognized statutorily and administratively as the national language of the Tamil speaking peoples in Ceylon. Tamil is to be made the language of administration and of the Courts of law in the Northern and Eastern Provinces, necessary provision, however, to be made for the non Tamil speaking minorities in these areas. The right of the Tamil speaking peoples throughout Ceylon to be educated in the Tamil language in all stages up to and including the University and the right of entry into the public services by competitive examinations in Tamil to be statutorily recognized. Every Tamil person should be entitled in law to transact business and correspondence with the Government in all parts of Ceylon in Tamil. All legislation, Gazette notifications, Governmental publications, notices and forms should be in Tamil also.

(3) The Ceylon Citizenship Act No. 18 of 1948 to be amended by deleting the words "before the appointed day" in Section 4 (1) of the Act and deleting of section 5 (1) of the act and by making such consequential amendments as may be necessary.

(4) Till such time as the question of Citizenship and the Franchise for the Estate Tamil population is settled representation in Parliament for these people to be provided by way of nomination to 4 out of the 6 appointed seats in Parliament and that a convention be created whereby the persons nominated will be the nominees of the political body which represents that population, namely the Ceylon Indian Congress.

Details and other points not covered by the foregoing paragraphs will be settled by negotiation between the Government and the party.

VIII

An Agreement*

reached between Mr Dudley Senanayake (on behalf of
the UNP) and Mr S.J.V. Chelvanayakam (on behalf of
the Federal Party) in March 1965

Mr Dudley Senanayake and Mr S.J.V. Chelvanayakam met on the 24.3.1965
and discussed matters relating to some problems over which the Tamil-speaking
people were concerned, and Mr. Senanayake agreed that action on the following
lines would be taken by him to ensure a stable Government:

1. Action will be taken early under the Tamil Language Special Provisions Act
    to make provision for the use of Tamil as the language of administration and
    of record in the Northern and Eastern Provinces.

    Mr Senanayake also explained that it was the policy of the Party that a
    Tamil-speaking person should be entitled to transact business in Tamil
    throughout the Island.

2. Mr Senanayake stated that it was the policy of his Party to amend the
    Language of the Courts Act to provide for legal proceedings in the Northern
    and Eastern Provinces to be conducted and recorded in Tamil.

3. Action will be taken to establish District Councils in Ceylon vested with
    powers over subjects to be mutually agreed upon between the two leaders.
    It was agreed, however, that the Government should have power under the
    law to give directions to such Councils in the national interest.

4. The Land Development Ordinance will be amended. ...Mr .Senanayake
    further agreed that in the granting of land under colonisation schemes the
    following priorities be observed in the Northern and Eastern Provinces.

    (a) Land in the Northern and Eastern Provinces should in the first
         instance be granted to landless persons in the District.

    (b) Secondly — to Tamil-speaking persons resident in the Northern and
         Eastern Provinces, and

    (c) Thirdly — to other citizens in Ceylon preference being given to
    Tamil citizens in the rest of the Island.

Sgd/Dudley Senanayake
24.3.1965
Sgd/S.J.V. Chelvanayakam
24.3.1965

[*The document we publish here appeared in the Sri Lanka press a few
weeks after the agreement was signed by the parties concerned. The
agreement itself was never officially released.]

IX

Resolution passed at a convention of the Tamil United Liberation Front held at Pannakam, Vaddukodai, on 14 May 1976

"Whereas thoughout the centuries from the dawn of history the Sinhalese and Tamil nations have divided between them the possession of Ceylon, the Sinhalese inhabiting the interior of the country in its southern and western parts from the river Walave to that of Chilaw and the Tamils possessing the northern and eastern districts,

And whereas the Tamil kingdom was overthrown in war and conquered by the Portuguese in 1619 and from them by the Dutch and the British in turn, independent of the Sinhalese Kingdoms.

And whereas the British Colonialists who ruled the territories of the Sinhalese and Tamil kingdoms separately joined under compulsion the territories of the Tamil to the territories of the Sinhalese kingdoms for purposes of administrative convenience on the recommendation of the Colebrooke Commission in 1833,

And whereas Tamil leaders were in the forefront of the Freedom Movement to rid Ceylon of colonial bondage which ultimately led to the grant of independence to Ceylon in 1948,

And whereas the foregoing facts of history were completely overlooked and power was transferred to the Sinhalese nation over the entire country on the basis of a numerical majority, thereby reducing the Tamil nation to the position of a subject people;

And whereas successive Sinhalese Governments since Independence have always encouraged and fostered the aggressive nationalism of the Sinhalese people and have used their political power to the detriment of the Tamils by —

(a) Depriving one half of the Tamil people of their citizenship and franchise rights, thereby reducing Tamil representation in Parliament;

(b) Making serious inroads into the territories of the former Tamil kingdom by a system of planned and state-aided Sinhalese colonization and large-scale regularization of recently encouraged Sinhalese encroachments calculated to make the Tamils a minority in their own homeland;

(c) Making Sinhalan the only official language throughout Ceylon thereby placing the stamp of inferiority on the Tamils and the Tamil language;

(d) Giving the foremost place to Buddhism under the Republican Constitution thereby reducing the Hindus, Christians and Muslims to second-class status in this country:

(e) Denying to the Tamils equality of opportunity in the spheres of employment, education, land alienation and economic life in general, and starving Tamil areas of large-scale industries and development schemes, thereby seriously endangering their very existence in Ceylon;

(f) Systematically cutting them off from the main-stream of Tamil culture in South India while denying them opportunities of developing their language and culture in Ceylon, thereby working inexorably toward the cultural genocide of the Tamils;

(g) Permitting and unleashing communal violence and intimidation against Tamil-speaking people as happened in Amparai and Colombo in 1956, all over the country in 1958, Army reign of terror in the Northern and Eastern Provinces in 1961, police violence at the International Tamil Research Conference in 1974 resulting in the death of nine persons in Jaffna, police and communal violence against Tamil-speaking Muslims at Puttalam and various other parts of Ceylon in 1976 — all these calcualted to instil terror in the minds of the Tamil-speaking people, thereby breaking their spirit and the will to resist the injustices heaped on them;

(h) By terrorising, torturing and imprisoning Tamil youths without trial for long periods on the flimsiest of grounds;

(i) Capping it all, by imposing on the Tamil Nation a constitution drafted under conditions of emergency without opportunities for free discussion by a Constituent Assembly elected on the basis of the Soulbury Constitution distorted by the Citizenship laws resulting in weightage in representation to the Sinhalese majority thereby depriving the Tamils of even the remnants of safeguards they had under the earlier constitution.

And whereas all attempts by the various Tamil political parties to win their rights by co-operating with the governments, by parliamentary and extra parliamentary agitations, by entering into pacts and understandings, with successive Prime Ministers in order to achieve the bare minimum of political rights consistent with the self-respect of the Tamil people have proved to be futile;

And whereas the efforts of the All Ceylon Tamil Congress to ensure non-domination of the minorities by the majority by the adoption of a scheme of balanced representation in a Unitary Constitution have failed and even the meagre safeguards provided in article 29 of the Soulbury Constitution against discriminatory legislation have been removed by the Republican Constitution;

And whereas the proposals submitted to the Constituent Assembly by the Ilankai Thamil Arasu Kadchi for maintaining the unity of the country while preserving the integrity of the Tamil people by the establishment of an autonomous Tamil State within the framework of a Federal Republic of Ceylon were summarily and totally rejected without even the courtesy of a consideration of its merits, and

Whereas the amendments to the Basic Resolutions intended to ensure the minimum of safeguards of the Tamil people, moved on the basis of the 9 point demands formulated at the Conference of all Tamil political parties on 7th February 1971 and by individual parties and Tamil Members of Parliament, including those now with the Government party, were rejected by the Government and the Constituent Assembly, and

Whereas even amendments to the draft proposals relating to language, religion and fundamental rights, including those calculated to ensure that at least the provision of the Tamil Language (Special Provisions) Act be included in the Constitution, were defeated resulting in the boycotting of the Constituent Assembly by a large majority of Tamil M.Ps, and

Whereas the Tamil United Liberation Front, after rejecting the Republican Constitution adopted on 22nd May 1972 put a 6-point demand to the Prime Minister and the Government on 25th June 1972 and gave three months' time within which the Government was called upon to take meaningful steps to amend the Constitution so as to meet the aspirations of the Tamil nation on the basis of the 6-point demands and informed the Government that if it failed to do so the Tamil United Liberation Front would launch a non-violent direct action against the Government in order to win freedom and the rights of the Tamil nation on the basis of the rights of self-determination, and

Whereas the last attempt by the Tamil United Liberation Front to win constitutional recognition of the rights of the Tamil nation without jeopardizing the unity of the country, was callously ignored by the Prime Minister and the Government, and

Whereas the opportunity provided by the T.U.L.F. leader to vindicate the Government's contention that their constitution had the backing of the Tamil people, by resigning from his membership of the National State Assembly and creating a by-election, was deliberately put off for over two years in utter disregard of the democratic rights of the Tamil voters of Kankesanturai, and

Whereas in the by-election held on the 6th February 1975 the voters of Kankesanturai by a preponderant majority not only rejected the Republican Constitution imposed on them by the Sinhalese Government but also gave a mandate to Mr S.J.V. Chelvanayakam, Q.C. and through him to the Tamil United Liberation Front for the restoration and reconstitution of the free, sovereign, secular, socialist state of Tamil Eelam,

The first National Convention of the Tamil United Liberation Front Meeting at Pannakam on the 14th day of May 1976 hereby declares that the Tamils of Ceylon, by virtue of their great language, their religions, their separate culture and heritage, their history of independent existence as a separate state over a distinct territory for several centuries until they were conquered by the armed might of the European invaders and, above all by their will to exist as a separate entity ruling themselves in their own territory, are a nation distinct and apart from the Sinhalese and this Convention announces to the world that the Republican Constitution of 1972 has made the Tamils a slave nation ruled by the new colonial masters, the Sinhalese, who are using the power they have wrongly usurped to deprive the Tamil nation of its territory, language, citizenship, economic life, opportunities of employment and education, thereby depriving all the attributes of nationhood of the Tamil people.

And therefore, while taking note of the reservations in relation to its commitment to the setting up of a separate state of Tamil Eelam expressed by the Ceylon Workers' Congress as a trade union of the plantation workers, the majority of whom live and work outside the northern and eastern areas,

This Convention resolves that the restoration and reconstitution of the free sovereign, secular socialist state of Tamil Eelam based on the right of self determination inherent to every nation, has become inevitable in order to safeguard the very existence of the Tamil nation in this country.

This Convention further declares —

(a)   that the State of TAMIL EELAM shall consist of the people of the Northern and Eastern Provinces and shall also ensure full and equal rights of citizenship of the State of TAMIL EELAM to all Tamil-speaking people living in any part of Ceylon and to TAMILS of EELAM origin living in any part of the world who may opt for citizenship of TAMIL EELAM;

(b)   that the constitution of TAMIL EELAM shall be based on the principle of decentralization so as to ensure the non-domination of any religion or territorial community of TAMIL EELAM by any other section;

(c)   that in the State of Tamil Eelam, caste shall be abolished and the observance of the pernicious practice of untouchability or inequality of any type based on birth shall be totally eradicated and its observance in any form punished by law;

(d)   that TAMIL EELAM shall be a secular state giving equal protection and assistance to all religions to which the people of the state may belong;

(e)   that Tamil shall be the language of the State but the rights of Sinhalese-speaking minorities in Tamil Eelam to education and transaction of business in their language shall be protected on a reciprocal basis with the Tamil-speaking minorities in the Sinhala State;

(f)   that Tamil Eelam shall be a Socialist State wherein the exploitation of man by man shall be forbidden, the dignity of labour shall be recognized, the means of production and distribution shall be subject to public ownership and control while permitting private enterprise in these branches within limits prescribed by law, economic development shall be on the basis of socialist planning and there shall be a ceiling on the total wealth that any individual or family may acquire.

This convention directs the Action Committee of the TAMIL UNITED LIBERATION FRONT to formulate a plan of action and launch without undue delay the struggle for winning the sovereignty and freedom of the Tamil Nation.

And this Convention calls upon the Tamil Nation in general and the Tamil youth in particular to come forward to throw themselves fully into the sacred fight for freedom and to flinch not till the goal of a soverign socialist State of EELAM is reached."

X

The TULF Amendment to the Statement of Government Policy

moved in the National State
Assembly on 18 August 1977

"As an amendment to the Motion on Acceptance of the Statement of Government Policy at the end add the words: —

"but regrets that while the Statement of Government Policy refers to the people's mandate to the Government to draft, adopt and operate a New Republican Constitution, the Statement studiedly refrains from referring to the mandate given by the people of Thamil Eelam to the Tamil United Liberation Front for the restoration and re-constitution of a free, sovereign socialist state of Thamil Eelam:

This Assembly further regrets that the statement of Government Policy has failed to take note of the fact that the Tamils are a separate nation by all internationally accepted standards by virtue of

(a)   their traditional occupation of a separate and well-defined territory in the Northern and Eastern parts of Ceylon;

(b)   their history of existence as a separate people for centuries prior to conquest by European imperialists;

(c)   their Common Economic life based largely on the agricultural, marine and other resources of their territory; and

(e)   their will to preserve their separate indentity and live together as a nation as has been unmistabkably demonstrated at the last General Election; and are therefore entitled to exercise their inalienable right of self-determination;

This Assembly further regrets that the statement of Policy does not indicate any recognition by the Government of the fact that the Tamil nation has, in the exercise of its right of self determination decided to live as a free people in the sovereign state of Thamil Eelam."

XI

An Extract from the
Dissent of Two Muslim Members of the
Presidential Commission on
Development Councils, SPV of 1980.

There is perhaps some confusion in the public mind that the Development Councils contemplated in our Terms of Reference are, or must be, the same as, or very nearly the same as, the Regional and District Councils contemplated in 1957 and 1968, both of which were intended to provide for certain demands by the Tamil Political parties. This was at a time when the constitutional background was different to what it is today. The constitutional background today relating to the Tamil language, which proceeds from the base of one country and one Nation, are contained in Articles 19 to 24 of the Constitution. They are too lengthy to reproduce here but their following broad effect may be noted —

(i)   While Sinhala is made the official language of the Republic, Sinhala and Tamil are declared to be the National Languages of Sri Lanka.

(ii)   A Tamil will be entitled to be educated thorugh the medium of the Tamil language.

(iii)   The Tamil language is also to be used as the language of administration for the maintenance of public records and the transaction of all business by public institutions in the Northern and Eastern Provinces.

(iv)   A Tamil in any part of the country shall be entitled to receive communications from and to communicate and transact business with any official in his official capacity, in Tamil.

(v)   A Tamil in any part of the country shall be entitled to certified copies of public documents in Tamil or if the original is in any other language a Tamil translation.

(vi)   Any local authority conducting its affairs in Tamil will be entitled to receive communications from and to communicate with any official in any part of the country in Tamil.

(vii)   A Tamil candidate for public or judicial office or for office in the Local Government Service will be entitled to be examined through the medium of the Tamil language subject to the condition that he may be required to acquire a sufficient knowledge of the Sinhala Language and provided that a person may be required to have a knowledge of Sinhala as a condition of admission to any public office if the duties of such office cannot be discharged without sufficient knowledge of Sinhala.

(viii) All laws and subordinate legislation have to be enacted, made and published in both Sinhala and Tamil.

(ix)   All existing written laws have to be published in both Sinhala and Tamil as expeditiously as possible after the adoption of the Constitution.

(x)   While Sinhala is made the language of the courts throughout Sri Lanka, the language of courts exercising original jurisdiction in the Northern and Eastern Provinces shall also be Tamil.

(xi)   Any party or any attorney representing a party is entitled in any court in the Island to submit pleadings and other documents and participate in proceedings in either Sinhala or Tamil.

(xii)   Any judge or juror or applicant or attorney if he is a Tamil and not conversant with the Sinhala language in a court where Sinhala is the only language of the court would be entitled to a translation to Tamil provided by the state.

Apart from these provisions relating to language, there is in the Constitution, a Chapter on Fundamental Rights, many of which are specifically directed towards the protection of minorities.

Article 12 of the Constitution which guarantees to all persons equality before the law and equal protection of the law, goes on further to provide in paragraph (2) that:

"No citizen shall be discriminated against on the grounds of race, religion, language, caste, sex, political opinion, place of birth or any one of such grounds;"

and in paragraph (3) that:

"No person shall, on the grounds of race, religion, language, caste, sex or any one of such grounds, be subject to any disability, liability, restriction or condition with regard to access to shops, public restaurants, hotels, places of public entertainment and places of public worship of his own religion."

Article 14 contains provisions guaranteeing freedom of speech, assembly, association; and religious belief and worship. Further, it entitles every citizen to the freedom to enjoy and promote his own culture and to use his own language; sub-paragraph (1) (h) of Article 14 ensures freedom of movement and of choosing his place of residence anywhere within Sri Lanka.

For the protection of these rights Article 17 read with Article 126 provides the machinery, viz., and application to the Supreme Court in respect of any infringment or imminent infringement by executive or administrative action, of any fundamental or language rights to which the applicant is entitled under the Constitution. A further safeguard is to be found in Article 156 which provides for the establishment of the office of Parliamentary Commissioner for Administration (Ombudsman) charged with the duty of investigating and reporting upon complaints or allegations of infringement of fundamental rights or other injustices by public officers and officers of public corporations or local authorities.

These and other provisions of the Constitution are directed to assuring to all minorities in Sri Lanka freedom from the danger of any tyranny by a communal majority so that the unitary character of the Republic may not be impaired by divisive politics which thrives on the magnification of accepted differences in race or religion.

Thus, the Constitution reflects the three basic principles or essentials of democracy — majority rule, minority rights and political equality; and in giving equal rights to all persons the Constitution is directed to breaking all barriers of race, religion or caste, or education, of culture and of want of opportunity.

In the light of all the safeguards provided for in the Constitution for all the minorities, we find it difficult to comprehend how our Terms of Reference can be read as authorizing this Commission to report on the advisability or possibility of resolving any minority or Tamil problems, by dividing the country politically or administratively into Nation states or regions by reference to any race, language or religion; or by recommending an unwarranted degree of freedom, from control by the Centre, to all or any of the 24 Administrative Districts part or a significant part of the legislative and executive sovereign powers of the people of Sri Lanka, exercised by Parliament and the President respectively, when there is not, except perhaps in the Northern Region, any demand or need for the adoption of such a course.

Even if there was any demand or need for the adoption of such a course, which inevitably will have an impact on the unitary state of the country, it will require an amendment to Article 2 of the Constitution. Any amendment to this

Article, which is one of the entrenched provisions, will require not only a two-third majority in Parliament, but also the approval of the people at a Referendum under Article 83.

Then again, Article 3 of the Constitution enacts —
"In the Republic of Sri Lanka sovereignty is in the people and is inalienable."

Among other things, this provision means that sovereignty of the people extends to every part of Sri Lanka, and to every person or section or group of persons. The sovereignty spoken of is an attribute of the whole people who are citizens of Sri Lanka. These sovereign, legislative, executive and judicial powers of the people cannot be granted — by whatever name called — be it separatism, federalism, devolution, autonomy or decentralization — to the people of a city, town, district, province or region.

The legislative sovereign powers of the people, exercised by Parliament consisting of elected representatives of the people, is expressly dealt with in Article 76 (1) of the Constitution which reads —
"Parliament shall not abdicate or in any manner alienate its legislative power, and shall not set up any authority with any legislative power."

Paragraph 3 of Article 76 goes on to provide for the only exception to this rule, viz.,
"It shall not be a contravention of the provisions of paragraph (1) of this Article for Parliament to make any law containing any provision empowering any person or body to make subordinate legislation for prescribed purposes . . . "

The word "subordinate" signifies the essential character of such laws, viz., that it must be the subject of control by the whole people of Sri Lanka whose representatives are the central executive and the central legislature.

The Muslim Minority

There is no question that in the demand for a separate, independent, sovereign state for the "Tamil Nation" in the Northern and Eastern Provinces of the country, the Muslim population is included in the "Tamil Nation" complex. This is evident from the 1977 General Election Manifesto by which the Tamil United Liberation Front launched its demand and sought a mandate for the establishment of such a State in the two provinces, for "all the Tamil speaking people" of the country, which expression yielding place in the Manifesto itself, to the expression "Tamils", "Tamil People" and "Tamil Nation." The Muslim population of 974,665 in the country which include, though they have a language of their own, the Malay population who are also Tamil speaking, thus became included as "Tamils" and "Tamil People" in the "Tamil Nation" complex because, and only because, they are Tamil speaking, and not because there is any racial, religious or cultural affinity between the Tamils and the Muslims in this country, or in any other part of the world. As a further reason for the inclusion of the Muslim population in the "Tamil Nation" complex, and as citizens of the separate, independent, sovereign state for the "Tamil Nation", the claim was advanced that the Muslim population realizing that their religion and language, lands and opportunities of employment were all being taken away from them, and that their lives and property, too, were insecure, and realizing also that movements that accepted the leadership of the Sinhalese political parties would not defend even these basic rights of theirs; had organized themselves into a "Muslim United Front" and made common cause for joint action with the Tamil population and the Tamil United Liberation Front, for the demand for a separate state for the "Tamil Nation" in which the Muslim population was to be included.

The "movements" that would not defend even the basic rights of the Muslim population referred to, though not named, were none other than the All Ceylon Muslim League and the All Ceylon Moors Association, which are the two main Muslim organizations in the country. These two organizations, and their leaders, as well as several other Muslim bodies which have made written representations to us, have rejected the thesis that the Muslims, because they are Tamil speaking, are in favour of dividing the country into a two-nation state — the Tamil speaking and non-Tamil speaking nation states.

Not having received any representation from the "Muslim United Front" referred to in the Manifesto, which had joined the Tamil United Liberation Front as a constituent unit in the demand for a separate state for the "Tamil Nation", in which the Muslim population was to be included, we made every effort to identify this Front, but without success. Our efforts, however, revealed that on the eve of, and for the purpose of the 1977 General Elections, some Muslims in the Eastern Province; the number remaining unknown and unascertainable, had joined the Tamil United Liberation Front which sponsored three of them as Tamil United Liberation Front candidates in three electoral districts in the Eastern Province. All three of them were defeated by the three Muslim candidates fielded by the United National Party, all the five Muslim candidates fielded by this party, which stood for a Unitary State and a united Sri Lankan nation, were returned to Parliament. There cannot be clearer evidence that the Muslim population even of the Eastern Province, 286,275 of the total Muslim population in the country of 974,665, are opposed to their inclusion in the demand for any separate state of which they are to be citizens — that they are not available for absorption in the "Tamil Nation" complex — that they are opposed to the division of the country by any means, for any reason — and that they will continue to live, as they have done for over 1,000 years, alongside with the rest of the country's national population, in all parts of the country. As it is not relevant for our purpose to examine whether even the Tamil population of the Eastern Province favoured or favour the establishment of a separate state, to include the Eastern Province for the "Tamil Nation", we refrain from doing so.

The Country, its People and their Living together

We consider it necessary, having regard to what we have stated, to examine the topography of the country, its multi-racial national population, and their spread and living-together, in the various parts of the country. If a Nation is as the word is defined and understood, the whole people of a country, organized as a separate political state, occupying a definite territory, Sri Lanka has, admittedly since 1833 at least, remained one country and the home of one Nation, consisting of the Sinhala, Tamil, Muslim and Burgher population of the country, so spread over the nine provinces and the twenty-four Administrative Districts, that the division of the country and its people, for any reason, will be as unimaginative as it is to unscramble the scrambled egg.

A table showing the population in each district, by communities, including the Indian Tamil, Indian Muslim in those classified as "others", is annexed as an appendix to this Note of Reservation.

As in the demand for a separate state for the "Tamil Nation" in the Northern and Eastern Provinces, the Muslim population of 974,665 is also included, it is necessary to set out the spread of the Tamil and Muslim population and also the Sinhala population in these two Provinces, and also the spread of the Tamil and Muslim population in all the other seven Provinces.

In the 3,429 square miles of territory in the Northern Province, which consists of the four Administrative Districts of Jaffna, Mannar, Vavuniya and Mullaitivu, there are 851,718 Ceylon Tamils; 45,370 Sinhala and 40,702 Ceylon Muslims. The Ceylon Tamil Population in the Northern Province is, therefore, half their total population in the country.

In the Eastern Province, which consists of the three Administrative Districts of Batticaloa, Ampara and Trincomalee, and 3,842 square miles of territory, there are 351,247 Ceylon Tamils, 286,275 Ceylon Muslims and 173,418 Sinhala.

The remainder of the Ceylon Tamil population of 405,022, which is a little over 25 per cent of their total population of 1,607,987 in the country, is spread over, and living alongside with the Sinhala and Muslim population, in all the other seven Provinces. There are 195,946 Ceylon Tamils in the Western Province and 89,767 in the Central, 8,127 in the Southern, 43982 in the North-Western, 16,308 in the North-Central, 24,928 in the Uva and 26,054 in the Sabaragamuwa Provinces respectively. The spread of the Ceylon Muslim population in the same seven Provinces is 247,592; 140,544; 49,744; 96,529; 42,248; 28,273 and 42,722 respectively.

The Muslim population having rejected their inclusion in the demand for a separate State in any part of the country, and not accepting their inclusion in the "Tamil Nation" complex, or as citizens of a Tamil state, and opposed to any interference with their constitutional right, as citizens of Sri Lanka, to choose their residence in any part of the country or be unsettled from their settled homes in any part of the country for settlement in any other part of the country, the demand for a separate State in the Northern and Eastern Provinces is only for the country's Tamil population. If 405,022 of them who are spread over the other 7 Provinces of the country are not to be unsettled, or are unwilling to be unsettled from these provinces for settlement elsewhere, they will continue to live and enjoy the citizenship rights of a state having the same mixture of communities as there are in Sri Lanka today. In such event, and assuming that the Tamil population in the Eastern Province opt to have them and the Province included in the separate State for the "Tamil Nation", the Eastern Province, with a territorial area of 3,842 square miles, will be a separate state for a population of 351,257 out of the total population in the Province, of 800,940. On the other hand, even if the entire Tamil national population of the country is to be settled in the separate State for the "Tamil Nation", the Eastern Province, with a territorial area of 3,842 square miles, will be a separate state for a population of 351,257 out of the total population in the Province, of 800,940. On the other hand, even if the entire Tamil national population of the county is to be settled in the separate State for the "Tamil Nation" in the Northern Province and the Eastern Province, the demand for the establishment of such a state in the two Provinces, in 7,371 square miles of the country's total territorial area of 25,332 square miles, will still be only for a population of 1,607,987, of the country's total national population of 13,330,360.

TABLE I

POPULATION IN SRI LANKA, 1871-1979: PATTERNS OF GROWTH

Census Year	Enumerated Population ('000)	Intercensal Increase ('000)	Average Annual Growth Rate %
1871	2,400	—	—
1881	2,760	359	1.42
1891	3,008	248	0.86
1901	3,566	558	1.72
1911	4,106	540	1.42
1921	4,498	392	0.91
1931	5,307	809	1.68
1946	6,657	1,350	1.52
1953	8,098	1,441	2.84
1967	10,582	2,484	2.65
1971	12,689	2,108	2.20
1981*	14,988	2,299	1.90

Source: *Census of Population 1971*, Vol. II,
    Dept. of Census & Statistics

*Source: *Economic & Social Statistics of Sri Lanka*, Vol. IV, No. 2 Dec. 1981
    Statistics Dept., Central Bank of Ceylon.

TABLE II
PERCENTAGE DISTRIBUTION OF POPULATION (CENSUS 1981)

District	Sinhalese	S. Lanka Tamil	Indian Tamil	S. Lanka Moor	Burgher	Malay	Others
Colombo	77.9	9.8	1.3	8.3	1.1	1.1	0.5
Kalutara	87.3	1.0	4.1	7.5	—	0.1	—
Gampaha	92.2	3.3	0.4	2.8	0.6	0.6	0.1
Kandy	75.0	4.9	9.3	9.9	0.2	0.2	0.4
Matale	79.9	5.9	6.7	7.2	0.1	0.1	0.1
Nuwara Eliya	35.9	13.5	47.3	2.8	0.1	0.2	0.2
Galle	94.4	0.7	1.4	8.2	—	0.1	0.2
Matara	94.6	0.6	2.2	2.6	—	—	—
Hambantota	97.4	0.4	0.1	1.1	—	1.0	—
Jaffna	0.6	95.3	2.4	1.7	—	—	—
Mannar	8.1	50.6	13.2	26.6	—	—	1.4
Vavuniya	16.6	56.9	19.4	6.9	—	—	0.2
Batticaloa	3.2	70.9	1.2	23.9	0.7	—	0.1
Amparai	37.6	20.1	0.4	41.5	0.2	—	0.1
Trincomalee	33.6	33.8	2.6	29.0	0.5	0.3	0.2

District	Sinhalese	S. Lanka Tamil	Indian Tamil	S. Lanka Moor	Burgher	Malay	Others
Kurunegala	93.1	1.1	0.5	5.1	—	0.1	0.1
Puttalam	82.6	6.7	0.6	9.7	0.1	0.2	0.1
Anuradhapura	91.3	1.4	0.1	7.1	—	—	0.1
Polonnaruwa	90.9	2.2	0.1	6.5	—	0.1	0.2
Badulla	68.5	5.7	21.1	4.2	0.1	0.2	0.2
Moneragala	92.9	1.8	3.3	1.9	—	0.1	—
Ratnapura	84.7	2.3	11.1	1.7	0.1	—	0.1
Kegalle	86.3	2.1	6.4	5.1	—	—	0.1
Mullaitivu	5.1	76.0	13.9	4.9	0.1	—	—

Source: Department of Census & Statistics 1982
Ministry of Plan Implementation - p. 32

TABLE III

**RELIGIOUS COMPOSITION OF THE POPULATION
OF SRI LANKA
1911-1981:
Percentage of Total**

	1911	1946	1971	1981
Buddhist	60.3	64.5	67.3	69.3
Hindus	22.9	19.8	17.6	15.5
Christians	10.0	9.1	7.9	7.5
Muslims	6.9	6.6	7.1	7.6
Others	--	--	0.1	0.1

Source: Department of Census and Statistics

TABLE IV
ETHNIC COMPOSITION OF THE POPULATION OF SRI LANKA: 1881-1981.

	1881	1901	1921	1953	1971	1981
All Ethnic Groups	2,760 ('000)	3,566 ('000)	4,498 ('000)	8,098 ('000)	12,690 ('000)	14,988 ('000)
			Percentage of Total			
Low-Country Sinhalese	) 66.9	40.9	42.8	42.8	42.8	) 74.0
Kandyan Sinhalese	)	24.5	24.2	26.5	29.2	)
Sri Lanka Tamils	) 24.9	26.7	11.5	10.9	11.2	12.6
Indian Tamils	)		13.4	12.0	9.3	5.5
Sri Lanka Moors	) 6.7	6.4	5.6	5.7	6.5	) 7.1
Indian Moors	)		0.7	0.6	0.2	)
Burghers and Eurasians	0.7	0.7	0.7	0.6	0.4	0.3
Malays	0.3	0.3	0.3	0.3	0.4	0.3
Veddhas	0.1	0.1	0.1	--	⎫	⎫
Europeans	0.2	0.2	0.2	0.1	0.1	0.2
Others	0.3	0.3	0.5	0.4	⎭	⎭

Source: Department of Census and Statistics.

TABLE V

MOVEMENT OF POPULATION — NATURAL INCREASE AND NET GAIN OR LOSS BY MIGRATION

1891 - 1981

Period	Actual Increase (+) or decrease (–) per 1,000 of population.	Net gain (+) or loss (–) by migration per 1,000 of population
1891-1901	186	+111
1901-1911	151	+50
1911-1921	96	+11
1921-1931	180	+32
1931-1946	254	+12
1946-1953	216	+17
1953-1963	476	–31
1963-1973	261	–9.9
1973-1981	135	–28

Source: Dept. of Census and Statistics
Ministry of Plan Implementation
1982, p. 60.

TABLE VI

EMPLOYED POPULATION BY LEVEL OF EDUCATION

All Island/Sectors — Sri Lanka 1980/81

Level of Education	All Island		Urban		Rural	
	Total	%	Total	%	Total	%
No Schooling	555061	11.7	58113	6.7	496946	12.8
Primary (Grade 1-5)	1784578	37.7	207909	24.1	1576668	40.7
Middle Grade (6-10)	1534100	32.4	320170	37.0	1213932	31.4
Passed G.C.E. (O.L.) N.C.G.E.	672415	14.2	210473	24.4	461943	11.9
Passed G.C.E. (A/L) H.N.C.E.	128030	2.7	34721	4.0	93308	2.4
Passed Degree or above	63487	1.3	33223	3.8	30264	0.8

Source: Labour force and Socio-Economic Survey 1980-81
Dept. of Census and Statistics, Ministry of
Plan Implementation.

TABLE VII

EMPLOYMENT AND ETHNICITY – SRI LANKA 1978/79

Percentage of the Total in the Ethnic Group

	Self Employed	Employer	Employee	Unpaid family worker	Total Employed
Kandyan Sinhalese	9.79	0.43	15.96	8.09	34.27
Low Country Sinhalese	7.03	0.59	19.52	3.35	30.49
Sri Lanka Tamils	8.63	0.30	16.23	2.81	27.97
Indian Tamils	0.93	0.08	47.50	0.45	48.96
Moors	6.79	0.70	13.64	2.12	23.25
Malays	3.14	0.45	20.63	1.35	25.57
Burghers	1.22	0.0	25.61	0.0	26.83
Others	10.00	10.00	20.00	0.0	30.00
Total	7.45	0.47	20.13	4.37	32.42

Source: Survey of Sri Lanka's Consumer Finances 1978/79
Central Bank of Ceylon - p. 72

TABLE VIII
UNEMPLOYMENT AND ETHNICITY — SRI LANKA 1978/79

Number unemployed as percentage of population in respective ethnic group

	1978/79
Kandyan Sinhalese	5.52
Low Country Sinhalese	6.92
Sri Lanka Tamils	3.43
Indian Tamils	2.91
Moors	3.73
Malays	6.73
Burghers	10.97
Others	0
Total	5.61

Source: Survey of Sri Lanka's Consumer Finances 1978/79
Central Bank of Ceylon - p. 82

TABLE IX

WELFARE LEVELS IN SELECTED ASIAN COUNTRIES — 1977

All Island/Sectors — Sri Lanka 1980/81

Country	GNP per capita (US $) 1979	Daily per capita calorie supply	Number enrolled in secondary school as percentage of age groups (1978)	Life expectancy at birth (years) 1979	Infant Mortality Rate (1979)
Sri Lanka	230	2126	52	66	3
India	190	2021	28	52	15
Thailand	590	1929	28	62	6
Indonesia	370	2272	22	53	14
Philippines	600	2189	56	62	6

Source: World Development Report - 1981.

TABLE X

REPATRIATION UNDER THE 1964 AGREEMENT
BETWEEN THE SRI LANKA AND INDIAN GOVERNMENTS

(1971 to end of 1982)

Up to the end of	Number of persons Issued with permits	Number of persons Issued with Indian Passports	Number of persons who have left Sri Lanka
1970	n.a.	75,228	30,194
1971	26,008	33,088	21,867
1972	29,502	40,859	27,575
1973	33,965	35,898	33,175
1974	37,459	43,325	35,141
1975	19,598	34,675	18,511
1976	39,387	21,670	33,321
1977	34,175	14,639	28,388
1978	21,736	19,267	20,281
1979	14,367	14,574	15,942
1980	14,889	24,434	17,735
1981	18,903	29,974	16,723
1982	24,276	24,984	18,214

Total from 1970 up to the end of 1982 —

412,615   317,067

Source: Economic and Social Statistics of Sri Lanka
Dept. of Census and Statistics, p. 12

GLOSSARY

ayurveda: indigenous system of medicine.

bhikkhu: monk or priest, member of the Buddhist order.

cetiya, dagoba: edifice built over a relic, generally a dome-shaped monument.

durava: Sinhalese caste, originally tappers of palm trees for production of spirituous liquors.

goyigama: Sinhalese caste, farmers, and generally recognized as the highest in the caste hierarchy.

karava: Sinhalese caste; originally fisherfolk.

nikaya: (Buddhist) sects into which the *sangha* (q.r.) or Buddhist order is divided.

pirivena: (Buddhist) educational institute attached to a temple *(vihara)*.

poya weekend: weekend holiday based on the phases of the moon.

purana village: ancestral village or old, long-inhabited village distinct from new village settlements in an area.

Rate Mahatmaya: chief of district *(rata)* in the Kandyan kingdom; this title was bestowed on native officials in the administrative hierarchy in the Kandyan provinces under British rule.

salagama: Sinhalese caste, originally cinnamon peelers.

sangha: Buddhist clergy: order of *bhikkhus.*

swabhasa: indigenous languages, Sinhalese and Tamil.

vellala: Tamil caste, farmers, and the highest in the Tamil caste hierarchy.

vihara: Buddhist temple.

INDEX